The
DISCIPLES'
JESUS

The
DISCIPLES'
JESUS

Christology as Reconciling Practice

TERRENCE W. TILLEY

ORBIS BOOKS

Maryknoll, New York 10545

Founded in 1970, Orbis Books endeavors to publish works that enlighten the mind, nourish the spirit, and challenge the conscience. The publishing arm of the Maryknoll Fathers and Brothers, Orbis seeks to explore the global dimensions of the Christian faith and mission, to invite dialogue with diverse cultures and religious traditions, and to serve the cause of reconciliation and peace. The books published reflect the views of their authors and do not represent the official position of the Maryknoll Society. To learn more about Maryknoll and Orbis Books, please visit our website at www.maryknoll.org.

Library of Congress Cataloging-in-Publication Data

Tilley, Terrence W.
   The disciples' Jesus : christology as reconciling practice / Terrence
W. Tilley.
      p. cm.
   Includes bibliographical references and index.
   ISBN 978-1-57075-796-9
   1. Jesus Christ—Person and offices. 2. Christian life. I. Title.
   BT203.T55 2008
   232.09'015—dc22
                                                    2008017530

For Bob and Elena DeStefano

and

Josh and Chris Dyer

whose lives and love bring joy to their parents

Those who do justice will live in the presence of the Lord.

O Lord, who may abide in your tent?
Who may dwell on your holy hill?

Those who walk blamelessly, and do what is right,
and speak the truth from their heart;
who do not slander with their tongue,
and do no evil to their friends,
nor take up a reproach against their neighbors;
in whose eyes the wicked are despised,
but who honor those who fear the Lord;
who stand by their oath even to their hurt;
who do not lend money at interest,
and do not take a bribe against the innocent.

Those who do these things shall never be moved.

—Responsorial Psalm for Sixteenth Sunday
in Ordinary Time, Year C
Psalm 15 (NRSV, adapted)

CONTENTS

Part III: God's Reign in Practice

Part IV: Implications

PREFACE

This book is an essay in a practical christology, a christology based in disciples' reconciling practices. Its fundamental insight is captured in Psalm 15: to live righteously, to do justice, is to live in the presence of the Lord, that is, where God reigns. It argues that seeing christology as a *practical,* rather than a theoretical, discipline reshapes our understanding of what christology is and does. Along the way, I think it resolves or dissolves some tangled problems in christology without abandoning the insights of the classic theological tradition. I am excited to present it to you; I hope it stimulates your faith and your reflection on your faith.

The book as a whole is the argument for this theological shift. Much more could be said than I have here, but the book is long enough to indicate how one might develop this work further. The introduction below outlines the structure of this book. The work has had a long gestation. What follows sketches the book's genesis and its place among my various essays in theology. It does not tell you much about the book and its argument but shows how it fits in its author's work.

This is my fourth authored book for Orbis Books. The first, *Postmodern Theologies* (1995) marked a slight change in perspective from my focus on narratives in previous theological work, for example, *Story Theology* (Michael Glazier, 1985), to a focus on practices. Practices, though, are typically understood through narratives, so "narrative" is not lost but placed as a different category in my later work. The shift is away from concern with narrative as a theological *locus* to assuming that narratives are a crucial theological *form* in which various theological *loci* can be traversed—especially "practices." I argued in *Postmodern Theologies* that a practice/praxis approach to theology was viable in this era and in *The Wisdom of Religious Commitment* (Georgetown University Press, 1995) that the evaluation of religious believing was not reducible to warranting or justifying particular religious beliefs but required the exercise of practical wisdom, asking whether one should participate in this form of life.

This trajectory led to *Inventing Catholic Tradition* (2000), which construed a tradition as a set of practices and set out briefly what that shift could mean for understanding revelation and authority, and to *History, Theology and Faith: Dissolving the Modern Problematic* (2004), which construed history and theology as professional practices ("disciplines") calling for role-specific responsibilities, and faith as a different sort of practice that called for person-specific responsibilities. Therein I argued that the traditional opposition of "faith and history" was a confusion of types of practice. Issues in christology and investigations of the "historical-Jesus" were among the topics explored in that last book. It had become clear to me that the next book I would write would have to be an essay in christology. This is that book.

I had once thought I might revise *Story Theology*, which was fairly well received and remained actively in print for a decade or more (and is still available in a reasonably priced "print-on-demand" edition from the Liturgical Press). Yet it was published just as the second quest for the historical Jesus was ending, unbeknownst to me, thanks to E. P. Sanders, *Jesus and Judaism* (1985). My book went to press before the influential book by George Lindbeck, *The Nature of Doctrine* (1984), could help shape my work; my disagreements with and debts to Lindbeck and the "New Yale School" (of which I am not a member) can be seen in my other Orbis books; my debts to Sanders and the research on Jesus of Nazareth in the wake of his work can be seen herein. I do not withdraw what I said in *Story Theology* here, but this is a quite different book with a different focus. Little, if anything, remains that is not amplified, refocused, and recast.

Much of what I wrote in *Story Theology*—five of its nine chapters—was christological. In a sense, then, this book is the product of a quarter century of thinking about christological issues. *Story Theology* was my first real essay in christology, although not titled as such. I expect this to be my final one.

I had also once thought that I should write a companion book to my analysis of the problem of evil, *The Evils of Theodicy* (Georgetown University Press, 1991). The working title for that imagined book was *Agents of Salvation*. The point of that book was to be to show how Christians should respond to the evils in this world, since I had found in *Evils* that the constructing of theodicies was itself an evil, part of the problem, not part of the solution. I knew then that the solutions would always be both partial and practical. While the intuition that generated the idea for *Agents of Salvation* remains, that book will never appear because the intuition could not come to fruition until the shifts noted in the previous two paragraphs had happened. That this book is my constructive response to the problem of evil will, I hope, be clear. Although I never refer to *The Brothers Karamazov* in what follows, it should also be clear that I find in Alyosha's response to Ivan a clue from "there and then" to how to think about responding to the evils in the world "here and now." With apologies to Alan Jay Lerner, our responses should not so much talk of Love but show it, for, insofar as we can do so, the practices of reconciliation are both the human responses to the problems of evils and the human responses and contributions to redemption.

I write as a theologian whose genre is the essay—even this book is a long essay—rather than the system. I am a practicing Catholic (still practicing; still not getting it right, either— writing a book like this helps its author see how short he falls of hitting the mark). I am neither a historian nor a New Testament scholar, although I do use the methods developed in both fields and occasionally reinterpret much scholarship in both fields throughout the course of this essay. What this means is that you will not find a set of footnotes that have systematically scanned to find everything dealing with the question under discussion to show the state of each particular question in New Testament or historical scholarship. My research has been broad, but I have not sought to display the *status questionis* for every issue. You will rather find references herein to key texts where you can find those discussions. This approach does *not* mean that I claim this essay should be exempt from critical examination by scholars in those disciplines; to the extent that what I write here is not at least compatible with the results of historical and scriptural studies, it is flawed. Admittedly, as a theologian, I go beyond what historians and scripture scholars can legitimately claim in the exercise of their disciplines. But so do most of them go beyond those disciplines when they doff their disciplinary chapeaux and don their theologians' caps, as they regularly do. What is here is a theological proposal, heavily dependent on a theological interpretation of history (an approach sketched in *History, Theology and Faith*, chapter 9).

I do not expect this to be the last word on this subject. Who Jesus is and was and how to follow him are topics of endless interest. This essay is only one voice in a multigenerational, multicultural conversation that will, *deo volente*, go on long after this book is forgotten. I hope that it is a useful contribution to that conversation—no more than that, but no less, either.

My debts are legion. Most of them are found in the footnotes as I rely, not uncritically, on the arguments and insights of many scholars. Those notes show some of my debts to those scholars. Not all will approve of my use of their work or agree with the arguments I have made herein. They are responsible for what they wrote, not how I used or abused their insights. I also owe numerous debts to colleagues and graduate students at the University of Dayton and Fordham University, where I have been offering seminars in christology. It has been and is a privilege to work with them. I am grateful for particular suggestions to Bill Portier, Beth Johnson, and Therese Lysaught.

An earlier version of portions of part 1 appeared as "Remembering the Historic Jesus: A New Research Program?" *Theological Studies* 68, no. 1 (March 2007): 3-35; I am grateful to David Schultenover, S.J., the editor, for permission to adapt that material here. The materials in the epilogue were written for particular occasions. I thank Paul Baumann, editor of *Commonweal,* for permission to revise a meditation he edited and published and use it in the epilogue. The material on *Dei Verbum* in the epilogue has not been published previously. Some paragraphs, as noted in the body of the text, are adapted from some of my earlier writings. Occasionally, one gets things about right and cannot do much better. Unless otherwise noted, New Testament translations are mine; I compare my renderings with the Revised Standard Version and the New Revised Standard Version with some regularity; I use other contemporary versions more sparingly.

I have discussed many of the ideas in this text, and numerous other theological matters, over the years with Dermot Lane, president of the Mater Dei Institute of Education, a college in Dublin City University; the work has become clearer as a result of his critiques. Maureen Tilley has read and commented on the entire manuscript; her love has sustained me. Our daughters and their husbands have brought joy to their parents. As one of those parents, I have dedicated this book to them. Susan Perry is a wonderful editor, patient and supportive as other duties interfered with finishing this text in as timely a manner as I'd like; Catherine Costello and her associates have caught numerous blunders and clarified points perfectly clear to an author, but that needed to be reworked so that a reader could understand the direction the author was actually going. My deep thanks to all.

I began thinking, researching, and writing on this particular book about a decade ago. I am happy that it has taken so long to finish it because so much important material has been published since the project began and I have been able to incorporate much of it. It is an experiment as much as an essay in christology. Welcome to the work!

INTRODUCTION

*T*he present essay is a constructive christology that begins in practice, not theory. It takes seriously the ancient insight that Jesus is the *autobasileia*, the reign of God in person, but transposes this insight into a practical, rather than theoretical, key. Jesus' empowering practices realize the reign of God. Thus, he is *autobasileia*, not alone but in and through his relationships with others who would live in and live out God's reign. They together form the Jesus-movement.[1] In this key, Jesus' remembered practices as carried on by his disciples are where the reign of God is. These practices, possible only in God's gracious presence, constitute living in and living out the reign of God, *basileia tou theou*.

The book can be approached in different ways. Some might prefer to begin where christology begins. They would do well to begin with part 2, where reflection on scripture occurs, arguing that christology begins in the disciples' imaginations, or part 3, where the substantial work is undertaken on the practices of God's reign. Some would prefer to see the way this theologian approaches the task of construction. They can begin with part 1, which displays the context for the rest of the work. It probably would not be good to begin with part 4, which draws out the implications of this approach for doctrine or with the epilogue, which deals with particular concerns.

Part 1, "Approaches," has six chapters. Chapters 1 and 2 locate the present work. The fundamental approach is that christology begins in disciples' imaginations and is realized by engaging in the reconciling practices that constitute discipleship.

---

1. I use the term "Jesus-movement" to refer to the community of Jesus' disciples. The term primarily covers the first generation of disciples but is extended to cover all of Jesus' disciples. I use the term partly in homage to Clarence Jordan, whose "Cotton Patch Version" of New Testament texts was a translation into idiomatic English of the U.S. South. Jordan rendered *basileia tou theou* as "the God movement." The Jesus-movement, then, is composed of all those who seek to follow Jesus by living in, living out, and living for God's reign, the *basileia tou theou*, that Jesus preached and instantiated. However, I am not suggesting, by using "movement" as my key term for the community rather than "church," that structures of authority are not part of the movement. The question that faces the churches—not addressed in any significant way herein because it is not directly relevant to the position I am developing—is not *whether* to have authority structures, but *how* those structures are to be instantiated in good practices so that the movement can begin and continue in creative fidelity to the tradition that is centered in remembering Jesus. I have written on the necessity of authority and institutions in "The Institutional Element in Religious Experience," *Modern Theology* 10, no. 2 (April 1994): 185-212; in *The Wisdom of Religious Commitment* (Washington, DC: Georgetown University Press, 1995) 45-53; and in *Inventing Catholic Tradition* (Maryknoll, NY: Orbis Books, 2000) 177-84. Thanks to William Portier for helping me see the need to clarify this point.

1

Chapters 3 through 6 display the scholarly approaches that help shape the approach taken in the rest of the book. Without the works featured in these chapters, this book could not have been written. I have learned from those scholars to take both the communal practices of memory recorded in the New Testament and the investigative work of historians as significant for attempting to write of the disciples' Jesus as inaugurating the reconciling practices of the reign of God.

Part 2, "Interrogations and Recognitions," explores four explicit interrogations and responses from the New Testament about Jesus and his significance. After showing that "where" one begins doing christology is in the practical imaginations of disciples, it turns to Mark's Gospel's version of Peter's confession at Caesarea Philippi—the first remembered use of *ho christos* of Jesus and the hinge that links the two halves of Mark's Gospel. The second interrogation is that of Mary and Martha as Jesus visits them after the death of their brother Lazarus—the hinge that joins the "book of signs" and the "book of glory" in John's Gospel. The third is Paul's use of a hymn in Philippians to show how Jesus is to be remembered and recognized in practice. The final interrogation is that of John the Baptist's disciples drawn from the Q source (a set of about two hundred verses composed mostly of remembered sayings of Jesus preserved in a stable form, presumably written, but possibly an oral saga that Matthew and Luke incorporated into their Gospels) and the practical response to it. My argument is that exploring these texts as the artefacts of actions, specifically of their human author's acts in recording the texts as they did, in light of the specific orientation of this essay laid out in chapters 1 and 2, reveals a very different way of understanding what christology is, a practical rather than theoretical christology.[2] Christology is carried on by engaging in the practices of the Jesus-movement.

Part 3, "Practices," displays the practices of the Jesus-movement: the wounded body of Christ is an agent of reconciliation and thus a secondary agency of the salvation wrought by the primary agency of God present in Jesus then and the power of reconciliation in the world even now. Here is the key point at which the link between discipleship, christology, and soteriology occurs. The distinctive practices of Jesus and his disciples, the Jesus-movement, are reconciling practices, practices that can heal the fractured persons and communities that we are. To engage in these practices reflectively is to do christology in and through practice. Chapter 12 shows the basis of the practical approach. The next four chapters are devoted to the reconciling practices that Jesus was perceived as empowering the other members of the Jesus-movement to perform: healing, teaching, forgiving, and table fellowship. Of course, this list is not exhaustive, but these are practices central to and distinctive of Christian discipleship.

Part 4, "Implications," discusses how the present approach is related to some traditional theological concepts relevant to a practical christology. Chapter 17 turns

---

2. Of course, there are many images of Jesus created by disciples. *Who Do You Say That I Am? Essays on Christology*, ed. Mark Allan Powell and David R. Bauer (Louisville: Westminster John Knox, 1999) displays a number of images that shape New Testament and other texts. The images here are ones remembered as being developed in interactions, explicable only by considering practices, and explicitly centered on the ways that Jesus walked and taught.

to the form and function of doctrine in a practical theology. Chapter 18 explores issues in christological doctrine, with extensive reflection on the contribution of the Council of Chalcedon. Chapter 19 recaps the discussion and reflects on the practical significance of the resurrection, atonement, and mission.

In one sense, the argument is simple: the texts of the New Testament are the first scripts that inscribe the community of disciples and the members of the community as engaging in the reconciling work exemplified by Jesus. The disciples, then and now, are empowered by the presence of the incarnate Word of Wisdom. That empowerment continues in contexts far removed from the context that gave rise to the Jesus-movement.

The epilogue reflects on the resurrection and on revelation in light of the main vision of the text.

Much more could be said about christology as reconciling practice than what I have sketched in this book. Yet if the argument is successful, then we will be able to see that christology always draws from and redraws the image of the disciples' Jesus. Who Jesus is and what God did through him for humanity are shown in and through the reconciling practices that this book claims fundamentally constitute christology.

Part One

APPROACH

One

WHY ANOTHER CHRISTOLOGY?

*T*he question is obvious: why yet another essay in christology? The past three decades alone have been littered with hundreds, if not thousands, of books on who Jesus was and what his significance is. Can there possibly be room for another? Can anything new be written after so much ink has already been spilt? Perhaps not. But perhaps replaying some familiar themes in a different key may be of use, even though, as German theologian Jürgen Moltmann put it, "No contemporary christology is ever completely new."[1]

Each of the essays in christology contributes to a conversation that began with the first followers of Jesus of Nazareth and will continue as long as Christianity continues. This particular essay approaches christology with a hermeneutical key that construes acts as more fundamental than texts and a perspective that sees practices as generating beliefs rather than beliefs grounding practice. The present approach is akin to some Latin American liberation theologies and some North American postliberal theologies. The differences with each will appear along the way.

Constructing Christology

In a previous book, I made three claims about doing theology.[2] I want to recall their significance here. In short, all theological work is construction undertaken on a particular site according to a building code.

First, theology is construction. Eternal truths are not simply "out there" to be unearthed and displayed. Whatever truths might be eternal, they are always uttered or written in language that is temporally shifting. The classical terminology of *prosōpon* and *hypostasis* in Greek, for example, does not have the same sense as the Latin *persona* or the English *person*. Hence, when one today hears talk of the doctrine of "three persons in one God," one may well not understand that utterance in the same way as the ancient church did. Nor is it clear that we understand the church's key christological claim (in Latin) that there are *duae naturae in una persona* in Jesus Christ as the early Latin theologians, much

---

1. Jürgen Moltmann, *The Way of Jesus Christ: Christology in Messianic Dimensions*, trans. Margaret Kohl (San Francisco: HarperSanFrancisco, 1990), 38.

2. Terrence W. Tilley et al., *Religious Diversity and the American Experience: A Theological Approach* (New York: Continuum, 2007), 1-63.

less the Greek writers, understood this claim. Nor is it clear that there is not a profound equivocation in the concept of *natura* in this formula, as divine nature and any other nature are clearly incommensurable. In all these crucial areas, our contemporary understanding may or may not be in line with that of the ancient church. Simply using contemporary English transliterations of the ancient words cannot guarantee that we mean the same as they did. As we move from ancient Greek and Latin to modern English, the "same words" are simply not certainly the same. Since all our claims are expressed in time-conditioned language, we cannot simply measure them against eternal truths to see if we got it right, because our language is not, and the sentences that express our claims also cannot be, eternal!

Even if God gives humans eternal truths, they must be in humans' time-bound language(s). Because no human language is eternal and every language, even Latin, shifts in meaning over time, there can be no final and definitive formula for expressing an eternal truth. This is simply a linguistic version of Thomas Aquinas's variously formulated dictum: *omnia quae recipiuntur recepta sunt secundum modum recipientis*, "all that is received is received according to the receiver."[3] As beings placed on this earth (not universally ubiquitous) and temporal (not eternal) who think and speak in local and temporally conditioned languages, we do not and cannot think or speak in a language that is eternal, universal and absolute. Such a language does not exist—at least this side of heaven. This point does not entail that there are not better and worse ways to speak of God—only that we cannot claim that any way we speak or anything we write is perfectly definitive, even if it is God-given. This is neither God's fault nor our fault. It is simply a fact: shifts in time, context, and translations can and unavoidably do alter the senses of words, even sacred words.

The key to understanding our heritage in the present is good communication, therefore, not mere signification marked by using "person" for *prosōpon*, and "persona," and "nature" to cover both *divinis natura* and *natura humana* (assuming, for a moment, a point in serious dispute, in other words, that we can say that God has or is a *natura*). Even God cannot guarantee that a specific, culturally and linguistic conditioned utterance will infallibly and eternally correctly and finally signify an eternal truth. Use over time shifts linguistic meanings. Premodern Christian theologians took "nature" as a God-given, stable, defining constituent of an entity. Modern people take "nature" as the realm of scientific investigation. Simply assuming that "nature" and *natura* communicate well enough to signify the same thing is unwarranted.

On the view presented here, reflecting eternal truth well is a *consequence* of, and *cannot be a criterion* for, our central Christian theological claims being communicated and understood aright. "Realism," that is, having our claims match reality, is not a foundation for our communication but the result of communicating

---

3. For this version of the saying, see Fergus Kerr, *Twentieth-Century Catholic Theologians* (Oxford: Blackwell, 2007), 58; the translation is mine.

well.[4] Distinguishing better from worse or true from heretical formulae is a matter not of finding a good metaphysical foundation or repeating ancient words in a wildly different contemporary context, but of warranting one's claims as well as one can in a particular situation, including the claim to be faithful to our old creeds in this new world.

Theological constructions contribute to the ongoing conversation that seeks to communicate the tradition as well as possible, thus, as a result—and only as a result—accurately signifying *pro tem* God's truth in human terms. And the criterion of good communication is the ongoing ability of those who communicate with each other to recognize how to live in and live out our tradition.

Theologians are like building contractors. A builder constructs or restores a house in a neighborhood. She does so as well as she can. There is no one perfect eternal house that she strives to build. Nor can any house be entirely new, or it cannot function as a house. Rather, she tries to build the best house she can with the resources available, to create a structure that will be a home for people to live in happily and relatively comfortably. Similarly, the theologian constructs or restores elements in an ongoing tradition. Her work cannot be eternal or entirely new. But each theologian attempts to build as good a theology as possible *ad majorem dei gloriam* ("to the greater glory of God") with the resources she has for the people who will live in and live out the tradition. Each does new work in a tradition that itself is invented and reinvented as language, cultures, environments, and people change. Theology, then, is a communicative practice of constructing a way to live in and live out a tradition faithfully.

Second, theological construction is undertaken on a particular site. Theologians each occupy a particular social location on that site. These locations increase the chances of particular insights and oversights. Latin American liberation theologians, for example, work from the perspective of the poor and oppressed. They have brought powerful insights to theology in general and christology in particular. In some early theology on that location, however, some theologians neglected the positive significance popular religion could have for theology, relied too heavily on neo-Marxist social theory, and overlooked the particular oppressions that afflicted and afflict women in Latin America—problems that were soon corrected by the liberation theologians themselves as a result of varying forms of constructive criticism.

Theologians' sites also include varying cultural terrains that provide particular challenges to theological construction. The U.S. site, for example, is characterized historically by being a nation that never had an established religion and so did not have to undergo the trauma of disestablishment. Presently the U.S. site is characterized by being a wealthy society, but one that is debt-ridden and increasingly socially and economically stratified. This society glorifies freedom of choice to the point of idolizing the individual and promoting consumerist

---

4. See Terrence W. Tilley, *Inventing Catholic Tradition* (Maryknoll, NY: Orbis Books, 2000), 170-77, for an application of this "consequentialist realism" to Avery Dulles's concept of revelation.

spirituality.[5] The result is a cultural tendency to tolerant indifference in religious matters, a tendency that reduces enduring religious commitments to temporary personal preferences. While theological constructs can do little to change the cultural terrain directly, theologians can attend to the characteristics of the site and build their theologies in ways that promote what is good about the site while being wary of systemic problems on the site.

Pope Benedict XVI, before and after his election, was especially concerned with a proliferating "indifferentism" in religious matters, an attitude that one is not better off to live in one religious tradition (or none) rather than another. He articulated this concern in opposition to "relativism," which concluded that, because all religious traditions are nearly on an epistemic par, no objective criteria could show one tradition to be more true than another.

While agreeing completely with the problem, the present approach has to find a solution different from the typical one that the pope articulated. Theologians often argue that they have a good foundation for their views, typically in metaphysics. Hence, this makes their views objectively true. The present approach rejects such foundationalism. The cultural fact of relativism in our global village and the ongoing conversations in contemporary philosophy have made foundationalism incredible and the tactic of finding foundations to demonstrate the truth of claims an ineffective strategy.[6] Socially and intellectually, the issues involve both the (doubted) possibility of discovering secure foundations for any beliefs and the fact that no particular philosophical foundations are beyond being reasonably contested by other philosophers. One cannot solve a dispute about which of a set of foundations is right by appealing to one's own! But that is what many theologians try to do. Rather, the position espoused here is that showing what it means to live in and live out a tradition to younger generations and to nonparticipants is how we can show that appraising our tradition as "true" is a reasonable thing to do. In a nonfoundationalist mode, justification of claims includes their being (and being recognized as) well-formed, coherent, reasonably based, accurate enough for the present occasion, and pragmatically effective.[7]

Third, the traditions in which we work provide a "building code" that each construction has to follow. These codes are, admittedly, often best stated negatively. In christology, for example, "do not deny either the true humanity or the true divinity of Jesus Christ" can be one way of formulating the classic Nicene-Chalcedonian orthodoxy. Any theological construct, such as Arianism, that fails to meet the code fails as a theology for Christianity. And occasionally some constructs that were once seen as not being up to code, such as the work of Nestorius, can be recognized as complying with the code. In soteriology, "do not attribute salvation to human works or human faith, but to divine gift" is one way

---

5. This particular characterization of the U.S. site is developed more fully in Tilley et al., *Religious Diversity and the American Experience*, 12-46.

6. This is not to deny the reality of "objective" truth, but to say that the project of finding foundations fails to demonstrate it any longer, if it ever did.

7. For a brief description of this approach, which sees finding a story, beliefs or tradition "true" to be an appraisal, see my *Inventing Catholic Tradition*, 156-70.

of formulating the classic doctrinal rule developed by Augustine and accepted by the tradition as prohibiting theological Pelagianism (although Pelagius may himself not have been a Pelagian[8]). Yet the relationship between faith and works may be formulated positively in a number of ways—so long as both faith and works are responses to God's gracious gift. In short, disputes in the tradition that generate firm and clear proscriptions show contemporary theologians which paths to avoid but not which way they must walk and talk (given the malleability of language) in their quests to communicate revealingly the Eternal One in and through thoroughly time-bound language.

The present essay is one of constructive christology. It is a construction, on the U.S. site, that seeks to work according to the ancient code ensconced as the *regula fidei* ("the rule of faith"). It does not use the same linguistic code as do contemporary transliterations of fourth- and fifth-century creeds. The creedal proclamations appear only in the penultimate chapter. Rather, it seeks to show ways of faithfully living in and living out the tradition that produced those creeds. It seeks not to repeat the past but to be creatively faithful in the present to that tradition. The context in which the ancient creeds were produced no longer obtains. The question is whether we can live in and live out the tradition in ways that are not only true to the past but true to God and can be appraised as true by our children, our friends, and perhaps even our opponents.

The Focus

The particular focus of this essay is that doing christology is a practice of discipleship. Contemporary christologists typically connect christology and discipleship.[9] The present approach treats christology specifically as enacted discipleship. To do christology—simply or complexly—is to engage in a practice that shows forth who Christ is. It is part and parcel of discipleship and can only be done by disciples. I admit this point "up front": christology is a production of disciples, not spectators. This is not in the least to gainsay the contributions of many scholars interested in discovering what we can know of Jesus apart from faith in him.[10] Their contributions are truly significant.[11] But such noncommitted

---

8. See B. R. Rees, *Pelagius: A Reluctant Heretic* (Wolfeboro, NH: Boydell Press, 1988).

9. Many others see this relationship, for example, Roberto Goizueta, *Caminemos con Jesús: Toward a Hispanic/Latino Theology of Accompaniment* (Maryknoll, NY: Orbis Books, 1995); Ada María Isasi-Díaz, "Christ in *Mujerista* Theology," in *Thinking of Christ*, ed. Tatha Wiley (New York: Continuum, 2003), 157-76.

10. The insights and oversights of this approach have been superbly summarized and reliably assessed in James D. G. Dunn, *Jesus Remembered*, vol. 1 of *Christianity in the Making* (Grand Rapids: Eerdmans, 2003), 1-97. This is the first of a three-volume work entitled *Christianity in the Making*. As of this writing, the second and third volumes have not been announced. Dunn shows especially clearly that we owe debts to many of the scholars whose work would be critical of the kinds of positions he or I would hold.

11. For example, the work of E. P. Sanders, *Jesus and Judaism* (London: SCM Press, 1985)

scholars are, from this perspective, engaging not in the practice of christology proper but in the practice of understanding the literature about an ancient messianic figure and the movement he inspired. They produce "studies" that may contribute to understanding the past in our present context, but their practice is not one in which they engage as a practice of discipleship.[12]

If there were no cloud of witnesses, no company of disciples, no body of Christ, there would be little interest in a treasonous troublemaker from Nazareth executed nearly two thousand years ago by a Roman procurator, Pontius Pilate. Modern scholars would have nothing to work on if disciples had not formed an enduring community that carried—and was carried by—the memory of him.[13] Scholars' investigations may yield results that support or oppose the images and understandings of Jesus that have become dominant in the Christian tradition. Their scholarly disciplines may support or contribute to the practices of discipleship, but they do not constitute discipleship. Historians' practices or claims cannot without

---

inaugurated a "third quest" for the historical-Jesus. In so doing, he made a profound contribution to christology, not as a "believer" but as an academic. Similarly, Paula Fredriksen and other Jewish scholars who work on the parting of the ways between late Second Temple Judaism and nascent Christianity have also contributed challenges and insights to those who do christology. But they are also not doing christology for the Christian community. Yet it is important to note that their scholarship is not uncommitted or neutral or in some sense "objective." While it is fallacious to reduce the worth of the results of an investigation to the acceptability or perspicacity of the investigators' religious or metaphysical beliefs, it is important to recognize how the scholars' work functions in its scholarly and social context. For one approach to this issue, see n. 14 below.

12. Elisabeth Schüssler Fiorenza (*Jesus and the Politics of Interpretation* [New York: Continuum, 2000]) has argued that this work is much less innocent than it appears. Much of the impulse of the modern quests for the historical-Jesus (her term, which I adopt; I use an analogous term for the group that gathered around Jesus and that endures after his death, the "Jesus-movement," as noted in the introduction) is directed not toward the man from Nazareth as remembered but toward creating an identity today: "In the past decade numerous scholarly volumes have appeared promising to tell us everything we want to know about the 'real' Jesus. By claiming to produce knowledge about the 'real' Jesus, malestream as well as wo/men scholars deny the rhetoricity of their research and obfuscate the fact that their reconstructive cultural models and theological interests are not able to *produce* the *real* Jesus but only creative *images* of him" (13). (Because "mainstream" scholarship is typically an occupation of men—and European and Euro-American men in particular— she uses the term "malestream.") Also see her *Jesus: Miriam's Child, Sophia's Prophet; Critical Issues in Feminist Christology* (New York: Continuum, 1994).

13. Compare Roger Haight, *Jesus Symbol of God* (Maryknoll, NY: Orbis Books, 1999): the memory of Jesus is a "constitutive dimension of the life" of the early Christian communities (270). That after his death he may have been "misunderstood" by the evolving church is entirely possible, but I find the claims of Amy-Jill Levine in *The Misunderstood Jew: The Church and the Scandal of the Jewish Jesus* (San Francisco: HarperSanFrancisco, 2006) overstated. While many of her claims regarding Christian anti-Judaism and misogyny are clearly warranted, they miss the significance of some Jewish views contemporary with Jesus that there were "two powers in heaven," for example, "God and God's Wisdom." This suggests not that Christians misunderstood Jesus, but that they applied an unusual form of monotheistic belief to the man Jesus (see Daniel Boyarin, *Border Lines: The Partition of Judaeo-Christianity* [Philadelphia: University of Pennsylvania Press, 2004], esp. 85-145). Nor is Levine concerned with early Christians' need to develop a particular identity that was neither rabbinic monotheism nor a part of a contemporary Greco-Roman polytheism.

confusion substitute for the specific practice of christology by disciples or even directly affect the faith of those who are Christian.[14]

The term "practice," as in "the practice of discipleship," is a term of art. The key here is that one learns *how* to engage in a practice; only then can one know *what* the practice is and *what* participation in the practice produces—including among the products of practices those dispositions we call "beliefs" and formulate in sentences. Practices are complex patterns of actions, like games. Novices typically learn how to engage in the practice from skilled participants in a community of practitioners. Participants strive for the goals of the practices by using means specific to the practices while being guided by rules inferred from exemplary exercises of the practice. Participation develops skilled practitioners (*phronimoi,* to use an Aristotelian term).[15] Learning how to drive a car is learning a practice; so is learning how to do research in physics. The finest practitioners develop the ability to make the practice better—though what counts as "better" cannot often be specified in advance or apart from participating in the practice.

For example, most Christian communities do not regard "foot washing" as a religious practice. A few see it as sacrament or ordinance. Most would agree with Raymond E. Brown, "But the majority of Christians from the beginning seem to have felt that what Jesus was commanding in [John 13:]14-17 was an imitation of the spirit of footwashing."[16] Rather than slavishly imitating this particular practice, Christians have seen the principle involved as one of service in love to others. The principle, then, becomes the key. One is to participate in the practice of service in love to others—which cannot be specified in advance as different circumstances require different ways of participating in the practices that can be grouped under the principle of loving service. What "counts" as carrying on the tradition begun with the foot washing—or with the anointing of Jesus by Mary of Bethany, as I

---

14. I have argued this point for historical investigations and their relationships to faith in general in my *History, Theology, and Faith: Dissolving the Modern Problematic* (Maryknoll, NY: Orbis Books, 2004), summarized at 186-91. A similar point has been made by Dunn (*Jesus Remembered,* 99-135), but he has "hermeneutics" mediating between history and faith, whereas I find that "theologians" (not an abstraction like "theology" or "hermeneutics") have the role-specific responsibility for engaging in mediating practice between the practices of historians and the practice of faith. And some of us engage in multiple practices of theologians, historians, and believers professionally and personally, which makes that "mediating" position possible but also tensive. For one useful understanding of this mediation, see Dermot A. Lane, *Christ at the Centre: Selected Issues in Christology* (Dublin: Veritas, 1991), 7. Lane focuses on the mediating work of his book. I would, however, emphasize the activity of theologians working over what those theologians produce.

15. I am indebted to Alasdair MacIntyre and James Wm. McClendon, Jr., for their work on practices. A rationale for my development of their views on "practice" and construing a religious tradition as a practice or set of practices can be found in my *Inventing Catholic Tradition,* chap. 2. Another account of practices with a focus on the community that sustains practitioners is Samuel Wells, *Improvisation: The Drama of Christian Ethics* (Grand Rapids: Brazos Press, 2004). Wells's approach sees Christian ethics "not as the art of performing the Scriptures but as faithfully improvising on the Christian tradition" (11), a theme that resonates with the present text. Wells centers on drama and dramatic interpretation; another image would be musical performance, especially jazz.

16. Raymond E. Brown, *The Gospel According to John: Introduction, Translation, and Notes,* 2 vols., Anchor Bible 29, 29A (Garden City, NY: Doubleday, 1966, 1970), 2:558.

discuss below—cannot be designated apart from the particular circumstances in which loving service is rendered to another. One sometimes wonders if pastors and bishops who ritually engage in actual foot washing on Holy Thursdays learn much of the spirit of foot washing and whether those whose feet are washed can recognize that spirit in many of the foot washers or learn how to accept such gracious hospitality and service.

A specifically religious practice involves the practitioners in learning *how* to live in and live out a religious tradition. In participating in the practices of the tradition, the participant learns *what* the tradition is and teaches, typically from exemplary practitioners who are the teachers and leaders in the community that carries the tradition. By engaging in the practices, participants develop a shared vision, that is, a web of convictions regarding both the goal(s) of human life and how such goal(s) can be reached. But the practices are primary; the doctrines are derivative. Insofar as the practices fail to show the point of the doctrine—perhaps as the actual ritual washing of feet may often show little of the "spirit" of foot washing—the practices become "mere ritual," irrelevant to the life of the ongoing tradition.

Christian discipleship, then, is the practice of following Christ. A person learns how to follow Christ; in learning how to be a disciple one learns who Christ is. To be a disciple is to learn how to have faith in God by following Christ. Discipleship involves, indeed *is*, a way of life.[17] This life is composed of various activities one learns how to engage in—prayer and worship; service with, to, and for others for the sake of righteousness and justice; reverence for all there is as God's gift; sustaining a community of disciples, and so on. One learns how to recognize and avoid engaging in activities one comes to recognize as sinful—revering the nation over God, making harmful and unnecessary divisions among people, self-centeredness, leading or being led by and with others into vile or violent behavior, and so on.

The rules guiding the practice are formulated in various ways. Most generally, the creeds incorporate the rule of the faith—but disciples seem to argue incessantly about how to form and follow those rules.[18] The goal of the practice

---

17. James D. G. Dunn writes that "Jesus' call to discipleship, then, is first and foremost *to recognize the reality of God's rule.*" See his *Jesus' Call to Discipleship* (New York: Cambridge University Press, 1992), 30. This recognition, however, is possible only in *practice*, not in theory. A "theoretical recognition" alone is no *recognition* at all.

18. However, this is not necessarily a bad thing. Alasdair MacIntyre has defined a living tradition as "an historically extended, socially embodied argument, and an argument precisely in part about the goods which constitute that tradition" (*After Virtue: A Study in Moral Theory* [Notre Dame: University of Notre Dame Press, 1981], 207). What makes it a bad thing is that we have allowed the arguments to degenerate into competitive shouting matches, with no one really listening to, understanding, and responding to others' positions critically, constructively, and persuasively—keys to the practice of real argument. We have failed to keep the conversation going about our practice of the Christian life and have excommunicated each other. The complete lack of real communication between Christian proponents of "pro-choice" and "pro-life" views of "abortion" is a prime example of such degradation. Such shouting matches are not part of the practice of argument but a degeneration of the practice.

is, in its broadest sense, salvation—a life accepted as from God through Christ to be even now eternally enjoyed in the Spirit—though how we ought to formulate our understanding of that goal is one of those items about which we argue. Nonetheless, as one engages in the practice one simultaneously learns how to be a disciple, that is, one who has the two-way relationship of "having faith in" and "being saved by" Christ.

The previous paragraph only barely indicates the richness and diversity of discipleship and barely pays lip service to the disputes that have all too often shredded communities of disciples into fractious disputation with and sometimes alienation from each other. On one level, plumbing the depths and mending the divisions of and in disciples' ranks are or ought to be fundamental concerns of theologians who serve the community. But my point here is a more focused one: doing christology is a practice of disciples, not spectators. And disciples are indeed followers of Christ *in practice*. The significance of this for theology appears in chapter 2.

Two

THE CHRISTOLOGICAL QUESTION

*N*umerous books and essays have used the question Jesus asks Peter in Mark 8:29, "But who do you say that I am?" as a title or a motif.[1] They tend to focus on *what* Peter says in the next verse, "You are *ho christos* (the anointed one)," rather than *who* is doing the asking or what Peter is *doing* in answering Jesus—save to assert that Peter's confession answers for all the disciples whom he represents.[2] I will have much to say about this scene set near Caesarea Philippi in chapter 8. It is, I argue, the place to begin christology because that is when and where christology began. But here I want to focus on some factors that are sometimes overlooked by those who approach christology today using this question.

First, no one can perform the act of asking that specific question except Jesus. For theologians or historians to address that question to themselves or their audiences, they must change it: Who do you say that he is/was? And that revised question does not have the same force as the original because it is not uttered by Jesus or addressed "in person" to a disciple. The act that Jesus performed in asking the question was not an academic test but a very personal challenge—in this case, from Jesus to an "exemplary" follower. Peter's confession is an act that testifies to his belief in Jesus—a very personal response *to the very one who asked him the question.* The first passion prediction and Jesus' description of discipleship that follows remind Peter of the hard truth that he did not want to accept the fact that just as Jesus will suffer, so will the disciples suffer.

Contemporary christologists cannot ask that question with either the same force or content. A contemporary respondent gives an answer that also has a different force and content. The question and answer in the Gospels are in the

---

1. For example, see the collection of excellent essays, *Who Do You Say That I Am? Confessing the Mystery of Christ*, ed. John C. Cavadini and Laura Holt (Notre Dame: University of Notre Dame Press, 2004); the collection of essays in honor of Jack Dean Kingsbury that focus on New Testament christology, *Who Do You Say That I Am? Essays on Christology*, ed. Mark Allan Powell and David R. Bauer (Louisville: Westminster John Knox, 1999); or Jacques Dupuis, *Who Do You Say I Am? Introduction to Christology* (Maryknoll, NY: Orbis Books, 1994).

2. For the former focus, see, e.g., Gerald O'Collins, S.J., "Jesus as Lord and Teacher," in Cavadini and Holt, eds., *Who Do You Say That I Am?* 51-62; James J. Buckley ("*Lectio Divina* and Arguing over Jesus: An Ascetic for Christological Rebukes," in Cavadini and Holt, eds., *Who Do You Say That I Am?* 87-108) does attend to what Peter and Jesus do with their words after the "confession."

second person; contemporary theologians' questions and answers must be in the third person.[3] They're not the same.

Both ancient and contemporary people can give testimony or witness. But theological analysis and exposition are supplementary to and derivative from the practice of faith, including the practice of giving witness. In any case, the contemporary theologian is not asking the addressee who she or he is, nor does the addressee respond with a confession of faith in the questioner. Christologists who focus on "Who do you say that I am?" can neglect the significance of the fact that they perform different acts in asking the question than Jesus did and the responses they elicit also can have a different force and audience from Peter's.

Second, no one can perform the act of answering Jesus' precise question except a disciple. The Gospels do not portray Jesus as addressing the question to "anyone" or "the crowds." It was a challenge to his disciples. If someone who is not a disciple hears and answers the question, the answer has a different force. It may be the expression of an opinion or an identification of a figure studied by scholars, but it is neither a confession of faith in Jesus nor a commitment to him. Again, as the act performed in asking the question shifts, the force and the meaning of the response can also shift.

What this means is that Peter's response cannot be replicated today any more than Jesus' question can. The reason is simple: no one who asks it of us is asking us for a confession of faith in the person asking the question. Or at least they shouldn't be asking for such a confession! Again, the force and content of the answers cannot quite be the same for the readers of modern christological texts as they were for Peter.

The typical content of the answers also is not merely different but of a different order from the original. The content is almost always about *what* Jesus was, not *who* he is *for Peter* or for his disciples. Consider the following, which begins a popular contemporary textbook in christology:

> In the light of Christian faith, practice, and worship, that branch of theology called Christology reflects systematically on the person, being, and doing of Jesus of Nazareth (*c.* 5 BC-*c.* AD 30). In seeking to clarify the essential truths about him, it investigates his person and being (who and what he was/is) and work (what he did/does).[4]

---

3. Talk about God in the third person should always be understood as derivative from second-person talk to God or with God. Third-person theology is derivative from the practice of the faith, always including the practice of prayer, of address to God in all we do—"omnia *ad majorem dei gloriam.*" For this point, see Terrence W. Tilley, "The Systematic Elusiveness of God: On the 50th Anniversary of Ian Ramsey's *Religious Language,*" *Horizons* 34, no. 1 (Spring 2007): 7-25.

4. Gerald O'Collins, S.J., *Christology: A Biblical, Historical and Systematic Study of Jesus* (Oxford: Oxford University Press, 1995), 1. This is not to say that O'Collins would disconnect christology from discipleship or that he wouldn't himself see his christological work as reflection on the faith he shares with his fellow Catholics. Other contemporary theologians typically do connect discipleship and christology; for example, see Haight, *Jesus Symbol of God*, 447-54; Lisa Sowle Cahill, "Christology, Ethics and Spirituality," in *Thinking of Christ: Proclamation, Explanation,*

Such a christological program wants to systematize the facts about and the Christian beliefs concerning Jesus as incarnate Son of God. It constructs a systematic, philosophically inflected account. It does not respond to "Who do you say that I am?"

In contrast, Peter was confessing *who* Jesus is *for him* (which does not in the least preclude the point that Peter was also trying to say who Jesus really was—Peter's answer is not on any account "merely a personal opinion" or a "functional, not ontological" claim).

Consider a parallel: When Romeo answers his own question, "Hark, what light at yon window breaks?" he does not answer it in terms of *what* Juliet is; his answer confesses *who* she is *for him*: "'Tis the East, and Juliet is the sun." His answer is relational and metaphoric—yet it shows the truth about what Juliet is for him and who she is, given that relationship.[5] The point of Romeo's answer is not to say *what* Juliet is but to show his love for her (in this soliloquy, of course, he shows it to the audience rather than to the actress playing Juliet). We *could* construct a theory that reflects systematically on the person, being, and doing of Romeo Montague. But would that help us understand him better? And might it help Juliet Capulet, who loved him and gave her life for him?

Analogously, this essay takes the primary christological issue to be not "what" Jesus is and does but "who" he is for us who follow him. Disciples love him and give their lives to—and may give their lives for—Jesus. The present approach is a theological exploration of christology in and as practice, specifically the reconciling practices that constitute the pattern of Christian discipleship. Of course, this approach does not preclude a more systematic and abstract theology. However, a systematic approach abstracts from, is derivative from, an approach that focuses on the Jesus who evokes disciples' faith. The primary christological issue is truly personal and truly an issue for those who are disciples, whether or not they are scholars.

The riot of metaphors in Shakespeare's balcony scene can be dissected just as the riot of titles for Jesus in the New Testament can.[6] But such analyses run the danger of blinding us to the force of Peter's confession or Romeo's declaration. We no more need a discursive analysis and clarification of the essential truths about Romeo or Juliet than we need such clarification about Jesus and Peter. We "get it" (as we get a joke) when we hear Romeo in the play say, "Juliet is the sun." We "get it" when we hear Peter in the Gospel say, "You are *ho christos*." We need to analyze those utterances only if we are scholars or pedants or do not get the

---

Meaning, ed. Tatha Wiley (New York: Continuum, 2003), 193-209; and any christology by a Latin American liberation theologian.

5. That figurative language can, as it stands, convey truth and truths is often overlooked. It is not only literal language that can have ontological force. This point is made repeatedly herein, but especially in chap. 18 in dealing with an ancient metonymy.

6. For recent explorations that focus on the titles, see Jon Sobrino, *Christ the Liberator: A View from the Victims*, trans. Paul Burns (Maryknoll, NY: Orbis Books, 2001), 113-218; and James D. G. Dunn, *Christology in the Making: A New Testament Inquiry into the Origins of the Doctrine of the Incarnation* (Philadelphia: Westminster, 1980).

point. In such analysis, all too often analysts tend to obliterate the fact that Peter's act is not merely *saying* what or who Jesus is, but is *showing* his faith in Jesus in his uttering his words.

This showing of faith is even more blatant in Matthew's Gospel. In Matthew's version of the scene, Jesus is so amazed by Simon Peter's answer that he has to attribute this powerful act of faith to the instigation of his Father in heaven. Whereas in Mark, Peter simply replies without need for divine inspiration, in Matthew Peter acts as a spokesperson for the Father, who must have told him what to say. The point is that much modern academic christology pays little heed to these shifts in the force of Peter's act as portrayed in the different accounts, evidently finding these differences not very relevant to their analytical task.[7]

I am not claiming that such analysis is unneeded or mistaken. Far from it. The better we can understand what Peter (or Romeo) confessed, the better we can understand how each responded to Jesus (or Juliet), and even the Jesus (or Juliet) to whom each responded. But whatever the point of literary criticism may be, the point of christology is lost if it loses the force of the acts performed in uttering a christological confession and attends only to the content of the act, to *what* is confessed. Objective philosophical or historical analysis cannot reach the goal of answering the key christological question but can provide one subsidiary means to help us understand how disciples might confess Jesus well in a context other than first-century Palestine.

To understand the force of what Peter said is to understand not merely *what* Peter said but what Peter *did* in saying what he said, and *how* Peter could be in position to say what he did. To understand that force is to understand not only what it meant and means to practice discipleship, but also what it is about Jesus that evoked and evokes that response. For just as Romeo's confession is a confession of love, so Peter's confession is a confession of faith. Understanding the confession begins with understanding how one can be able to utter it properly, what kind of person one has to be or has had to become, in order to confess it. The utterances cannot have the force they do except as an act of love/faith in the context of a relationship. If we remove from our analysis of the utterance any understanding of the relationship, or of the force of the loving/faithful act we perform in uttering our love/faith, we lose its meaning. We see it as an aesthetic object to be dissected, not an act that we can or should perform. Dissecting *Romeo and Juliet* or the Gospel according to Mark can be interesting and informative, but

---

7. The best analyses of New Testament christology move beyond this "objectifying" approach. A prime example is Dunn's *Christology in the Making.* I have long been indebted to his work (see my *Story Theology* [Wilmington, DE: Michael Glazier, 1985; reprint, Collegeville, MN: Liturgical Press, 1990, 1991, 2002], esp. chap. 7) and I continue to appreciate his scholarship on behalf of Jesus' followers, especially as carried further in *Jesus Remembered,* vol. 1 of *Christianity in the Making* (Grand Rapids: Eerdmans, 2003). Although the present project was first conceived and contracted before *Jesus Remembered* was published, most work on it was deferred until after the publication of my *History, Theology, and Faith* and the completion of other duties that arose in the meantime. As Dunn's work has helped shape some of the material and given support to the basic vision of the project, it is fortunate that the project was not too far along for me to learn from his work. See chap. 5 below.

such analysis does not get to the heart of appreciating who the Capulets and the Montagues were or of confessing Jesus as *ho christos*.

Certainly, many Christian scholars might not disagree with the point of the last paragraph. They would agree that lovers should perform loving acts and disciples should engage in faithful acts. They might also advert that their analyses, however academic, would not be intended to preclude such acts; it is just that performance of acts of faith like "confession" or "witness" is not what their work is about. Analysis is what they do—and as scholars, all they do.

And that precisely is the problem: the practical significance of what scholars do. Put rather baldly, scholars typically study texts as texts, not as records of actions. For many academic christologists, the *text* of the New Testament is the beginning and—save for references to the hypothesized "Q" document contained in Matthew and Luke, and a few references to the extracanonical works—the end of "New Testament christology." Other scholars focus on the affirmations of Nicaea and Chalcedon, finding that the task is to explain just how those conciliar texts got things right. Scholars focus on the meaning of the *text*, what it meant in its original context and sometimes what it can mean now. New Testament scholars give lip service to the process of oral transmission, but rarely attend to the actions and interactions that were performed and only then preserved in a written text— whose meaning they seek to analyze.[8] Scholars of Nicaea and Chalcedon give lip service to the shifts in meaning in the technical Greek philosophical terms used by those councils and the various translations of the terms outside of a Greek philosophical context into Latin or English or other languages. This is the problem: the force and meaning of the act of love or the act of faith that gave rise to the texts under study have been reduced to the meaning of texts apart from the force and meaning of the acts that produced them. In such a reduction, there is a great loss, if for no other reason than that the significance of texts is constituted in part by the force of the acts that produced them.[9]

The text does not give meaning to our deeds. Our acts produce texts that others read and respond to. Our actions, what our actions produce in words or texts, and the reception of those words or texts are meaningful.[10] Our confessions—from

---

8. However, this is changing. Dunn (*Jesus Remembered*) focuses on what studies of the oral transmission of stories and sayings can do to help us understand the growth of the gospel tradition. He summarized his basic insight pithily: "Mark's Gospel may be *frozen* orality, but it is frozen *oral-ity*" (202). Since Dunn recognizes that the oral transmission is tradition, this implies that scripture is *frozen* tradition, but it is frozen *tradition*. So much for *sola scriptura*.

9. The separation of theory from practice is not a new problem but one that has afflicted the Christian community practically since the beginning. Jon Sobrino highlighted this in his discussion of such a separation in Chalcedonian christology: "For whatever reasons, following, *doing*, became divorced from *theoretical* christology. The Christian life, as ascesis or spirituality, was of course encouraged, but christology—as an exercise of the intelligence—was gradually changed into a conceptual exercise, separated from the practical life of embodied faith and basing itself only on visualized faith" (Sobrino, *Christ the Liberator*, 229). As discussed in chap. 18 below, the vicious disputes about this Chalcedonian visualization among the monks could be rendered benign by a focus on the practice of spirituality.

10. This is a central claim of "speech-act theory." When a person speaks and is heard (or, analogously, writes and is read), a person performs an act. That act falls into one of five classes: it states

performing to receiving— are meaningful acts. These acts, performed and heard as one of the practices of discipleship, give force and meaning to the words, whether oral or written, we produce.[11] It is not that the act of writing an essay in theology in general or christology in particular is one thing and an act of faith is something entirely separate. While writing theology is *one* of the acts faithful folk perform, it is itself an act done in light of and out of faith. As such, its first force is from the act performed; the reception of the text—whether oral or written text—is second. By focusing on texts alone, scholars can all too easily obscure this important relationship of a person's speaking to the content of what the person says and the ways that speaking is heard.[12]

This approach emphatically does not disparage or disregard the mountains of textual work done on the New Testament or the great conciliar formulae. This legacy is a great gift to us. Nor do I want to reduce the meaning of a text to the author's meaning or intention or even the meaning and force it had when originally produced. We have learned to avoid the "intentionalist fallacy,"[13] in

---

facts, makes a commitment, directs/requests another to act, expresses feelings, or declares a new state of affairs to exist and it then does exist (as when each member of a couple in proper circumstances says, "I do," a new state of affairs—a marriage—is created). The act performed is called the "illocutionary act" or "illocutionary force"; the sentence or expression used is the "locution"; and the uptake by hearers is effected by a "perlocutionary effect." For present purposes, it is enough to note that there are varieties of acts, and only *one* of them has a locution that can be true or false, the act of stating. The locutions of the other acts, such as warnings (a kind of directive), may require conditions to be a certain way for the act to be proper (e.g., yelling "Fire!" when there is none would be improper—not a "lie" but a vicious act nonetheless), but their locutionary content is neither true nor false in themselves. If one does not know the force of the act, one cannot know the meaning of the locution. A similar point goes for writing, but in that case the perlocutionary effect may be completely outside the author's intent, whereas for most spoken acts, the speaker's intent is pretty clear to the hearer. For further discussion of these points in terms of speech-act theory and, to a lesser extent, poststructuralist accounts of language, see my *The Evils of Theodicy* (Washington, DC: Georgetown University Press, 1991; reprint, Eugene, OR: Wipf & Stock, 2000), 9-81.

11. This does not mean that we can arbitrarily give meaning to our words or sentences. Our speaking is structured by the language we speak, by our competence in using it, and by the ways our hearers or readers can respond to our acts.

12. Similar points could be made regarding "conciliar christology," where the focus on the texts of the creeds and *what* they say can obscure the creeds as communicative acts performed. To be faithful to those creeds cannot be simply repeating what they say, but must be communicating how and what they communicate to their audiences. To be faithful to the tradition does not mean repeating a form of sound words, but carrying on the tradition and communicating it. This point is discussed more extensively below in chap. 13, where the form and function of religious doctrine are distinguished from asserting one's faith; a creedal text can be use for both purposes, but have different functions. See pp. 203-5.

13. It is not easy, however, to say what replaces "author's intention" to give validity to interpretations. Sandra Schneiders (*The Revelatory Text: Interpreting the New Testament as Sacred Scripture*, 2nd ed. [Collegeville, MN: Liturgical Press, 1999]) suggests the "ideal meaning" that can be actualized in varied interpretations in different contexts (xxx-xxxiv). Schneiders suggests analogies in music and sport—the perfect rendition of a score is an ideal never realized, but one can recognize better and worse performances; some play golf well, some poorly, but they are nonetheless playing golf, not baseball or tennis. Schneiders focuses here on the *conditions* that make for valid interpretation; she only briefly discusses *criteria* by which we can judge good interpretation (164-67). It is the criteria, however, that are crucial.

which the meaning of a text is reduced to the author's intentions as carried out in the acts that produce the text. Nor do I want to reduce the meaning of a text to an audience's reception of the text. This would be a "receptionist fallacy" that finds significance in the way a text is received. Nor do I want to devalue the multiple forms of "higher criticism," whether literary, form, source, redaction, social scientific, narrative, or other forms of textual studies that have taught us much. Yet studies that approach the product and that downplay the roles of the producer or the act of production of the text and the community that receives the text are incomplete in their analyses. Understanding the force and purpose of acts that produced texts may sometimes contribute practically nothing to our understanding the meaning of a text. But the force and purpose of acts do not "factor out" when considering "personal" acts and their texts—such as acts of testimony or witness—key genres in christology.

The question that centers this essay in christology is not, What was and is the meaning of *what* Peter confessed? but How can we embody and understand in and through our own practice the significance of Peter's *exemplary act of confessing* Jesus as *ho christos*? The question is not the meaning of the words, or of the sentence, or of the text, or even of the text in its literary (canonical) and extraliterary (sociohistorical) context—although investigations of each of those provides grist for our mill. The question is the meaning and force of the *act*—and only once we understand the force of the act can we then understand the meaning of the sentence uttered in performing the act of confessing.

Obviously, the present work is necessarily in debt to centuries of scholarship on the texts and their genres and contexts. The purpose here, however, is different: to understand what disciples did and do, not merely to understand the texts they left behind and which were canonized by the church. The question is first to understand how to be a disciple of Jesus of Nazareth or to know what it means to be a disciple of Jesus of Nazareth. The answer is not in understanding the meaning of a text but in learning how to live out a commitment. It is learning how to act, or as I shall argue below, to engage in reconciling practices, including undertaking the practice of speaking rightly.

In sum, the present essay begins with a different question from that asked by most christologists, not merely, What is the meaning of the text? but What is the significance of Peter's act? an exercise in discipleship preserved in the community's lore.[14] That different beginning means a different set of issues to be

---

14. Much modern and contemporary christology is devoted to making the meaning of the affirmation of Jesus as the Christ accessible to nonbelievers—and the nonbeliever in each of us. For example, Roger Haight (*Jesus Symbol of God*) has taken the approach that the task of christology is to make the content of the old affirmations, preserved in the texts of creeds and scripture, accessible to the postmodern mind. Haight wants to show how Christians can talk of Jesus as the symbol/sacrament of God's presence in and to the world without sacrificing either fidelity to the tradition or resorting to claims *prima facie* easily dismissed by modern and contemporary thinkers. Haight writes with the diversity of religious traditions always in sight, a notable advance over much christology which accords that diversity little importance. He has come under significant criticism for an underdeveloped sense of the incarnation and an attenuated concept of the symbolic. By working in a tradition of modern theology circumscribed by Troeltschian presumptions about the practice of history and what is credible to

confronted and a different pattern of development in understanding the force of christological claims.

Most scholars treat faith in Jesus as "Christian belief in Jesus,"[15] an attitude of trust and commitment on the part of disciples. For some purposes in christological work, this is sufficient. But all too often this focus on belief means that the scholar has little or nothing to say about how faith in Jesus as the one who brings salvation affects the disciples' understanding of who Jesus is.[16] Such faith is faith in practice, and discipleship is reconciling practices—our practices, which in limited ways instantiate the healing that God has brought to disciples through Jesus.

Typically, christology is sundered from the practices of disciples and taken to be an ahistorical theological endeavor. One of Elisabeth Schüssler Fiorenza's insights provides the angle of vision from which to see the problems with that practice. What she writes about one community applies, in my view, to all the communities of Christians: "I want to argue . . . that for the Q people this prophetic tradition is an open ongoing tradition. Jesus of Nazareth, whom they understand as an eminent prophet of Sophia, *does not close this tradition but activates it.*"[17] Schüssler Fiorenza's work challenges those who think that focusing

---

those who accept the axioms of historical study, he is open to criticism for being too "modern," and not "postmodern" enough (see my *History, Theology, and Faith*, 38-48). His methodological approach is an example of what George Lindbeck called "experiential expressivism" (*The Nature of Doctrine: Religion and Theology in a Postliberal Age* [Philadelphia: Fortress, 1984], 16-17), characteristic of modern liberal theology; for one crucial example, see Haight's discussion of the reports of the "resurrection experiences" of the disciples, summarized in *Jesus Symbol of God*, 123. Haight does not deny the reality of the resurrection, as indicated at various points in his text (75, 124-27, 141-43, 145, 150, 179, 181, 196, 207-8, 347), although some critics have thought he has done so (such as Donald Gelpi, *Peirce and Theology: Essays in the Authentication of Doctrine* [Lanham, MD: University Press of America, 2001], 79-89, who takes him to reduce the reality of the resurrection to subjective experience because he conflates methodology and rhetoric). While much is to be learned from Haight's work, it asks and seeks to answer a very different question from that which concerns us here.

15. For instance, Dunn, *Jesus Remembered*, 12.

16. Dunn's monumental book *Jesus Remembered* focuses on *what* is remembered about Jesus more than on *how* those who remembered him were shaped by the encounter and engaged in the practice of discipleship, which has left behind the artifacts we call Gospels. Dunn is properly interested in the *fact* of faith and its effect on the remembrance of Jesus. His work is shaped by an understanding that the practice of remembering by narrating is the ground from which the New Testament springs. He thus gives the texts the status of the artifacts of disciples' acts of remembering. In so doing, Dunn is going beyond the text-centered approaches of much contemporary christology. But this does not exhaust the significance of discipleship for the work of salvation and how the disciples carried not only the stories of and about Jesus, but his practice.

17. Elisabeth Schüssler Fiorenza, *Jesus: Miriam's Child, Sophia's Prophet: Critical Issues in Feminist Christology* (New York: Continuum, 1994), 142 (emphasis added). Feminist scholars are often criticized for their use of "sophia." Yet even non-feminists recognize that in the Gospels and "in Pauline Christianity Christ may have been seen as the human expession of God's attribute of wisdom, which in Jewish sources is often portrayed in personified form" (Larry W. Hurtado, *Lord Jesus Christ: Devotion to Jesus in Earliest Christianity* [Grand Rapids: Eerdmans, 2003], 119). Hurtado attributes this position to Dunn, *Christology in the Making*, in the course of arguing against Dunn's rejection of "preexistence" in the *kenōsis* hymn in Philippians 2. But Hurtado never contradicts the point about identifying Christ with wisdom, only that such identification is insufficient reason to reject the belief in preexistence most find displayed in the hymn.

on the linguistic meaning of the "reign of God" (*basileia tou theou*) in Jesus' talk can be understood apart from the relationships that empowered the practices that constitute the Jesus-movement (a term to designate the faction of Jews who evidently called themselves "the Way," but were first known polemically as the "Nazarenes" and who, along with some gentiles, eventually became called "Christians"). The Jesus-movement was one of the emancipatory movements in late Second Temple Judaism and if disciples today are faithful followers of Jesus, Christianity remains such.[18]

Larry Hurtado also approaches the New Testament as an artifact created out of the practices of devotion to and even worship of Jesus among even the very earliest Christian communities.[19] He focuses on "Christ-devotion" rather than christology because the latter has to do with beliefs, he says, about Jesus, whereas the former can focus on the liturgical practice—which developed quite early—of devotion to Christ. This focus on a key practice in the Jesus-movement is a significant contribution. But worship is not the only practice of the community, no matter how central.

But what if one were to write a christology in which the particular focus was on how the various practices of discipleship related the disciples to Jesus, on how that commitment was exercised and that trust developed? Might such a christological essay show how Christians whose purpose is to practice their faith (as sketched so lightly above) have in the past and can in the present engage in that practice well? Might that essay notice not as an intrinsically christological moment merely Peter's confession on the way to Caesarea Philippi that Jesus is "the christ" but also Jesus' rebuke of Peter? And Peter's denial of knowing Christ in the passion narratives as not merely a failure in his commitment but an instructive failure not only in fidelity but also in christology? The point would not be so much to bring scholarship to faith as to realize what faith has to say to scholarship.

Faith is not merely belief or trust or even both. Faith is living in and living out a set of reconciling practices that give rise to expressions of that trust, formulated as beliefs and inscribed in texts. Admittedly, an attitude of trust is sometimes hard to sustain in the face of adversity.[20] This particular focus, on practice as

---

18. Schüssler Fiorenza consistently writes of the *basileia* as an emancipatory movement and often has used the term "commonweal" to translate *basileia*. "Commonweal" suggests both the function of ruling and the realm ruled by God; as such it is a promising way to understand the *basileia*. But the notion of "emancipation" remains a rather open concept and clearly a modern one that we hear in, perhaps, a political way in a political context that is quite different from the politics of late Second Temple Judaism. It is important not to separate, but to distinguish the *basileia tou theou* from the community that carried it, the "Jesus-movement" (chap. 4 contains a rationale for using "movement"). In this essay, I will not much use the term "emancipatory" as I find it "too modern," although I find that the practices of the Jesus-movement can, for the most part, be helpfully characterized as emancipatory.

19. Hurtado, *Lord Jesus Christ,* 3-4.

20. Lest I be accused of Pelagianism, I do not in the least think that one can enter into or participate in the practice without divine grace. Nor do I think that participating in the practice "earns" one "salvation." Learning how to practice the faith enables a Christian to realize what salvation is and to come to know who Jesus is and even to know how to know, love, and serve God in this world and be happy with God forever in the next (to paraphrase the *Baltimore Catechism,* question 2). These are

primary and beliefs as dependent on practice, is at the heart of this essay, as it has been at the heart of Schüssler Fiorenza's, Dunn's, and Hurtado's work. But neither worship nor memory is sufficient as practice for the life of discipleship. Considering the life of discipleship more broadly leads to a new perspective in christology—christology as a reconciling practice.

The Vision

This particular focus on practices makes possible a vision: that discipleship is christology and soteriology in practice; soteriology and christology are inseparable from discipleship. And discipleship is a matter of imagination, of creatively extending the patterns set in the Jesus-movement in the first century into new times and places.

Hence, christology begins in disciples' *imaginations*. If we are not faithful disciples, well-disciplined in our lives, if we do not "have his mind within us" (Phil. 2:5), if our ways are not "God's ways" (Mark 8:33), then our imaginations about who Jesus is and what God brings to humanity through him will go wrong. If the New Testament shows us the patterns for being Christian disciples, and if we have read these earliest christologies rightly, then attempting to begin christology in some other place breaks with this pattern. Christology begins in *disciples'* imaginations, not the imaginations of the people—a point developed in chapter 8 below.

Of course, the practices of discipleship displayed in the New Testament carry many other christological themes. Yet all are connected with discipleship and its significance: if we are disciples we are/will be saved. And just as Peter needed correction from Christ, and the Philippians needed exhortation from Paul, sometimes our imaginations need to be shaped and formed by our fellow disciples,[21] like Mary perhaps showing Jesus how to serve.[22]

Other approaches may be needed at times. It may be that as times have changed, our way of understanding who Jesus is must also change. Some seem to think that we should begin in places other than the imagination. Perhaps we should begin with dogmas or definitions or comparative studies or historical investigations. But in the New Testament, christology begins from none of these places. It comes not from studies or theoretical explanation, but from the disciples' imaginations.

These other places should be understood not as beginnings but as bearings

---

not three separate things (practicing, realizing, knowing). They are constituents of the grace-given relationship with God.

21. Buckley ("*Lectio Divina* and Arguing over Jesus") proposes to use the patterns he sees in the rebukes in the Gospels as examples for disciples to follow even today when they "rebuke" each other in the context of christological debates. The practice of Jesus in correcting the "minds" of the disciples is a practice that the disciples can and must take up. Paul is an exemplar in this, but it remains a way in which those who follow Jesus can incarnate atonement.

22. See below, pp. 98-107. The order of events in John's Gospel can be read imaginatively as suggesting that Jesus learned the service of foot washing from Mary of Bethany.

for our christological journey. Sometimes on our journeys, we stop and "get our bearings." We look around us to see how to get where we're going from where we are. We seek directions from others on the journey and look to landmarks to help us. History, comparative studies, and dogmas are landmarks that help us find our bearings. Just as persons of practical wisdom have sometimes to correct their judgments by considering factors previously unavailable, so we can use dogmas, comparative studies, or historical investigations as additional guides for our imaginations.

We can continue to understand christology as beginning in disciples' imaginations, not in the findings of church fathers, ecumenical councils, comparative religionists, or questers for the historical-Jesus. Christology begins with how the community of the Spirit, past and present, has imagined him and followed him. But imaginations can go wild. And so those fathers, councils, comparativists, and questers can provide guidance to their fellow members of the community of the Spirit. They can help us correct our undisciplined imaginations. Or so we shall show in subsequent chapters. In this, they cannot give us the goal for our christological journey nor our direction, but they can give us bearings for the journey to guide us on our way.

To begin christology in the disciples' disciplined imaginations is not for us to tell tall tales or to make our christology the imaginary product of our imaginations. Yes, christology past and present must be imaginative. But it is our ability to imagine connections that makes it possible for us to have a life, a story, a community, and a world. Imagination glues the disparate together and slices the similar apart. The imagination is fertile ground. But our growth in faith needs guidance. In that we are like Peter. He needed correction. Otherwise his imagination would have led him away from the actual path to an imaginary one. Jesus rebuked Peter directly. Mark told the story to guide us. Paul exhorted the Corinthians. Many disciples' voices shape the mind of the community that has Christ's mind in it.

To do christology we must learn how to be in and of that community of the Spirit. For if we would be disciples of Christ, we must know how to understand and enact the proper "ways." We must know both how to live in and how to live out the story. For it is living in and living out the story of Christ present in the community of the Spirit that we come to know "who he is" and can come to be in position to give a true answer to the question, "Who do you say that I am?" Living in and living out that story shapes and corrects our imaginations.

Christology is not an intellectual matter, at least not exclusively. Doing christology is coming to know the mind of (in the particular sense of Phil. 2:5, discussed in chapter 10) another person. We come to know others by living with them, walking with them. We can only do so if we know how to live in community. We must reach out to them and allow them to reach out to us, to become "of one mind." And that is how we come to know who Christ is. We come to be of one mind with him through those who are one in mind with him.

The point of christology is not theory. Rather, its point is to grow from and guide the life of discipleship. The purpose of christology is to shape our imaginations which give us the "mind" that shapes our life. If we are well shaped, we will be images of him as well. To imagine Christ and to image him for others is the central purpose and point of doing christology, of being able rightly to say "who he is" according to Mark and Paul.

But we do not live in the Roman Empire of the first century. Our imaginations are shaped by a wildly different set of communities from those that shaped the imaginations of Mark and Paul and their immediate readers. We cannot simply ask today, What would Jesus do? since Jesus as a living, breathing human being with a body just like ours is of another time and place. Nor can we ask simplistically, What would the first disciples do? since those members of the Jesus-movement were also women and men of another time and another place. But as the "mind" of the community of disciples, as the sender of the Spirit of the community, as the one whose body we are, he is truly present and has been present for us, with us, in us, and through us even after his resurrection and exaltation. We can and must allow our imaginations to be corrected as was Peter's. We can listen to the voice of *ho christos,* who corrects our confused minds and distorted imaginations. But now he speaks to us from the community which has his mind, which has learned the lessons Mark and Paul and John and a cloud of witnesses have taught. To be faithful, we may need to be creative.

One of the most pervasive features of traditional patterns in Christian theology is the separation of christology ("who and what Jesus is/was") from soteriology ("what Jesus did") and of both from discipleship ("what we are to do," often treated as "spirituality" or "morality"). Theologians wrote—and write—as if one could answer one of the questions without regard to the others. Typically, discipleship is treated as if it were limited to the realm of "applied" or "pastoral" theology. Theology proper dealt with christology, Trinity, atonement, and the other "big" intellectual and academic issues, not "mere" pastoral practice. The big loser in this pattern was soteriology.

Soteriology became reduced almost fully to the mechanics of atonement.[23] Separated from christology and theologies of grace, debates over "exemplary," "substitutionary," "ransom," "rescue," and "victory" theories of the atonement (all based on various New Testament texts) raged in Christian circles until an exhausted theological community turned to other, more ponderable issues. While defenses of a substitutionary theory of atonement remain *de rigeur* in some evangelical circles, atonement theology—and the soteriological concerns that

---

23. One recent graphic example of this is Mel Gibson's film *The Passion of the Christ*, which treats Jesus' atoning death entirely apart from his ministry and God's raising him from the dead. Theologians have started to connect salvation with the gift of the resurrection of the dead, anticipated and promised in Jesus' resurrection. See, e.g., Dermot A. Lane, *Christ at the Centre: Selected Issues in Christology* (Dublin: Veritas, 1991), 106-7, 124. Stephen Finlan (*Problems with Atonement: The Origins of, and Controversy about, the Atonement Doctrine* [Collegeville, MN: Liturgical Press, 2005]) provides a useful and readable survey of the issues—in short, no theory of atonement avoids vexing theological problems, but abandoning the doctrine seems to put other essential Christian doctrines in jeopardy. Lisa Sowle Cahill ("The Atonement Paradigm: Does It Still Have Explanatory Value?" *Theological Studies* 68, no. 2 [June 2007]: 418-32) recognizes these problems and argues for a way to retain the imaginative heart of the doctrine; also see below, pp. 163, 248 n. 21, 249-52.

it stood for—had mostly languished until liberation theologians reopened the issue.[24]

Despite unwarranted accusations of confusing political liberation and economic empowerment with salvation, most liberation theologians[25] have reconnected soteriology, however inadequately from some perspectives, to discipleship and christology. The key here is the primacy of *praxis*. Gustavo Gutiérrez defined liberation theology as "a critical reflection on Christian praxis in the light of the word of God."[26] The spirituality and pastoral practice of the community are primary. "Theology *follows;* it is the second step. What Hegel used to say about philosophy can likewise be applied to theology: it rises only at sundown."[27] The goal of Christian *praxis* is liberation—spiritual, personal, and social liberation.[28] In this

---

24. One of the issues that the Congregation for the Doctrine of the Faith (CDF) has raised regarding Jon Sobrino's work is that Sobrino construes Jesus as the "exemplary cause" or the "symbolic cause," not the "efficient cause" of salvation. The CDF then incorrectly infers that, because the cause is "exemplary," Sobrino reduces salvation to "moralism." But Sobrino's approach is to focus on the practice of Jesus, not merely on his death, as salvific. Moreover, that practice makes possible life in the kingdom of God—an "exemplary cause," in practical terms, just *is* effective as a *gracious*, compelling example that provokes the practices of the kingdom. Jesus' cause is "exemplary," but it also conveys, in traditional terms, the grace needed to enact the example. Moreover, the CDF "Notification on the works of Fr. Jon Sobrino SJ" (http://www.vatican.va/roman_curia/congregations/cfaith/documents/rc_con_cfaith_doc_20061126_notification-sobrino_en.html [accessed March 16, 2007]) relies on proof texts to show Sobrino's work not in line with the tradition. In doing so, the text effectively demands transliterations, literalistic translations, rather than interpretations of classic terminology in a world that is wildly different from the one in which the classic terms were used. The CDF effectively is demanding that theologians repeat a form of sound words, rather than develop a communicative practice that expresses how living in and living out the faith is living the life of the saved. Given the differences in our locations and methodologies, I follow Sobrino in accepting a version of exemplarism that construes Jesus' "example" as an empowerment that is a true source of the grace of reconciliation, mediated in and through the community. For further discussion of this matter, see chap. 17 below.

25. Gustavo Gutiérrez makes the integrity of liberation clear in connecting the varied realms of salvation/redemption: the social (including economic and political) realm, where there are numerous structural evils or social sins that cannot be isolated from (but must be distinguished from) the personal realm, where there are numerous sins and their effects, and the spiritual realm, where there is the evil of separation from God. Gutiérrez's work may underplay the natural realm, where there are evils such as ecological degradation and perhaps even entropy, but this charge is rarely raised seriously against liberation theologians. Integral redemption/salvation is not merely the salvation of individuals into a posthumous kingdom, but the taking up of each and all into the eternal life of joy in God. The most likely candidate for being an exception to this claim is José Porfirio Miranda. His provocative works, for example, *Communism in the Bible*, translated by Robert Barr (Maryknoll, NY: Orbis Books, 1981), are among the more extreme statements in liberation theology and ought not to be taken as typical. Moreover, whether the theological supporters of the Sandinistas in Nicaragua and the FLN (National Liberation Front) in El Salvador a quarter century ago confused the part (political and economic liberation) for the whole (reconciliation of all in the divine mystery) is an issue that evidently cannot be resolved, given the lack of agreement on what would constitute evidence to support claims one way or the other.

26. Gustavo Gutiérrez, *A Theology of Liberation*, trans. Sr. Caridad Inda and John Eagleson, 2nd ed. (Maryknoll, NY: Orbis Books, 1988), xxix. In that such praxis is Christian, it is presumably grounded in God's grace and cannot be a purely human achievement.

27. Ibid., 11-12.

28. Ibid., xxxviii.

approach, understanding how to be a disciple is inseparable from understanding who Christ is and realizing what the salvation that God brings to the world through Christ is. The liberating grace of Jesus is the empowerment of disciples to bring reconciliation in these proximate areas. Disciples are empowered or graced by God to be agents of reconciliation and salvation.

Roberto S. Goizueta has found an ambiguity in the concept of liberating praxis in liberation theology:

> Is liberation the *result* of praxis, that is, the "product" of our struggle to transform society? Or, is liberation a *concomitant*, or *by*product, of praxis— i.e., the change that takes place in us *as* we engage in that struggle? Do we become liberated only *after* and *as a result of* our social action, or do we become liberated *in the course of* our action? Is praxis, or human action on its own end and, thus, valuable in and of itself, or is praxis valuable only insofar as it leads to a liberated society?[29]

Goizueta's answer—an answer that many liberation theologians would not reject, I think—is that as "revealed in popular Catholicism, human action or praxis is 1) sacramental; 2) essentially and intrinsically communal, or relational; 3) an end in itself; 4) empowering; and, therefore, 5) liberating."[30]

An analogous pattern of giving primacy to practice can be found in the work of some "narrative"[31] and "postliberal"[32] U.S. theologians. Their focus on learning how to be faithful disciples as the first practice of Christians has reshaped theological discourse in this country. The disciplines of Protestant Christian ethics and Catholic moral theology have especially been reformed by the recovery of "virtue ethics," an ethic of practice, not rules.[33] Sometimes explicitly (in some

---

29. Roberto S. Goizueta, *Caminemos con Jesús: Toward a Hispanic/Latino Theology of Accompaniment* (Maryknoll, NY: Orbis Books, 1995), 86-87. Goizueta reads the ambiguity of praxis in liberation theology as analogous to the ambiguity of praxis in Marxist theory. I am not so sure that liberation theologians, at their best, do not transform the concept in such a way as to come to basically the same conclusion as Goizueta does.

30. Ibid., 103.

31. James Wm. McClendon, Jr., *Biography as Theology: How Life Stories Can Remake Today's Theology* (Nashville: Abingdon, 1974), and *Systematic Theology,* vol. 1, *Ethics* (Nashville: Abingdon, 1985). My *Story Theology*, like McClendon's early work, focuses on narratives rather than practices, but the shift in focus represented in this book is not my abandonment of an earlier position. Showing how disciples perform faith, how we can put it virtuously into practice, requires narrative display and understanding. But narrative is a *form* of good theology, not a theological *topic*. The shift is one from a concern with *form* to a concern with more material issues in theology.

32. Stanley Hauerwas, *Performing the Faith: Bonhoeffer and the Practice of Nonviolence* (Grand Rapids: Brazos, 2004), is a recent example. Many works by McClendon, Hauerwas, L. Gregory Jones, Brad Kallenberg, and others influenced by their works and the works of Yale theologian George Lindbeck are in this category. My own debts to them are deep, despite my distance from some of them (which is exemplified in my far more positive attitude to liberation theology than most of the aforementioned).

33. Stanley Hauerwas's early works are landmarks for this shift. See his *Character and the Christian Life: A Study in Theological Ethics* (San Antonio: Trinity University Press, 1975); *Vision and Virtue: Essays in Christian Ethical Reflection* (Notre Dame: Fides, 1974); and *Truthfulness and*

works of James W. McClendon), sometimes more implicitly (in many of Stanley Hauerwas's essays), an understanding of reconciliation as a practice in part constitutive of God's work for humanity sheds light on ways to reconceptualize soteriology. Indeed, the position developed in this book has some parallels to, and has been influenced by, McClendon's practical work on atonement and Hauerwas's work on discipleship.[34] Their approach would recognize and accept Goizueta's clarifying of the liberationist approach to praxis—save that the "therefore" might be omitted in the quotation above and liberation defined simply as learning how to engage in these practices in the grace of God. I would also be inclined to dispute the "therefore," as "liberation" seems a constitutive goal in, rather than a consequence of, good practices.

We have not yet fully realized what the postliberal and liberationist turn to practice means for our ongoing theological work outside of ethics. I see a number of implications.

Negatively, the "practical turn," like the various "linguistic turns" in philosophy, marks the exhaustion of the Enlightenment's project in philosophy and theology, the "turn to the subject" and the "turn to experience." The Enlightenment individual subject has been replaced by the community-shaped agent, and experience has been replaced by practice. Whereas a subject could be anyone, anywhere, at any time, an agent is a particular embodied person, located in a particular time and place and constituted in large part by a web of relationships that empower and restrain her or him. Whereas experience is something that happens to a subject, an agent engages in practices.[35]

Positively, the "practical turn" marks a realignment of theology as a constituent in shared Christian practice. Not all Christians are or should be professional theologians; but theologians have the responsibility of discerning, proposing transformations when necessary, and proclaiming when appropriate a properly theological component in that shared practice.[36] Theology does not in some way give a "foundation" to practicing the faith. As Gutiérrez claims, theology is "second" and reflective, not first and foundational. If doctrines are rules, as postliberals argue, then doctrinal theology is the practice of reflection on rules inferred from practicing the faith.[37]

One felicitous implication that can be drawn from "the priority of practice" is

---

Tragedy: Further Investigations into Christian Ethics (Notre Dame: University of Notre Dame Press, 1977).

34. See especially Hauerwas and James Fodor, "Performing Faith: The Peaceable Rhetoric of God's Church," in Stanley Hauerwas, *Performing the Faith: Bonhoeffer and the Practice of Nonviolence* (Grand Rapids: Brazos, 2004), 75-109.

35. Lest it be thought that this approach ignores the importance of "reception" or of "contemplation," it recognizes the importance of "listening" as a demanding practice and of contemplative absorption as possible only by those who are far advanced in contemplative practice. While there is a danger for a "practical" approach to become fascinated with what we do, the proper approach is on what God does for us, to us, and enables us to do as God's devoted agents. "Obedience" in such a perspective is not passive acceptance of authority but active acceptance of empowerment to act gracefully.

36. I develop this view in *History, Theology, and Faith*, chap. 11.

37. I argue for this claim in *Inventing Catholic Tradition*, chap. 4.

a retrieval of a Thomistic distinction between primary and secondary agency.[38] It is clear that God in Christ is the primary agent of our salvation. God saves, we don't. Yet in some sense we are also agents of salvation—for ourselves, for each other, and for the world. It is not that "we do it" and God does not. Rather, when we practice our faith gracefully, we are God's agents through whom God works. God is the primary agent, we are secondary. When we engage in those practices we should avoid, we effectively obstruct God's action. We cannot finally obstruct God's purpose, of course, nor can we think that we are the only secondary agents God uses—the entire created world is in some way God's secondary salvific agent. In a practical perspective, the "Great Commission" of Matthew 28 is just that—a commissioning of Jesus' disciples to be God's agents of salvation.[39]

Just as creation of all there is may best be construed as an act of infinite divine power, so salvation of all there is may also best be construed as an act of infinite divine power. But such power does not preclude either the need for or the usefulness of finite powers exercised in this world by finite agents who participate in and further the agency of infinite love. God's infinite agency and infinite power are not on the same level with or exercised in the same way as finite power. Finite and infinite power and agency cannot be in competition with each other.[40] How one acts for God in contributing finitely to the ongoing work of reconciling all-that-is in divine love gives force to how one understands who Christ is— the primary agency of God most wonderfully really present in and through the (noncompetitive) secondary agency of Jesus—and what he does—reconcile the world unto God's own "self" through the acts he performs in, through, and with his body.[41]

---

38. This is obviously analogous to more typical formulations of primary and secondary causality. I had been unsuccessful in finding a way to put together the points made in this paragraph until remarks by Robert Barron reminded me that God's infinite power and humans' finite powers cannot be "in competition." That crystallized my understanding. This is developed in dialogue with Robert Barron, pp. 221-28 below.

39. Regarding primary and secondary agency, Austin Farrer wrote, "God works omnipotently on, in, or through creaturely agencies without either forcing them or competing with them" (*Faith and Speculation: An Essay in Philosophical Theology* [London: A. & C. Black, 1967], 62; cf. 65, 82, 154). This fundamentally Thomistic understanding of the relationship between divine and human agency will be explored later. How these activities have dual authorship is not a soluble problem in Farrer's view: "Both the divine and the human actions remain real and therefore free in the union between them; not knowing the modality of the divine action we cannot pose the problem of their mutual relation" (66). The argument in chap. 18 below follows Barron in making claims that could also be found in Farrer's work. However, we can, at least abstractly, suggest something about the modality of divine action. The importance of mission recurs in chap. 19.

40. In this perspective, sin is not competing with God, but, as noted above, obstructing God's purpose.

41. Robert Barron has also commented that understanding a heresy as obscure as monothelitism is important because it shows the problem of conflating as one will the infinite will of God with the finite will of Jesus of Nazareth. If these two could be conflated, then they could be in competition. But since one is an exercise of divine nature or primary agency, and the other of human nature or secondary agency, they can be in perfect harmony without the possibility of competition. Barron, of course, is not responsible for any misuse I may make of his comments. These points are developed in dialogue with his work in chap. 18 below.

By the end of this book, I hope that this vision—here rather briefly and even abstractly construed—of how theology in general and christology and soteriology in particular cannot be sundered from discipleship will appear in more vivid detail.

The Place of Christology

By now it is obvious that this vision repositions christology from a realm of "dogmatic" theology into "practical" theology. Indeed, this vision construes all dogmatic theology as reflection upon praxis/practice. This carries implications for the relationship of christology to other disciplines in theology. While the "practical turn" carries similar implications for all theological loci, the way the christological question is posed here, the particular focus on practices, and the vision of a practical theology in which discipleship is inseparable from christology and soteriology (and each are inseparable, of course, from the other) could also lead to a fundamental rethinking of the concepts of grace, revelation, and creation. This book cannot do so, but the paths to such rethinking can be indicated.

Most contemporary theologians construe faith and revelation reciprocally.[42] Revelation both shapes and presupposes faith. Faith is not in some way possible without revelation, at least implicitly, if not explicitly, received. Yet if faith is construed as a practice—echoing Aquinas's understanding of faith as a theological virtue—how can faith and revelation be reciprocal? In an attempt to navigate between objectivist accounts (God whispers propositions in some ears and the hearers write them down) and subjectivist accounts (some individuals discern an internal light or feeling or focal awareness and express that discernment in writing), Avery Dulles focused on the symbolism of revelation. But, rather than focusing on *what* God is using (symbols)[43] in communicating, a practical approach would focus on *how* God is communicating. But we only have evidence for either how or what God communicates by considering the responses God evokes. We cannot get to "God's side" of the table or lay out the conditions under which God

---

42. See, e.g., Avery Dulles, *Models of Revelation*, 2nd ed. (Maryknoll, NY: Orbis Books, 1992), 279-80. I have discussed Dulles's approach in *Inventing Catholic Tradition*, 170-77. My point there was to show that the epistemological position I had taken ("consequential realism") was compatible with, and could even clarify, a clearly orthodox Catholic theology of revelation. I had not then worked through how a practical approach to theology would reposition the doctrine of revelation.

43. In *Models of Revelation*, Dulles finds that symbols are signs that "contain and mediate the reality they signify" and "give rise to true affirmations about what is antecedently real" (267). Specifically, Christian revelatory symbols are "the persons, events, and other realities whereby God brings into existence the community of faith we call the Christian Church" (266). In particular, I find the use of the concept "symbol" to obscure the fundamental claims about God and the world that I find need to be put in terms of divine acts first and foremost. Roger Haight (*Jesus Symbol of God*), for example, writes that "Jesus the individual human being is a religious symbol" (203). This is a fundamental claim for Haight, but it makes no sense to talk of Jesus as a "concrete symbol" remembered in "conceptual symbols" like texts unless Jesus did and was perceived as doing something by the power of God. Making symbols, rather than actions, the fundamental category for analysis is a less felicitous path than focusing on actions—or so I hope the work in this book shows.

can perform a speech act.[44] So whether we focus on the content (the symbols) or the communication (the act or interaction that produces those symbols), we only have the finite side of the transaction available to us. The epilogue develops these points.[45]

Our first witnesses are the most famous. Our own imaginations must be disciplined by the early practices of the Jesus-movement. They set the tone for discipleship, for they are the first among us who remembered Jesus and had his "mind" in them. But the question of how to approach and understand those witnesses is vexed. The next chapters show how historical work helps us understand the Jesus-movement and its practices.

---

44. Nicholas Wolterstorff (*Divine Discourse: Philosophical Reflections on the Claim that God Speaks* [Cambridge: Cambridge University Press, 1995]) develops a theory of divine communication as a pattern of divine agency, specifically God's speech acts. As will become clear below, my own view differs dramatically from Wolterstorff's despite our mutual concern with speech-act theory. Wolterstorff's account ties an understanding of infinite divine agency so closely to finite agency that it allows the possibility that divine and human agency might be in direct competition, a position that does not fit well with a "practical" theology or any understanding of divine agency that leaves human agents sufficiently free to be held responsible for their actions.

45. I would like to suggest that we can again draw on a Thomistic category to help us understand this. God's revelation is what Thomistic theologians might call an exercise of primary agency. As uncreated grace, it is God's very presence as an agent to us. Faith is revelation considered as secondary agency. Uncreated grace produces created grace, that is, the grace that possesses and is possessed by disciples (and even others!). We can know of uncreated grace only through the reality of created grace. If we are recipients of grace, the grace that is created in us is the result of our relationship with God; the created grace of our actions and our secondary agency result from the very relationships we have with God who is uncreated grace. The key is that grace is not some "thing" superadded to our being, but it is what we are as humans, as creative agents whose creative potential is unleashed in various ways, but especially in the practices of discipleship. To put it quickly, to be graced is to be graceful in what we do.

Three

ORIENTATION

$\mathcal{T}$he present essay relies on a number of presumptions about how to do christology. The first and foremost is that Jesus lived and died an observant and faithful Jew, specifically a Jew from Galilee. Indeed, claims about Jesus bar Joseph cannot be sensibly made without reference to his Jewish environment. His way of life is shaped by a pattern of Torah observance. His teaching makes sense only in the context of a long tradition of Jewish prophets and sages. His disputes with his fellow Jews—sometimes intensified and reshaped in the context of the transmission of the memories about Jesus by his disciples, who also disputed with their fellow Jews—are intra-Jewish disputes about Jewish life, worship, and belief. In all this, "Jesus does not have to be unique in all cases in order to be profound," as Amy-Jill Levine put it.[1] Jesus' teaching, his interpretation of (*not* rejection of) Torah, his prayer, and his parables, though remembered as central and distinctive to his work and message, are variations in the many approaches to God, the world and everything, the theological themes, and the practical quotidian concerns of Jews living in the (late, as we now know) Second Temple period under Roman occupation of Palestine.

Of course, Jesus was a unique person, as is each of us. Levine's comment is not denying that. But his practices and teaching were not unique. Others taught in parables, contested with friendly opponents, and called for reform of socio-politico-religious patterns and persons' lives as did Jesus. But his followers found something in him that led them to respond distinctively to him and to proselytize others, both Jews and gentiles, to live out a life of discipleship in response to the living power of Jesus after his death.

Second, the only significant written records that we have of Jesus' work and teaching are in the New Testament. Although there are a few scattered references to Jesus and his disciples in extra-Christian sources, and possibly some sayings of Jesus preserved in noncanonical works, the memories transmitted from Jesus' time and finally written decades after his death are our fundamental sources. These records, however, were written by disciples who sought both to be faithful in remembering Jesus and to construct their own distinctive identity as a movement that grew in and then beyond the context of Judaism. To read the New Testament without recognizing its roots in Judaism and without allowing for these factors

---

1. Amy-Jill Levine, *The Misunderstood Jew: The Church and the Scandal of the Jewish Jesus* (San Francisco: HarperSanFrancisco, 2006), 23.

(and others to be discussed below) that shaped the rhetoric of the language that transmitted those memories is to misinterpret the significance of the texts and the practices and memories they record.

For example, the disputes in the New Testament are often crafted by the writers in such a way as to be "identity markers," that is, stories that differentiate "us" from "them." Some of these disputes are internal to the Jesus-movement, such as those about whether gentiles who joined the movement had to observe Jewish law, and, if so, what sort of observance was to be required of them. Other disputes occur between the Jesus-movement and the other movements or parties in Second Temple Judaism. Many of these disputes that occurred after Jesus' death likely colored the memories of the Jesus-movement in such a way that disagreements occurring at the time the texts were written were "remembered" as happening during Jesus' own ministry. Thus, when the New Testament texts treat "the Jews" or some party in Judaism as the opponent or enemy, one must understand that not only was one Jew, Jesus, disputing with other Jews, but that later some Jews (those in the Jesus-movements) were fighting with other Jews (those who were not part of the Jesus-movements).

Hence, one cannot simply "read" the New Testament texts. One must place them into their rhetorical context: these are texts meant not only to preserve memories and guide discipleship when the first generation is gone, but also to shape a movement's identity in opposition to other movements. Far too many readings of the New Testament—and particularly of its significance for christology—neglect the contexts that determine the range of the possible meanings the authors could have intended the text to have and the rhetorical strategies that the authors used in part to establish the identity of the Jesus-movement in those crucibles of conflict. Failure to account for the context, rhetorical strategy, and purposes of the acts inscribed in, by, and through the texts distorts our understanding of those texts.

Third, the present work finds the now-common division of christological work into "from above" and "from below" to be confused. The confusion is that it conflates epistemological issues with ontological ones. The question, How do we come to know about Jesus? is different from the question, Who is Jesus, really? The former question always necessarily is a historical question, rooted in the place from which the question is asked, that is, "from below." The latter may be answered with a narrative that begins with God ("from above") or with a narrative that begins with Jesus the Galilean Jew ("from below").[2] However, a more unified

---

2. In this, I allude to the work of my teacher, the late James Wm. McClendon, Jr. He worked through the various issues in classic conciliar christology in light of the New Testament. He found that the "two natures in one person" doctrine, however important and clarifying in the Greek and Latin disputations of the fourth and fifth centuries, simply did not and could not convey the same significance in the modern, scientifically inflected languages of the present. He therefore suggested that we need a "two-narrative" christology. See *Systematic Theology,* vol. 2, *Doctrine* (Nashville: Abingdon, 1994), 274-79. We do see that dual pattern in the New Testament: in some texts the basic structure is "God made a man his Son" while in others "God made the Son a man" (see my *Story Theology* [Wilmington, DE: Michael Glazier, 1985], 121-27). Robert Barron (*The Priority of Christ: Toward a Postliberal Catholicism* [Grand Rapids: Brazos, 2007], 64-67) also shows sympathy with a "two narrative" interpretation of the New Testament patterns.

approach shows how the "two narratives" are linked, as in the pattern discerned by Reginald H. Fuller.[3] I would suggest that this also stands behind the classic orthodox christology of later centuries. First, it begins with the earthly Jesus that the disciples knew, remembered, and emulated. He is a human being whom they knew. But they found that he drew out of them wisdom and power like no other person ever had. Whether they were wo/men or men, marginal or elite, poor or wealthy, urban or rural, they realized how to live in and live out the coming reign of God in his company. Second, if he is all that, then the Jesus whom they remember as empowering them must be sent from God in a special way. The New Testament presents Jesus as a prophet "and more." Though called "messiah," he was other than a pretender to the Davidic throne. He is imagined as being with God even before he was sent, of being God's wisdom or word or son even before he became the human being they remembered. Third, for what he drew from them and gave to them, he is construed as the incarnate presence/power of God, bringing from and to the Jesus-movement the power of God and the empowering of God. Some called him God's son (though the Creator does not have procreative equipment) or God's word (though the unoriginate One does not have vocal cords) or as God's wisdom (even though God's wisdom is God's presence). Fourth, God is seen so strongly as present in the one who empowers the Jesus-movement that the Spirit, Wisdom, or Logos of God is seen as descending to be present in the life, ministry, death, and resurrection of Jesus, Miriam's son. Fifth, Jesus is exalted or raised up to return to God. Thus the sequence can be understood as follows:

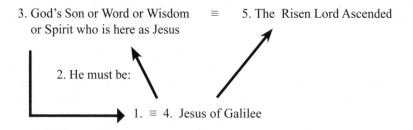

(1) The disciples encounter and remember the empowering Jesus, so transforming of their own lives that they (2) find that he must be divine as they recognize the divine acting in and through him and cannot but think that (3) he came from God

---

3. Reginald H. Fuller, *The Foundations of New Testament Christology* (London: Collins, 1976). He discerns the "descending-ascending pattern" which is the basis of my comments here. I have developed that to bring out the obvious "step 1." The implication that this is a very early pattern results from reading Fuller's work in light of Hurtado's analyses in *Lord Jesus Christ: Devotion to Jesus in Earliest Christianity* (Grand Rapids: Eerdmanns, 2003). Hurtado's work argues that Fuller's finding that a "high christology" emerges late in the history of the development of christology in the New Testament is incorrect. Nonetheless, Fuller's work is especially helpful in overcoming the dichotomies in christology over the last fifty years, especially among Catholic theologians, of "christology from above/christology from below" and "ascending/descending" christologies. These terms are not antithetical.

and was with God as God-in-action who (4) descends to be what we recognize in Jesus whom we know and (5) who is no longer captive of the earth but exalted by God despite his execution, and whose empowering presence—*the Real Jesus*—is yet with us in the movement.

If this is accurate, then there is no such thing as "christology from above" or "christology from below." The Jesus-movement began with "where they were," for there was no other place to begin. They remembered Jesus in what they did. Indeed, so does *every* christology follow this pattern. We must begin where we are. The common disjunction between from above/from below christology obscures the fact that christology always arises in disciples' imaginations. We start with Jesus as he is perceived and imagined on this earth. We start telling the story *here* even if the story we tell begins in heaven.

Fourth, the quests for the historical-Jesus[4] are misguided. Their goal, from the first, was to isolate Jesus from his Jewish environment and make him "available" for contemporaries. Perhaps dissatisfied with institutionalized religion, the questers have sought to find a historical-Jesus to play off against the inherited, often unhistorical, presentations of a Christ who seemed all-too-little human. Yet, like the responses that unmasked the pretensions of the first quest in the nineteenth century,[5] the contemporary responses directed against the second (1953-1985) and third (roughly 1985-present) quests,[6] especially the "neo-liberal" version of the

---

4. I adopt this term coined by Elisabeth Schüssler Fiorenza to signal that the "historical-Jesuses" that are "discovered" by scholarship are actually constructs of scholars who may or may not be disciples. See her *Jesus and the Politics of Interpretation* (New York: Continuum, 2000), 2 n. 3.

5. Three different works are usually credited with bringing about the collapse of the first quest (although it must be noted that one of the classic expositions of the historical-Jesus that emerged from the hand of the liberal questers, Adolf Harnack, *What Is Christianity? Sixteen Lectures Delivered in the University of Berlin during the Winter Term, 1899-1900* [London: Williams & Norgate, 1901; 1st German ed., 1900], was published at the height of these attacks). Albert Schweitzer (*The Quest of the Historical Jesus* [London: A. and C. Black, 1910; 1st German ed., 1906]) undermines the liberal quest's ignoring of the apocalyptic element in Jesus' teaching. Martin Kähler (*The So-Called Historical Jesus and the Historic Biblical Christ*, ed. Carl E. Braaten [Philadelphia: Fortress, 1964; 1st German ed., 1892]) argued that distilling a historical-Jesus was isolating him so baldly from his historic significance given in the faith of the disciples in him, with the result that the Jesus thus found was insignificant. William Wrede (*The Messianic Secret* [Cambridge: J. Clarke, 1971; 1st German ed., 1901]) showed that the Synoptic tradition yielded Gospels that were not only documents of faith, but were structured by theological motifs of their authors—effectively undermining them as historical sources almost as much as John (more obviously theological) had been undermined earlier. Regrettably not often mentioned is Alfred Loisy (*The Gospel and the Church*, trans. Christopher Home [London: Isbister, 1906; 1st French ed., 1902]), who anticipated Schweitzer's criticism and whose approach clearly recognized the Gospels as documents written in and for a community of faith.

6. N. T. Wright was the first to use this term. He finds the quest beginning earlier and a group of four works as the "climax, thus far, of the Third Quest": Ben F. Meyer, *The Aims of Jesus* (London: SCM, 1979); A. E. Harvey, *Jesus and the Constraints of History* (Philadelphia: Westminster, 1982); Marcus Borg, *Conflict, Holiness, and Politics in the Teaching of Jesus* (New York: Edwin Mellen, 1984); and E. P. Sanders, *Jesus and Judaism* (London: SCM, 1985); see Stephen Neill and Tom Wright, *The Interpretation of the New Testament 1861-1986*, 2nd ed. (Oxford: Oxford University Press, 1988), 381. However, Wright also recognized that *Jesus and Judaism* "refuses to begin with the sayings, and starts instead [with] his action against the Temple" (N. T. Wright, "Quest for the

latter associated with the Jesus Seminar, take various forms. But they all share a common insight analogous to the counter-responses to the first quest: the historic Jesus, the man from Nazareth, is the Jesus remembered by, imitated by, worshiped by the disciples whom his actions and words empowered. The individual human being abstracted from all that, the "historical-Jesus," is not only a creation of the quest, often in the quester's own image,[7] but also historically insignificant— without Jesus' *historic impact*, how could anyone ever take this itinerant healer, exorcist, teacher from an outpost of the Roman Empire in the first century to be *historically* interesting?

Luke Timothy Johnson has been one of the toughest critics of the "neo-liberal" quest for the historical-Jesus.[8] What the questers do, finally, is not "history" but "theology," the construction of a Jesus to believe in—but a Jesus not presented in the tradition carried by the Christian church. Moreover, most of these scholars have explicit or implicit agenda that include "presenting" the historical-Jesus in a way that enables contemporary audiences to appreciate him (usually over against "stale" traditional views). But in so doing, they risk making Jesus appear as not strange to us, as someone, however, from that distant time and place must be.

The historical-Jesuses are constructed not merely for historical purposes, but to give Christians a new identity in the present. As Paula Fredriksen has put it:

> To regard Jesus historically . . . means allowing him the irreducible otherness of his own antiquity, the strangeness Schweitzer captured in his closing

Historical Jesus," in *The Anchor Bible Dictionary*, ed. David Noel Freedman, 6 vols. [New York: Doubleday, 1992], 3:801). It is this shift to *actions* done by and to Jesus in the context of late Second Temple Judaism, rather than Jesus' *teaching*, that marks the decisive orientational shift that I find most significant in the third quest. While the other authors also move away from the second quest into a more sociohistorical approach, Sanders's move is the key breakthrough.

7. The sharpest formulation of this point was in a book first published in 1909 by the Catholic modernist George Tyrrell. He commented on the work of liberal Protestant theologian Adolf Harnack as follows: "The Christ that Harnack sees, looking back through nineteen centuries of Catholic darkness, is only the reflection of a Liberal Protestant face, seen at the bottom of a deep well" (*Christianity at the Crossroads* [London: Allen and Unwin, 1963], 49). Tyrrell's point applies *mutatis mutandis* to many contemporary questers. Elisabeth Schüssler Fiorenza makes a similar point in *Jesus and the Politics of Interpretation*, 13; a brief account of her position is her "Jesus of Nazareth in Historical Research," in *Thinking of Christ: Proclamation, Explanation, Meaning*, ed. Tatha Wiley (New York: Continuum, 2003), 29-48.

8. Luke Timothy Johnson, *The Real Jesus: The Misguided Quest for the Historical Jesus and the Truth of the Traditional Gospels* (San Francisco: HarperSanFrancisco, 1996). Walter Wink ("Response to Luke Timothy Johnson's *The Real Jesus*," *Bulletin for Biblical Research* 7 [1997]: 1-16) portrays Johnson and the questers as opponents in a boxing match he referees. I discuss some of the problems with the quest as a historical enterprise in *History, Theology, and Faith: Dissolving the Modern Problematic* (Maryknoll, NY: Orbis Books, 2004), chap. 9. See also Elisabeth Schüssler Fiorenza, *Jesus: Miriam's Child, Sophia's Prophet: Critical Issues in Feminist Christology* (New York: Continuum, 1995), 82-88, for a feminist critique of the neo-liberal quest. This is *not* to say that the church's tradition and memory are to be rendered immune from criticism and revision. Far from it! The practice of understanding that memory and tradition in contexts that are wildly unlike those in which the tradition was first lived in and lived out requires creative invention to be faithful followers of that tradition; or so I argued in *Inventing Catholic Tradition* (Maryknoll, NY: Orbis Books, 2000).

description: "He comes to us as One unknown, without a name, as of old, by the lakeside." It is when we renounce the false familiarity proffered by the dark angels of Relevance and Anachronism that we see Jesus, his contemporaries, and perhaps even ourselves, more clearly in our common humanity.[9]

Jesus does not fit our familiar categories; we need to acknowledge his strangeness to us. The quests for the historical-Jesus all too easily fall prey to the desire for relevance.

Moreover, what does rigorous historical research yield as historical facts, not reconstructions? E. P. Sanders lists eight historical facts that are almost indisputable:

1. Jesus was baptized by John the Baptist.
2. Jesus was a Galilean who preached and healed.
3. Jesus called disciples and spoke of there being twelve.
4. Jesus confined his activity to Israel.
5. Jesus engaged in a controversy about the temple.
6. Jesus was crucified outside Jerusalem by the Roman authorities.
7. After his death Jesus' followers continued as an identifiable movement.
8. At least some Jews persecuted at least parts of the new movement . . . and it appears that this persecution perdured at least to a time near the end of Paul's career.[10]

Even these items are not perfectly stable as historical conclusions, as minimal as they are. Fredriksen has argued rather persuasively that nos. 1-5 cannot be certainly sequenced in that order and that no. 5 cannot be affirmed on historians' grounds to be a cause of no. 6.[11] Other scholars might reformulate no. 3 (to exclude reference to the Twelve) and no. 4 (as not quite as reliable as the others). Many Muslims would argue, on the basis of the Qur'an, that no. 6 is not historically accurate. Of course, the list of "historical facts" might also be expanded.[12]

---

9. Paula Fredriksen, *Jesus of Nazareth, King of the Jews: A Jewish Life and the Emergence of Christianity* (New York: Knopf, 1999), 267-68.

10. Sanders, *Jesus and Judaism,* 10-11; I think Jesus was not merely a healer but an exorcist, a point too often downplayed in the quests for relevance. Compare Norman Perrin, *The New Testament: An Introduction* (New York: Harcourt, Brace, Jovanovich, 1974), 277-78, for a similar list by a scholar sympathetic to the second quest. These factoids are not sufficient for a biography of Jesus.

11. Paula Fredriksen, *From Jesus to Christ: The Origins of the New Testament Images of Jesus*, 2nd ed. (New Haven: Yale University Press, 2000), xxii. Fredriksen, against a very wide consensus, argues that the cleansing of the temple (the key action signified in item 5) never actually occurred but should be attributed to the early church. I am not persuaded that she can sustain her argument (see my "Teaching Christology: History and Horizons," in *Christology: Memory, Inquiry, Practice*, ed. Anne M. Clifford and Anthony J. Godzieba, Annual Publication of the College Theology Society 48 [Maryknoll, NY: Orbis Books, 2003], 275-76 n. 18), but it clearly is a floating pericope articulating a memory that had different anchorings in the memories of different communities, reflected in the fact that the authors of John and Mark could place it into their texts at different points.

12. In his more popular *The Historical Figure of Jesus* (London: Penguin, 1993), 10-11, Sanders

Even if these eight items were completely reliable as historical facts, they are not enough to warrant a reconstruction of a historical-Jesus. They are but parts of a skeleton that scholars have unearthed and that they imaginatively expand by adding more bones they think "must have been" part of the skeleton and by layering on flesh to give their readers a portrait the readers can recognize. In doing so, scholars often fail to portray the significance of the historic Jesus. The quest cannot reach the goal of portraying objectively the actual man Jesus in any substantive way—the data are simply not there, even if it were possible to "reconstruct" a person from his dry bones.

What marks contemporary critics of the quests is not merely their opposition to the questers' goal and methods. Indeed, sometimes that opposition is almost ironic, since many of the techniques the critics use and positions they take are possible only because of the quests. The present work will also use those methods, and like the contemporary critics of the quest will seek not to construct a "historical-Jesus" but the historic Jesus who led a faction in Second Temple Judaism that eventually became a distinct faith tradition.[13]

The next three chapters of part 1 articulate the key elements in the orientation of the approach in this book: the status of Jesus of Nazareth, the practice of remembering the historic Jesus and its implications for christology, and the significance of the early worship of Jesus as God's agent. Instead of questing for a "historical-Jesus," scholars have begun to seek to understand the "historic Jesus," the Jesus remembered by the community of his disciples. Like the quests, the new program has sought to present a critical, not naive, understanding of Jesus. Like the quests, the new program has sought to use serious methods developed by historians and has not based its claims on "faith." But unlike the quests, this new program for remembering Jesus makes it possible to explore Jesus not primarily in terms of his "words," but in terms of his "deeds," his practices—including his practice of teaching. The new program also makes it possible to see how the disciples carried on those practices that they found him empowering.

The new program is characterized by three main components: a shift from the "great man" approach to Jesus to a "first among equals" approach (especially Elisabeth Schüssler Fiorenza); a shift from a focus on scripture as written text to a focus on scripture as script (as for a play) that takes seriously the orality of the tradition (especially James D. G. Dunn); and a shift from understanding the acceptance of Jesus' divinity as a late, even Hellenized, accretion to an early recognition (especially Larry Hurtado and Daniel Boyarin). Overall, the new program shifts from constructing theories about the "historical-Jesus" to understanding the practices in which Jesus was remembered.

---

expands this list. He adds Jesus' year of birth, his childhood in Nazareth, his preaching the kingdom of God, his going up to Jerusalem for Passover about the year 30, and an arrest by Jewish authorities, and he writes more extensively about the effect of the disciples' seeing Jesus after his death. In the second edition of Perrin's *New Testament: An Introduction* (1982), Dennis Duling also made a similar expansion (411-12). Even these expanded versions are not sufficient to give a biography of Jesus.

13. For a recent analysis of the process of the development of Christianity as a separate tradition, see Daniel Boyarin, *Border Lines: The Partition of Judaeo-Christianity* (Philadelphia: University of Pennsylvania Press, 2004).

Four

JESUS AS FIRST AMONG EQUALS

*F*eminist historian/theologian Elisabeth Schüssler Fiorenza has argued that the quests for the historical-Jesus are a discourse that is simply misguided or distorted. The questers look for a "great man," a key individual who was so important that he and he alone reshaped history. Schüssler Fiorenza argues that this discourse has the historical emphasis all wrong. If a disciple has faith in Jesus Christ, then construing him as a great world historical figure like Socrates or Buddha or Muhammad or Napoleon or Hitler is insufficient. And as a historian investigates the context in which and the conditions under which an individual worked as well as what actions and movements his or her work brought about, the quest for an individual's self-understanding may be interesting ("What did Lincoln really think about African slaves in the U.S.?"), but is not the important work that historians do. Hence, the quests are of little properly historical relevance and religiously suspect.[1]

Unfortunately, many members of the "third quest" have ignored her work. For example, John Dominic Crossan in his own work on the historical-Jesus fails to refer even to her own major methodological work, *In Memory of Her*, "although he ends his 'big Jesus' book as well as his 'little' one with the headline, 'In Remembrance of Her,' which seems an unmistakable allusion to it."[2] The omission of feminist authors with relevant insights from third quest authors' publications, however, is

---

1. For an extended reflection on the issues usually treated under the "faith and history" problematic that lies behind the present paragraph, also see my *History, Theology, and Faith: Dissolving the Modern Problematic* (Maryknoll, NY: Orbis Books, 2004).

2. Elisabeth Schüssler Fiorenza, *Jesus and the Politics of Interpretation* (New York: Continuum, 2000), 63; see also 32-33. She cites John Dominic Crossan, *Jesus: A Revolutionary Biography* (San Francisco: Harper-Collins, 1994), 190, and refers to her *In Memory of Her: A Feminist Theological Reconstruction of Christian Origins* (New York: Crossroad, 1983); Catherine Keller, "The Jesus of History and the Feminism of Theology," and John Dominic Crossan, "Responses and Reflections," both in *Jesus and Faith: A Conversation on the Work of John Dominic Crossan, Author of the Historical Jesus*, ed. Jeffrey Carlson and Robert A. Ludwig (Maryknoll, NY: Orbis Books, 1994). Schüssler Fiorenza's own contribution was *Jesus: Miriam's Child, Sophia's Prophet: Critical Issues in Feminist Christology* (New York: Continuum, 1994). More startling is Larry Hurtado's omission of any references to her work in his *Lord Jesus Christ: Devotion to Jesus in Earliest Christianity* (Grand Rapids: Eerdmans, 2003), as her work is clearly relevant to his. Schüssler Fiorenza has noted that ideas generated by feminist reconstructive work like hers can be co-opted and used in ways that support the very structures of domination she opposes (*Jesus and the Politics of Interpretation*, 134). Whether the present work does so is not for me to decide, but I have tried not to co-opt her work, but to dialogue with it and use it creatively.

not the main point of contention. Nor is it that they construct the historical-Jesus in their own image.[3] Rather, the problem is that "academic biblical discourses on Jesus" too easily "support the rhetoric and structures of domination."[4]

Key to Schüssler Fiorenza's argument is discourse analysis. She identifies the quests for the historical-Jesus as an identifiable practice of academic discourse.[5] Her key point: "Discourses do more than designate things; they are practices that 'systematically form the objects of which they speak.'"[6] The historical-Jesus is just such an object. The actual man Jesus is not the historical-Jesus; the historical-Jesus is a construct of the discourse, just as the actual planet denominated "Venus," "the morning star," or "the evening star," while not completely a construct of our discourses, can be talked of only *as* a construct of our astronomical or astrological discourses. That discourses construct objects does not make the objects in some sense phony or deny the reality of what is objectified in the discourse. That discourses construct objects is the only way that they are available for us to talk about—as constructions in and of a discourse.

That there was an actual person[7] Jesus or is an actual planet we call Venus is not an issue. The question is how they function in our religious and astronomical discourses. With regard to Jesus, the key issue is whether the image or understanding of that man from Galilee in the discourse of the questers is harmful or helpful to

---

3. "Whether they imagine Jesus as an existentialist religious thinker, a rabbinic teacher, an apocalyptic prophet, a pious Hasid, a revolutionary peasant, a wandering Cynic, a Greco-Roman magician, a healing witch doctor, a nationalist anti-Temple Galilean revolutionary, or a wo/man-identified man, the present flood of Historical-Jesus books and articles documents that despite their scientific positivist rhetoric of facts and historical realism, scholars inescapably fashion the Historical-Jesus in their own image and likeness" (Schüssler Fiorenza, *Jesus and the Politics of Interpretation*, 6).

4. Ibid., 11.

5. For a sketch of what a discourse practice looks like, see my *The Evils of Theodicy* (Washington, DC: Georgetown University Press, 1991), 31-32. Of course, one (relatively) nondiscursive way to show the referent of a discourse is to point at it, but Jesus is unavailable for pointing at.

6. Schüssler Fiorenza, *Jesus and the Politics of Interpretation*, 15, quoting Michèle Barrett, *The Politics of Truth: From Marx to Foucault* (Stanford, CA: Stanford University Press, 1991), 130.

7. I use the rather bland "person" here in part because Schüssler Fiorenza also problematizes "man" and "woman," the very words we use as constituents of discourse constructs about sex. She claims that the modern versions of these categories with which we habitually and not unreasonably work are quite different from ancient and medieval categories (*Jesus and the Politics of Interpretation*, 9-11). Sandra Schneiders distinguishes between the actual Jesus (both the man who was born in Nazareth—what most scholars mean by the "actual Jesus"—and the one we encounter today), the historical-Jesus constructed by historians, the proclaimed Jesus (the actual Jesus as witnessed to and believed in by Christians), and the textual Jesus rendered in the New Testament books (*The Revelatory Text: Interpreting the New Testament as Sacred Scripture*, 2nd ed. [Collegeville, MN: Liturgical Press, 1999], xxi-xxx). Luke Timothy Johnson (*The Real Jesus: The Misguided Quest for the Historical Jesus and the Truth of the Traditional Gospels* [San Francisco: HarperSanFrancisco, 1996]) makes a similar distinction with even more theological verve, finding the *real* Jesus to be the one encountered in and through the practices of the Christian community. I differ in nomenclature, following Van Harvey, *The Historian and the Believer* (New York: Macmillan, 1966), 268, regarding the distinction between the actual Jesus as the man who lived and died in Second Temple Judaism and the historians' construct. I would also underline the plurality of proclamations and textualizations of Jesus more strongly than Schneiders does.

following him in realizing the *basileia tou theou*. That is, does this discourse help the life and work of disciples?

The term "discourse" is a term of art. A discourse forms a distinctive linguistic system. In any discourse, there are powerful connections between the constituents of the system. A person who enters a discourse practice (for instance, "is converted" to a fundamentalist Christian group or "becomes an intern" in an American hospital) learns how to accept some beliefs as unquestionable. The participant learns how to use language in particular ways, for example, to designate some as preachers or elders or doctors and others as parishioners or patients and how to take some texts (in the former case, the Bible, usually the AV; in the latter, medical textbooks) and persons (the pastor; the attending physician) as authoritative. The participant recognizes that some practices (boozing, dancing, gambling; fee kickbacks, ambulance chasing, euthanasia) are forbidden or impossible without leaving the discourse practice and other practices (referring all things to God; professional courtesy, diagnosing) as expected. The participant can usually take an institutionally determined place (worshiper in the church, parent and supporter of the Christian school; physician in the hospital, diagnostician in the clinic), which gives the participant a status in the discourse community. Such status and power relationships make it impossible for an ordinary church member to give an "authoritative" interpretation of a text or for a non-physician to render a diagnosis or write a prescription. It is practically impossible for a preacher not to give an authoritative reading of a text or a physician to render an opinion (as opposed to a diagnosis or prescription). A discourse both limits the possible acts that can be performed by those engaged in it and determines the roles people can play, some as patients (versus clients, payers, and the like) and others as physicians—noting that in some circumstances a person can be both.

Discourses need to be tested and assessed. One cannot, however, do so by comparing a discursive object with a nondiscursive object. This is the error of naïve realism. Naïve realism is rooted in a serious confusion: that we can compare what we say about something with something that we talk about—while at the same time not talking about that something. It assumes that you can tell me what you are talking about (at least when you cannot point at it without ambiguity) without using language. Rather, we test discourses by assessing the reliability of the discourse, including the effects it has.[8] Schüssler Fiorenza finds that the focus on the historical-Jesus is shaped by an unacknowledged methodological focus of questionable reliability and has had some deleterious effects.

The discourse of the historical-Jesus construes him as a great man. The practices of historical-critical interpretation of the Bible based in academic study in the university are as normal as the practices of diagnosis or surgery are in a hospital. That Jesus is a "great man" in this discourse is nowhere clearer than in the tactics of the second quest, which sought to separate Jesus from his own Judaism and from the movement in which he participated by using a criterion of dual dissimilarity.

---

8. For one view of the criteria to be used in such assessment, see my *Inventing Catholic Tradition* (Maryknoll, NY: Orbis Books, 2000), 156-70.

Schüssler Fiorenza quotes Dieter Georgi to great effect on this point: "This view that Jesus had been a genius of some sort became the dominant view in the late eighteenth, nineteenth, and twentieth centuries, not only in Germany but also in Western Europe and North America, among both Protestants and Catholics."[9] That this "great man" or "genius" was a Jew from Galilee became irrelevant. It would be like saying that it was irrelevant that Socrates was an Athenian philosopher.

Why did Jesus come to be viewed as a "genius"? Part of the reason likely has to do with dominant historiographical trends and a version of the "Great Man" view of history that are part of the assumptions in the discourse. But another factor could also be the waning in the credibility of the incarnation in the face of the more general collapse in the credibility of miracles in modernity.[10] As Jesus was presumed to be only a man, not God incarnate, how could "his" deeds and words inspire a movement that became Christendom?[11] The answer is easy, too easy: he was an original genius, a great man. No longer believable as God incarnate, Jesus was best thought of, then, as the best and greatest of men, whose genius could not be reduced to ambient Judaism or developing Christianity.[12] Why did the leaders in Jerusalem reject him and the early church "corrupt" his message? To answer a bit baldly: The former did not understand or rejected his genius. The latter had to routinize, and thereby corrupt, his charismatic leadership. (That these answers are produced more by the presumptions of academic discourse than the evidence seems obvious). Given these views about miracles, late Second Temple Judaism, and the development of that early Catholicism (seen even in the later texts of the New Testament) that is so repugnant to liberal Protestant noses, almost naturally the "scientific historical liberal Jesus research understands Jesus as the exceptional individual, charismatic genius, and great hero."[13] Hence a trajectory begun in the first quest and continued in the second and third quests—and a reflection of the ideology of the "Great Man" even if not of the image of the questers.[14]

---

9. Schüssler Fiorenza, *Jesus and the Politics of Interpretation*, 61, quoting Dieter Georgi, "The Interest in Life of Jesus Theology as a Paradigm for the Social History of Biblical Criticism," *Harvard Theological Review* 85, no. 1 (1992): 76. The prominence of the "original genius" who created novelty and broke old rules, as found in eighteenth-century aesthetics and romantic philosophy may also be an influence, but I have not found documentation of such.

10. For a sketch of this factor, see my *History, Theology, and Faith*, 71-76.

11. Of course it is possible that this strategy is an unacknowledged and inappropriate seepage of the concerns of theological presumptions into the practice of historians. Then, the "Great Man" approach would seem to give some historical weight to the religious belief in the incarnation, as if that act of God, discernible in faith, was more significant for understanding history than the discoverable historical facts about Jesus' environment or the Jesus-movement, including its central figure.

12. This notion may be a development of Friedrich Schleiermacher's christology. See F. D. E. Schleiermacher, *The Christian Faith*, ed. H. R. MacKintosh and J. S. Stewart, trans. of 2nd German ed. (Edinburgh: T&T Clark, 1928; German ed., 1830), 377-90.

13. Schüssler Fiorenza, *Jesus and the Politics of Interpretation*, 60.

14. Schüssler Fiorenza connects the issues of the myth of pristine Christian origins and anti-Judaism more extensively in *Jesus and the Politics of Interpretation*, 128-44. Some have seen as anti-Jewish the Christian egalitarian feminist interpretation of early Christianity. Schüssler Fiorenza notes that some of her language in *In Memory of Her* might have been less careful than it could have been,

This strategy creates two problems: separating Jesus from his environment and separating him from the Jesus-movement. The third quest made real headway on the former problem,[15] but the latter one remains. Modern and contemporary scholarship tends to neglect the significance of the circles of disciples that formed the Jesus movement; it still focuses on understanding Jesus as if he were an isolated individual to whom the movement responded—and as if that response were not important. Moreover, some scholars still tend to focus on Jesus' teaching as if it were not one of his practices; as Schüssler Fiorenza put it, "feminist liberation theologians in general have asserted that it is Jesus' historical practice and humanity that is theologically important."[16] Separating Jesus from his practices as the disciples either carried them on or abandoned them is another way that questers can separate Jesus from his environment and his historic significance. It is as if this one man were so utterly important that we—as historians, not as disciples—have to understand *him* without regard to his movement. As Schüssler Fiorenza and Luke Timothy Johnson have noted from rather different perspectives—echoing a point Martin Kähler made a century ago—the construction of the "historic event" of the man Jesus *as a historical figure* (and as allegedly more significant than the much more historically significant Jesus-movement) is not a function of the man Jesus but a creation of the questers' discourse.[17] It is unwarranted for historians to separate the historical-Jesus from the movement that remembered and imitated him in its distinctive practices.

Schüssler Fiorenza finds that an effect of the questers' discourse is to continue to support structures of domination and oppression, rather than movements for liberation. She makes sweeping claims about the guilty entanglements of much "malestream" scholarship in oppressive political, economic, and social structures, and calls for scholars to disentangle themselves. She writes: "If Historical-Jesus discourses are to position themselves not in the spaces of domination but in the critical alternative spaces of emancipation, I argue, they need to shift their theoretical focus and frame of reference away from the Historical-Jesus, the exceptional man and charismatic leader, to the emancipatory Divine Wisdom movement of which he was a part and whose values and visions decisively shaped him."[18]

Whether Schüssler Fiorenza's overall indictments of academia in general and of the historical study of early Christianity are sustainable is beyond the scope of

---

and that some of the "Jesus and women" writing others have done has led unwittingly to anti-Jewish or supersessionist writing. However, she argues that her feminist interpretation and reconstruction reject the myth of a pristine earliest Christianity that is the root of anti-Judaism (and perhaps of supersessionism); also see 153-54. For another example of a thoroughly Christian theological work that both is feminist and assiduously avoids anti-Judaism and supersessionism, see Elizabeth A. Johnson, *Truly Our Sister: A Theology of Mary in the Communion of Saints* (New York: Continuum, 2003).

15. See especially E. P. Sanders's watershed text *Jesus and Judaism* (London: SCM, 1985).

16. Schüssler Fiorenza, *Jesus: Miriam's Child*, 48. She is here arguing against the typical presumption of the alleged importance of Jesus' maleness and the downplaying of his liberating praxis.

17. See Schüssler Fiorenza, *Jesus and the Politics of Interpretation*, 42-47; and Johnson, *Real Jesus*, 81-86.

18. Schüssler Fiorenza, *Jesus and the Politics of Interpretation*, 21.

this book.[19] Yet at least one critical point is clearly sustainable and one strategy commendable. The critique of sexism is sustainable. Traditional Christian doctrine, some feminist theology, popular religious culture, and the discourse of the historical-Jesus all presume the maleness of Jesus. A running motif through *Jesus and the Politics of Interpretation* is that this presumption of those discourses is not necessarily benign. At least four issues are involved.

First, the presumption of Jesus' maleness tends to conflate biological male sex with socially constructed men's roles.[20] Jesus is a (biological) male, so he is a man (a social role). Both terms, "male" and "man," are considered to be at least relatively stable with at least a core meaning that does not change. This is debatable; it is not clear that having male genitalia is either necessary or sufficient to make one a "man."

Second, it is unwarranted, even wrong, to presume that the male Jesus was a "man" in the sense of ancient society. Ancient discourses constructed "man" far differently from modern discourses. To put it broadly, for ancients the "other" of "man" was not (as in the present popular dualist anthropology) "woman." "Man" was primarily the property-holding head of household and "man's" "other" was his property, whether human (slaves, children, spouses, dependents, servants) or nonhuman (land, cattle, trade goods, etc.). Obviously, this characterization is simplified, as different ancient societies constructed "man" and "his other" differently. Schüssler Fiorenza's point can be sustained if something like this characterization is a "core meaning" of "man" in relevant ancient societies. I see no reason to think something like this characterization cannot be sustained. Egalitarian movements, in any social context of the ancient world, were counter-cultural. There is no reason to think that any ancient society was egalitarian. This fact about human cultures supports the plausibility of the wide application of the generalization, as does the limitation of the right to vote in some of the original United States to property-owning white males over twenty-one years of age. Jesus evidently did not own property, did not head a household, and so on, so he may well not have been a "man" in that context.

One might note that the great councils of Nicaea and Chalcedon focused on Jesus' humanity, not his maleness. This is entirely true. However, the issue is not the nomenclature that the council used, but that the culture modeled what it meant to be human in terms of a male stereotype. The councils can be used to mitigate these points about Jesus' maleness, but to do so, one has to raise the question of whether females were as fully human as males. Fourth-century Cappadocian theologian Gregory Nazianzen formulated a motto for the full humanity of Christ: "whatever has not been assumed has not been redeemed." Christ assumed a full human nature, so all humanity can be redeemed. However, this motto does not clearly include females *qua* female in the human nature that Christ has assumed if that human nature is defined by the male's nature. While the council documents

---

19. See ibid. 4-5, and passim.

20. While I am aware of the problems with separating issues of anatomy and physiology from the social construction of gender, some distinctions need to be made. Until a better set is constructed, the familiar biological sex/social gender roles will have to do.

may provide a resource for inclusivity, they, like any other ancient texts, would have to be purged of their kyriarchal content.

Third, the ranking of a man was determined by his status, especially his property status. A nonpropertied, independent man, if there were such, would not be much of a man in such a society and might not be treated as a real man by other men. Hence, Schüssler Fiorenza suggests that it is possible to construct a historical-Jesus, as part of the underclass, as a "wo/man."[21] Yet it must be admitted that this appellation seems a stretch because a wo/man is typically owned by someone else, and no one seems to have been able to own Jesus.

Fourth, the function of the maleness of Jesus for women is to support a modern, "traditional" man/woman anthropology.[22] The Christian right is an obvious focus for this criticism of the ahistoricism of this concept, but the more generalized claim applies beyond that discourse. Schüssler Fiorenza put the attractiveness of the man Jesus this way: "On the religious Right, for example, the combination of Protestant revival methods with the cultural romance narrative—Jesus loves me so!—seeks to secure the loyalty of Christian wo/men. Jesus becomes commodified and commercialized in terms of heterosexuality and wo/men's desire for the perfect man, the knight in shining armor who will rescue and truly love them."[23] Jesus becomes "the answer" for women, even a proto-feminist who loves women. Hence, at least on the count of "sexism," the claim that contemporary scholars fail to problematize the construction of gender and that this can contribute to perpetuating patriarchy is sustained.

For instance, when Dunn writes that "there is no hint in the Jesus tradition that Jesus thought of women as disadvantaged as a class in the way that the 'poor' and 'sinners' were,"[24] his readers may well take the reference to "women" to be unproblematic—because he has not problematized the term as Schüssler Fiorenza has. The readers take the text to mean what they ordinarily mean by "women,"

---

21. Schüssler Fiorenza, *Jesus and the Politics of Interpretation*, 12. At this point, she writes "Jesus" rather than "Historical-Jesus," but she does place this usage in scholarly discourse; thus, given what she has written about discourses, "Historical-Jesus" is appropriate. She uses the term "wo/men" for two purposes: first to interrupt (/) our habitual thinking about "woman" and "women" and our presuming that those terms have a stable meaning rather than being socially constructed; second, to recognize and include those men who are also subordinated along with women (see *Jesus and the Politics of Interpretation*, 4 n. 10).

22. This function of Jesus' maleness creates the problematic that Schüssler Fiorenza identifies as "Jesus and women" (*Jesus and the Politics of Interpretation*, 34-41).

23. Ibid., 145. The material in this quotation seems to me to fail to take seriously enough the social construction of gender roles by writing "wo/men" instead of "women." Those persons are socially constructed as women, not as wo/men, or they would not be so vulnerable to seduction by the romance, whether fundamentalist, liberal, or feminine feminist. Schüssler Fiorenza relies on Donna Minkowitz, *Ferocious Romance: What My Encounter with the Right Taught Me about Sex, God, and Fury* (New York: Free Press, 1998). It is also not clear, as I argue below in reliance on feminist theologian Mary McClintock Fulkerson, that Jesus is always invoked as a knight in shining armor. We need to see how "Jesus" functions in the particular discourses; Schüssler Fiorenza's point applies to many, but not all, constructions of Jesus.

24. James D. G. Dunn, *Jesus Remembered*, vol. 1 of *Christianity in the Making* (Grand Rapids: Eerdmans, 2003), 537.

that is, "women" as constructed in the modern, dual-gender anthropology where the difference in reproductive equipment is taken to be "essential" and other differences "accidental," or at least "less important." We "take it for granted." It is "common sense" that women are women, no matter where or when.

And that is the problem. Of course there is no concern for women's place in Jesus' work, if one takes "women" in the modern sense, because *there just were no such people at that time.* Nor was Jesus a proto-feminist. He simply could not have such a concern at that time because *there just were no feminists at that time.* Being a feminist was not a live option There was no discourse in which he could participate that would give a first-century Jew the ability to talk or think or act this way. Women, as constructed in the discourses of modernity, did not exist. Females' social identity was constructed then and there otherwise than here and now. It is not that Dunn wants to perpetuate discrimination against women in the churches or society[25]—far from it. His point is that women were full members of the Jesus-movement (with the corollary that the refusal to ordain women based on Jesus' practice is simply unwarranted). But if one fails, as he does, to problematize the construction of gender and the differences between ancient and modern constructs, one's text can be read in such a way that it continues to support oppression even if one would oppose it. Hence, Schüssler Fiorenza's point about scholars' (often unwitting) entanglements in a sexist culture as continuing to perpetuate gender stereotypes unless they problematize gender as a construct of discourses is a point well made.

Schüssler Fiorenza summarizes her recommended strategy by arguing that historical-Jesus research "must develop a reconstructive social-scientific model patterned after grass-roots social movements for change"[26] in order to do justice not only to the freedom that scholarly work gives the scholar but also to extending that freedom to other groups beyond the academy in contemporary culture. What she is arguing for is, in effect, a profound reform of the discourse.

Her argument requires a shift from questing for the Great Man in historical-Jesus studies to discerning the memories and practices of the Jesus-movement and Jesus as a "crucial member"[27] of that movement.[28] She construes that movement as a "discipleship of equals."[29] The key is remembering:

---

25. See especially the whole section on women in *Jesus Remembered*, 534-37.

26. Schüssler Fiorenza, *Jesus and the Politics of Interpretation*, 27; I have quoted selectively, as her language at this point presumes more familiarity with previous material in the chapter than I can provide here.

27. Ibid., 136.

28. Ibid., 167. Schüssler Fiorenza finds that the "part" Jesus plays is that of *primus inter pares* in the movement. Missing here is advertence to the fact that any movement has different roles that one rather than another person may be fit to play. They may well not be on a par with each other in every respect. More importantly, Paula Fredriksen notes that it was *only* Jesus who was crucified—his followers were not, and evidently were not even pursued with any great vigor by any authorities (see her *Jesus of Nazareth, King of the Jews: A Jewish Life and the Emergence of Christianity* [New York: Knopf, 1999], 8-10). It is Larry Hurtado's amply documented thesis (discussed below) that the worship of Jesus began very early in the tradition. Certainly his role was "crucial," but much of Schüssler Fiorenza's justifiable focus on the Jesus-movement seems to make it difficult to see why he *alone* was executed, unless his role was "crucial" enough to merit crucifixion, and why he *alone* became worshiped in a religiously monotheistic culture. I will return to this point.

29. Schüssler Fiorenza's understanding of early Christianity as a "discipleship of equals" has

To understand Jesus research as a critical practice of *re-membering* . . . rather than as a quest for certainties, engenders a shift from a rhetoric of scientific or theological positivism that seeks to produce scientific certainty to one that aims at critical retrieval and articulation of *memory*. *Memory* and *re-membering* as a reconstructive frame of meaning do not require one to construe a dualistic opposition between history and theology, objectivity and interestedness, Jesus and Judaism, Jesus the exceptional individual and Jesus shaped by his community; between the pre-Easter Jesus and the post-Easter Jesus, the historical Jesus and the kerygmatic Christ.[30]

Schüssler Fiorenza is not alone in calling for the re-membering of the Jesus-movement as a historical task. Indeed, in the next chapter we focus on one attempt to do just that: James D. G. Dunn's monumental *Jesus Remembered,* which is one example of such an approach done in dialogue with and opposition to the patterns found in contemporary historical-Jesus research.[31]

The important point, for present purposes, is that Schüssler Fiorenza teaches us to highlight the significance of the movement. Historically, Jesus can be understood as the first among human equals. Theologically, he can be seen as empowered by the divine in the movement "of which he was a part and whose values and visions decisively shaped him"[32] into the person the movement in turn kept in memory and came to worship as truly God's agent.

---

received significant corroboration from John Howard Yoder's different methodological and ideological perspective. In *The Politics of Jesus: Vincit Agnus Noster*, 2nd ed. (Grand Rapids: Eerdmans, 1994), 188-92, Yoder also finds an egalitarian movement at the beginning of the Jesus-movement, but (apparently following Schweitzer) he also seems to think that Schüssler Fiorenza argued for the "declination" of early Christianity into patriarchy, an interpretation of her own work she has rejected (see n. 14 above).

30. Schüssler Fiorenza, *Jesus and the Politics of Interpretation*, 75. She attributes the term "re-membering" to Mary Daly and goes on to note a key implication of this approach: "If the memory of Jesus' suffering and resurrection, understood as an instance of unjust human suffering and survival, is at the heart and center of Christian memory, then the critical ethical and theological line must be drawn between injustice and justice, between the world of domination and a world of freedom and well-being" (75-76). In *History, Theology, and Faith*, I argued that history is a professional practice with role-specific responsibilities for the historian and that faith is a person-specific practice with person-specific responsibilities for the believer. The theologian as a person of faith and also a professional has (among others) the role-specific responsibility to mediate between historians' work and faithful practice, including belief. Hence, I would take a view of the "history and theology" matter different from Schüssler Fiorenza's, fully agreeing that they are not opposites but noting that they must be related in a way that does not undermine the legitimate autonomy of the historians' work. But I would also note that theologians' articulation of faith claims cannot be limited to validation in the ecclesial community, but must be enlightening and defensible in the academy as well.

31. As noted above, Dunn does not problematize gender issues clearly, which makes it crucial to use his work carefully.

32. Schüssler Fiorenza, *Jesus and the Politics of Interpretation*, 21. For a more nuanced statement of her approach, see 165-67. Also see eadem, *Jesus: Miriam's Child* (49), where she puts it this way: "Jesus' practice as a Galilean prophet who sought to renew the Jewish hope for the reign of G*d, his solidarity with the poor and despised, his call into a discipleship of voluntary service, his execution, death and resurrection, in short, Jesus' liberating practice and not his maleness is significant." The focus on Jesus' maleness, whether ancient or contemporary, misses the point.

Five

REMEMBERING THE HISTORIC JESUS

*M*any theologians do christology from a "faith perspective." Some even recognize that we cannot know anything about Jesus except as he was remembered by those who had faith in him, as James D. G. Dunn demonstrates.[1] Both historians and theologians must recognize that there are no facts about Jesus that are separable from the disciples' perspectives and from their reactions to him—including their speaking and writing about him. As we have argued, a "historical-Jesus" in some way "as he actually was" apart from those faith-filled perspectives is a chimera.[2]

We have no texts authored by Jesus, but only the record of the impact Jesus' actions, including his teaching, had on his followers. What we have are memories of him carried in the practices of discipleship, practices the disciples attributed to his initiation.[3] Moreover, these memories are necessarily partial. Whatever he may have been, he is far more as a human being than the impact he had on his followers. Even I am far more as a human being than the impact I have on my students and that they might record. If even as a mere human I am different from how I appear to my students, why should we think that how Jesus appeared to his disciples for a year or so can be sufficient evidence to show us who he is apart from the impact he had? And as is frequently noted, the memories of Jesus

---

1. See James D. G. Dunn, *Jesus Remembered*, vol. 1 of *Christianity in the Making* (Grand Rapids: Eerdmans, 2003), 128-35, for an exemplary formulation of this point. Nor did this faith begin with the resurrection. As Edward Schillebeeckx put it, "There is not such a big difference between the way we are able, after Jesus' death, to come to faith in the crucified-and-risen One and the way in which the disciples of Jesus arrived at the same faith" (*Jesus: An Experiment in Christology* [New York: Seabury, 1979], 346). Roger Haight interprets Schillebeeckx to mean that there is an analogy between the disciples' faith in Jesus before and after their experiences of his resurrection (*Jesus Symbol of God* [Maryknoll, NY: Orbis Books, 1999], 128). I argue below that the continuity of the practices of the disciples is a key to understanding the continuity of their way of faith.

2. The actual person of Jesus, the man who lived in "the world behind the text," is historically inaccessible to us. We can "get to" him only through a world, a world that is constructed in the realm of kyriarchy. Nonetheless, we can make arguments about which memories are accurate, which distorted. The results of those arguments can provide touchstones, if not formal criteria, for linking our present practices with those inaugurated in the Jesus-movement (which at the beginning, of course, included Jesus). That the disciples included females as well as males seems obvious from New Testament studies; that Jesus' practice can warrant the practice of limiting leadership roles in the community to males is untenable if Jesus' practice is to be the touchstone or criterion for contemporary practice.

3. For a similar point about memory, see Elisabeth Schüssler Fiorenza, *Jesus: Miriam's Child, Sophia's Prophet: Critical Issues in Feminist Christology* (New York: Continuum, 1994), 90.

were recorded by males who were literate Greek speakers. We have only a partial picture, as the voices of other disciples, females, illiterates, and Aramaic speakers are preserved only in the Greek texts we have. Even as we try to appreciate him as he was in the Jesus-movement, our imaginations will be necessarily partial—both because the data available to us are very limited and because our location in a particular time and place shapes our imagination and understanding. Nonetheless, as Dunn ably demonstrates, the quest for knowledge of a historical-Jesus apart from the community that remembered him in faith, however limited that memory, is at best quixotic and at worst deceptive.

The limitations of memory have led scholars to assume a "gap" between Jesus and his followers. Christopher Tuckett has discussed the problem of that "gap" as follows: "At the risk of making a sweeping generalization, one might say that the existence of a possible gap between Jesus' self-consciousness and later Christian claims about him has been felt to be more of a problem for English-speaking scholarship and/or theology than it has been for German-speaking theology."[4] While I do not think we can say much about Jesus' "self-consciousness," the presumption of a huge gap between Jesus and his disciples that has pervaded much biblical scholarship to the point of suggesting that there was little, if any, connection between Jesus and the other members of the Jesus-movement is untenable.[5] Both Schüssler Fiorenza and Dunn recognize the partiality without assuming there is a gap. Jesus was present to his disciples and is remembered by them. That there is partiality is inevitable; that there is a "gap" is an unnecessary construct, one made to separate Jesus from his context and from those who carried on his work as his disciples.

The key point that we can take from Dunn's work is that he takes orality seriously. He argues for a change in "default settings" from presuming that the Gospel texts are literary creations like novels to presuming them to be transcriptions of oral performances: "The default setting means that when you want to create something different, you need constantly to resist the default setting, you need consciously to change or alter it. But when you turn your attention elsewhere, the default setting, the pre-set preference, reasserts itself."[6] In so doing, he focuses on the performance practice of the Jesus-movement.[7] Scholars recognize, for example, the "breathless" quality of Mark's Gospel. They understand that Mark wove together oral sources, but they do not seem to take seriously the possibility that Mark is a *script*, not a generic text.[8] It is a script built from memories of

---

4. Christopher Tuckett, *Christology and the New Testament: Jesus and His Earliest Followers* (Louisville: Westminster John Knox, 2001), 228.

5. See ibid., 227-33.

6. Dunn's methodology is explicated in "Altering the Default Setting: Re-envisaging the Early Transmission of the Jesus Tradition," *New Testament Studies* 49 (2003): 139-75 at 140.

7. Dunn is not unique in this focus. Bruce Chilton and J. I. H. McDonald (*Jesus and the Ethics of the Kingdom*, Biblical Foundations in Theology [London: SPCK, 1987]), for example, highlight the concept of performance: "'Performance' . . . refers both to the activity which results in the telling of a parable, and to the activity which may attend the hearing of a parable" (16). Chilton and McDonald, however, do not develop this insight as extensively as Dunn does.

8. The entire Gospel of Mark, save for a bit of repeated material, can be declaimed in a two-hour

oral performances, a script recording the tradition and setting it for the future. As Dunn put it, "Mark's Gospel may be *frozen* orality, but it is frozen *orality*."[9] Hence, the primary interpretive category for discerning the materials Mark used to form his narrative is *not* the normal "default" of literary criticism, that is, "layers of tradition" that are revised in various editions of a written text of which Mark is a "final" one (though one used in later editions by Matthew and Luke). Rather, the default position should be that the Markan (and other Gospel) texts are transcriptions, that is, "records of performances." Such an approach recognizes that the tradition develops into a text rooted in hearing and recording multiple oral performances of stories of what Jesus did and said and how he was treated.[10] The shifted default setting also makes the text not the object of interpretation but a tool for understanding the Jesus-movement then as a key for understanding how we can live in and live out that movement now.

Dunn shares the basic counter-response to the quests identified at the beginning of the previous chapter: the only reasonable object of historical research is Jesus remembered by and in the Jesus-movement. Dunn's main methodological contribution is a theory of the oral transmission of tradition. Like the scholars of the third quest, Dunn assumes that Jesus makes sense only in his social environment; the more we know about that environment, the more we can understand the significance of the Jesus-movement's memories of him (not his significance alone apart from the movement). Like Schüssler Fiorenza, Dunn assumes a real continuity between Jesus and the Jesus-movement. Given that assumption, he writes, "Sociology and social anthropology teach us that such groups would almost certainly have required a foundation story (or stories) to explain, to themselves as well as others, why they were designated as 'Nazarenes' and [later] 'Christians.'"[11] Jesus' disciples remembered him as a teacher, an exorcist, a healer; their stories told of their preserving his teachings and imitating his doings. Eventually, these memories were organized into Gospels, a distinctive form of ancient biography.[12] Dunn concludes that the Jesus-movement would have wanted to remember the Jesus tradition and that the spread of the Gospels attests to an interest in "knowing about Jesus, in preserving, promoting, and defending the memory of his mission and in learning from his example."[13]

---

performance (with an intermission), as American actor Frank Runyeon has shown in his one-man chancel play performed in numerous colleges and churches in the United States.

9. Dunn, *Jesus Remembered*, 202.

10. The pervasive "written text" default setting can be illustrated from numerous authors. One example is Luise Schottroff's important *The Parables of Jesus*, trans. Linda Maloney (Minneapolis: Fortress, 2006), which has reshaped my understanding of the parable tradition. Her point is to understand the text in its sociohistorical context. Hence, she writes, "Attempts to discover pre-Lukan material in the Lukan text remain hypothetical and do not help us to understand the text" (132).

11. Dunn, *Jesus Remembered*, 175.

12. Dunn notes that the stricture against taking the Gospels as biographies applied to modern forms of biography (ibid., 184-85). Larry Hurtado (*Lord Jesus Christ: Devotion to Jesus in Earliest Christianity* [Grand Rapids: Eerdmanns, 2003], 277-80) canvasses the scholarship that has led to the conclusion that the Gospels are like ancient *bioi* or *vitae*, literary forms more or less like biographies.

13. Dunn, *Jesus Remembered*, 186. The more usual modern approach is to take the writings of

This conclusion may be true, but Dunn finds that there clearly was "prophecy" in the early church, that is, that inspired disciples would speak in Jesus' name after his death. One might say that they "channeled" Jesus. Did this practice corrupt the memories of the disciples by distorting their memories? Many scholars are wary of the effect of such "prophecy" and assume that the deliverances of the prophets may have had little to do with what Jesus stood for and may have even obscured the original memories kept alive in the Jesus-movement. Dunn notes, however, that the Jewish communities, including the Jesus-movement, had to discern false from true prophecy—a challenge that likely continued as Christianity developed into a distinct tradition, growing out of one of the two factions of late Second Temple Judaism that endured in some way long after the destruction of the temple (the other being rabbinic Judaism). On what grounds would one judge prophecies? Dunn ingeniously shows how this process likely went and its implications:

> First, . . . *any prophecy claiming to be from the exalted Christ would have been tested by what was already known to be the sort of thing Jesus had said.* This . . . implies the existence in most churches of a canon . . . of foundational Jesus tradition. But it also implies, second, that only prophetic utterances which *cohered* with that assured foundational material were likely to be accepted as sayings of Jesus. Which means, thirdly, that—and the logic needs to be thought through here carefully—any *distinctive* saying or motif within the Jesus tradition as we now have it is likely to have come from the original teaching of Jesus, since otherwise, if it originated as a prophetic utterance, it is unlikely to have been accepted as a saying of Jesus by the church in which it was uttered. In other words, we have here emerging an interesting and potentially important fresh criterion for recognizing an original Jesus tradition—a reverse criterion of coherence: the *less* closely a saying or motif within the Jesus tradition coheres with the rest of the Jesus tradition, the *more* likely is it that the saying or motif goes back to Jesus himself.[14]

---

the Gospels as a narrative of an event, rather than as frozen oral stories of memories of actions. For example, Roger Haight wrote, "I presuppose the principle that all contact with God is mediated historically, and that for the Christian faith Jesus is the event in history where that encounter occurs" (*Jesus Symbol of God*, 2nd ed. [Maryknoll, NY: Orbis Books, 2000], 88). The problem is that Jesus is not an event but a person—and a person seen as especially an *agent* of God who *acted* (not merely was present to be "encountered") in and through Jesus. Moreover, it is not the individual "event" or person that is the locus of encounter, but the Jesus-movement, even during his lifetime, is what mediates the action of God. We must move not only from textuality to orality as our default, but to action rather than text or event as our default mode of understanding the significance of Jesus and the Jesus-movement. For a discussion of the significance of distinguishing acts from events, see my *History, Theology, and Faith: Dissolving the Modern Problematic* (Maryknoll, NY: Orbis Books, 2004), 49-54, 60.

14. Dunn, *Jesus Remembered*, 191-92. For a recent reformulation and defense of the criteria, see Gerd Theissen and Annette Merz, *The Historical Jesus: A Comprehensive Guide*, trans. John Bowden (Minneapolis: Fortress, 1998), 115-21. However, given the critiques of Schüssler Fiorenza noted above, Theissen and Merz's confidence "that it is humanly possible to be *certain* in dealing with the historical Jesus that we are not engaging in 'dialogue' with a product of our imagination, but with a concrete historical phenomenon" (121; emphasis added) may be too strong. See also Gerd Theissen

While such prophecies might elaborate on the tradition, any that would change it in significant ways would likely be accounted "false prophecy." Hence, the presence of prophecy in the early church does not count against the fidelity of the oral traditions of the remembered Jesus but makes possible the use of a new, and benign, form of a criterion of dissimilarity unlike the one used by the second quest and properly rejected by the third quest.

Oral transmission does not produce a series of literary layers but is a set of distinct performances. The significance of this point is crucial, for scholars have usually used tools of literary criticism rather than analyses of performance practice to explore the development of the tradition. Undoubtedly, these performances began while Jesus was alive (see Luke 9:1-10; 10:1-17); the notion that "tradition" began only after the resurrection is untenable. For example, Mark could not have used the "messianic secret" motif unless people were remembered as talking about Jesus' words, deeds, and significance. And these performances were heard and replicated by other narrators.

An implication of recognizing the orality of tradition methodologically is that "audience response" criticism has a fundamental role to play. For the transmission of tradition orally requires both a speaker and a hearer who then becomes a speaker for new hearers—a pattern that is of prime importance for this work. Memories are preserved in performance. Tradition is carried in such performance practice. The audience's response—in both hearing the stories told as authentic and retelling those authentic stories themselves (and being unable to pass on inauthentic stories)—is intrinsic to the process.

It is a commonplace of speech-act theory and reader-response criticism that the audience has to "fill in" gaps in what they read or hear with their previous understandings—a point illustrated above in discussing how modern readers might fill in the understanding of "women" with modern constructs when they read texts about wo/men in the ancient world (to borrow Schüssler Fiorenza's interruptive term).[15] We hear and read what others say and write, and fill in the meanings we understand from our culture and traditions. Dunn applies this point to ancient practice: "Oral traditional texts imply an audience with the background to respond faithfully to the signals encoded in the text, to bridge the gaps of indeterminacy and thus to 'build' the implied consistency."[16] Following Richard Horsley, Dunn notes that "Q should be seen as the transcript of one performance among many of an oral text, 'a libretto that was regularly performed in an early Jesus movement.'"[17]

---

and Dagmar Winter, *Quest for the Plausible Jesus: The Question of Criteria*, trans. M. Eugene Boring (Louisville: Westminster John Knox, 2002), 210-12, for their summary of criteria of historical plausibility, which they see as a "correction" to the criterion of dissimilarity.

15. An influential version of this practice of filling in the details is H. Paul Grice's notion of "conversational implicature," developed in lectures in the 1960s and published in his *Studies in the Ways of Words* (Cambridge, MA: Harvard University Press, 1989); for a development of this concept to account for both "implicit" and "implied" senses, see Kent Bach, "Conversational Implicature," http://userwww.sfsu.edu/~kbach/impliciture.htm (accessed February 22, 2005).

16. Dunn, *Jesus Remembered*, 205.

17. Ibid., 205, citing Richard A. Horsley and Jonathan A. Draper, *Whoever Hears You Hears Me: Prophets, Performance, and Tradition in Q* (Harrisburg, PA: Trinity Press International, 1999), 160-

But did the audience that heard the story then tell the story just as they heard it? Did they write the story they heard? Dunn develops interesting answers to both questions.

It has been a commonplace that stories "expand" as they are retold in an oral traditioning process. Many scholars believe that this embellishment may have happened to the stories of miraculous feedings in the Gospels. However, following Kenneth Bailey, Dunn notes that in oral societies there seem to be three patterns of communicating tradition: First, "formal controlled tradition" is rigid; the text is set as if it were in writing; the narrator may not deviate; poems and proverbs may fit best in this class. Second, "informally uncontrolled tradition" (Bultmann's concept) is free; there is no set text or "right way" to tell jokes or communicate news. However, a third pattern, "informally controlled tradition," allows some flexibility in performing the text, but also significant control by the community that "knows" the story it is hearing: "'The central threads of the story cannot be changed, but flexibility in detail is allowed.'"[18] Typically this material is composed of memories of "parables and recollections of people and events important to the identity of the community."[19] Much of the tradition transcribed in the Gospels, then, is informally controlled tradition.

One example of informally controlled tradition would be the empty tomb narratives. The constant would be the fact that the empty tomb was found by women disciples. Which women, whom they saw, and what they said to whom varied (so this is not a strongly controlled narrative). But the constant of women, not men, finding the tomb empty suggests that there was a crucial control even for these varying performances of the "news." Throughout his text, Dunn recognizes that code words and narrative structures seem to work as cues for the various performances of telling the stories about Jesus and his doings.

Memories preserved in the Jesus-movement are best understood as communicated in informally controlled tradition—from the beginning when Jesus was alive until they were frozen into written texts. Dunn's conclusion brings out the significance of this approach:

> In particular, the paradigm of literary editing is confirmed as wholly inappropriate: in oral tradition one telling of a story is in no sense an editing of a previous telling; rather, each telling starts with the same subject and theme, but the retellings are different; each telling is a performance of the tradition, not of the first, or third, or twenty-third "edition" of the tradition. Our expectation, accordingly, should be of the oral transmission of the Jesus tradition as a sequence of retellings, each starting from the same storehouse

---

74. I suspect that it might be more accurate to talk of performances, texts, and movements in the plural rather than in the singular.

18. Dunn, *Jesus Remembered*, 207, citing Kenneth E. Bailey, "Informal Controlled Oral Tradition and the Synoptic Gospels," *Asia Journal of Theology* 5 (1991): 42-45.

19. Dunn, *Jesus Remembered*, 207.

of communally remembered events and teaching, and each weaving the common stock together in different patterns for different contexts.[20]

The hearers likely know the stories being recited; the teller will want to be a good communicator of the tradition. While there will be performance variants (and probably exaggerations), reciters who go off track should be corrected, if by nothing else, by not having their story survive in the tradition because it fails to accord with the rest of the tradition.

This approach clarifies remarkably the process of the composition of the written Gospels and our understanding of minor and major variations. To illustrate this process, consider an analogous case. In the mid-twentieth century, musicologists and folklorists collected Appalachian folk music that might otherwise have been lost. They went out into the country, listened to performances, and recorded them—not on phonograph records or tape, but as sheet music with tune and lyrics. They might have heard the same song performed a number of different ways on different occasions by different performers. They could then either write down the variants or combine them into a collected or critical or "frozen" version. Another musicologist in another part of the country might hear different songs or variations of the same song that the first musicologist heard. When asked which version is right, they could respond that each is rightly a record of a performance.

The Gospel writers did something similar. Mark and the compiler of Q composed their texts from the performance or performances they heard, perhaps using some written materials. When Luke and Matthew worked from those written texts, they likely knew oral traditions in their own community that they had heard performed and substituted them in their own narratives or revised the ones they received according to their own oral performance tradition or included both stories (in Luke, for example, the sending of the twelve and the sending of the seventy look remarkably like different performances of the same story). John transcribed different performances and probably included material that was more fully developed in oral lore than the Synoptics' material; yet the differences and parallels in some of the material, for example, the passion narrative, and the inclusion of Synoptic-like stories, for example, Jesus and the woman caught in adultery (John 8:3-11), clearly suggest that some of the oral performances the author(s) of John heard were related to those of the tradition that led to the Synoptics.

As with the modern musicologists, so with the ancient evangelists: we can assume that they strove hard to get things right. When asked which of them is "right," we can first note that they would claim to record rightly the performances that kept alive the memories of Jesus. But critical theologians may propose that some of the recorded performances incorporate innovations, or that one remembered and recorded performance is better than the others. Critical practice puts questions to the scores and texts that might well not be raised by those who

---

20. Ibid., 209.

engaged in the practices of remembering what they heard and transmitting that memory.

If this account is basically correct—and I think it must be—it enables us to discern the performances that were frozen into scripture. It also provides another reason to think that we cannot "get back" to an actual man, Jesus, and certainly not to his "self-consciousness"—for all we have are records of performances of the Jesus-movement. What we get is the historic Jesus, Jesus remembered in and through the practice of tradition, which he is also remembered as having initiated by his own powerful and empowering practices. We may make inferences about his self-consciousness, just as we may about Moses and Buddha and Lincoln and Hitler, but given the minimal material we have available on ancient figures (at least in comparison with figures of the last few centuries) our inferences can be minimal and very tentative, at best.

What Dunn has surfaced, however, is an important factor in understanding the Jesus-movement. The movement's performances did not merely keep the memory of Jesus alive, but *constituted* the memory of Jesus. Dunn naturally focuses on the memories of Jesus' sayings and doings. What falls out of his picture is the other kinds of actions the Jesus-movement performed—and the radicality of the challenge of this movement to the authorities—who certainly do not fall into our presumed categories, which facilely distinguish "religious," "political," "social," and "intellectual" authorities, a point made far more clearly by Schüssler Fiorenza, among others.

The perplexing question in all this is, what did Jesus do to get himself executed by the Romans? And, yes, this was a Roman execution. As Dunn notes, "At the very least, however, the primary responsibility for Jesus' execution should be firmly pinned to Pilate's record, and the first hints of an anti-Jewish tendency in the Gospels on this point should be recognized and disowned."[21]

Of course, in the context of disputed interpretations of what constituted the way of being a Jew and the demands of the law, some devout Jews could have had reason to oppose Jesus. At that time religious opposition could not be separated from political, social, and economic opposition because these discourses and practices—which we treat as relatively independent of each other today—were not separable. "Religious" opposition could and sometimes did lead to violence. The disputes Jesus engaged in were disputes among Jews. Hence, some Jews, perhaps some leaders, could turn Jesus over to the Roman authorities because Jesus might be a threat to all the interlocked authorities in Roman Palestine.[22]

There is little reason to think that Pilate was duped. He was not stupid; on

---

21. Ibid., 776-77.

22. Raymond E. Brown, *The Death of the Messiah: From Gethsemane to the Grave: A Commentary on the Passion Narratives in the Four Gospels*, Anchor Bible Reference Library (New York: Doubleday, 1994), 383-97. Brown notes that if the authorities handed Jesus over to Pilate, it would not be a unique case. Citing Josephus, *The Jewish War* 6.5.3 §§300-304, Brown notes that Jewish leaders arrested Jesus son of Ananias, who protested against Jerusalem and the temple sanctuary (Brown, *Death of the Messiah*, 383).

the contrary, he was evidently an effective and perhaps even ruthless governor.[23] However Jesus came under his authority, he—as the responsible authority—bears the responsibility for the execution. The Gospels indeed are too interested in laying the blame on the Jewish authorities for us to be sure to what extent Jewish authorities were involved. In the interlocking authority structures of Roman occupiers and indigenous elites, it is hard to imagine them totally uninvolved. Thus, we can have little confidence in saying how accurate the portrayals of Jesus' trials were.[24]

Moreover, insofar as Jesus was or was seen as a political challenge, it is unlikely that Pilate could have released Jesus or did release Barabbas. "Releasing a political insurrectionary, especially during the Passover holiday celebrating the Jews' release from an oppressive, enslaving government of Egypt, would have been political folly."[25] However ruthless he may have been, Pilate was not a fool.

We shall return to this topic later, only noting here that the reason Jesus was killed is rooted in what he did—the practices he engaged in that evoked opposition and execution. But after that execution, something strange happened: his disciples began to worship him. The significance of that practice as a presumption of the work here is detailed in the next chapter.

---

23. Dunn, *Jesus Remembered*, 774-75.

24. This argument simply prescinds from attempting to harmonize the various stories. They are so differently told that any harmonization of them into a coherent narrative inevitably distorts one or more of the stories so that it is substantially changed in emphasis.

25. Amy-Jill Levine, *The Misunderstood Jew: The Church and the Scandal of the Jewish Jesus* (San Francisco: HarperSanFrancisco, 2006), 99.

Six

GOD'S SAVING AGENT

One of those actions downplayed by both Schüssler Fiorenza and Dunn (at least so far)[1] is the practice of the worship of Jesus. In his monumental *Lord Jesus Christ,* Larry Hurtado argues that devotion to Jesus as in some sense God incarnate originated very early in the Jesus-movement, *contra* the position of many of the various questers for the historical-Jesus who thought it a late development.[2] Hutardo recognizes a remarkable "intensity and diversity of expression" in the practice of devotion to Jesus. He sees this worship practice as not contradictory to, but developed as a variant form of, Jewish monotheism.[3] He also wants to bring those who do christology to recognize that it is not merely belief, but devotional practice, that is relevant to our understanding of the development of the earliest tradition in christology.

---

1. James D. G. Dunn, *Jesus Remembered,* vol. 1 of *Christianity in the Making* (Grand Rapids: Eerdmans, 2003). Anticipated volumes may develop this point.

2. Larry Hurtado (*Lord Jesus Christ: Devotion to Jesus in Earliest Christianity* [Grand Rapids: Eerdmanns, 2003], 2) follows Martin Hengel in having to posit "a virtual explosion" of devotion to Jesus before 50 C.E.. Hurtado cites Hengel and Anna Maria Schwemer, *Paul between Damascus and Antioch: The Unknown Years* (Louisville: Westminster John Knox, 1997), 283-84; and Hengel, "Christology and New Testament Chronology," in idem, *Between Jesus and Paul* (London: SCM, 1983), 30-47. Hurtado has also published a more accessible version of his argument as the first four chapters of *How on Earth Did Jesus Become a God? Historical Questions about Earliest Devotion to Jesus* (Grand Rapids: Eerdmans, 2005). The other four chapters reprint scholarly studies.

3. Hurtado, *Lord Jesus Christ,* 2-3. Hurtado opposes the prevailing assumption that the worship of Jesus arose late in the tradition. See, e.g., Roger Haight, *Jesus Symbol of God,* 2nd ed. (Maryknoll, NY: Orbis Books, 2000): "Jesus was interpreted as sharing various degrees of divine election and closeness to God. Some time in the course of the first and second centuries, Christians began to worship Jesus" (206). What Hurtado makes clear is that Jesus is very early seen not as a symbol of or mediator for God but as God's agent who, as such, participated in the very divinity of God, a point Haight acknowledged. Haight also notes that the results of Hurtado's earlier analysis, *One God, One Lord: Early Christian Devotion and Ancient Jewish Monotheism* (Philadelphia: Fortress, 1988), show that this worship can be explained by and is consistent with both later orthodoxy and later Arianism: "The New Testament remains ambiguous" (256 n. 27). The New Testament may be ambiguous theologically, but it is, on Hurtado's account, very clear in terms of the religious responses to Jesus it portrays and the devotion it alludes to. Hurtado has offered a strong argument for his claim that the mutation of monotheism that allowed devotion to Jesus as divine may well have been a major factor in the opposition of other Jewish factions to the Jesus movement and thus in the parting of the ways (see Hurtado, "Early Jewish Opposition to Jesus-Devotion," in idem, *How on Earth?* 152-78). However, Daniel Boyarin (*Border Lines: The Partition of Judaeo-Christianity* [Philadelphia: University of Pennsylvania Press, 2004]) has argued that this "variation" was already extant in Judaism before the Jesus-movement. Boyarin's view is discussed below.

Hurtado writes to oppose two approaches, a naïve ahistorical approach and a form of the "history-of-religions" approach. The anticritical apologists refused to take historical analysis of the materials seriously because "the theological and religious validity of traditional Christian devotion to Christ would be called into question if it were really treated as a historical phenomenon."[4] The history-of-religions approach found that devotion to Christ was merely an instance of "the deification of heroes and the emergence of new gods rampant in the Roman world" that corrupted the simple movement "in which ideas of Jesus' divinity could not have appeared."[5] Hurtado successfully argues that "the chronological data do not readily support a claim that devotion to Jesus as divine . . . emerged in the late first century."[6] His argument dates such striking devotion to Jesus to within a few years of his death—as evinced by the intensity of Paul's conversion and the evidence from Paul's letters (supported by other New Testament texts) that "the really crucial period for the origin of remarkable beliefs about Jesus' significance is 'the first four or five years' of the early Christian movement."[7]

Hurtado finds that the early traditions recorded in various sources support the claim that the practice of worshiping Jesus is early in the tradition. When we recognize that what the scriptures preserve is based in oral performances, including devotional performances, the diversity is not surprising. But why is there such intensity, an intensity significantly greater than the devotion to or worship of other divine agents in Judaism or of the various gods of the Greco-Roman world? Hurtado's answer is clear:

> Early Christians saw Jesus as the *uniquely* salvific agent of the one God, and in their piety they extended the exclusivity of the one God to take in God's uniquely important representative, while stoutly refusing to extend that exclusivity to any other figures. . . . Both the "privileging" of Jesus over any other figure in their beliefs and religious practices and the characteristic definition of Jesus with reference to the one God show recognizable, indeed identify, influences of the Jewish "monotheistic" tradition.[8]

Hence, worship of Jesus is undertaken by Jews in the context of Judaism, not in imitation of the polytheism of the Greco-Roman world.

Such worship is grounded in a particular culture with an image of the divine different from ours. Paula Fredricksen has noted, "*Theos* in ancient monotheistic imagination—pagan, Jewish, and Christian—was a much more flexible term than is "God" in its modern avatars."[9] Divinity was graded, not absolute. Divinity

---

4. Hurtado, *Lord Jesus Christ*, 5.
5. Ibid., 6.
6. Hurtado, *How on Earth?* 19.
7. Ibid., 37, quoting Hengel, *Between Jesus and Paul*, 44.
8. Hurtado, *Lord Jesus Christ*, 204-5.
9. Paula Fredricksen, "What Does Jesus Have to Do with Christ? What Does Knowledge Have to Do with Faith? What Does History Have to Do with Theology," in *Christology: Memory, Inquiry,*

stretched from a "high god" at the top through various celestial beings and humans who functioned as divine agents, to the emperor. Jews and Christians did not worship lower gods, but did tend to recognize their power. This is the context for claims about Jesus' divinity. As Fredricksen put it:

> Thus claims about Jesus' divine status originally appeared within a culture where such a thought was thinkable, without *eo ipso* calling into question the integrity of Jesus' humanity or the high god's (God the Father) distinctive difference. Theologically, the claim cohered with contemporary constructs of monotheism (one god at the top, others of varying degrees below). Chalcedon affirmed an extreme version of this more traditional concept of graduated divine personalities. It bordered on paradox. But it was not nonsense.[10]

The Council of Chalcedon, of course, affirmed more than graduated divine personalities. But it was in this context of a monotheism different from ours that such affirmations were possible.[11]

Yet Jesus was worshiped. How can Jesus be worshiped, given Jewish monotheism? Given that Christians did not accept a form of Greco-Roman polytheism that allowed worship of "lesser" divinities, and given that Israel was monotheistic, the worship of Jesus obviously raises questions about the fidelity of Jesus' early followers to Jewish monotheism. If we grant, as Hurtado put it, "the exclusivist monotheism of Roman-era Judaism . . . are we to think of this constraint [of monotheism] only as maintained or as 'broken' in early Christian circles, as some scholars . . . have formulated the question?"[12] If there was a "break," however, it was occasioned not by the introduction of Hellenistic categories but by the practice of devotion to Jesus that amounted to worship.

Yet Daniel Boyarin has persuasively argued that Jewish monotheism was not so monolithic as it is often presented to be. Boyarin has argued that Jews held a *logos* theology or a wisdom theology. There were, in Judaism, Boyarin writes:

> several variations of a doctrine that between God and the world, there is a second divine entity, God's Word (Logos) or God's Wisdom, who mediates between the fully transcendent Godhead and the material world. This doctrine was widely held by Jews in the pre-Christian era and after the beginnings of Christianity was widely held and widely contested in Christian circles. By the fourth century, Jews who held such a doctrine and Christians who rejected it were defined as "neither Jews nor Christians" but heretics.[13]

Practice, ed. Anne M. Clifford and Anthony J. Godzieba, College Theology Society Annual 48 (Maryknoll, NY: Orbis Books, 2003), 10.

10. Ibid.

11. I discuss Chalcedon more fully in chap. 18.

12. Hurtado, *Lord Jesus Christ*, 51.

13. Boyarin, *Border Lines*, 30-31.

In the fluid religious world that the first Christians and their fellow Jews inhabited, there were "non-Christian Jews who believed in God's Word, Wisdom, or even Son as a 'second God,' while there were believers in Jesus who insisted that the three persons of the Trinity were only names for different manifestations of one person."[14]

What comes to distinguish Christian forms of Jewish *logos* theology is the claim that the *logos* or wisdom of God has become incarnate in Jesus of Nazareth. Boyarin notes:

> The structure of the Prologue [to John's Gospel], then, according to this mode of interpretation, moves from the pre-existent Wisdom/Logos that is not (yet) Christ, a notion subsisting among many first-century Jewish circles, to the incarnation of the Logos in the man Jesus of Nazareth, who is also the Messiah and thus called the Christ. Far from a supersessionist move from the particularistic Torah to the universalistic Logos . . . the movement of the narrative is from a universal Jewish Logos theology to the particularism of Johannine Christology. . . . Of course, for the Evangelist the incarnation supplements the Torah—that much is explicit—but only because the Logos Ensarksos [incarnated] is a better teacher, a better exegete than the Logos Asarkos [not embodied].[15]

Whether this exegesis of John 1:1-14 as a narrative rather than a poem or hymn, interpeted in light of contemporary Jewish hermeneutical practice and thought, can be sustained is an open question. Yet Boyarin's work answers the difficult question of how Jesus could be considered divine by Jews who were his disciples: the way was prepared by Jewish *logos* theology. All they did was to apply it to Jesus.

Boyarin's further argument needs to be mentioned here as well. The split between Judaism and Christianity occurred only because heresy hunters on both sides condemned the "heretics" on their own side as well as their opponents on the "other side." While this movement can be read as a constituent in a process of identity formation, Boyarin's thesis is both more radical and more political:

> In the first and second centuries, there were Jewish non-Christians who firmly held theological doctrines of a second God, variously called Logos, Memra, Sophia, Metatron, or Yahoel; indeed, perhaps most of the Jews did so at the time. There were also significant and powerful Christian voices who claimed that any distinction of persons within the godhead constituted ditheism. In short, the vertical axis—between believers in Jesus versus nonbelievers in Jesus—did not form the boundary between believers in Logos theology and the deniers of Logos theology. Rather, that distinction,

---

14. Ibid., 90.
15. Ibid., 107.

like a horizontal axis, crossed through both categories defined by the vertical axis.[16]

Boyarin goes on to claim that it is the work of "heresiologists" that created a partition between Jews and Christians. Hence, there may not even be a "small step" from what we now tend to identify as a particularly Jewish view to what Hurtado calls a Christian "binitarian" pattern of worship."[17]

The practice of worshiping Jesus may be practically no step at all, save to apply the "two powers in heaven" theology that identified the "second God" in heaven as an actual person. The worship is "binitarian" because

> there are two distinguishable figures, God and Jesus, but they are posited in a relation to each other that seems intended to avoid a ditheism of two gods, and the devotional practice shows a similar concern (e.g., prayer characteristically offered *to* God *through/in the name of* Jesus). In my judgment this Jesus-devotion amounts to a treatment of him as recipient of worship at a surprisingly early point in the first century, and is certainly a programmatic inclusion of a second figure unparalleled in the monotheistic tradition of the time.[18]

In developing—very quickly—such a worship practice, the faction of Jews (and including gentiles early on) that formed the Jesus-movement created an innovative pattern of "monotheistic" worship performance based in an extant Jewish theology.

Boyarin argued that the ways between Judaism and Christianity were not "parted," but that leaders among the apostolic fathers and the rabbis "partitioned" a religiously and theologically diverse whole. Rabbis eliminated "binitarianism" as a live option by labeling those who held for two powers in heaven *minim,* heretics, and the apologists and church fathers developed a heresiology that labeled those who rejected the form of binitarianism of the *logos* incarnate "heretics." In so doing, each leadership group developed the polemics present in the New Testament and established an identity of "our group" over against the "other group." Both claimed to carry on the authentic tradition of Israel. The rabbis and the fathers thus established the separate identities of the two traditions by partitioning the diverse multitude that had formed "Judeo-Christianity."

Nonetheless, if this story of moving from a shared *logos* theology, to the identification (or rejection) of an incarnate *logos,* to a separation is relatively accurate, the questions it raises are significant. First, why did the Jewish followers of Jesus develop such a worship practice? What in their corporate life evoked it? Second, what does it mean? What are its theological implications? What are its implications for understanding the shape of the Jesus-movement? A third set of

---

16. Ibid., 92.
17. Hurtado, *Lord Jesus Christ*, 52.
18. Ibid., 53.

questions about the Jesus-movement's relationship to other factions in Judaism could also be addressed, but extensive discussion of that issue is beyond the scope of this book. Assuming Hurtado to be correct about the early emergence of this pattern of worship, we can say this: The evidence shows that the early members of the Jesus-movement developed their own eucharistic worship practices (which likely contributed to their recognizing Jesus as divine) *and* participated in Jewish worship as well, perhaps into the fourth century. Perhaps this dual worship practice was one reason for the early clash between Jewish temple authorities and the Jesus-movement.

Hurtado argues that four forces or factors are relevant to answering the question why the disciples worshiped Jesus. The first factor is Jewish monotheism: the earliest Christians were not Roman polytheists but committed Jewish monotheists. Hurtado finds that, rather than being influenced by Greco-Roman patterns, Christians tended to resist them even when considering Jesus divine. Second, Jesus' impact was significant. Just as opposition to him was extreme, so those who followed him were extremely positive about him. Whatever his status, he and his movement were persecuted. His followers strongly bonded, at least partly in response to this opposition. They exalted his name above every other. And if they were persecuted, no wonder. As Amy-Jill Levine provocatively put it, "Might Christ-confessors have sought to replace Torah with Jesus as the center of worship? That would get someone booted out of my synagogue."[19] Third, they had "revelatory religious experiences, which communicated to circles of the Jesus movement the conviction that Jesus had been given heavenly glory and that it was God's will for him to be given extraordinary reverence in their devotional life."[20] If Boyarin is right, that is just what they did. Moreover, whatever one thinks of the historicity of the resurrection, followers of Jesus were convinced that their experiences of seeing him after his death grounded their devotion to him. Fourth, the movement had to distinguish its practices both from the other factions in Judaism and from the Greco-Roman religious environment. Hurtado argues that the distinctiveness of Christian worship of Jesus can be explained by the profound response to Jesus and his practices in a context shaped by these four factors and reinforced by the developing leadership of the community.

According to Hurtado, Jesus' words and deeds led his followers to regard him as God's salvific agent. But in what did they find "salvation" to consist? Two fundamental factors seem to have influenced the disciples' sense of "salvation" from Jesus. First, they were empowered to engage in the same sort of practices Jesus did. The early Christian communities remembered that any "dispute regarding questions of status and hierarchy was roundly rebuked by Jesus: the model of discipleship is precisely *not* the stratified hierarchy of typical social organisations and national structures."[21] It is a commonplace that, as disciples,

---

19. Amy-Jill Levine, *The Misunderstood Jew: The Church and the Scandal of the Jewish Jesus* (San Francisco: HarperSanFrancisco, 2006), 108.

20. Hurtado, *Lord Jesus Christ*, 78.

21. Dunn, *Jesus Remembered*, 607. In particular, Dunn notes, "There is no suggestion of the twelve functioning as 'priests' to others' 'laity'" (607 n. 292).

they were in the role of students to Jesus' role as teacher.[22] But it is usually thought that Jesus taught *about* the reign of God. However, what Jesus did and taught was not merely *about* the *basileia tou theou*; it *was* the reign of God! He did not merely model it or teach about it, but showed them *how* they could live in the *basileia*, how to serve actively in it, how to be the *basileia*.

For example, Jesus was remembered as an exorcist and a healer as well as a teacher; indeed, that he was a healer-exorcist is exceptionally well attested in the New Testament.[23] When the other members of the Jesus-movement went out, they too exorcised, healed, and taught (see Luke 9:1-2; 10:16-17).[24] They remembered him as "sending" them, and they marveled at the power of his name over the demons—as if Jesus' name was as sacred and powerful as God's. The disciples continued what Jesus began.[25] He had empowered them to do so, and they were so overwhelmed at their empowerment that they came to worship him. It is not that he was merely God's agent; they too became agents of God in spreading the commonweal of God through their own practices—which were also Jesus' practices. Hurtado highlights the disciples' awe in the face of Jesus' words and deeds, but he consistently sees these experiences as something "received," not enacted. However, Hurtado focuses so strongly on cultic or religious (in the modern sense) experience that he neglects to consider the active responses of disciples in spreading the reign of God. While Hurtado writes of the experiences that lay at the root of the disciples' developing worship of Jesus, he leaves the content of these experiences undetermined.[26] The adherents of the movement would remember and worship Jesus not merely because he affected them, but because they perceived him as empowering them: he gave them his power, including the use of his name to cast out demons. Jesus was worshiped as God's divine agent, as the incarnate *logos,* not because he (though now dead) had affected his first followers, but because he (alive among them although exalted into God's presence) empowered them to act. The adherents of the movement today should remember and worship Jesus because they find him alive among them although exalted into God's presence empowering them to act and to speak even now.

What grew over the decades of early Christianity was not only devotion to Jesus as God's own divine salvific agent incarnated but also an attempt to account for this devotion in the context of monotheism and in light of the philosophical concepts available in late antiquity. Hurtado put it this way:

> In the doctrinal language that began to be favored in the second century and thereafter, the Son shares the same divine "nature/being" (Greek:

---

22. Ibid., 556-57.

23. See ibid., 673-83.

24. See Hurtado, *Lord Jesus Christ*, 203-6.

25. Lest it be thought otherwise, I am not suggesting that Jesus was unique as a healer, exorcist, or teacher. Just as there were other emancipatory movements in late Second Temple Judaism, as Schüssler Fiorenza noted, so there were other exorcists, healers, and teachers. In these roles, Jesus is not a unique or unsurpassably great man.

26. See Hurtado, *Lord Jesus Christ*, 64-74.

ousia) with "the Father." Of course, in the classic expression of Christian teaching about God, the doctrine of the Trinity, the "Holy Spirit" comes to be included as well as the third constituent of the divine triadic unity. But the main concerns in this long and complex disputation and development of the Christian doctrine of God were to express Jesus' genuinely divine significance and status, and, equally firmly, to maintain that God is "one." In this latter concern especially, we see the continuing influence of Second-Temple Jewish monotheism.[27]

The later doctrinal developments, then, were rooted not so much in apologetics or religious practices in the Greco-Roman world as in the actual religious life of the Jesus movement from its beginning—perhaps even in the lifetime of Jesus of Nazareth.

It is clear that the doctrinal positions of the fourth and fifth centuries are rooted in the records of the disciples' memories of Jesus. Historically speaking, the Chalcedonian formula resulted from a combination of factors, including ongoing political intrigues, intellectual debates, and the need to fashion a distinctive identity over against the patterns both of rabbinic Judaism and of the diverse religiosity of the Roman Empire. From a historical point of view, the formula is contingent—it might have been different. However, the actuality of historical contingency does not warrant any speculations about how it might have gone otherwise, only the recognition that the way it happened was not historically necessary. Christians may believe, of course, that events developed as God wanted—or at least as one of the ways God wanted them to go. The issue was how to preserve a memory of Jesus as both the one who was first among equals and the one who was also recognized and remembered as God's empowering agent. That Jesus was truly human, truly divine, both one in being with us and one in being with God—however difficult to understand that formula might be—is the way the Jesus-movement sought to understand Jesus the Christ whom they remembered in their midst, especially in and through the practices of discipleship, the topic of part 3 below.

---

27. Hurtado, *How on Earth?* 55.

CONCLUSION TO PART ONE

What can we harvest from these varied approaches to the New Testament for use in the present work?

Like Schüssler Fiorenza and Dunn, Hurtado dethrones the regnant patterns of interpretation of the early Jesus-movement. Schüssler Fiorenza highlighted the significance of the movement. Historically, Jesus can be understood as the first among human equals. Theologically, he can be seen as empowered by the divine in the movement "of which he was a part and whose values and visions decisively shaped him"[1] into the person the movement in turn kept in memory. That memory was transmitted in practice, especially the oral practices of telling and listening and retelling—some of which, at least, is "informally controlled tradition" that allows us to see how the historic Jesus was construed and remembered by the early movement, possibly even during his lifetime, as Dunn notes. Part of that construal, of course, resulted in a devotion so intense that it required a mutation of Jewish monotheism in practice and in theory.

While not all the scholars whose work we have examined would agree about the methods or the aims of their scholarship, we are in position to develop an understanding of the disciples' Jesus that has two foci: (1) not the historical-Jesus but the historic Jesus; not the Jesus constructed from the thin results of critical scholarship but the Jesus who matters as a historic person; and (2) the historic community that began to worship Jesus as divine practically from the beginning. If I have accurately described this approach to the remembered historic Jesus, what are its theological implications?

More concretely, first, remembering the historic Jesus supports the christological pattern discerned by Reginald Fuller.[2] If this pattern is accurate, then there is no such thing in the New Testament as "christology from above" or "christology from below." The adherents of the Jesus-movement began their christology "where they were," that is, with their practices of remembering Jesus. They remembered Jesus in what they did, including their practice of "binitarian" worship, and in where they imagined Jesus the Christ to be. Indeed, *every* christology follows this pattern.

---

1. Elisabeth Schüssler Fiorenza, *Jesus and the Politics of Interpretation* (New York: Continuum, 2000), 21. For a more nuanced statement of her approach, see eadem, *Jesus: Miriam's Child, Sophia's Prophet: Critical Issues in Feminist Christology* (New York: Continuum, 1995), 49, 165-67.

2. See the discussion above, pp. 36-37, of R. H. Fuller, *The Foundations of New Testament Christology* (London: Collins, 1976).

The common disjunction between christology from above/from below obscures the fact that christology always arises in disciples' imaginations. We start with Jesus as he is perceived and imagined on this earth. *We* start his story here even if we imagine or infer that it really began in heaven. If the "binitarian" worship of Jesus is the community's recognizing in him the unique and profound agency of God in and through the movement God constituted as the Jesus-movement, and if this worship is quite early, then the pattern of christology charted above is also probably quite early.

One obvious objection to this approach might be made based in the work of Schüssler Fiorenza. In a "kyriarchal social system and kyriocentric world view, Jesus is understood not only as the divine son and extraordinary man but also as the lord and master over the world." By "kyriarchy" Schüssler Fiorenza means "the domination of the lord, slave master, husband, the elite freeborn educated and propertied man over all wo/men and subaltern men."[3] If kyriarchy was inscribed in our traditional worship practices, then simply continuing traditional practices may be implicitly supporting the same sort of social structure that crucified Jesus and continues to damn true emancipatory movements.

However, in the first quotation in the previous paragraph, Schüssler Fiorenza writes in the passive voice. In so doing, she obscures who is doing the understanding. Of course, she presumes that it is elite, academic males doing it. And—unless we (for I am of that tribe) can work to subvert the discursive formulations that perpetuate this unjust social structure she calls "kyriarchy"—we are part of the problem, not part of the solution.

But what if it were oppressed women who used the notion of the lordship of Jesus and the power of his name to resist and counterbalance the lordship of husbands and other males whose roles are constructed by the kyriarchal discourse Schüssler Fiorenza seeks to undermine? Could it be that buried in the tradition is a notion—altogether too prone to abuse—that God as Lord of creation and Jesus as Lord can empower resistance to the lords of this world? Mary McClintock Fulkerson has argued that in one contemporary discourse practice, that is exactly the case: some Appalachian Christian women use what is available and powerful in the kyriarchal discourse that constructs them as subservient and dependent in order to resist the lordship of their husbands and other dominant males. They appeal to their Father in heaven against the power of their fathers and husbands on earth. They can use pertinent passages in scripture—recognized as an authoritative source by the dominant men of their culture—to undermine patterns of their domination. If there is no other Lord but Jesus, then there is an opening in that discourse for oppressed subalterns to call on the Lord and thus practice resistance

---

3. Schüssler-Fiorenza, *Jesus and the Politics of Interpretation*, 95. Schüssler Fiorenza is more concerned with texts and discourses than with worship. When she writes of the cult, e.g., the worship reflected in Philippians 2:5-11, she presumes that early Christian claims were influenced by Greco-Roman religions and formed a "foundational mythology that created its own cult" (*Jesus: Miriam's Child, Sophia's Prophet*, 148). This is an area of contention. That the discourse of worship could be bent in kyriarchal ways seems undeniable; that it is based in a kyriarchal myth is not so clear.

to the earthly lords who control women's lives. Calling on Jesus for help may even help them discern rays of emancipatory light in a dreary situation.[4]

It is interesting that there seems to be a difference in the New Testament texts that call on Jesus as Lord and those that call Jesus "Lord." In the former, the vocative *kyrie* is usually a request for help from Jesus to rescue a person from a problematical situation or to have Jesus effect a cure. In John 11, for example, Martha and Mary call on Jesus as lord seven times before he raises Lazarus from the dead. Here, it is not the power of patriarchy or kyriarchy that is inscribed but cries of women and men who need Jesus to save them or another from an illness, affliction, or death.

I do not want to challenge Schüssler Fiorenza's approach of finding traces of suppressed discourses and changing the basic presuppositions regarding gender for interpreting the texts. Rather, I suggest that if we can understand the subversive practices of resistance that create "other possibilities" in the nooks and crannies of the system, if we can discern how to use the power of the sacred name to create leverage for resistance even when it is not possible to overthrow the system of oppression, then even we educated elite can learn from the discourse practices of the oppressed. We can learn not only something about how the confession "Jesus is Lord" has been abused in the past and is abused in the present to support "kyriarchy" but also how to critically reconstruct, theologize about, act in the service of—and even pray to—the Lord Jesus in our own discourses in a manner like that of the Appalachian wo/men to whom Fulkerson gives a voice. Yet we can never forget how easy it is to tame or hijack a practice of resistance and emancipation that uses the Lord's tools to deconstruct the lords' controlling discourses.

Second, in this way it is possible to see that the "binitarian" worship pattern in the very early Jesus movement may not be a practice that is a creation of oppression but a worship practice subversive of oppressive structures. This dangerous pattern of worshiping Jesus as the empowering agent of the one God was in tension not only with other movements in late Second Temple Judaism, evidently even those that accepted a "two powers in heaven (not one on earth) theology," but also with the Greco-Roman social structures that provided the matrix for developing Christianity both before and after the destruction of the temple in 70 C.E. Those matrices could then be seen as the context in which the resistant practice was tamed by oppressive "default" habits in those cultures, as the tradition developed, into a pattern supportive of a dominant class. With Schüssler Fiorenza, I find no reason to think that this "default" habit was not present from the beginning. There was no time when the power of oppression was not. It has always been a factor in the communities of disciples, a factor to be resisted.

Third, these presumptions open up the possibility of exploring a broader range of practices that constitute the exercise of Christian faith in Jesus. Bearing one another's burdens (Gal. 6:2), living so as to be worthy of the gospel of Christ

---

4. Mary McClintock Fulkerson (*Changing the Subject: Women's Discourses and Feminist Theology* [Minneapolis: Fortress, 1994], 239-98) develops this point. Fulkerson, a theologian working out of the Reformed tradition, warranted her claims about this "subaltern" discourse in part by ethnographic fieldwork.

(Phil. 1:27), and a host of other practices define discipleship. These orientational chapters have focused on practices that must be rethought: approaching the historic Jesus, considering ways of re-forming the patriarchal discourse practices that shaped the texts, the significance of forms of oral transmission, and the rationale for worship of Jesus. The fundamental methodological point we can take from their work is crucial: practices like living in and living out the *basileia tou theou*, worship, and remembering in the community do not merely count in understanding the significance of christological claims but in fact constitute the context of discipleship, the only context in which the imaginative and faithful christological claims in the developing tradition can have significance.

All the scholars discussed in these orientation chapters regard the practices of the early tradition as a resource for christology. But my point is more radical. These linked practices *are* christology. When John's messengers ask Jesus whether he is the one who is to come, he responds that they should tell John, "the blind receive their sight, the lame walk, the lepers are cleansed, the deaf hear, the dead are raised, the poor have the good news brought to them"—precisely what the Jesus-movement effects. The question about Jesus' identity is answered by "what has been and is being done."[5] It is not just what the individual man Jesus does but what his disciples are remembered as doing even before the death of Jesus. Just as the practices of transmitting the oral tradition are remembering (or misremembering) Jesus, and the practices of worship are the "presencing" of Jesus, so the practice of imaginatively confessing Jesus as *ho christos* is both a rejection of the lords of this world and a declaration of allegiance to the Lord whom Jesus makes present in his own empowering practices—practices that led and lead to reconciliation and the construction of a community that lives in (even if proleptically) the *basileia tou theou*. What Schüssler Fiorenza perhaps overstates—in response to the "Great Man" assumptions of the academic "historical-Jesus" discourse, that Jesus was *primus inter pares* in the Jesus-movement—is an important insight for my thesis: that the historic Jesus was and is the first person among those who recognized the empowering presence of God, the prophet of Sophia recognized as incarnating Wisdom who teaches the members of the movement not what is wise but how to exercise wisdom in practice; who does not reveal truths but draws out from members of the movement insights that help them to see how to live truthfully; who graces the movement not by infusing its members with something from on high but by surfacing the divine creative grace in the movement and helping shape an ongoing movement of created, creative grace; who refuses to make the disciples into wholly dependent patients who respond to God's powerful Agent in passive acceptance but empowers them to become creative and graceful reconciling agents of the commonweal divine. How they came to imagine him as the anointed one, *ho christos*, and how those imaginations are always in the context of discipleship is what we explore in part 2.

---

5. That this response echoes 4Q521 suggests that Jesus and/or the transmitters of the tradition knew this passage from Qumran and applied it to the work of the messiah. See James D. G. Dunn, *Jesus Remembered*, vol. 1 of *Christianity in the Making* (Grand Rapids: Eerdmans, 2003), 447-52.

Part Two

RECOGNITIONS
AND
INTERROGATIONS

Seven

BEGINNING CHRISTOLOGY
AT THE RIGHT PLACE

*T*he New Testament does not have christologies in the modern sense. Scripture does not systematically reflect on who Jesus of Nazareth was/ is and what he did. Rather, it uses a wide variety of images, titles, role designations, and metaphors to show Jesus' significance. It does not seek to investigate Jesus or clarify "truths" about him. Rather, it proclaims what he meant in and for the communities of those who followed him. It is not so much a book or composite text in the modern sense, but a script for, or a transcript of, oral performances. The Gospels, Paul's letters, and most of the other "texts" in the New Testament were *scripts* meant to be performed by a literate disciple and heard by a community, and then performed again and again by those who heard the performance. Even the letters to a community might often be a supplement to or a script for a spoken performance by the one bearing the letter. The New Testament is not a set of theological treatises to be read by individual scholars and interpreted or explained for others.

Considered as scripts that reflect and structure performances, the New Testament is neither a book of doctrine for Christians to learn nor a book of morals to enact. Disciples performed them when they gathered together, especially when they gathered to worship and to remember in the communion of the Lord's Supper the one whom they followed and who was present in and to them as the agent empowering the practices of their discipleship.

To learn how to interpret these scripts well by playing them out in one's life is to learn how to be a disciple. One learns how not only to tell the story, but to live the story in new ways. One develops a repertoire of practices that constitute discipleship. Learning how to act shapes a person into a disciple, for we are what we do. Or, if one prefers, what we do reflects who we are—philosophical debates about "being" being prior to "doing" or vice versa were not of much interest to practitioners. Which, if either, was "prior" made no difference in practice.

Proclaiming the faith is one sort of practice. Some texts in the New Testament are the equivalent of lyrics for chanting, as the *kenōsis* hymn in Philippians 2 may be. Some are scripts of model proclamations, such as that of Peter at Caesarea Philippi or Martha at Bethany or Paul's speech in the agora in Athens "recorded" in Acts. Others are simply stories that proclaim the faith of the disciples of Jesus by showing others addressing him as "Lord."[1]

---

1. The literature on *kyrios* (Lord) as a title for Jesus is fairly consistent in finding that "Lord"

Believing is another sort of practice—we have to learn how to believe. As we become disciples, we are schooled in ways of believing. Belief or trust or faith in Jesus and the Jesus-movement is not a prerequisite or foundation for discipleship—it is a constituent of following Jesus. In the sense that a virtue is a habit or practice, then faith or trust or belief is a virtue. Just as a married couple over the years may learn not only what love is but how to love better as they grow in their shared life, so disciples learn both what faith is and how better to exercise that faith as they grow in the community of disciples. They even write down their memories so that "you may believe that Jesus is the Christ, the Son of God, and that believing you may have life in his name" (John 20:31). Believing permeates what committed disciples do. In short, the New Testament is not a text to be analyzed so much as a set of scripts for forming a company of performers, a movement that will be Christianity.

Of course, some texts, including some passages in Paul's letters, are more like directives on how to succeed—or to avoid failure—in the practices of discipleship. Because stories can't interpret themselves, sometimes guidance in how to live and tell the stories is necessary. Directives can provide guidance for the practical interpretation that is living out and living in those stories.

These scripts vary widely, both in form and content. Images of God, testimonies of witnesses, and clues about who Jesus really was and what he really did are imbedded in them.[2] They are not perfectly consistent with each other—in part because good performance practice requires that one tailor performances to the circumstances, including being aware of the audiences one is performing for and with, and the distinctive contexts, needs, and idiosyncrasies of one's audience. Disciples' hearing and reenacting those stories will also be shaped by contexts. As contexts, needs, and idiosyncrasies change, so will the way the stories are told.

Some scripts require substantial rewriting or deep reinterpreting because their texts have become misleading. New Testament texts written by Jews rhetorically distancing "us" from those "other Jews" who are our opponents cannot simply be enacted today by gentiles. The long history of Christian anti-Judaism is due, in part, to Christians neglecting the contexts in which the texts were written and the purposes for which they were written. Texts written to establish identity in what seem to be sometimes vicious intra-Jewish disputes nearly twenty centuries ago, as the Jesus-movement was attempting to establish its identity vis-à-vis other Jews

---

was not a title used by Jesus during his lifetime although common among his followers; see the discussion in Larry Hurtado, *Lord Jesus Christ: Devotion to Jesus in Earliest Christianity* (Grand Rapids: Eerdmans, 2003), esp. 20-22.

2. For example, Richard A. Horsley and Jonathan A. Draper (*Whoever Hears You Hears Me: Prophets, Performance and Tradition in Q* [Harrisburg, PA: Trinity Press International, 1999], 160-74) argue that the Q document lying behind Matthew and Luke is best understood as a transcript of one (or more) oral performance(s) in a performance tradition that was remembered and recorded in (one or more) written formats; also see James D. G. Dunn, *Jesus Remembered*, vol. 1 of *Christianity in the Making* (Grand Rapids: Eerdmans, 2003), 205.

and the prevailing Greco-Roman religions, cannot mean the same thing when that context, those rhetorical practices, and dissimilar cultural roles obtain.[3]

Beyond such tailoring, consider the widely varying stagings and settings for performances of *Hamlet* or *Macbeth*, the transformation of Bizet's *Carmen* into an all African-American film, *Carmen Jones*, or the multiple genres—stage versions, opera, ballet, films (including *West Side Story*)—that show and tell the classic tale of *Romeo and Juliet*. Each way of performing these classics is remarkably different from the others, but they still show and tell the story. The first performers (authors) of each do not create an archetypal staging to be slavishly emulated in each future production. Rather, all, including the first, are creative performers. The performers transform the play as they discover what works and what does not. Scripts, music scores, and dance scores are not the performance. They preserve the lineaments that make the work what it is. But actual performances may deviate from them, sometimes successfully, sometimes not. As stories and plays move from one genre to another, the actual performers in each genre may have to exhibit different sets of skills, for different skills are needed to perform in different genres. If the tradition of interpreting *Romeo and Juliet* is so varied, why would one expect less of Christianity?[4]

If one begins by recognizing that the texts in the New Testament are first scripts to be performed, one will not be surprised at their variations. One also can seek to discern the original performances remembered in these scripts—and likely often transformed because of shifts in context and genre as each story is reenacted in a performance practice tradition. In short, we can work as drama or music or dance critics engaged in a very specific task: to discern through the texts a reflection of Jesus' disciples' anamnestic practices as they sought to keep his memory alive in their faithful performances so that we can keep his memory alive as we become disciplined performers.

Christians' primary performance practice is remembering who Jesus was and is, a practice that gave them their own identity—and should give us our identity—as his disciples. They first remembered him in practice, not theory. This is not to say that they did not use numerous theoretical concepts in their performances, but notes that theory was not the point of what they did and how they lived. Hence, what one does not have in these texts are theoretical christologies, even if today we see in the various texts of the New Testament a host of christologies in the making and a myriad of theological/theoretical reflections on who Jesus was and what he did for those who had faith in him. We have guides to performance, both theoretical and practical.

---

3. For a clear, critical, yet sympathetic discussion of these issues, see Amy-Jill Levine, *The Misunderstood Jew: The Church and the Scandal of the Jewish Jesus* (San Francisco: HarperSan-Francisco, 2006), 87-117.

4. In *Inventing Catholic Tradition* (Maryknoll, NY: Orbis Books, 2000), I construe a tradition as a set of practices (implicitly performance practices) that must be invented anew in each context. Whether any instantiation of the tradition is faithful or not is a matter of assessment—which is sketched in the final chapter of that book.

The image of the New Testament as a score to be performed or a script to be enacted, rather than as a text to be read and interpreted, requires a reorientation in one's approach to the text. A practical approach to the text as a record of oral performance does not reject the work of scholars who have focused on the text as a book or set of books to be interpreted as literary productions. Indeed, the present approach is deeply indebted to such interpretations. Rather, a practical approach to christology re-places the interpretive work of textual scholars and literary critics in the constellation of theological interpretive practices.

In the next four chapters, I take four New Testament texts that christologists have frequently analyzed. I approach them as guides for the practice of discipleship, a practice that gives rise to beliefs in Jesus. In rereading these texts as records of performances ("frozen orality," as discussed above in chapter 5) and scripts for disciples' further performances, I believe these texts take on new significance. They do not first set patterns for belief, as some christologists seem to think, beliefs that Christians may accept, reject, modify, or develop. Rather, they set patterns for practice that Christians are to reenact to be part of the "running performances" of discipleship—performances that take widely varying forms. Believing (having faith) is carried out by engaging in those practices, but beliefs are not the "foundations" of practice, but shorthand guides abstracted from performance practice. And as I argued in *Inventing Catholic Tradition*, a tradition *is* a practice or set of practices. The patterns of practices are necessarily not rigid;[5] one cannot say just how they are to be put into practice before one begins the practice; we can only act as well as we can and show as well as we can what it means to live in line with those patterns, to perform those practices well, to be a disciple, a member of the ongoing Jesus-movement.[6]

---

5. Dunn (*Jesus Remembered*, 205-10) used work of Kenneth Bailey on oral transmission and performance practice to make a similar point about the malleable reliability of oral transmission performance. Dunn uses Bailey's category of "informal controlled tradition" to great effect in analyzing the Gospels as recording at some points various performances of the same story. Neither uncontrolled (and therefore fully flexible) nor formally controlled (and therefore inflexible in performance) this performance tradition is more like cool jazz in which a recognizable classic tune, for example, "On Green Dolphin Street," can be played in numerous ways both by different performers and on different occasions by the same performers. It is the same tune, but performed (and recorded) differently each time it is performed (rather than just lazily replayed).

6. At this point, the question of "criteria" of good performances may arise. A performance is presumed to be acceptable unless the community finds it unacceptable. If there are criteria, they are "negative" ones that exclude bad performance, not "positive" standards that performances must meet to be accepted as "good." Dunn, for example, finds that the worries of critical historians, especially their worry that prophetic speech (given by disciples who claim to be speaking for or in some odd way "channeling" Jesus; compare *Didache* 11) may have influenced or reshaped Jesus material, may be overstated because there was much concern in the New Testament churches and in their ambient culture to exclude false prophecies. These communities would have tested the prophetic speech for its fidelity to Jesus and to the received traditions of the community; this process likely antedates Easter. This means that even if the tradition has been developed and elaborated in performance, it is quite likely that the early Christian community used a criterion of fidelity as at least an informal norm to recognize bad performance, that is, to exclude false prophecies—a problem that evidently plagued at least some early Christian communities. The interesting upshot of this viewpoint is that what "odd" material may remain in the texts that we have inherited receive some

Modern scholars tend to focus not on these specific texts as records of oral performances (both of the narrators and the subjects of the narration) in a predominantly oral culture, but as literary creations to be understood in terms developed in a sophisticated literary culture. Yet rooting out the actions the narrators were performing in speaking their lines and the actions the subjects performed opens the door for understanding not only the disciples' Jesus, but also why christology is not to be rooted in systematic thought but in reconciling practice.[7]

But we will begin here at the beginning—the first time someone called Jesus "the Christ."

---

support for its authenticity, for there needs to be an explanation of why such material which might well have failed the test of fittingness was retained; one possibility is that some of it was retained because it was strongly remembered as Jesus' material. See Dunn, *Jesus Remembered*, 186-92.

7. Focusing on these texts may seem arbitrary in that numerous other christological texts and images can be found within and without the New Testament canon. We cannot ignore "the exuberance of Jesus' followers that created in the first decades of the movement's existence, the wildest diversity of mythic portraits of Jesus" (Wayne Meeks, "The Man from Heaven in Paul's Letter to the Phillipians," in *The Future of Early Christianity: Essays in Honor of Helmut Koester*, ed. Birger A. Pearson in collaboration with A. Thomas Kraabel, George W. E. Nickelsburg, and Norman R. Petersen [Minneapolis: Fortress: 1991], 329-36, at 329). However, no other "mythic portraits" of Jesus are connected so clearly with the wisdom of the practice of discipleship as are the scene at Caesarea Philippi and the *kenōsis* hymn, and the nuances of recognition by two of Jesus' key disciples presented by the scene of the raising of Lazarus and its following pericopes make these texts especially relevant for the present work. It is undeniable that there were many other images of Jesus in the New Testament and other early Christian writings; but for a practical discipleship, these texts are clearly among the most relevant.

Eight

CONFESSING JESUS AS *HO CHRISTOS*

Peter at Caesarea Philippi

*T*he argument of this chapter begins by showing that Peter's confession of Jesus as the Christ was the first ever recorded use of the term *ho christos*[1] for Jesus. This means that Peter's action, portrayed in the Gospel of Mark, marks the beginning of christology proper. Hence, Peter's imaginative response to Jesus' question is the right place for us to begin our consideration of christology as reconciling practice.

Mark never uses the term *ho christos* earlier in the Gospel. Peter's confession is its first reported use—and the only time reported in the Gospel that a supposedly "right" understanding of this term appears.[2] Here, in the first part of the Caesarea Philippi scene, begins christology proper:

> And Jesus went out with his disciples to the villages of Caesarea Philippi and on the way he was questioning his disciples saying to them, "Who do the people [*hoi anthrōpoi*] say I am?" and they spoke to him saying, "John the Baptist, and others Elijah, others one of the prophets," and he questioned them, "Who do you say that I am?" Peter, answering, says to him, "You are the christ [*ho christos*]," and he warned them that they should tell no one about him. (Mark 8:27-30)

Stylistically, this passage is a "hinge" in the Gospel of Mark, a centerpiece of the whole. But why claim that here begins christology?

---

1. I will generally leave this term in transliterated Greek. While Peter's use of the term may not be metaphorical, the term clearly has many nuances. Literally, it is "the anointed one," and is often taken to mean "the messiah" or "the king," and is probably taken that way here, but it has other echoes, such as the one prepared for death or burial.

2. Although scholars acknowledge that the term *ho christos* was used very early about Jesus, quite possibly even during his lifetime, by his followers (and perhaps others) to designate him, they have long debated whether Jesus used the term *ho christos* to assert that he was the messiah. The general consensus is that it is unlikely that he did. Raymond Brown, for example, accepts this point, but also thinks it also unlikely that he *denied* that he was the messiah and that even if he had accepted the title, that it would not have been in terms of a Davidic messiahship which his followers and opponents may have expected. As chap. 11 shows, the "one who is to come," presumably the messiah, inaugurated a reign quite different from what a conquering Davidic messiah would have done; see Raymond E. Brown, *An Introduction to New Testament Christology* (Mahwah, NJ: Paulist, 1994), 79-80.

The Origin of the Story

Does the story in Mark record the memory of an actual event from the time of Jesus' ministry? The answer is that it is possibly a historical memory, but this is not certain. Yet it is not clear that any significant arguments against its historicity can be mounted, save that most scholars have assumed that giving Jesus the title of messiah, *ho christos*, the anointed one, is a product of the later development of the tradition, rather than of the disciples' memory.

What are the relevant issues? First, presuming that Mark is the earliest Gospel we have, and only the Pauline writings predate it,[3] this is the very first recorded use of *ho christos* as a title for Jesus in the entire New Testament. Earlier writings by Paul rarely use the expression *ho christos* and never use it as a title or a role for Jesus to play.[4] Paul and those who write in his name much more typically use "Christ Jesus," and not "the Christ, Jesus."

Second, Peter's response originates the "title" *ho christos*.[5] It is possible that Mark's attribution to Peter of the first use of *ho christos* for Jesus does date from an actual event while Jesus was alive. If this is so, then we may be glimpsing the written memory of an actual oral performance that itself constitutes the beginning of christology proper. Mark's text can be seen as inscribing the first, although flawed, realization of Jesus' identity by his followers.

One objection that can be raised against a claim for the historicity of Peter's confession is the assertion—quite likely accurate—that the entire Caesarea Philippi scene is literarily composite. Many scholars have argued that the scene is woven together by an author from multiple strands in the tradition.[6] While the

---

3. The hypothetical Q document or documents or oral performances that constitute Q are not relevant here. Beyond the fact that the Q document or documents are modern scholars' constructs rather than extant texts, they do not use *ho christos* as a title. The dating of the *Gospel of Thomas* is so unclear that it cannot function as evidence; there is little reason to think that it is earlier than Mark.

4. Of the 270 uses of *christos* in the seven undisputed Pauline letters, only two (Rom. 9:3 and 9:5) use the term with the definite article. In these uses Paul refers to Jesus, but does not clearly address him with the title of "the Christ." The force of Paul's use is not to give Jesus a title or to debate about its significance. Rather, he simply assumes the designation. It is clear that the term connotes Jesus' status as messiah and is not simply a "surname" throughout Paul's writings. But its use is that of a definite description more than a proper name, and clearly not a title of honor as in the Synoptics. Compare Larry Hurtado, *Lord Jesus Christ: Devotion to Jesus in Earliest Christianity* (Grand Rapids: Eerdmans, 2003), 98-101; Hurtado also notes that for Paul "'Christ' functions almost like a name for Jesus . . ." (264 n. 11) and rarely as a title—and it may be that the "rarely" is an understatement.

5. For a discussion of the Caesarea Philippi scene in Mark, its significance for christology, and a review of recent literature on the scene, see my essay, "O Caesarea Philippi: Starting Christology at the Right Place," in *Theology and Sacred Scripture*, ed. William P. Loewe and Carol Dempsey, Annual Publication of the College Theology Society 47 (Maryknoll, NY: Orbis Books, 2002), 135-61.

6. For example, see Rudolf Bultmann, *The History of the Synoptic Tradition*, rev. ed., trans. John Marsh (New York: Harper & Row, 1968), 257-59, 431. Bultmann rejects views that treat the Caesarea Philippi pericope as unified and historical, such as Oscar Cullmann's view, which is characterized by Bultmann as a "psychologizing interpretation."

scene may have multiple sources, it is not clear when that composition occurred.[7] The composition may have occurred quite early, even within Jesus' lifetime, as the story was told. There is no good reason not to think that a very early performance conveying Jesus' significance was the point at which the parts of the story were woven together. There is no reason to think that the weaving occurred only when the final scribe of Mark was writing the story.[8]

Moreover, the Caesarea Philippi scene is an important event in the Markan narrative. Mark placed it at the center of his story—it is the hinge on which the Gospel turns. To place the scene there underlines its significance. As Dunn put it, "Over all the probability must be deemed quite high that in Mark 8:27-30 [and parallels] we see recalled an episode within the mission of Jesus in which the issue of Jesus' messiahship was raised."[9] As the story plays a pivotal role in Mark's Gospel, it is a pivotal story for the Jesus-movement. And it is the first remembered use of *ho christos* in the tradition.

---

7. Pheme Perkins has argued that each of the units in the story, the Petrine confession, Jesus' command to silence, the passion prediction, the rebuke of Peter, and the call to discipleship can reasonably be viewed as reflecting actual events, even if their literary form has been shaped over time; see her *Peter: Apostle for the Whole Church* (Columbia: University of South Carolina Press, 1994), 29-31. Brown (*Introduction to New Testament Christology*) suggests that the scene might not be unhistorical ("If we were to judge that the confession itself is not implausible historically . . ." [75]). Yet Brown *uses the subjunctive* in answering the question of whether Jesus affirmed himself to be the Messiah, so it is not clear whether he would find the scene as a whole historical.

8. Although Dunn doesn't make the point explicitly, the parallels and divergences between Mark 8:27-30, Matt. 16:13-20, and Luke 9:18-21 suggest that behind each of these texts may be multiple performances of "informally controlled" narrations of the tradition. The parallel lists of who they (people or crowds) say he is, his question, the core of Peter's answer, and the command to tell no one are identical; the rest of the items vary slightly although Matthew adds 16:17-18 and Luke adds Jesus praying with the disciples and drops out the location. Perhaps Matthew and Luke had heard other versions of the story and "corrected" the Markan account—based on yet a slightly different way of performing the tale—with the stories they knew. Dunn also finds that the recollection of a turning point in Galilee recorded in John 6:66-69 with a Petrine confession in response to a challenge from Jesus, combined with the Synoptic texts and literarily unrelated to them, leads to the conclusion that it is historically probable that "both attest a memory of some such event" (James D. G. Dunn, *Jesus Remembered*, vol. 1 of *Christianity in the Making* [Grand Rapids: Eerdmans, 2003], 645). While this multiple attestation is *not* sufficient to warrant a claim that such an event actually occurred with a very high degree of historical reliability, the reality of a crisis or turning point in the life of the Jesus-movement and the challenge of Jesus coupled with a response from Peter is, in my judgment, more probably reflective of an actual event than not. Additionally, placing the elements together in one scene, with a visit to one specific town, may well be the creation of the oral performance behind the Synoptics or Mark's contribution. But an argument that the scene as a whole is a literary creation of the Markan redactor is not evidence against the historicity of the individual elements woven together in the scene, and certainly not for the significance of the story as a whole in the life of the Jesus-movement.

9. Dunn, *Jesus Remembered*, 645. It is not clear that Jesus ever called himself the messiah in any sense of the term; the historical evidence simply is not conclusive (see ibid., 648, and the literature cited in nn. 159, 160). Dunn recognizes that the text is a literary composite. He notes that the passion prediction was "a core saying which has been thus elaborated" (800), but also claims it unlikely that the rebuke of Peter in 8:33 was interpolated into the text (645). Like Perkins, Dunn finds that though the scene may be a composite, its components each have some claim to echo actual events in Jesus' life.

It also might be objected that Mark does use *ho christos* a few times later in the Gospel, and that such literarily "later" usage might well not have been later in fact, since Mark's sequencing of the events in Jesus' life cannot be trusted for historical reliability, as noted in chapter 3. This point is significant, not because it undercuts the claim to historicity, but because it opens up a crucial theme in Mark's Gospel: no standard understanding of *ho christos* is right.

Portraying Confusion

Everyone in Mark is confused about *ho christos*. Perhaps that is why Jesus is portrayed as silencing the disciples. Perhaps this "silencing" is not to keep a "messianic secret" but to stop spreading a "messianic confusion."

First, the texts in which *ho christos* is used are varied. In each of them, a different sort of speech-act[10] is performed. Once, Jesus mocks the scribes while he is teaching in the temple. They can't tell higher from lower, or sons from fathers. They think *ho christos* is David's son. *Ho christos*, though, cannot be David's son. Jesus points out that David called him "Lord," so *ho christos* (and Jesus if he is *ho christos*) cannot be David's *son* (Mark 12:35)—what father calls his son "lord"?[11] Later, Jesus warns about the end-days, when people will mistakenly identify the wonder-workers here and there as *ho christos* (Mark 13:21). In the passion narrative, the high priest asks Jesus if he is *ho christos*, son of the Blessed One; Jesus responds "I am" (Mark 14:61).[12] Finally, the chief priests and scribes mock (among themselves) the crucified Jesus as *ho christos, ho basileus Israel*. They deride Jesus' failure, sarcastically identifying him as "the anointed one" and "king of Israel" as he hangs on the cross, executed by Roman justice for his treason.[13]

Second, what is common to all these uses is that whoever uses the term gets its significance wrong. Each performance is flawed because it connects the title *ho christos* with a Davidic king. And none of them is a response to Jesus by a disciple. Jesus was not the expected messiah or a king.[14] It is not inconceivable

---

10. See chap. 2, n. 10, pp. 20-21, for a brief sketch of speech-act theory.

11. This scene is clearly christological and generally believed to be a retrojection of later christological thought back into the memories of Jesus. The wordplay remembered here is typical of oral culture, so it cannot certainly be excluded as an authentic memory of Jesus' performance, but neither can it be relied on historically. See Dunn, *Jesus Remembered*, 634-35. None of the disciples is present at this point in the passion narrative; this also counts against the likelihood of this being historical.

12. See Dunn, *Jesus Remembered*, 651-52, for the issues regarding the reliability of this saying coming from Jesus.

13. Dunn concludes lucidly: "Moreover, since the royal Messiah translated readily enough as 'king of the Jews,' the obvious deduction is that Jesus was 'handed over' to Pilate's jurisdiction on the charge of claiming to be David's royal successor, in the full knowledge that one who claimed to be a king was likely to receive short shrift from the prefect. . . . But for the moment it is sufficient to have demonstrated the high historical probability that the issue of Jesus' messiahship was the decisive (legal) factor in (or, should we say, excuse for) Jesus' execution" (*Jesus Remembered*, 634).

14. It is possible that the point (recorded not in Mark but in Q) of Jesus' blessing one who does

that each of the uses in Mark's Gospel gets the significance of *ho christos* wrong because the reign of God that *ho christos* inaugurates is not what they expected.

Third, *everyone* who identifies Jesus as *ho christos* is mistaken about the significance of that appellation. From Peter to the chief priests and scribes, they all imagine wrongly the reign of God brought by the anointed one. They may get the words right (Peter and the high priest especially), but they don't really know who or what *ho christos* is. A text, like the Gospel of Mark, that portrays such repeated blundering raises the suspicion that something tricky is going on.

It is not merely that they *did not* get the significance of calling Jesus *ho christos* right. They simply *could not* get it right. In short, they all blundered because their "minds" (English cannot do justice to the Greek here—more about that later) were wrong. Even less than Peter's, the ways of the others were not God's ways. They were not the kind of people who could bring off the imaginative performance of properly confessing Jesus as *ho christos* because they didn't "get" what Jesus was about. Both Peter and the accusers and executioners of Jesus may have known the right words to use, but they never could say who Jesus really was because their heads were "in the wrong place." Peter's ways were a human's ways, not God's— Peter's head was in the wrong place. (What could it mean to be in the right place? That is material for discussion of Philippians 2 in chapter 10. Here a hint: both texts use the same concept that we translate "ways" in Mark and "mind" in Philippians.)

Indeed, not only are all those who identify Jesus as *ho christos* mistaken about the significance of that term as applied to Jesus, but so is everyone else who tries to identify him. The other possible identities Mark places in his narrative are also false leads. Jesus' family and neighbors got it wrong. They could not imagine him to be more than a carpenter—and perhaps a crazy carpenter. Herod's crew got it wrong as we shall see. Their answers were imaginative but nonetheless wrong. The scribes got it remarkably incomplete and thus wrong. Their answer was imaginative but fundamentally confused—he was not a son of David, in the Davidic line of kings of Israel. The imagined people of an apocalyptic future got it wrong. They would equate *ho christos* with a wonder-worker. The high priest got Jesus to admit finally that he was *ho christos*. But he misunderstood what Jesus meant—he too likely expected a Davidic kingdom that would upset the political status quo with Rome. And Mark makes another clever connection here—or rather a disconnection. When *Pilate* asks Jesus a similar question, whether Jesus is king of the Jews, Jesus does *not* respond, "Yes." Rather, he refuses to accept that title. He replies, "You have said it." Not I—*you*! Perhaps he accepts the title *ho christos* from the high priest but not the title *basileus tōn Ioudaiōn* from Pilate. And later the chief priests and the scribes mock Jesus as a king. But how can it be that the one who preached and enacted the nearness of the coming of the reign of God is identified as the king of Israel, of the Jews? Only God is the king of Israel! At best, they are confused and mocking him; at worst they are blaspheming. In each of these cases, confusion reigns.

---

not find him a scandal was to differentiate his understanding of God's reign from that of John the Baptist. See below, pp. 116-22, 175-77.

Peter, like the high priest later on, got the title right. But Peter and the high priest got the significance wrong. Like the high priest, Peter got the *title* right, but as Stanley Hauerwas once put it, he got the *story* wrong[15]—just as Pilate would have misunderstood if Jesus had accepted the title of "king." Peter, the high priests, the scribes, and the lovers of miracle-workers may have had the words right. But the words alone don't tell us what the words mean; the words need a story to tell us what they mean. And all of them told the wrong story—the story of a conquering Davidic messiah, rather than a suffering messiah. Since they told the wrong story, they could not but be confused about the significance of the title.

Mark portrays Jesus as silencing those who could not get the story right. They were not his followers, his disciples. Like Peter, they might have the words, but not their significance. It would be better to be silent than to say words or tell stories that mislead one's hearers! In short, might it be that Mark's clues lead us to understand that christology must begin in *disciples'* imaginations, and not in their imaginations alone but in those imaginations as disciplined by Jesus (and after his death, by the Jesus-movement that kept him alive in its midst in its active remembering of his presence).

An obvious problem with this view would seem to be the problematic narrative structure of Mark. Choosing between the sequence of events and time-line of Mark (singly attested period of ministry of a year or less) and that of John (singly attested period of ministry of over two years) for Jesus' public activity seems arbitrary. Either or both patterns may be arbitrary.[16] Hence, that *ho christos* is used incorrectly earlier in Mark's Gospel cannot be evidence that it was not used earlier than Peter's confession in actuality.[17] What is evidence, however, is

---

15. Stanley Hauerwas, "Jesus: The Story of the Kingdom," in *A Community of Character: Toward a Constructive Christian Social Ethic* (Notre Dame: University of Notre Dame Press, 1983).

16. Dunn notes the consensus that John is not in the same league as the Synoptics as a source for Jesus material, but some details in his narrative may contain early tradition (*Jesus Remembered*, 166), and some, including Dunn himself, find the longer ministry narrated by John more plausible, as well as John's chronology of Jesus' last days. But the language of the Gospels, including the use of *ho christos* as a description of Jesus before the "turning point" in John 6:66-69, is not reliable enough to be used as counterevidence to the issue under discussion.

17. Paula Fredricksen has argued that this arbitrariness has important ramifications for the "cleansing of the temple." Mark locates this pericope just before the passion. John narrates it at the beginning of Jesus' ministry. This difference means that we cannot place that crucial event historically with any reliability. Thus, asserting that this act is the triggering event that led to the arrest, trials, and crucifixion of Jesus goes beyond the evidence. Fredricksen goes further and argues that the incident is an invention of the early church. This argument founders on several grounds. First, it argues against a consensus in scholarship that accepts the Markan placement. This consensus is established by scholars using significantly different methodologies. While she may bear the burden of proof against the certainty of Mark's placing the incident, the consensus makes it quite a heavy burden. Second, the fact that the event has multiple attestations in oral traditions behind Mark and John makes it difficult to attribute such a distinctive incident to a creation *ex nihilo* by an inspired prophet that early in the development of the tradition. Third, it fits too well with what we know about Jesus: that he was executed as a messianic and/or royal pretender who evidently evoked the wrath of the Jerusalem leadership. Fourth, it is portrayed as a lone act of Jesus, which coheres with the fact that his followers were active in Temple worship after his death. However, its timing—and the sequence of any events in the life of Jesus save for his last days—remains uncertain. For example,

that *the performance of the speech act of confessing in response to a question of Jesus occurs nowhere else in the Gospel*. Indeed, the only other point in the Gospel when Jesus accepts the title is perhaps in response to the high priest—who evidently also does not understand what sort of messiah Jesus is. Chronologically, it is part of the passion narrative and thus must be *after* a "turning point" in Jesus' ministry placed by both John and Mark in Galilee. Hence, the problems with Synoptic sequencing do not affect the present claim that the Caesarea Philippi scene records the first use of *ho christos*, at least as a confession of faith.

I find no good reason not to think that confessing Jesus as *ho christos* began at this turning point in the development of the Jesus-movement, probably at Caesarea Philippi during Jesus' own lifetime. It also seems likely that the scene has been developed in the tradition in such a way to show that Jesus is not a "royal" messiah. However, if Dunn is right about the practices of oral performance and the oral transmission of tradition as informally controlled, then that development should be consistent with the disciples' memory of Jesus. Hence, Caesarea Philippi can also be seen as the right place for us to visit as we begin trying to understand the disciples' Jesus.[18] Whether oral performers composed the scene from stories of disparate events or from a story of a single event is no longer relevant: Jesus' questions and his responses to the replies of the disciples and Peter are clearly actions performed by the disciples' Jesus and recorded for their memories.

Performing the Caesarea Philippi Story

Mark sets the scene as Jesus and the disciples are walking over to the villages near Caesarea Philippi. They leave the crowds behind in Bethsaida. Thus, Mark or his source makes this a story not about Jesus teaching the crowds or his mission to Israel. This is an "in-house" story, a story of and for the Jesus-movement (see Mark 8:27ff.). Mark sets the tale at a turning point in the life of the Jesus-movement. The story starts when Jesus asks his disciples how people size him up. They come up with some possibilities they have heard. Jesus then asks them what they say

---

Dunn does not place it in the narrative and notes the problems the Markan placement creates (see *Jesus Remembered*, 636-40, 795-96; for Fredriksen's arguments, see *From Jesus to Christ: The Origins of the New Testament Images of Jesus*, 2nd ed. [New Haven: Yale University Press, 2000], xxii; eadem, *Jesus of Nazareth, King of the Jews: A Jewish Life and the Emergence of Christianity* [New York: Knopf, 1999]; and "What Does Jesus Have to Do with Christ? What Does Knowledge Have to Do with Faith? What Does History Have to Do with Theology?" in *Christology: Memory, Inquiry, Practice*, ed. Anne M. Clifford and Anthony J. Godzieba, College Theology Society Annual 48 [Maryknoll, NY: Orbis Books, 2003], 3-17; also see my "Teaching Christology: History and Horizons," *Christology: Memory, Inquiry, Practice*, ed. Clifford and Godzieba, 275-76 n. 18).

18. In what follows, I will analyze the earliest form of the scene we have, that of Mark, as I find that construing his Gospel as a script for an oral performance makes sense of the oft-noted "breathless" structure of the Gospel—and that such an approach helps surface some verbal connections that might have struck early listeners' ears in ways they don't ordinarily strike us who are formed by literary cultures.

about it. Peter pops out the "right" answer. Jesus silences them—they are to tell no one. Then Jesus explains what Peter's answer means. Peter opens his mouth again. He refuses to accept Jesus' explanation. Jesus rebukes Peter: he calls him a "Satan"! Yet later in Mark's narrative, Jesus lifts him up by taking him along for a marvelous sight—for what follows shortly thereafter is the transfiguration scene.[19]

The story looks pretty straightforward, but it is more complex than it appears. The questions ask more than meets the eye. The answers tell more than they say. No one really "gets" the right answer to the big questions, and the "wrong" answers reveal more than the "right" ones.

Mark's text gives up clues that enable us to sort out the complexity. From the beginning there is the secret.[20] Jesus tells all the creatures who knew the secret to keep it to themselves, yet his reputation spreads. Mark's Gospel invites the reader to draw obvious conclusions, but he also leaves clues to other conclusions we can draw.

We who read the Gospel tend to focus solely on *the* question Jesus asks and *the* answer Peter gives. Jesus' questions are now terribly familiar to us. "Who do you say that I am?" has become a hackneyed sermon title. Sometimes it seems like a question on a multiple choice test. The disciples report imaginative answers (a, b, c), but they're the wrong answers. Then Peter gives his imaginative answer (d). And we think he's right. In a way he is—at least he didn't answer "none of the above" or "all of the above."

Yet the trickiness of Mark's Gospel suggests that we need to look beyond the obvious "right answer." Many, if not all, of Mark's sources were orally performed, and Mark itself is amenable to oral performance.[21] Mark's story is not really about Peter identifying Jesus correctly as the Christ. His identification of Jesus as *ho christos* begins well, but then Peter gets off-track. The clues in Mark's story point to "the right track."

---

19. The next passage in Mark (8:34-9:1) is directed to the disciples and the multitude, so there is clearly a "scene shift" here. But the next scene is the transfiguration (9:2-8) with only Peter, James, and John present. Whatever the significance of this story, Mark's placing it where he does suggests that the rebuked Peter was nonetheless not anathematized.

20. Dunn (*Jesus Remembered*, 624-26) argues that the "messianic secret" motif is too varied to be a monovalent motif, as Wrede had assumed. Dunn finds that the issue of Jesus' messiahship likely did arise during his ministry, but that it was a title he refused (647ff.).

21. I have heard the Gospel of Mark performed as a one-man chancel play (in English) in a "two act" performance by actor Frank Runyeon a number of times at the University of Dayton (he has taken this performance on tour to many venues). He provided a brief setting that gave the audience the role of an ancient Christian community of the Diaspora hiding in fear and hearing the story from an emissary from another community. He finished a moving and powerful performance of the whole Gospel (leaving out only some duplicated materials—which might have been an alternate oral or manuscript tradition at one point) in under two hours. In a predominantly oral culture, such a feat—while perhaps not commonplace—could easily be done by an accomplished storyteller, especially one bringing comfort to a community that was afraid.

The First Question and Answer

The first question comes out of the blue, as Jesus and his disciples are walking along. He asks his disciples, "Who do people [*hoi anthrōpoi*] say that I am?" (8:27). A good question. Jesus must have a reputation. After all, Mark has spent seven-and-a-half chapters of his book narrating Jesus' deeds. So, Jesus asks the disciples how people see him.

Those who were listening to the narrative had heard a lot. Jesus was baptized in the Jordan by John and was driven into the desert for forty days by the Spirit. Then he walked the villages of the Galilee. He preached, healed, exorcised demons, stilled a storm, multiplied food, ate with tax collectors and sinners, and argued with Pharisees. He sent out his twelve henchmen "two-by-two," and they did deeds of exorcism and healing in other places (a point to which we return in chapter 13). He commanded demons to be silent about his identity. He told the people he healed *not* to tell *anyone* about his works, "but the more he charged them, the more zealously they proclaimed it" (Mark 7:36). Who would tell this secretive, teaching, healing, arguing, ritually suspect miracle-worker to his face who, or what, he was reputed to be—especially when his family thought he might be mad?

A person's reputation varies: some people think well of one, some ill. Some identify a person positively, others negatively. Mark litters his story with identities for Jesus. The demons identified him as the holy one of God. (Those demons didn't know him just by reputation: he threw them out of those they possessed.) A voice from heaven said he was a beloved son. A grieving father, a hemorrhaging woman who touched the fringes of his garment, some friends of a paralytic, and a Syrophoenician woman saw him as a healer. Some Pharisees took him for an opponent who arguably violated the Sabbath (though Mark caricatures the Pharisees' views). His family thought him crazy. His neighbors were skeptical—he was merely the carpenter they knew. "What is this wisdom that has been given to him?" (6:2) they asked sarcastically. They probably thought him a fraud since he did not perform wonders for them. Some scribes who came down from Jerusalem to see his deeds found him a man possessed by the prince of demons. Many who saw the wonders he worked were afraid. But they all had him pegged—as a prophet, or healer, or charlatan, or some such. Or so they thought.

Hearers of the story have been so far bombarded with events and actions and images. The "breathless" pace of Mark in oral performance portrays a scene of nearly ceaseless action. The images briefly canvassed above are more than varied—they are wildly conflicting. The storyteller then brings us to this incident where Jesus asks about his own reputation.

His disciples gave different answers to his question on the road to Caesarea Philippi. They said some people thought him to be John the Baptist (who had been executed by Herod); others thought he was Elijah, the great Hebrew prophet of the past returned to his people; and others saw him as one of the prophets, but without specifying which one (8:28). Why did the disciples give these answers? Or, more accurately, why does Mark's tale narrate these as their responses? Why these three answers? Mark doesn't say. All we have is the story he told and the clues he left. We have to listen for the connections.

The first clue is from an earlier episode in the Gospel. The NRSV renders the episode this way:

> So [the Twelve] went out and preached that all should repent. They cast out many demons, and anointed with oil many who were sick and cured them. King Herod heard of it, for Jesus's name had become known. Some were saying, "John the baptizer has been raised from the dead; and for this reason these powers are at work in him." But others said, "It is Elijah." And others said, "It is a prophet, like one of the prophets of old." But when Herod heard of it, he said, "John, whom I beheaded, has been raised." (Mark 6:12-16)

Here is the very same set of answers the disciples will give to Jesus' question later in the story! But Mark 6 puts it in the mouths of Jesus' *enemies*, not the mouths of his disciples. Herod and his cronies develop the same short list of possibilities for Jesus' identity as the disciples do in reporting what the people say—but two chapters earlier in the Gospel than the disciples' report.[22] Herod himself identifies Jesus with the man he has had murdered. Should we hear this as an anticipation of another execution? As a chilling warning? And should we note that this is quite an imaginative list—all of the identities attributed to Jesus were those of dead men?

Herod was a puppet king, sustained by the occupying power of the Roman army. His courtiers had imaginatively identified Jesus as John, Elijah, or one of the prophets. Is it just a coincidence that when Jesus asks his disciples who people (*hoi anthrōpoi*) say that he is, the disciples answer as Herod's men did? Or is it a clue to a connection?

Jesus had warned his disciples against the "yeast of the Pharisees and the yeast of Herod" (8:15). That these short lists are the same suggests a connection of these enemies of Jesus to the Caesarea Philippi scene. Mark gives us no reason to think that the disciples might have gotten this list from Herod or one of his familiars at court. The identity of the lists is Mark's clue. Whom did Jesus mean when he asked about *hoi anthrōpoi*? Either Jesus was not asking who *anybody* in the crowds imagined him to be, but who his enemies imagined him to be, or his disciples understood him to be asking who his enemies imagined him to be, even if he was asking about the people in the crowds in general. In either case, the disciples' answer connects the road to Caesarea Philippi to the palace of Herod and the murder of John the Baptist. But what connection does this clue help us to make?[23]

---

22. An audience would hear these lists only about ten minutes apart, presuming that the story-teller included both feeding miracles. Less than a minute before the beginning of the Caesarea Philippi scene, they would have heard Herod's name again (8:15).

23. Luke's version of this story substitutes *hoi ochloi* for *hoi anthrōpoi*, "the crowds" for "the people." In doing so, Luke erases the connections to Herod's henchmen. In Luke's version, the crowds who do not understand are those who have just participated in the feeding of the five thousand—a point underlined by Luke's changing Mark's and Matthew's sequence of scenes imme-

Moreover, the disciples do not say, "Some take you to be a fraud, others a wonder-worker, others an exorcist, others a wandering cynic-sage, an itinerant magician, a charlatan."[24] The disciples' report brings Jesus' enemies into the scene.

The second clue is that Jesus is identified with the dead. Herod may have accepted the views of the Sadducees that there would be no resurrection of the dead, or Herod may have accepted views associated with the Pharisees that God would raise the dead *en masse* in the future. But belief in an individual resurrection would be truly odd. Why would Herod and his courtiers imagine that Jesus was a dead man risen to life? Were they spooked? Superstitious? The resurrection of the dead—whether believed in or denied—was a future event. But they identified him as a dead person already returned. Whatever the reason may be for this hard-hearted lackey of Roman oppressors to imagine Jesus as the dead John, the clue points to Herod's *imagination* of Jesus' identity.

Mark's story of the early Jesus-movement coming to the villages of Caesarea Philippi begins with a question from Jesus and an answer from his disciples that has Herod and his cronies as the "people" who imaginatively identify Jesus with the return of a dead man.

Second Question and Answer

Jesus then asked his disciples "Who do you (plural) say I am?" Grammatically, this question looks like the previous one. Grammar, though, can be misleading. The second question is not a request for information about Jesus' reputation. The second question is not directed to the people or the enemies, nor is it even about the beliefs of Herod or any other absent people. The second question challenges the disciples to testify: it is not, "Who do *they* say that I am?" but "Who do *you*

---

diately before the Caesarea Philippi scene. For the significance of this, see William C. K. Poon, "Superabundant Table Fellowship in the Kingdom: The Feeding of the Five Thousand and the Meal Motif in Luke," *Expository Times* 114, no. 7 (April 2001): 224-30, and chap. 16 below.

24. Elisabeth Schüssler Fiorenza has wittily retold the rabbinic story of the return of Moses to this life in order to visit the renowned scholar Rabbi Akivah in his academy. "Sitting in the back of the classroom, Moses listened in wonder as Akivah with great eloquence, exegetical skill, and intellectual breadth expounded the unfathomable mysteries of the Torah. When Moses asked, amazed, who had written such great things about which he had never heard, Rabbi Akivah answered, 'These are the words of the Torah given by G*d to Moses at Mount Sinai.'" She then riffs on this story: "If Jesus, like Moses, were to return to earth, read all his biographies and attend the Jesus Seminar or the Society of Biblical Literature annual meeting, he also would marvel and ask with amazement: 'Who is this person they are talking about?' Is it Jesus, the apocalyptic prophet, the Cynic peasant, the millenarian seer, the magician, the wisdom teacher, or the witch doctor? But, unlike Moses, Jesus might not just marvel at the rich diversity of meanings ascribed to him by distinguished scholars. Rather, most likely he would have an identity crisis and fall into deep depression. He rightly would ask: 'Who am I if I take seriously what they say?'" (*Jesus and the Politics of Interpretation* [New York: Continuum, 2000], 1). Perhaps he would not take their ways or words as friendly any more than he once took what *hoi anthrōpoi* said and did; for it was the disciples who seemed to have counted.

say that I am?" He asks, "What is *your* mind about me, how do *you* imagine me, or what image do *you* have of me?" This question demands an entirely different kind of answer. It seeks no report about others, but a confession of their own "take" on him. Peter declared, "You are *ho christos*." Jesus responded by charging them—as Peter may have spoken for all of the disciples—to keep silent about him.[25]

Fervent Gospel readers can be so aware of Matthew's expanded version of this story that the early version constructed by Mark seems incomplete. Peter's answer is taken as so brilliant, so unexpected, that Matthew has Jesus say that only his father could have told Peter that Jesus was the Christ, so he makes Peter the first pope (as Catholics have sometimes read the story; see Matt. 16:13-20).[26] Note that in Mark's version, Peter is not really brilliant or inspired. No father in heaven was needed to reveal it to Peter. He just answers the question. We know Matthew's story, and so we can easily, and incorrectly, read Mark as telling the same story. We remember the amplification, especially about Peter, in Matthew. But Mark's story is not Matthew's. Mark's earlier story is, so far, merely ho-hum and matter-of-fact. Peter merely gives his imaginative answer. Jesus doesn't even directly acknowledge that Peter got the answer right. All Jesus says is that the disciples must not tell anyone.[27]

Peter's response is quite imaginative and quite literally original in the Christian tradition. We have noted above the other uses of this title in Mark. We also noted that everyone who identifies Jesus as *ho christos* doesn't understand the meaning of *ho christos* as applied to Jesus. The accusers and executioners of Jesus may have known the right words to use, that he was *ho christos*, but they never could say who Jesus really was because their minds were "in the wrong place."

The Story of Christ and His Disciples

Mark's story of Peter's response at Caesarea Philippi is emblematic. Peter got the story wrong because his imagination had gone haywire.[28] His "mind" was

---

25. Dunn finds that "the command to silence functions more to indicate a messianic misunderstanding than a messianic secret" (*Jesus Remembered*, 649). Mark presumably indicated that by the next several verses, wherein Jesus "corrects" Peter. The "right" understanding of Jesus as the anointed one of God is evidently not in the realm of a "royal" messiahship, but in a quite different power given by God to and through Jesus, a point developed in part 3 below.

26. Dunn reflects the widespread consensus among scholars that Matt. 16:18 is "probably redactional and indicative of later developments" (*Jesus Remembered*, 513).

27. I speculate that perhaps the force of Jesus' command to silence was not to keep a secret but to say "shut up and stop talking such foolishness." At least that may be as good an interpretation of the occurrence of this injunction as the numerous hypotheses propounded by scholars since Wrede.

28. The use of "imagination" in this book is not an appeal to a "faculty," but to the practice exemplified by those who have the virtue of *phronēsis*, "practical wisdom." The *phronimoi* have the ability to imagine how standards, rules, or universals apply in specific situations. In Aristotle's *Nicomachean Ethics*, this is the virtue that bridges intellectual and moral virtues, the practical (but not theoretical) capstone of the mind (see 1140a:24-28). To a modern eye, it looks like a "bridge"

wrong (and all the others were "wrongheaded," too). The way Mark or his source continues the story on the way to Caesarea Philippi after v. 30 is important. The passage can be rendered thus (compare the RSV and the NRSV):

> And he began to teach them that the Son of Man must undergo great suffering and be rejected by the elders and the chief priests and the scribes, and be killed (and on the third day rise again).[29] He said this quite openly. And Peter took him and began to rebuke him. But turning and looking at his disciples, he rebuked Peter and said, "Get behind me, Satan! For you are not setting your mind [*ou phroneis*] on things of God [*ta tou theou*] but on human things [*ta tōn anthrōpōn*]." (Mark 8:31-33)

Peter is "wrongheaded." He has his "mind" in the same place that *hoi anthrōpoi* have their mind—the same place that Herod and his cronies have their minds (if we have read the clues correctly), the same places that the chief priests and the scribes have their minds, and even the same place Pilate has his mind. *Ho christos* is the anointed one. But which anointed one? And anointed for what purpose? To be *ho christos* is to be anointed. An anointed one is appointed by God for a purpose, for a task. Kings are anointed for God's work, as are priests. The prophet Elijah was supposed to anoint Elisha, but it is not recorded that he did so—he just threw his cloak over him. To figure out what it means for someone to be *ho*

---

between the intellectual, theoretical virtues or ability and the moral, practical virtues one must have to be a good person and a good friend. A case study of one form of such an imaginative practice in a specific religious cultural context (for Aristotle's account was also specific to an androcentric, slaveholding culture even if its basic insights can be extended to other contexts) can be found especially in chaps. 3 through 5 of Robert A. Orsi, *Thank You, St. Jude: Women's Devotion to the Patron Saint of Hopeless Causes* (New Haven: Yale University Press, 1996), 70-184. Some would find this a rather questionable exercise of practical wisdom, but the problems with the St. Jude devotion were not with the women who were devoted or even the highly fictionalized saint to whom they were devoted, but the social, economic, and religious contexts that made this devotion one that "fit" (and still "fits") for the devout. Orsi clearly criticizes the trivialization of the practice, which, for some, simply "masked what was in fact a deeply passive and alienated experience of reality" (197). Yet in theological terms foreign to Orsi's work, Jude was an occasion of grace for many of the devout (see 198). For contemporary theological work on the virtue of *phronēsis*, see my *The Wisdom of Religious Commitment* (Washington, DC: Georgetown University Press, 1995), esp. chaps. 4 and 5. The point Orsi made about the trivialization of some women's use of Jude in their devotion is, in my terms, an exercise of practical wisdom at the most minimal level or a failure to exercise practical wisdom at all.

29. The phrase in parentheses is almost certainly a postresurrection addition. As Dunn put it, "The tradition has been so elaborated here in the light of Easter faith that it is difficult to discern whether there was a pre-Easter form" (*Jesus Remembered*, 495). When dealing with the passion prediction of Mark 8:31, he writes, "Clearly the tradition intends to recall that Jesus predicted his death, including the 'handing over' and attendant suffering" (799). He noticeably omits the resurrection. He infers that Luke and Matthew have altered the tradition, but does not draw the rather obvious conclusion that even in Mark, the phrase is likely introduced in the postresurrection narrating of the story—otherwise why would Peter be rebuking Jesus for going through a tough trial and coming out with renewed life by rising (active verb) again?

christos, one has to tell the *story* of the anointed one—what does the anointed one do? Otherwise "the anointed one" could mean almost anything. But Mark is too clever an author to leave such a key term totally indeterminate, even if his oral source(s) did.

The story has Peter, like many others, imagining *ho christos* as the anointed king in the line of David. Such a king would gloriously throw off the Roman oppressors. He would fight the Romans and win, and he would live to rule. But Jesus was to die. He would not fight the Romans. He would not be a military victor. He would not replace Herod or Pilate or both of them. So Jesus had to rebuke Peter. For mistaking Jesus for an anointed king like David? For denying that Jesus would be rejected and die? The text does not say, but what else could Mark have had in mind in his telling of this story, especially including the resurrection prediction? Otherwise, why would Mark have Jesus turn around and practically curse Peter as a "Satan"?

Jesus cursed Peter because Peter's "mind" was with Jesus' accusers. Here is the height of wrongheadedness. Peter's mind is with *hoi anthrōpoi,* with Herod, and the high priests, Pilate, and the scoffers. Peter's mind is in the wrong place. Peter has not "set his mind" on God. Or, in other translations, Peter's "ways" are said to be "man's ways, not God's ways." This "mind setting" or "way" must be very important to get right, especially if Peter was cursed by Jesus for being so wrongheaded. Whether or not the rebuke was connected in the actual course of events with the confession, the importance of the rebuke for the disciples hearing this performance cannot be overestimated.[30]

The verb Mark uses here, a form of *phroneō,* which we translate as "set your mind," is very distinctive. *Phroneō* is not used elsewhere in Mark's Gospel. The only use of the verb in Matthew's Gospel is in Matthew's version of the same story. When Luke tells his version of the Caesarea Philippi incident, he rewrites Mark's story dramatically: it is no longer placed on a hike in Galilee, Peter is not rebuked (nor named the rock of the church as in Matthew), and Luke thus never uses this verb! This verb itself is a clue.

Phroneō as a verb is found fourteen times in the epistles of the New Testament and once in Acts. Nouns from this root are scattered in the New Testament, with the most (seven) in Matthew's Gospel. What does it mean to be told to "have a mind on [*phroneite*] God's things"? But in the Gospels, this verb is found only in the Caesarea Philippi scene. What does it mean *here*? How would have it been heard?[31]

---

30. Dunn (*Jesus Remembered*) mentions this verse only in passing (645 n. 149; 648 n. 160).

31. The verb has a curious history. In the Septuagint, it is found almost exclusively in wisdom literature. In the New Testament, it is used either to indicate a way of understanding that is reprobated (when it is used with οὐ) or to indicate a way of understanding that is supported, given that there are other "live options," mentioned either explicitly (as here) or implicitly, as in Phil. 2:5, typically translated, "Let the same mind be in you that was in Christ Jesus" (NRSV). We will explore this passage below. Connecting this concept with extrascriptural uses goes beyond present needs. G. W. H. Lampe (*A Patristic Greek Lexicon* [1961; reprint, Oxford: Clarendon, 1987], 1490-91) does not list the verb, so evidently he thinks it has no different meaning in the patristic period.

Well, we know what it doesn't mean. It doesn't mean to have a mind that is on the side of the people. *Hoi anthrōpoi* have their heads in the wrong place. They misunderstand the meaning of *ho christos*. In Mark's telling of the story, Jesus admits to being *ho christos*, the anointed one (the Christ, the messiah) and is identified as the king of the Jews—the reason or excuse for his execution (see n. 13 above). So identifying Jesus as the anointed Davidic king is not stupid or naïve or impossible. It is just wrong. Even if the title is right, the story is wrong: Jesus as the anointed one is not appointed by God to be a Davidic king.

To understand what *ho christos* means requires one to have a mind (*phroneite*) for God's things. To have such a mind is not merely to "think right." One cannot think right unless one actually walks in the way of the Lord.

This is the importance of the verb *phroneō*. It designates not merely a mental idea or belief, but a *practical* wisdom. It begins by having one's imagination properly engaged, disciplined, and put into practice. Practical wisdom is the exercise of good imagination, rightheadedness in understanding and practice. Such a "mind" realizes that Jesus is the one anointed not to save people by inaugurating a new rule like that of David, but to save people by beginning a new reign, the divine reign seen in and through the practices of living in and living out the reign of God—which, for Jesus, leads to the cross (and resurrection). Mark uses this verb as a clue to show that christology begins in the disciples' disciplined, practical *imagination*.

At least some who heard this story or later read Mark would understand Mark's use of *phroneō*. It had been used with roughly the same meaning for hundreds of years. To be a "prudent" or practically wise person—to have *phronēsis* or be a *phronimos*—was to be a person who knew how to get things right, not only in theory but in practice. This is a person who knows *how* to do things the right way. But such getting things right is to imagine how general principles apply here and now. In practical situations there can be disagreements about which principles apply and how to apply them. And there is no way to appeal to a principle to say how a principle is to be put into practice. Even people of good judgment, or apparently good judgment, might differ. As one understands the meaning of a title such as "the anointed one" by understanding the right story, the story of *ho christos* who would suffer and die, to show the title's significance, so one understands the right application of a principle by understanding how the story plays out when one uses that principle. Both are exercises of creative, practical imagination, of *phronēsis*. The right-minded disciple should know that fleshing out the "code" of *ho christos* is not to imagine and act on the coming of a Davidic kingdom headed by Jesus, but that it is a different story entirely. It is the story of a divine way that was the mission of Jesus—a mission in which the Twelve participated two by two earlier—and even the story of his execution. After all, that is what happens to great prophets—as Herod's execution of John showed.

In the New Testament, to get things right in practice is to know how to follow Jesus and to know who he is. "Practice" and "theory" are inseparable. One cannot properly imagine one without the other. Understanding *ho christos* is not a matter merely of intellectual understanding. One has to know how to do what the anointed one did in order really to understand, and one has to learn how to do this. In learning this practice of becoming a disciple, one learns how to have a disciplined imagination. But discipline—being a disciple—takes know-how. And know-how comes from practice.

To have a mind for God's things, to be rightheaded, then, is to be able to follow the story of *ho christos*. But that following is certainly not merely getting the title right, nor is it a merely abstract or theoretical understanding, a "knowing what" the story is. To follow the story of *ho christos* is precisely the following that is discipleship. One must follow the story by being able not merely to tell it, but to know *how* to live it. This verb of imaginative wisdom in practice, *phroneō*, is a "knowing how" to live out the story of *ho christos*. It is knowing how to live and how to die, not as king or baptizer or prophet, but as a member of the Jesus-movement that God is inaugurating. It is knowing how to imagine how to free people from their torments and how to imagine that death, a defeat according to human ways (*ta tōn anthrōpōn*), can be the hoped-for victory divine (*ta tou theou*).

Only those who know the story by living in it and living it out can rightly answer the christological question, "Who do you say that I am?" Mark's clues connect discipleship and imagination. Christology begins as an enterprise of disciples' imagination. The characters in Mark's Gospel imagined Jesus in certain ways. But none of them knew how to walk the ways of God, or—which is the same thing—had their minds set on the things of God. Hence, they got the christological answers wrong. Even Peter needed to be disciplined so as to learn how to follow the story. Christology begins in the imagination of those who learn how to live in and live out the story of *ho christos*. So christology is an enterprise not only of Jesus' followers' imaginations, but of their *disciplined* imagination.

In one sense, Mark does not spell out the right answer to Jesus' question at Caesarea Philippi. He never explicitly narrates the story that gives *ho christos* its significance. There is no tidy way to understand what *ho christos* means. Rather, the whole Gospel sets the pattern. But it allows readers to craft their own understanding. They, too, are carriers of tradition—and a tradition is a practice or set of practices including living and telling the "informally controlled" stories that carry on the tradition in practice. Even when the oral tradition becomes frozen in textual form, the question of how to carry on the Jesus-movement in new circumstances and contexts is not answered by the story of the life and death of Jesus. That story can function only as a principle to be put into practice by those whose mind is *ta tou theou*. The disciples who read the final version of Mark's story as text did not live in the temporal, social, religious, or political context that drove the situations and the plot of the story. They could not mimic the story mindlessly. They could only carry on what had been handed to them and hand their own way of living out the story on to others who would be shaped by their predecessors and who would shape their successors in the tradition.

Mark's story crosses up the reader by refusing to say what the right answer is. It shows readers what they need to *do* to answer the question. We readers need to have the right mind and thus be imaginative disciples who will accept corrections to our imagination and understandings just as Peter did. At its best, the Jesus-movement is a self-correcting movement as the disciples become teachers, the called callers, the healed healers, and hearers become tellers of the Word.

Peter is a paradoxical sign of hope for the other members of the Jesus-movement. Peter never did get it right. The last we hear of him in the story is his weeping in repentance or shame for his denial of Jesus after the cock crowed thrice. If even the first disciple can fail so miserably and still be accounted one of the movement, there is hope even for us sinners who may be shackled by our fear. For there is one final mention of Peter in this story: a young man in a white robe, sitting alongside the tomb where they had laid Jesus, tells the women who come to anoint the body with aromatic spices that Jesus is risen. "But go, tell his disciples and Peter that he is going before you to Galilee; there you will see him as he told you" (Mark 16:7). Peter gets yet another chance to get it right—even though Mark ends the Gospel by writing that the women "said nothing to anyone, for they were afraid" (16:8).[32]

Yet how can that be? We have heard of the resurrection. Somehow the story got out even though Mark says they kept the secret. Perhaps this is Mark's last irony. In telling the story, in declaiming it to an audience, the secret is told! If the story of the secret is told and heard, the secret cannot be kept. Someone in the movement must have cast off their fear and told the story; they could not have said nothing. When we keep in mind that the Gospel is not merely a text but the result of the tradition of the performance of powerful and life-shaping communicative actions, then those who hear and understand this good news must live with their fear but must nonetheless live in and live out the stories to be disciples who know how to follow Jesus, to be able to first *show* what that story is through what they do and only through that showing be able to *say* correctly who Jesus is. Evidently Peter got it right finally—or so the legend of his martyrdom upside down on a cross suggests.

Remembering that Mark's Gospel is a compilation of oral performances can lead us to see his story anew.[33] His Gospel is a story of *ho christos*. But one cannot

---

32. I accept the view of most New Testament scholars that this is the end of Mark's Gospel, even if abrupt, and that subsequent material in the canonical text was added to harmonize it with Matthew. Of course, there may have been additional verses, but if there were, they are lost.

33. While it is relatively easy to show that Mark is a script, rather than a text, the fact that Luke and Matthew apparently had written texts to work from (Mark and Q) suggests that the oral component is less important for them. However, four factors apply. First, they have unique material that is likely rooted in oral traditions in their own communities. Second, they showed considerable freedom in working with both their apparently written sources. They have reworked material. Some of these reworkings are so extensive that it is possible that they knew different forms in their own communities of material they also found in Mark or Q. Hence, they could be relying on oral traditions in those instances. Third, it is not entirely certain that they had written versions of Mark and Q before them. The arguments scholars make are based almost exclusively on verbal similarities and identities that they argue could not be coincidence, as oral transmission would develop more differences. But this presumes a "literary default." Other possible explanations abound. It might be that some of those sources were "formally controlled oral tradition" (see pp. 55-56 above) so that substantial verbal identity might be expected in an oral culture. It is even possible that the same person or group of persons narrating Mark and Q did so for each community; that would explain

understand what that means unless one has a disciplined imagination that leads one to know how to have a mind and to live a life focused on the things of God. If we would do christology, if we would say "who he is," then we must know how to live in and live out that story. Otherwise, we may be addressed as Peter was—Satans who have our minds on the enemies' ways, not on God's. Mark's Gospel especially puts christology in the context of discipleship. That discipleship will walk in the ways of God, and those ways lead to the chance of persecution and death for being a disciple and for enacting *basileia tou theou*. For the whole Gospel is about how to have the mind of a disciple, and at its key turning point, and only there, do we get the beginnings of christology proper, where Jesus is remembered as rebuking those who do not have their minds on God's things.

And who would these people be who need no rebuke and who have their minds shaped properly as disciples? That takes us into another story and another chapter.

---

how the "inherited text" was both different in parts and identical in other parts. Fourth, even if they had written texts, they were scripts; hence, their work was further development of scripts—in light of other oral performances for which they wrote scripts. In short, for the Synoptics, it is "orality all the way down"; the written texts are derivative.

Nine

CONFESSING JESUS AS *HO CHRISTOS*

Martha and Mary at Bethany

*I*n contrast to the bumbling disciples, especially Peter as portrayed in Mark, the Gospel of John portrays two disciples whose faith is nigh unto perfect: Martha and Mary. They appear in John 11 and 12, at the end of the "book of signs."[1] They also appear in the Synoptic tradition (Luke 10:38-42).[2] In considering the responses to Jesus by Martha and Mary at Bethany, both the similarities to and differences from Peter's performance at Caesarea Philippi are instructive.

Many scholars note that there are linguistic and stylistic indicators that strongly suggest that the two women would also have been well known in the earliest Christian community. James D. G. Dunn argues that these texts remember actual disciples who were at the center of Jesus' followers. In the Johannine version under consideration here, Martha "is given the more impressive role."[3] In Luke's Gospel, Mary seems to have the better role. However, Elisabeth Schüssler Fiorenza gives a very persuasive rhetorical interpretation of the Lukan version as prescriptive, not descriptive. The Lukan version has Mary doing the "one thing necessary," listening to Jesus, while Martha is busy in the diaconal work of hospitality. That Jesus-in-Luke valorizes Mary's receptivity rather than Martha's activity is,

---

1. Raymond E. Brown found that John 11 and 12 "were a late addition to the plan of the Gospel" that had earlier ended with John 10. See Brown, *The Gospel According to John: Introduction, Translation, and Notes,* 2 vols., Anchor Bible 29, 29A (Garden City, NY: Doubleday, 1966, 1970), 1:427.

2. Elisabeth Schüssler Fiorenza (*But She Said: Feminist Practices of Biblical Interpretation* [Boston: Beacon, 1992], 66-68) argues persuasively that placing this story in the midst of other stories about Christian practice, specifically the Good Samaritan parable and its interpretation in Luke 10:36-37 and Jesus' instruction on prayer in Luke 11:1-4, is an instruction in Christian practice—but one that the tradition Luke inherited construed as valorizing Mary's role over Martha's. Given the discussion of the significance of table fellowship and Jesus' place in it below (pp. 175-87), I cannot but agree that the valorizing of one over the other seems not to fit with Jesus' other practices. Schüssler Fiorenza also notes that "although Luke's rhetorical strategy acknowledges women as members of the Christian movement, it downplays their apostolic leadership" (67). Mary and Martha are indeed part of the circle of disciples, but Luke puts them in their (inferior) place in his telling of the story.

3. James D. G. Dunn, *Jesus Remembered*, vol. 1 of *Christianity in the Making* (Grand Rapids: Eerdmans, 2003), 535.

in Schüssler Fiorenza's analysis, a strategy characteristic of the evangelist. He employs this strategy repeatedly in his Gospel—he puts women in their "proper" (inferior) place. Hence, it is not warranted to claim that this text, which plays off one sister against another, reflects a strategy of Jesus.[4] Rather, it is Luke's way of placing women in his story of the community. Although they do not appear by name in other parts of the Gospel, their names and their actions are remembered among those who were disciples of Jesus.

Jesus has performed many wonders in the first half of John's Gospel. These are signs of his significance and power. The last of the signs in the "Gospel of Signs" is the raising of Lazarus from the dead. In John's rendition of the story, this sign is also the "last straw," which provokes a meeting of a council, identified as the Sanhedrin by John, that plots to assassinate Jesus.[5]

John's way of connecting these two events is hardly credible historically. He portrays the council's motive as stopping Jesus from throwing in with the Roman occupying forces.[6] Connecting the raising of Lazarus with a conciliar plot to oppose Jesus lest he be allied with the Romans is a function of John's literary and rhetorical approach rather than historical information about the meeting of the Sanhedrin or its connection with the raising of Lazarus. After all, crucifixion was a Roman manner of execution—whatever Jesus was imagined to be, to take him as an ally of Rome seems ludicrous.

This juxtaposition of events reminds us of an important point. It must be noted that much of the material in these chapters of John goes well beyond the memory of actual events.[7] The plot against Jesus may be a fictional foreshadowing of the passion narrative that attributes to "the Jews"—always Jesus' opponents in John—the instigation of his execution by the Romans. The connections between one event and another can often be attributed to the author's plot rather than to actual historical sequence. Nonetheless, the actuality of the women as disciples and the tradition of an anointing, a chrismating, of Jesus seem based in reliable memories.[8]

---

4. Schüssler Fiorenza, *But She Said*, 55-68.

5. For a useful survey of work on these texts, see Alexander J. Burke, Jr., *The Raising of Lazarus and the Passion of Jesus in John 11 and 12* (Lewiston, NY: Edwin Mellen, 2003). Burke argues that these chapters are a complex but unified eschatological narrative that bridges Jesus' ministry to the world to his ministry to his disciples (223-24). Burke's basic claim about the unity of the chapters helps warrant the present connecting of the raising of Lazarus with the Bethany "family scene" (80-82, 90-94).

6. Raymond Brown also finds the connection between the raising of Lazarus and the planning of the Sanhedrin to be not connected historically but to be a connection John drew for his own "pedagogical and theological purposes" (see Brown, *Gospel According to John*, 1:427-30).

7. Nonetheless, in the conclusion of an exhaustive commentary on the story, John P. Meier is inclined to think that the richly elaborated story "ultimately reflects some incident in the life of the historical Jesus" (John Meier, *A Marginal Jew: Rethinking the Historical Jesus,* vol. 2, *Mentor, Message, and Miracles*, Anchor Bible Reference Library [New York: Doubleday, 1994], 831).

8. See Dunn, *Jesus Remembered*, 534-37, regarding discipleship and the likelihood of the historicity of the anointing.

The Encounter at Bethany

In the plot of the Gospel of John, the encounter at Bethany marks, like the Caesarea Philippi scene in Mark, a literary turning point in the Gospel narrative. In John's Gospel, the "book of signs" is complete and the "book of glory" is about to commence. This very positioning suggests that this is an important narrative for recognizing who Jesus is.

John 11 starts by turning the corner. Jesus delays going to Bethany to see (and presumably heal) Lazarus whom he loved, even though his sisters Mary and Martha had sent for him. In giving his reason for dawdling, Jesus voices the Gospel's impending shift in emphasis: "This illness is not to death, but is for the glory of God so that the son may be glorified through it" (11:4). It is now explicit. The "book of signs" is about to be transformed into the "book of glory." This phrase about glory is stylistically the very center of the hinge on which the Gospel turns, the meeting at Bethany.[9] The sign of the raising of Lazarus is the glory of God. The text can be rendered as follows:

> When he came, Jesus found Lazarus had already been in the tomb four days. Now Bethany was near Jerusalem, about two miles away. Many of the Jews had come to Martha and Mary to console them about their brother. Martha, when she heard Jesus was coming, met him. But at the same time Mary sat home. Martha said to Jesus, "Lord, if you were here, my brother would not have died. Even now I am sure that whatever you ask God, God will give you." Jesus says to her, "Your brother will rise again." Martha says to him, "I am sure that he will rise in the resurrection on the last (*eschatē*) day." Jesus said to her, "I am the resurrection; one having faith in me though dead will live, and each who lives and has faith in me never dies at all. Do you have this faith?" She says to him, "Yes, Lord, I have faith that you are *ho christos*, the son of God, the one who is coming into the world." (John 11:17-27)[10]

By the time Jesus gets around to coming over to Bethany, Lazarus is four days in the tomb.[11] Martha and Mary were grieving with a number of people, presumably friends and family. Martha went out to greet Jesus, Mary stayed in the house. Jesus assured Martha that her brother would rise again. Martha seemingly (mis)understood this as Jesus' reminding her of the resurrection of all on the last

---

9. See Burke, *Raising of Lazarus*, 223.

10. Meier thinks that Martha's confession is an addition to the story and that the story makes sense without it. He advocates "removing" it as unhistorical (*Mentor, Message, and Miracles*, 816-17). Meier never considers that John may be weaving in another oral tradition that he has inherited. While this may be woven into the story for John's purposes from another source, it is not certainly a redactional addition, although Meier seems to think so.

11. As Raymond Brown put it, "This detail is mentioned to make it clear that Lazarus was truly dead. There was an opinion among the rabbis that the soul hovered near the body for three days but after that there was no hope of resuscitation" (*Gospel According to John*, 1:424).

day.[12] When Jesus responds, without hesitation Martha confesses her faith in Jesus as *ho christos*.

Like Peter, Martha is sure about him and God. What is often read as her "rebuking" Jesus for not doing what she might have wished, is rather an expression of her trust. When she seems a bit disappointed, Jesus asks her to reiterate her faith in him and she does. Unlike Peter, who began to remonstrate with Jesus, Martha can confess her faith without challenging Jesus' understanding of what it is to be *ho christos*. Unlike her fellow Jews, who cannot even believe in the signs Jesus gave them, Martha is a Jewish disciple who has faith without signs. As Schüssler Fiorenza noted, Martha confesses her faith in Jesus in the classic Johannine understanding:

> Jesus is the revealer who has come down from heaven. As such it [her use of *ho christos*] has the full sense of the Petrine confession at Caesarea Philippi in the synoptics, especially in Matt 16:15-19. Thus Martha represents the full apostolic faith of the Johannine community, just as Peter did for the Matthean community. More importantly, her faith confession is repeated at the end of the Gospel in 20:31, where the evangelist expresses the goal of her/his writing of the Gospel: "But these are written that you may believe that Jesus is the Christ, the Son of God, and that believing you may have life in his name."[13]

Martha here is portrayed as the true disciple, the one with unhesitating faith in Jesus, whom God had sent into the world.

Later, when Martha returned to the house and secretly told Mary that Jesus had come, Mary went out to Jesus. The mourners followed her, evidently to console her if she was going to the Lazarus's tomb to weep (11:31). Coming to Jesus, she fell at his feet, weeping, and repeated what Martha had said, "Lord, if you were here my brother would not have died" (11:32). When Jesus saw her and the other mourners weeping, he "shuddered, moved with the deepest emotions."[14] She wept not at the tomb, but at his feet. He inquired where Lazarus had been laid, and the friends and family consoling the sisters said, "Lord, come and see." And then

---

12. See Adele Reinhartz, "The Gospel of John," in *Searching the Scriptures,* vol. 2, *A Feminist Commentary,* ed. Elisabeth Schüssler Fiorenza (New York: Crossroad, 1994), 581.

13. Schüssler Fiorenza, *In Memory of Her: A Feminist Theological Reconstruction of Christian Origins* (New York: Crossroad, 1984), 331. The use of "belief" in English may conceal that the verbs here are from *pisteuō,* the key verb for having faith. Belief, in John, is not a propositional attitude but a way of living; in my own translations, I have used the more complex "have faith" in order to bring out this dimension.

14. For this rendering, see Brown, *Gospel According to John,* 1:421. Brown comments that the verb translated as "shuddered" suggests "an articulate expression of anger." This "usage is also found in Mark xiv 5. The verb also describes Jesus' reaction to the afflicted (Mark i 43; Matt ix 30). . . . While it does not seem that Jesus would have been angry at the afflicted, he may very well have been angry at their illnesses and handicaps, which were looked on as manifestations of Satan's kingdom of evil. (It should also be noted that the use of the verb in such Synoptic passages is associated with the stern command to keep the secret of what Jesus has done and of what he is)" (425-26).

Jesus wept, confronted by the reality of the death of one he loved, that is, of a disciple. He went to the tomb. Martha warned him that Lazarus would stink as it was the fourth day since his death. Jesus again told Martha that if she had faith, she would see the glory of God. Then Jesus called Lazarus out and he emerged. Many of the mourners had faith in Jesus, but some went to the Pharisees and the Sanhedrin, who then determined to kill him according to John's construction of Jesus' significance—since Jesus was performing many signs, "If we leave him go on, all will have faith in him" (11:48) and the Romans will favor him (!!!) over "us," that is, the Pharisees and Sanhedrin (an odd conjunction as well).

The key element in the story is not Jesus' miracle, but the act of confessing faith by one of the members of the Jesus-movement. As Schüssler Fiorenza puts it:

> Jesus' public ministry climaxes in the revelation that Jesus is the resurrection and the life (11:1-54). Whereas in the original miracle source the raising of Lazarus stood at the center of the story, the evangelist has placed the dialogue and confession of Martha at the center of the whole account. Central to the dialogue with Martha is the revelatory saying of Jesus in 11:25f, "I am the resurrection and the life . . ." as well as Martha's response in v. 27: "Yes, Lord, I believe that you are the Christ, the son of God, who is coming into the world."[15]

Numerous commentators have noted that Martha's act, which expresses her faith, precedes the sign Jesus is to work. Her faith is first, the sign comes later.

It should be noted that the verb here is *pepisteuka*, a form of *pisteuein*, often translated "believe," but this is better rendered as "have faith in" to bring out the relationship of Jesus and the disciples. Like *phroneō*, *pisteuō* is not merely a "cognitive" attitude or disposition but an act of the "whole person." The former centers on practices, the latter on a fully trusting commitment; they are not interchangeable verbs, but both indicate the pattern of discipleship. Having faith is not merely believing with one's head, but acting with one's whole self, including confessing one's faith. Throughout this scene, "believing" in Jesus is performing an ongoing act of trusting in him, of following his ways, an act or strong disposition possible for those who recognize Jesus as God's Son, the resurrection and the life. It is not merely belief in a claim.

The context of this story is the whole "book of signs," the previous nine chapters. This is brought into focus in the carefully constructed scene that is often called a "summary narrative" in John 10. Again, as noted above, the connection between this narrative and the narrative centered in Bethany is far more likely theological than historical. The point is to contrast the response of Jesus' opponents and his disciples, Martha and Mary.

In John 10:24-25, "the Jews" ask Jesus if he is *ho christos*. He responds that he has told them, but that they do not have faith (*pisteuete*) in him. They then want to stone him for blasphemy. After some more disputing, Jesus then concludes:

---

15. Schüssler Fiorenza, *In Memory of Her*, 329.

"If I am not doing the works of my Father, then do not have faith in me. Yet if I do them, even if you do not have faith in me, have faith in the works, so that you know and understand that my Father is in me and I am in the Father" (10:37-38). They don't have faith, of course, but try to arrest him. He escapes.

The contrast with Mark seems great. Unlike Mark, where there is constant blundering about the significance of *ho christos,* here there is an inability to recognize *ho christos.* If in Mark, the disciples all blundered because their ways were not the right ways (*ou phroneis*), here they fail because their minds were wrong in a different way. They could not confess Jesus as *ho christos* because they didn't "get" what Jesus was about. They asked the right question, but could not see the answer. Here they cannot recognize Jesus as *ho christos* as they do not have faith in him; they do not follow him. Unlike Martha, who expresses her faithful commitment *before* Jesus does the wondrous deed of raising her brother, the others who can see the signs do not have faith even with the signs.

What is significant about this dispute is the focus on the "works." These are the practices that are the signs of what life is like in the *basileia tou theou.* These are the signs of a life that reflects God's gift of life. Jesus in John, unlike in the Synoptics, claims to have "told them" that he was *ho christos,* but his opponents did not accept that he was *ho christos.* What he then does is to focus on the works: if this is what *ho christos* does, then why do you not have faith in me? They could see the works; even if the works did not lead to faith and discipleship, at least they could recognize the works as a sign of the presence of the reign of God. If Mark's foils blundered about Jesus, John's foils are blind.

The contrast of Jesus' opponents, "the Jews," with Martha's confession is obvious. She has faith in him. She needs no "works" to show her who he is; rather, her faith as a disciple enables her to recognize his works. She already recognizes, follows, and confesses him as *ho christos.* Her only problem, at the beginning, is that he did not come soon enough to save her brother from death. Her expectation of a healing was dashed.

"The Jews" cannot recognize the works as signs that Jesus is from God, and they cannot have faith in Jesus even with the signs. Hence, they do not know who he really is. The opponents' failure echoes the confusion of Herod's cronies and the people about Jesus' identity in Mark. In both narratives, Jesus' opponents are characterized as not "getting it," as being confused about who he is. They simply do not recognize him. As the discourse early in Mark between Pilate and his cronies displays Herod's (and the people's) mistakes about Jesus' identity sets up the Caesarea Philippi scene, so the opposition of "the Jews" in John sets up the Bethany scene.

Whatever the historical provenance of this brief dispute, it clearly reflects an opposition between the Jesus-movement and other movements in Judaism. Whether this is a product of later times or a memory of actual disputes is not the point. The point is that the works are there for all to see, if they would see. *Ho christos* is present—the works are not independent evidence for that, but do show that, as more common to the Synoptic tradition, the *basileia tou theou* is at hand.

The Supper at Bethany

But this is not the end of the sisters' exemplification of discipleship. At the beginning of the "book of glory," the first person to anoint Jesus is Mary:

> Six days before the Passover, Jesus came to Bethany. . . . There they made him a supper; Martha served, and Lazarus was one of those at table with him. Mary took a pound of costly ointment of pure nard and anointed the feet of Jesus and wiped his feet with her hair; and the house was filled with the fragrance of the ointment. (John 12:1-3)

The recognition of Jesus as *ho christos*, the anointed one, is made explicit in Mary's action of hospitality. As Schüssler Fiorenza put it in discussing these two episodes in the Gospel of John, "While Martha of Bethany is responsible for the primary articulation of the community's christological faith [in John 11], Mary of Bethany articulates the right praxis of discipleship [in John 12]:" Right speech and right practice fit together like sisters. And Lazarus is present—thanks to Jesus.

Schüssler Fiorenza sees Martha as performing the role of a *diakonos* in John 12, which may have been the only established "office" in the Johannine community. She also notes, "In John, Mary and Martha are not seen in competition with each other, as is the case in Luke. They are characterized as the two ministers at a supper, which takes place on a Sunday evening, the day on which the early church celebrated the Eucharist."[16] That the author of John has placed this pericope after the confession of faith and the raising of Lazarus in chapter 11 suggests that both of them are now expressing their faith again, this time in practice.

This event of the anointing of Jesus is narrated not only in John but also in the Synoptic Gospels (Mark 14:3-9; Matt. 26:6-13; Luke 7:37-38). The chrismating of Jesus, however, illustrates the difficulty in figuring out just what happened and what the most reliable recorded memories are. Mark 14:3-9, paralleled in Matthew 26:6-13, recollects an anointing of Jesus' head in Simon the Leper's house in Bethany by an unnamed woman using expensive perfume made from nard carried in an alabaster jar. Luke 7:36-38 places an anointing of Jesus' feet with perfume from an alabaster jar by a sinful woman during the Galilean ministry. John 12:1-8 has Martha serving a dinner while Mary anoints Jesus' feet. Whether Luke has disconnected the story from Martha and Mary or John has connected the story to those disciples, whether Jesus' head or foot was anointed, or whether there were multiple anointings or only one cannot be determined on textual grounds. That storytellers adapted their narration of the anointing story for different purposes seems obvious; the similarities and differences of the story suggest what Dunn calls "informally controlled tradition." There is flexibility in the text, but the central thread of the story—that a woman anointed Jesus with nard—is unchanged.[17] That this story was variously told and incorporated into

---

16. Ibid., 330.

17. Dunn, *Jesus Remembered*, 207, citing Kenneth E. Bailey, "Informal Controlled Oral Tradition and the Synoptic Gospels," *Asia Journal of Theology* 5 (1991): 42-45.

the existing Markan, Lukan and Johannine frameworks seems likely. That these accounts are also rooted in the memory of events, however much that memory was shaped by narrators and authors, also seems likely. That they are ripe for various interpretations is certain.[18]

The elements of the story overlap in the various versions. The variants, including what part of Jesus' body was anointed (feet or head), the use of expensive nard, and the alabaster jar, suggest that this was an oft-told story, but one that did not have a content that was tightly controlled by the community (see n. 2 above). While some elements were "informal controlled tradition," others seem rather freely composed. Unlike Peter at Caesarea Philippi, Mary does not remonstrate with Jesus. Indeed, in John's telling, the next event is Judas's remonstrance that the ointment could have been sold for money for the poor. It is the traitor who remonstrates.

As Peter did not understand what *ho christos* would have to undergo and what it meant to be *ho christos*, neither did Judas get the point of the work, the action performed by Mary. The anointing by Mary is the recognition *in practice* of the one who has crystallized the power of God in and for the community. She chrismates *ho christos*. She responds to his work that reconciles her brother who had been dead to his family with a complementary work of her own.

Judas wants to do the conventional right thing. Yet Judas's remarks are "off key." That they literarily foreshadow for the listener his later betrayal of Jesus seems obvious. Judas doesn't have the imagination to recognize Jesus as the anointed one. As Adele Reinhartz puts it, Mary "is the counterpart to Judas; the true female disciple is an alternative to the unfaithful male disciple [Judas]."[19] Mary knows how to practice a disciples' faith; Judas does not.

Moreover, the Johannine version of this anointing anticipates the Johannine "Last Supper" scene with the exemplary foot washing of Jesus. As Schüssler Fiorenza notes, "Moreover, the centrality of Judas in both this scene and in the foot washing scene emphasizes an evangelistic intention to portray the true disciple Mary of Bethany [not to neglect Martha] as counterpart to the unfaithful disciple Judas Iscariot."[20] As with the Caesarea Philippi scene in Mark, the events at Bethany have resonances throughout the Gospel that suggest that true discipleship is faith in action—articulated by Martha, enacted by Mary, and misunderstood by Peter.

However, another possibility looms. Perhaps Mary *did* anoint Jesus' feet rather than his head. In anointing Jesus' feet, then, Mary *teaches Jesus* how to serve.

---

18. Brown also suggested that there might be a connection between the parable of the Good Samaritan, whose journey was from Jerusalem to Jericho, and the following narrative of Mary and Martha, whose home in Bethany would have been on the road the Samaritan had followed (even though Luke places them in Galilee or Samaria). Brown suggests some "latent reminiscence" in the juxtaposing of these two texts; see *Gospel According to John*, 1:422-23. If Dunn is right about oral performance, an oral performer of the Lukan text might well interpolate a story from the family at Bethany. Alternatively, as Schüssler Fiorenza suggests, this may be another case of Lukan redaction that pairs stories about males with stories about females.

19. Reinhartz, "Gospel of John," 583.

20. Schüssler Fiorenza, *In Memory of Her*, 330.

Perhaps Jesus, at the Johannine Last Supper, gestured to Mary's anointing in his own act of hospitality. But the possibility is real: perhaps Mary did show Jesus a way to live as a servant.

Scholars have noted that all the Gospels are structured theologically, not chronologically. Hence, constructing a chronology of events of Jesus' lifetime is always precarious.[21] Yet Mary is remembered as anointing him before the final events of his life. While washing feet is an example of loving service, it is often connected to Jesus' death. As Raymond E. Brown summarizes his approach to the scene, "The footwashing is presented as a prophetic action symbolizing Jesus' death in humiliation for the salvation of others."[22] But why interpret the foot washing *forward* into Jesus' death, rather than *backward* as a symbolic summary of his life of loving service? The injunction "you are to do exactly as I have done for you" (John 13:15b) may, of course, refer to foot washing (but then it is notable that few since engage seriously in this practice). But why ought we not assume that this is an action symbolizing Jesus' life of reconciling service for the salvation of others? Why not connect it with Mary and Martha and the service they render Jesus and that Jesus renders them? Why assume that it is Jesus who always taught but was never taught in the ways of God? An assumption that the anointing foreshadows his death more than it recapitulates his service and his instructions to his disciples to continue that service seems unwarranted. Rather, the true disciples—Martha and Mary—show by contrast (to Judas) what discipleship is, show by contrast (to "the Jews") what it means to have faith in Jesus, and perhaps show Jesus (or, more likely, the hearer or reader) that each member of the Jesus-movement, even the first among equals, is to engage in the practices that effect God's reign.

John and the Synoptics

As historical records, the Synoptic Gospels are preferred by many historians to the Gospel of John. The scholars' reasoning is complex, but in the end they believe that John is more distant in time and in conceptual framework from the events of

---

21. The point made by Paula Fredriksen (*From Jesus to Christ: The Origins of the New Testament Images of Jesus*, 2nd ed. [New Haven: Yale University Press, 2000]) regarding the placement of the "temple incident," noted above (p. 39 n. 11), applies *mutatis mutandis* to other events in Jesus' life. Some events have to come before others, such as the trials (if any) before the crucifixion, the killing of John the Baptist before Jesus' execution. But given the multiply attested sequence of meal, arrest, trial, and execution for Jesus, it seems likely that the anointing took place before that sequence.

22. Brown, *Gospel According to John*, 2:562. Brown's extensive survey of research on this scene warrants strongly that the scene is a composite, for example, in harmonizing "sacramental" and "exemplary" understandings in John 13:1-20. But I find no reason to think that what is harmonized are written rather than oral sources. Brown seems not to have often worked with a "default understanding" of orality (see pp. 50-51). More interestingly, if these are the two interpretations of Jesus' action, there is much flexibility in taking up either a ritual or exemplary understanding—foot washing is not a characteristic practice of Christians, although loving service should be. Save in some Holy Thursday liturgies where a most stylized, even sanitized, version is undertaken as part of the commemoration of the Last Supper, the tradition of the washing of feet has not been a major part of Christian practice.

the ministry of Jesus of Nazareth. John's Gospel has gone through substantially more "theological development" than have the Synoptics, in their view. While none of the authors of the New Testament texts is without religious and theological concerns, John is considered the most theologically inflected Gospel.

But the "high christology" of John's Gospel, exemplified in the prologue, may be neither an incursion of Greco-Roman philosophy nor an unprecedented view that took a long time to develop in a Christian community "separated from" mainstream Judaism in theology, if not always in worship. In other words, if Daniel Boyarin's thesis has some credibility (see pp. 61-64 above), John may reflect a strand in ambient Judaism of the first century that the Synoptics do not. Although the Gospel of John is a more thoroughly theologically inflected document than the Synoptic Gospels, and the theology of the Gospel of John is a "*logos* theology" that leads to a binitarian and eventually a trinitarian doctrine of God, it is not merely possible, but likely, that the historical core of John is both rooted in the memories of disciples and shaped in telling and retelling by those who accepted the Jewish theology of "two powers in heaven."[23] The notion that Jesus could be addressed as "the Son of God who is in the world" suggests, in this context, the very theological shift that would mark the difference between Jews in the Jesus-movement and other Jews who accepted the "two powers in heaven" form of Jewish monotheism: the second power in heaven not only acted in the world, but had come into the world.

Amy-Jill Levine's provocative line, quoted earlier, is relevant here. "Might Christ-confessors have sought to replace Torah with Jesus as the center of worship? That would get someone booted out of my synagogue."[24] Throughout John's Gospel, Jesus is addressed as *kyrie*.[25] While non-disciples and non-Jews

---

23. It is interesting to note that over forty years ago, Raymond E. Brown argued against despising the historicity of John's Gospel in "The Problem of Historicity in John," in *Gospel According to John*, 1:143-67. At that time, Brown perceived a more open attitude to historical elements in John, an attitude that would wane in the more recent quests for the historical Jesus. A number of Brown's claims about the separate oral performances of a narrative of feeding leading to the duplicated stories in Mark 6-7 (154-56) and about the lack of multiple attestation for one or another chronology are again in the fore. Moreover, Brown also implied that some substantial differences in texts portraying what seem to be the same episode are due to different narrations, and some unexpected convergences between the Synoptics and John are also due to the oral sharing of stories in different contexts.

24. Amy-Jill Levine, *The Misunderstood Jew: The Church and the Scandal of the Jewish Jesus* (San Francisco: HarperSanFrancisco, 2006), 108.

25. The address is also found almost as often in Q, less often in parts of Matthew and Luke that do not depend on Q, and only twice in Mark. Ben Witherington III finds *kyrie* to be one of the "names" of Jesus. He argued that the "names" or "titles" Jesus accepted (Son of Man, Son of God, Lord, Christ) define him in the context of relationships with God and others. Jesus is not an "individual" in the modern sense, but a central member in a social network who, like others in the network, is defined by relationships. Witherington's claim that Jesus had a "christology" has been met with some resistance. Among other issues is whether the task of making claims about Jesus' self-understanding "by examining his relationships with other significant figures" has enough reliable data to make such inferences; after all, the memories of his disciples were necessarily selective. See his "The Christology of Jesus," in *Who Do You Say That I Am? Essays on Christology*, ed. Mark Allan Powell and David R. Bauer (Louisville: Westminster John Knox, 1999), 1-13, at 1; and his *The Christology of Jesus* (Minneapolis: Fortress, 1990).

are often portrayed as addressing Jesus as *kyrie* ("Lord, will you cure my son?") when their lives are disrupted and in need, this address also occurs when disciples address questions to Jesus. *Kyrie* is used often in the Septuagint to designate God. It also functions as a title of address to a superior in a hierarchical society, as "Sir" does in English. No evidence supports a conclusion that the Gospel writers did or did not intend to connect *kyrie* when addressed to Jesus with Yahweh. However, since *kyrie* is an address to God in the Septuagint, hearers of the Gospel, especially Hellenized Jews who read the Septuagint rather than the Hebrew text of the Jewish Bible, might have been at least ambiguous about what *kyrie* would mean when people addressed Jesus. If John is written in the context of the "two powers in heaven" theology, then the split between those who had faith in Jesus and those who did not could also be the split between those who would see Jesus as worthy of address as *kyrie* as the Wisdom of God and worthy of worship, and those who would not. The latter might well want to remove those who worshiped Jesus from the synagogue, even if they had some sympathy with the "two powers in heaven" theology: "Those who walk Jesus' way think that the Second Power has come to Earth as a man!!!" The point is that the overtones of *kyrie* for the hearers of the rest of the Gospel may well harmonize with the high christology of the prologue.

The previous paragraph is rather inferential, even speculative. Other inferences are quite possible. But it is not impossible that the shaping of the Gospel reflects a conflict between those Jews who followed Jesus as an incarnated "second power from heaven" and those who refused to do so. Only the latter group is denominated "the Jews" in John's Gospel, but it is possible that the opposition between groups of Jews in the Gospel would have been instructive for—and perhaps articulated in the context of the beliefs of—those Jews who at least considered the possibility that there were "two powers."

While the Johannine material has undergone substantial recasting and is shaped according to the literary and theological interests of the author,[26] the presentation of the encounter of Jesus with Mary and Martha at Bethany may well recollect an event that was told so as to characterize both who Jesus was and what discipleship meant. The connection of Martha's confession of Jesus in words with Mary's confession in the deed of anointing the anointed one suggests the intimate connection of practice and belief.

Word and deed are like sisters. To have faith in Jesus is to engage in the appropriate practice and to confess in the appropriate words. If belief without deeds is dead, then deeds without belief are blind. Or, as noted much earlier, one of the practices of the faith is the practice of believing, trusting in, *ho christos*. But discipleship is not belief. As John has Jesus say at the Last Supper:

---

26. Brown (*Gospel According to John*, 1:xliii-li) finds at least five layers in the Gospel, making it more difficult for historians to mine the Gospel for memories of the historic Jesus that are not heavily inflected.

Now, if I washed your feet, even though I am Lord and Teacher,
you too must wash one another's feet.
For it was an example that I gave you:
you are to do exactly as I have done for you.
Let me firmly assure you,
no servant is more important than his master;
no messenger is more important than the one who sent him.
Now, once you understand this,
happy are you if you put it into practice. (John 13:14-17)[27]

And those who put it into practice a few chapters earlier were those model disciples Martha and Mary, who were sure that he was from God, the anointed one who brought about the ultimate reconciliation—he brought their brother back to them from the dead.

---

27. This translation is from Brown, *Gospel According to John*, 2:548-49.

Ten

THE WISDOM OF
CHRISTIAN PRACTICES AT PHILIPPI

*T*he scenes treated in the previous two chapters in particular and the Gospels in general are not unique in connecting discipleship with christology. To recognize Jesus properly as the Christ, one has to have the right "mind" or have faith in Jesus. These are complementary ways of speaking of the practice of discipleship, one focusing on actions and the other on attitude. Both are exercises of the imagination. Doing christology is impossible without properly practicing the wisdom of God's ways or the faith in *ho christos*.

Interestingly enough, a quite similar point is made by another author, in another time and place, using a different literary genre. Here the key is not a *story* about Jesus, but what was likely a *hymn* or *poem* about Jesus that Paul uses in his letter to the Philippians. It is interesting to note that those hearing oral clues when this poetic text was read could connect it not only with the Johannine text, especially the midrash or poem or hymn that forms the prologue to John's Gospel, but also by linguistic association to the scene at Caesarea Philippi.

Hymns to Jesus

One of the earliest Roman, non-Christian references to Christian life is from a letter of Pliny the Younger, governor of Bythinia, written in 112 c.e. He reported that the Christians met "on a certain fixed day before it was light, when they sang in alternate verses a hymn to Christ as to a god."[1] No one knows if we still have the hymn he reported. But we do have a number of early Christian hymns embedded in the New Testament.[2]

---

1. See Everett Ferguson, ed., *Encyclopedia of Early Christianity* (New York and London: Garland, 1990), s.v., "Pliny the Younger" and "hymns." The quotation is from *Epistles* 10.97, 98: *carmenque Christo quasi deo dicere* is the key phrase.

2. The classic study of the *kenōsis* hymn is Ralph P. Martin, *Carmen Christi: Philippians 2:5-11 in Recent Interpretation and the Setting of Early Christian Worship*, rev. ed. (Grand Rapids: Eerdmans, 1983). Martin also discusses other New Testament hymns to help provide the context for the hymn. The importance of Paul's rhetoric in his use of this hymn is highlighted by Maureen A. Tilley, "Philippians 2:6-11 and the Question of Pre-Existence" (M.A. Thesis, St. Michael's College, Vermont, 1985). My understanding of the *kenōsis* hymn and its use is much indebted to these works, although neither focuses on the "exemplary" use of the hymn as strongly as the present discussion. The work of Larry Hurtado, discussed above, is also important in this regard.

Why are ancient hymns important? The very fact that they were passed on and recorded strongly suggests that they both shaped and expressed the faith of the people who sang them. Of course, we cannot simply read ancient faith from ancient hymns. Would that it were so easy! We simply don't have many of them, at least not from the first century of Christianity. We don't know if the few we have are a "fair sample."[3] The preserved hymns may be selected from a set that is quite different from the whole. We simply cannot generalize from the hymns we have.

Nor can we be sure that the hymns were preserved because they expressed the people's faith or for some other rhetorical purpose. Nor do we know if the ones we have were widespread. Of course, they spread as the Gospels and letters of the New Testament spread—quite widely! But we can sometimes use a specific hymn as a clue to the practice and life of a specific community and as a clue to understanding an author's point in quoting a hymn.

The *kenōsis* hymn in Paul's letter to the Philippians (2:6-11) may be the earliest Christian hymn we have. Paul had organized the Christian community in Philippi about 49 c.e. He wrote to the community in Philippi no more than seven or eight years later, possibly earlier. He claims to be writing from prison. He prays "that your love may abound more and more, with knowledge and all discernment, so that you may approve of what is excellent, and may be pure and blameless for the day of Christ, filled with the fruits of righteousness which come through Christ Jesus to the glory and praise of God" (Phil. 1:9-11). He encourages members of the community at Philippi to let their "manner of life be worthy of the gospel of Christ" (Phil. 1:27). He recognizes that there are opponents, people who are of "other minds," but he encourages the Christians in Philippi not to fear (1:28) but to stand together with all looking not only to their own interests but also to the interests of others.

Paul quotes the hymn, likely well known in the community, to make a point by showing the community that its hymn had important implications for the practice of discipleship. His rhetorical skill in quoting the hymn provides a clue to Paul's purposes. The hymn itself probably went something like this:

> Though he was in the form of God,
> he did not count equality with God
> something to be grasped,
> but emptied himself taking the form of a slave,
> born like humans;
> and being in the human pattern,

---

3. Indeed, we are not even certain that all the passages traditionally identified as hymns or poems are actually such. For example, Daniel Boyarin has argued that the Johannine prologue may not be a hymn or poem at all, but may be rooted in a midrash on Gen. 1:1-5. He suggests that it can be seen as "a strictly chronological narrative" that is actually a "piece of perfectly unexceptional non-Christian Jewish thought that has been seamlessly woven into the christological narrative of the Johannine community." See *Border Lines: The Partition of Judaeo-Christianity* (Philadelphia: University of Pennsylvania Press, 2004), 93-111, at 111.

> he humbled himself and became obedient unto death,
> (even to death on a cross).[4]
> So God highly exalted him and
> bestowed on him the name above every other name
> so that at Jesus' name,
> every knee should bow
> and every tongue confess
> Lord Jesus Christ to the glory of God the Father.

This precious hymn was sung by Christians long before the Gospel of Mark was written. Whatever else it is, it is a treasure of early Christian devotion.

Theologians want to analyze the hymn. One of the key questions they debate is whether the hymn implies the preexistence of Christ. Did the early Christians in Philippi believe that Christ existed as divine before Jesus was born? He was "in the form of God" (*en morphē theou*), according to the hymn, perhaps even as God's Wisdom was in the form of God. Many have argued that the hymn does imply preexistence; others are not convinced. Some have suggested that even if the *text* of the hymn suggests preexistence, Paul's *use* of the hymn would make sense even without Paul's having to presume or accept "preexistence."[5] Paul's point was not to assert preexistence. He is quoting back at the Philippians a hymn they likely knew. He used the hymn rhetorically, so that every point that the *text* of the hymn makes may not be a point *he* was making in using it (just as not all cantors who are required to sing "Amazing Grace" believe they are "wretches" in need of salvation, despite the original lyric— "revised" in some "liberal" versions found in some hymnals to omit that term so harsh to gentle ears). However, if one takes the debate over the question of preexistence as crucial to understanding Paul's christology, one misses the force of Paul's letter and misses Paul's point.[6] What point was he making in using the hymn?

---

4. Most scholars see this line as a Pauline addition to the extant hymn.

5. This argument is made stronger if one considers the hymn to be the "locution" and if one recognizes different illocutionary acts in Paul's use of it and adaptation of it and in the Philippians singing of the hymn. One cannot always assume that a text used in an act with one illocutionary force has the same significance or meaning as when it is used with another illocutionary force. The meaning of "she is an angel" is quite different if one is using it with different forces, such as literally (as in some television shows of the last decade about heavenly beings), metaphorically (to express one's admiration for another who engages in virtuous activity), or ironically (to describe a wicked person). To understand the meaning of a text, one has to understand the force with which it is uttered or written and read or heard. I am indebted to Maureen Tilley for seeing the significance of this point.

6. Larry W. Hurtado (*Lord Jesus Christ: Devotion to Jesus in Earliest Christianity* [Grand Rapids: Eerdmans, 2003]) spends some space (119-23) on the issue of preexistence, but mostly in dialogue with James D. G. Dunn, who has argued against the concept of preexistence in Paul. Morna D. Hooker thinks that the "figure in view" is more Adam than a preexistent one, although she finds it impossible to not accept a Pauline (or pre-Pauline) assumption of preexistence ("*Adam* Redivivus: Philippians 2 Once More," in *The Old Testament in the New Testament: Essays in Honour of J. L. North*, ed. Steve Moyise, Journal for the Study of the New Testament Supplement Series 189 [Sheffield: Sheffield Academic Press, 2000], 220-34). Hurtado argues that this is a pre-Pauline hymn that

Paul's Use of the Hymn

The introduction to the hymn is crucial to understanding Paul's rhetorical purpose. "If there is any empowering (*paraklēsis*) in Christ, any incentive in love, any community in the Spirit, if there is any compassion and sympathy, fulfill my joy by having the same mind (*phronēte*), the same love, the same accord, the same spirit" (2:1-3). Paul urges the Philippians to do nothing from selfishness but "in humility to count others better than yourself. Let each look not only to his own interests but look also to those of others" (2:4).

Then the final command of the introduction: No English translation can really bring out its power. *Touto phroneite en hymin ho kai en Christō Jesou.*[7] In this sentence Paul does not tell the Philippians not to "believe" something or to "do" something. Rather he introduces the hymn by saying, "Have in yourselves the mind (*phroneite*) which is also in Christ Jesus" (2:5) and he seems to quote the hymn in the same sentence.[8] Paul's point is to instruct his readers in the "mind" or "ways" of discipleship. The hymn then tells the Philippians what this "mind," this practical wisdom is.

---

shows that very early Christian worship demonstrates a belief in the preexistence of Christ; but he also recognizes that the use of the hymn in the context of the letter is to shape Christian practice (134). My own understanding of the affirmation of preexistence (and, like Hurtado, I think it early) is that such belief is not so much an implication of the views of Jesus but an (unavoidable) outgrowth of participation in the practices of the Jesus-movement, especially the worship practices. Hurtado thinks that such participation is rooted in profound "conversion" experiences that bring the Jewish members of the Jesus-movement to a variant of monotheistic language that is "binitarian," but subordinationist, to convey the significance of Jesus as a divine agent. See Hurtado, *How on Earth Did Jesus Become a God? Historical Questions about Earliest Devotion to Jesus* (Grand Rapids: Eerdmans, 2005), 25-30, 53, 88-107). Dunn's magisterial *Christology in the Making: A New Testament Inquiry into the Origins of the Doctrine of the Incarnation* (Philadelphia: Westminster, 1980) saw the only real alternative to his view that the hymn was to be understood in the context of a "new Adam" christology to be the Hellenistic "divine man" view (125). Boyarin's view of the "two powers in heaven" theology raises significant questions that may undermine Dunn's interpretation. But Paul is *using* the hymn whether or not one accepts the "two powers" or "preexistence" view. In Paul's use of the hymn, that issue simply "factors out." His purpose is other than asserting or not asserting preexistence.

7. Wayne A. Meeks ("The Man from Heaven in Paul's Letter to the Philippians," in *Where Christology Began: Essays on Philippians 2*, ed. Ralph P. Martin and Brian J. Dodd [Louisville: Westminster John Knox, 1998], 232) has noted that this clause has "perplexed not a few interpreters."

8. It is remarkable that much scholarship ignores v. 5. Few of the essays in *Where Christology Began* attend to it. In that collection, only Stephen E. Fowl, "Christology and Ethics in Philippians 2:5-11," devotes significant space to the use of the hymn (145-48). Other essays mention an "ethical understanding" of the hymn, but focus so much on its difficult vocabulary, translation problems, and the significance of the imagery that the point of the hymn in the context of the letter is simply left aside. Brian J. Dodd, "The Story of Christ and the Imitation of Paul in Philippians 2-3," reviews various authors who suggest that it is not Christ but Paul who is to be imitated only to oppose that understanding (154-62). Meeks ("Man from Heaven," 333) notes the significance of the rhetoric of the hymn. Also see Stephen E. Fowl, *The Story of Christ in the Ethics of Paul*, Journal for the Study of the New Testament Supplement Series 36 (Sheffield: JSOT Press, 1990). Hurtado, however, writes essays on both Phil. 2:5-11 and 6-11. See *Lord Jesus Christ*, 121 n. 95.

It is not coincidental that Paul uses the same verb Mark used for Jesus' rebuking Peter. In Paul's use of the hymn, following Jesus and knowing who he is are the same thing. Paul is insisting on the Philippians' getting it right, including the death on the cross, which may well be the price of discipleship. Proper discipleship is good christology.

The verb *phroneite* is most typically used in the New Testament and the Septuagint with a negation: *ou phroneite*. The verb serves to urge or command people *not* (*ou*) to follow the wrong way of life or to accept a path of false wisdom. In Mark's Gospel, Jesus told Peter he was following false wisdom—a fairly typical way of using the verb. But in Philippians 2:5, Paul uses it without the negative, without the *ou*. He tells them how to imagine the right path, the path they are to follow.

This latter exhortation implies that those who have other minds have been or might be "in" the community at Philippi that Paul addresses. Later in the letter, he makes this explicit: "Brethren, join in imitating me, and mark those who so live as you have an example in us. For many, of whom I have often told you and now tell you even with tears, live as enemies of the cross of Christ. Their end is destruction, their god is the belly, and they glory in their shame, with minds set on earthly things" (Phil. 3:17-19).[9] When one is trying to discern and follow the wise path among the many available, the imaginative practice of wisdom is what one is doing—and one learns this through imitating those who know how to do it—Aristotle's *phronimoi* or, in the present case, disciples whose minds are mature (3:15).

The use of the *kenōsis* hymn in Philippians connects *phroneō* to discipleship. To have the "mind" of Jesus is to conform one's understanding in practice to Jesus—*given that other options are possible*.[10] Other uses are similarly suggestive. When Mark portrays Jesus castigating Peter, it is for his taking the wrong path, for conforming to human, not divine ways. The curious use of *phroneo* as an admonition—apparently it is used only when multiple options of life patterns are available—seems to differ from classic uses of the verb and of the noun connected with it, practical wisdom, *phronēsis*.

Another link between Mark's story and Paul's use of the hymn is that each is followed by a characterization of the proper path as one of suffering, sacrifice, and death. The first passion prediction in Mark is part of the Caesarea Philippi scene. It is followed by Jesus' prediction of his passion and death. Paul adds "death on a cross" to the hymn after urging the Philippians to let "this mind" be in them. Paul's letter is strongly hortatory, and Mark's scene can be read as a warning to those who think or thought that Jesus would be a Davidic messiah. These are both instructions, in different forms, in practical wisdom for those who would be Jesus'

---

9. Although Paul here calls upon his readers to imitate him, it is not because of his excellence, but because for him "to live is Christ" (1:21).

10. Meeks ("Man from Heaven," 331-32) is explicit in calling the letter "parenetic," not in a sense of urging the following of some moral rule, but in showing that Christ models the Christian life; in this he refutes an argument by Ernst Käsemann that the Pauline use of the hymn is exemplary in the manner suggested herein.

disciples. The way of following Jesus is not in the practices of the world but in the practices of the reign of God.

Paul's letter portrays the way of life of this path at great length. But Paul also hints at other ways not to be followed. *Phroneite* is an imperative verb. Paul uses it with persons who might walk one way or another, who might live in one story or another, who might develop one practical pattern of wisdom or another. In using it, Paul exhorts the Philippians to have the right "mind" when one's "mind" might well be other. Whereas we might translate *ou phroneite* as "don't you all be wrongheaded," *phroneite* says "be rightheaded"—and here's how to do it.

The point of Paul's use of the hymn is not academic. He is not offering a theory of preexistence. He uses the hymn to remind the Philippians how to be disciples. He does not quote their own hymn back at them to exalt Jesus. He quotes their hymn to remind them that, as Jesus did not hold on to his status but humbled himself to be a slave, so must they if they are to follow him. And as he would suffer hideous execution as a criminal, so might they have to pay the final price. The point of his use of the hymn is to show them what it means to have the mind of Christ in them; the point of his adding to the original hymn "even to death on a cross" is to help them understand the cost of discipleship. It is a summary of his purpose in the whole letter. As Morna Hooker put it, "Writing to those who were his 'joy and crown', Paul ensured that his understanding of *how the gospel should be lived* was preserved. The Philippians were surely encouraged and inspired by his letter to them, not rebuked."[11] The Philippians knew the text of the hymn. If the Philippians were to understand the significance of their own hymn, they must live it—as modified by Paul. That's Paul's point. If they are to know who Christ is, they must follow Christ by living out the gospel, not suffering for the case of suffering, but suffering with and for each other.

What is that "mind" of Christ? The whole point of the letter seems to be to lay it out for the Philippians: "Only let your manner of life be worthy of the gospel of Christ, so that whether I come and see you or am absent, I may hear of you that you stand firm in one spirit, with one mind striving side by side for the faith of the gospel, and not frightened in anything by your opponents" (1:27). Paul tells them, among other things, not to grumble (2:14), to rejoice in the Lord (3:1; 4:4), to look out for the dogs, evil workers, those who demand circumcision (3:2), to press on for the goal (3:13-14), to stand firm in the Lord (4:1), pray (4:4) and to think about what is true, honorable, pure, gracious, and excellent (4:8). In all of these, Paul is urging harmony on the community. Harmony is possible only when one is reconciled with one's opponent, so that the community may be united in Christ, not divided into parties fighting over less important things. Paul's rhetorical strategy was to call them into unity and to avoid the practices of division that characterize the way of "the dogs."

Mark was addressing a community that had issues different from those of

---

11. Morna D. Hooker, "Philippians: Phantom Opponents and the Real Source of Conflict," in *Fair Play: Diversity and Conflicts in Early Christianity: Essays in Honour of Heikki Räisänen,* ed. Ismo Dunderberg, Christopher Tuckett, and Kari Syreeni (Leiden: Brill, 2002), 377-95, at 294.

the Philippian community. It is possible that one of Mark's rhetorical strategies was to encourage a community that had been fearful by portraying the reality of fear in the earliest disciples—even when Jesus had been raised (Mark 16:8, probably the last words of the Gospel). Mark's point may be to say that faith is not incompatible with fear, for even those leaders in faith had great fear but led anyway. Another possible exploration would be the relationships of fear and faith, for Paul seems to be doing much the same thing as Mark, rhetorically speaking: saying how to live in Christ even in the face of fearsome opponents or attractive options. Discipleship is not easy.

Both Paul and Mark are showing in their texts that the way the disciples imagine Christ and the way they live are intimately connected. To identify Christ as a "slave" who embraced death on a cross is to imagine him as emptying out all exaltation for the sake of humanity. To follow Christ is to let the mind of this slave be in us, to do the same. As he was a slave for us, so must we be slaves for each other. Paul is not urging a notional or abstract understanding. The mind of Christ is exhibited by wisdom in practice. Indeed, the whole letter to the Philippians, like the whole Gospel of Mark, can be seen as instruction in the practice of discipleship. The community, each and all, is to keep their minds, their pattern of life, their practical wisdom, and their lives the same as one who became a slave to serve them. For they will in and by so doing come to be glorified just as Christ was.

Discipleship and Christology

As in Mark, so in Paul. To understand who Jesus is, to do christology, requires one to know how to follow Jesus. One can do this only as a member of Jesus' community of followers. One can then exercise one's disciplined imagination to say "who he is." Mark, writing some four decades after Jesus' death and resurrection, addressed his Gospel to his fellow Christians. Even if Mark's addressees were afraid, so were the first disciples. Even if Mark's readers failed in understanding, so did the first disciples. Even if Mark's readers had trouble following Jesus, so did the first disciples. Even if Mark's readers were unfaithful, they knew that Peter—the "Satan" who would later betray Jesus—saw the transfiguration a week after the Caesarea Philippi scene. He would hear from the women that Jesus had been raised. The community would be there for them. As in Mark, so in Paul. The practice of discipleship is possible only in a community of support, a communion of saints.

Only if one can learn how to follow Jesus, can one imagine "right-mindedly" who he is and learn what he is for us. Only if we have a community of disciples that both imagines who he is and also images him for the rest of the world, can we come to imagine who he is and be an image of him for the world. Only an imaginative community of disciples can teach us what it is to follow Jesus. Paul uses the hymn not merely to encourage moral life or to present a paradigm. He uses the hymn to show how living well in community and salvation are connected: when one knows who Christ is and how to follow him, the circle is complete.

Paul does not instruct an individual disciple. In Mark's Gospel, Peter took the brunt of Jesus' rebuke or curse. Peter alone—but standing perhaps for all who fail to walk the way of God because their mind is not on God's things—is denominated "Satan." Paul's letter was written long after the scene at Caesarea Philippi happened, according to Mark, but written long before Mark's Gospel. In his letter, it is the community as a whole, the community (*koinōnia*) in the Spirit who must live in and live out the story of Christ if they are to understand who he is—their savior.

Both Mark and Paul present christology in the context of discipleship. Only disciples in community can properly imagine who Jesus is. Their imaginations need instruction and correction. Those who know how to have a mind for the things of God or, as Paul puts it, are mature, are the guides. "I press on toward the goal for the prize of the upward call of God in Christ Jesus. Let those of us who are mature be thus minded (*phronōmen*) and if in anything you are of a different mind (*phroneite*), God will reveal that to you, too" (Phil. 3:14-15). Those of another mind are enemies of the cross of Christ (Phil. 3:17). They know how only to destroy themselves. They cannot know Christ, nor, I infer, do christology.

As in Mark and Paul, so in John. In this Gospel we see Jesus engaging in the same sorts of actions as Mary. Earlier I suggested that Mary's action of anointing Jesus might be an anticipation of the Johannine Last Supper. But perhaps this act is even more significant. Perhaps Jesus learned from Mary what service was and what to be the anointed one was and that these were identical: to be the anointed one is to be a servant. We have often assumed that the Bethany scene foreshadows the Last Supper. Can we not also imagine, as suggested above, that the Bethany scene offers a key to understanding the service of being *ho christos*, that Jesus learned the importance of serving others from Mary's action? As any professor can tell you, when teaching really happens, the students teach the teacher as well as the teacher teaching the students. Perhaps the disciple has taught the Master here—a point that fits with the interpretation of the Jesus-movement as a discipleship of equals, discussed in chapter 5 above.

The anointed one had to serve, and the servant is *ho christos*. The connection of discipleship with christology and vice versa appears again in John. If multiple attestation from differing sources in the New Testament written in different genres carries the weight the "New Quest" for the historical-Jesus put on it, then we have extremely strong attestation of the connection between christology and discipleship: attested by Mark, John, and Paul.

But what is this pattern of discipleship? What are the practices that disciples engage in? Interestingly, the beginning of an answer to these questions is found in a "confrontation" between Jesus and the disciples of John the Baptist. In this scene, the connection of the practices of *ho christos* and the practices of the expected reign of God is made clear. That is matter for chapter 11. How the disciples carry the story on in practice is matter for part 3.

Eleven

THE INTERROGATION
BY THE DISCIPLES OF
JOHN THE BAPTIST AT NAIM

A fundamental claim of this work is that christology begins in disciples' imaginations and can be done only in the contexts of the practices of reconciliation that constitute discipleship. Yet we conclude the constructive section of part 2 with a story that does *not* reflect the discourse of disciples, at least not directly. This story does tell us something crucial: it offers an early account of the practices of the reign of God that Jesus points out as indicators of the kind of messiah he might be and the sorts of practices by which one could recognize someone who was living in and living out God's reign. This narrative makes explicit the connections of the practices of reconciliation and the reign of God inaugurated by the anointed one.

Obviously, the story is remembered by the disciples of Jesus. Most scholars would attribute it to the Q source. Yet these memories are of Jesus' encounter not with his disciples but with disciples of John the Baptist. Whatever difficulties there are with the chronology of the Gospels—and there are many—this story is likely rooted relatively early in Jesus' career while John was still alive. Even if the story has been elaborated (as it most likely has been because the Baptist movement continued in competition with the Jesus-movement after the Baptist's death, and Jesus' disciples' telling of the story would tend to exalt Jesus and to minimize the Baptist), it is nonetheless an indicator of what the Jesus-movement and the reign of God are to look like. The story helps us to show that disciples can do christology as reconciling practice.

The story comes in two very similar versions. Matthew and Luke refashioned their source in their own ways. It is, of course, possible that these versions of the story provide an example of an oral tradition that is "informally controlled," as discussed in chapter 5. There is some flexibility in telling the story as well as significant control by the community that "knows" the story it is hearing: "The central threads of the story cannot be changed, but flexibility in detail is allowed."[1] The community will not allow a storyteller to "get away with" telling a story that does not reflect or refract the Jesus it remembers. The practice of

---

1. James D. G. Dunn, *Jesus Remembered*, vol. 1 of *Christianity in the Making* (Grand Rapids: Eerdmans, 2003), 207, citing Kenneth E. Bailey, "Informal Controlled Oral Tradition and the Synoptic Gospels," *Asia Journal of Theology* 5 (1991): 42-45.

memory keeps the imagination in check. Just as Jesus corrected Peter's defective imagination at Caesarea Philippi, so the community does not accept those stories that are defective.

James D. G. Dunn notes that informally controlled tradition is often composed of memories of "parables and recollections of people and events important to the identity of the community."[2] This story provides an identity for the Jesus-movement, not one that has ideological requirements but an identity built of reconciling practices. Even non-disciples might recognize this movement in its practices. Here's the story in both canonical versions:

The disciples of John told him about these things. John summoned two of his disciples and sent them to the Lord to ask, "Are you the one who is to come, or should we look for another?" When the men came to him they said, "John the Baptist has sent us to you to ask, 'Are you the one who is to come, or should we look for another?'" At that time, he cured many of their diseases, sufferings, and evil spirits; he also granted sight to many who were blind. And he said to them in reply, "Go and tell John what you have seen and heard: the blind regain their sight, the lame walk, lepers are cleansed, the deaf hear, the dead are raised, the poor have the good news proclaimed to them. And blessed is the one who takes no offense at me." (Luke 7:18-23)

When John heard in prison of the works of the messiah, he sent his disciples to him with this question, "Are you the one who is to come, or should we look for another?"

Jesus said to them in reply, "Go and tell John what you hear and see: the blind regain their sight, the lame walk, lepers are cleansed, the deaf hear, the dead are raised, and the poor have the good news preached to them. And blessed is the one who takes no offense at me." (Matt. 11:2-6)

The interrogation by John's disciples in the story is not straightforward. Their question asks for a yes or no answer. Jesus' answer is neither yes nor no. Rather, Jesus answers with a recital of a set of practices. This list of practices closely echoes a text known among the Essene community at Qumran (4Q521, "The Messianic Apocalypse"). The list in the Gospels is identical save that it adds the curing of lepers. This particular list of practices is a distinctive catalogue that is not found in extant texts except in the Qumran text. All the elements in the list are drawn from various parts of the Old Testament,[3] but the list is almost certainly one

---

2. Dunn, *Jesus Remembered*, 207.

3. The passage is filled with quotations from the scriptures. As Joseph A. Fitzmyer notes, the "One who is to come" is in effect a title, drawn from Mal. 3:1; the expressions the blind see, the deaf hear, the dead live, and the poor have the good news preached to them come from Isa. 61:1; 35:5; 26:19; and 61:1, respectively (Fitzmyer, *The Gospel According to Luke: Introduction, Transla-*

that Jesus and John would both have known *if* they had been associated with the Essene community. As with Jesus' interrogation of his own disciples at Caesarea Philippi, discussed earlier, this simple text both hides and displays important insights about Jesus, his practices, and the reign of God.

Biblical scholars generally agree on a number of factors that influence the reading of this text: Jesus and his disciples had been associates of John the Baptist. Perhaps they were participants with John and his disciples in an Essene community like that at Qumran. Perhaps Jesus and his disciples had been followers of John. At least some of Jesus' disciples had been disciples of John before becoming Jesus' disciples. Perhaps they came to different understandings of the meaning of living in and living out the reign of God. This dialogue makes clear, however, that Jesus and John were clearly remembered as having different ideas about how to prepare for the reign of God: John focused on repentance for sin/reorientation of one's life and baptism in light of a coming judgment, while Jesus focused on the reorientation of life in light of the kingdom being at hand in the practices that characterized the reign of God that would come with *ho christos*.

Although the ancient Jewish historian Josephus mentioned John the Baptist, we know about John primarily from the fifteen "vignettes" that appear in the New Testament.[4] These stories are not unbiased. In reading them, we need to recognize that they were shaped, probably both in oral transmission and in their final written form, by the opposition or competition between the disciples of Jesus and those of John decades after the death of both Jesus and John. Most scholars are willing to accept that it is likely that the "decrease" of John and the "increase" of Jesus may have been developed in the polemics between the communities. But as John P. Meier suggests, given their respective situations during Jesus' ministry, the narrative likely reflects an understanding of Jesus during his ministry, not after his death.[5] Another factor testifying to its fundamental reliability is that the Synoptic version of the story includes no acknowledgment from John of Jesus' superiority—an unlikely omission if the story had been created out of whole cloth.[6] Hence, the heart of this dialogue represents an important memory in the community of Jesus and his relationship with John.

John was a prophet of purity. John baptized in or near the Jordan River. "In his preaching, he emphasized the importance of behavioral conversion subsequently

---

tion, and Notes, 2 vols., Anchor Bible 28, 28A [Garden City, NY: Doubleday, 1981, 1985], 1:662; similarly, Catherine M. Murphy, *John the Baptist: Prophet of Purity for a New Age* [Collegeville, MN: Liturgical Press, 2003], 66). However, the combination of these practices, including cripples walking and the dead being raised echoes 4Q521; see Dunn, *Jesus Remembered,* 447-52. The Qumran text was released in 1991, and interpretations began to appear shortly thereafter, for example, Michael O.Wise and James D. Tabor, "The Messiah at Qumran," in *Biblical Archaeology Review* 18, no. 6 (1992): 60-61, 65.

4. Material in this paragraph and the next two paragraphs relies, not uncritically, on Murphy, *John the Baptist,* esp. 41, 83-84.

5. John P. Meier, *A Marginal Jew: Rethinking the Historical Jesus,* vol. 2, *Mentor, Message, and Miracles,* Anchor Bible Reference Library (New York: Doubleday, 1994), 132-33.

6. The claims of Jesus' superiority are in conjunction with the baptism of Jesus by John and are found mostly in the Gospel of John.

marked in the flesh by his purifying baptism."[7] He seems to have expected an eschatological judge for whom he was preparing people to be worthy—though it is not clear whether that would be a prophet, an angel, or God. He was executed by Herod Antipas.

Both Jesus and John were evidently strange prophets. They were open to fraternizing with social outcasts, called people to reorient their lives, spoke of the nearness of God's promised reign, and provoked opposition from other Jews, including some Jewish leaders. In a factionalized context with numerous parties or sects contesting each other in this period, such opposition would not be surprising. Jesus, unlike John, evidently did not demand ascetic rigor such as fasting. Differences between John's movement and the Jesus-movement in their varying practices and in their varying understandings of the reign of God provide the background for the Gospels' portrayal of the interrogation of Jesus by the disciples of John the Baptist. When John's disciples ask Jesus if he is the one who is to come, presumably the one who will be the eschatological judge or the one to inaugurate God's reign, Jesus is remembered as responding not with talk about God's reign, but by inviting them to report what they saw and heard—the practices of God's reign, not the judgment that John might expect.

The list of practices quoted in the Gospels is associated with the messiah in the Qumran text.[8] Jesus' act of quoting of this text "back to John" through John's disciples has the rhetorical effects both of challenging the Baptist movement's conception of the reign of God and of claiming that God's reign was already present. If Jesus is "the one who is to come," then the "evidence" is that the reign of God comes not so much in judgment as in healing and reconciliation.

In his response to their interrogation, Jesus does not claim to be the messiah, but he does not have to do so. Rather, by invoking the practices associated with the messiah at Qumran, he implies that he is the one John was expecting to bring God's reign. He also very indirectly admonishes John with a beatitude—don't take offense. The reign that the Jesus-movement is bringing might proceed rather differently from the reign of God that John was expecting.

The interrogation reveals the difference between John's conception and Jesus' conception of God's reign. John P. Meier put it this way:

Although Jesus' mission retained from John's the practice of baptism and the threat of destruction soon to come, its emphasis lay elsewhere: the good news of God's kingly rule, already powerfully at work in Jesus' healings and exorcisms, as well as in his welcome and table fellowship extended to sinners and toll collectors. . . . Though Jesus' "star" was already "on the rise" while John was still active, the overturning of John's expectations must have had a greater, not to say crueler, impact on the Baptist once

---

7. Murphy, *John the Baptist*, 83-84.
8. Dunn, *Jesus Remembered*, 447-52.

he was imprisoned and his personal activity of preaching and baptizing terminated.[9]

As Meier notes, the notion of judgment, prevalent in John, is not eliminated in the Jesus-movement. Nonetheless, there is an implicit christological claim here, a claim made not directly, but by enumerating the practices of the expected messiah.

That Jesus is "the one who is to come" is shown to John's disciples by his practices. Echoing the list associated with the messiah at Qumran, Jesus is not *saying* he is the one to come, but *showing* what the one to come is like. The point of this dispute may well be that the reign of God is recognized by those who can recognize these practices as characteristic of it. Evidently John's disciples did not recognize or accept this. It is not clear if this is because their "minds" were in different places or because they did not have faith in Jesus—reasons for not walking the path of discipleship discussed in the three previous chapters. But because John's movement endured after John's death, at least some of his disciples remained faithful to him and did not become disciples of Jesus.

But Jesus is remembered as adding a practice to the list from 4Q521. By claiming that the lepers are healed, Jesus is remembered as shifting, ever so slightly but significantly, the signs of the kingdom: the lepers were cleansed. Lepers[10] were outcast; they were considered to be ritually "unclean." Leviticus 13:45-46 says that the "person who has the leprous disease shall wear torn clothes and let the hair of his head be disheveled; and he shall cover his upper lip and cry out, 'Unclean, unclean.' He shall remain unclean as long as he has the disease; he is unclean. He shall live alone; his dwelling shall be outside the camp" (NRSV). Leviticus 13 and 14 prescribe various practices and rituals for priests to examine leprous people and dwellings, to quarantine or declare "unclean" those who suffer the disease, and to mark their recovery. In curing lepers, Jesus works to reconcile people to the community, to bring them back "into the camp." In both stories of the healing of lepers in the Gospels (Mark 1:40-45 and parallels; Luke 17:11-19) Jesus instructs the healed lepers to show themselves to the priests so that they can be reconciled to the community.[11]

The point of those healings—a characteristic practice of Jesus and explicitly added to Qumran's messianic list—is not to demonstrate works of power. Rather, it cures the condition that has alienated the afflicted persons from the community of the healthy. Jesus was likely not unique in curing lepers, but whoever would

---

9. Meier, *Mentor, Message, and Miracles*, 132-33. Meier repeatedly claims that this interrogation does not evoke a "christological" response (e.g., p. 400), but if the response so strongly alludes to 4Q521, it is a very strong but "coded" claim to be the one whose practices are the practices of the reign of God. Meier may be correct about the response not implying or assuming a christological *theory*, but in it Jesus is portrayed as identifying messianic *practice* with his practice.

10. "Leprosy" in the scriptures is not limited to Hansen's disease (which was probably unknown at the time of Leviticus, but could be found in the ancient Near East by the time of Jesus), but likely includes psoriasis, eczema, and vitiligo. See Meier, *Mentor, Message, and Miracles*, 700.

11. Interestingly, some of the lepers try to become disciples of Jesus, a statement not made about other people Jesus cured.

cure them would make it possible for them to be outcasts no longer. Curing lepers may be a "healing miracle," but it is also a reconciling practice.

The addition of this practice to the text is significant. Rather than remembering Jesus as quoting a text, the Gospels remember him as altering the text. The particular practice introduced here is explicitly a reconciling practice that makes possible the reintegration of the outcast into the community as "healthy" and "whole." It gives the outcast—in Latin—*salus*. And *salus* is the root of our word "salvation."

The connection of salvation to reconciliation is obvious. What makes healthy people healthy is their ability to be part of and to function in a community. To be part of and functioning in a community, then, is to be saved. The heart of salvation is reconciliation. And it is a practice of the *basileia tou theou*, the reign of God, which is appearing with the one who is to come, the one who will inaugurate God's reign, not by mounting a Davidic throne but by empowering the members of the Jesus-movement to engage in the healing practices that are a constituent of, but certainly not the whole of, salvation.

Why would Jesus be a scandal? Certainly his nonascetic behavior could be a scandal. So could his associating with sinners, prostitutes, and toll collectors. But why would John have to be urged indirectly not to be scandalized by Jesus? Jon Sobrino has argued that the scandal would come in Jesus' preaching the good news to the poor,[12] but that was a Qumran expectation of the messiah that John and Jesus and the disciples presumably would have known. Rather, the scandal might be that Jesus himself has changed the basic direction of the preaching of the reign of God. The "blessing" then functions as a warning or a challenge to John that Jesus has gone his own way. Meier put it this way: "Thus, behind the discreet formulation of a sweeping beatitude, 'happy is he who. . . ,' stands a delicate appeal to one particular person. Jesus is tacitly entreating his own rabbi to recognize in his former pupil the unexpected—and for John, disconcerting— consummation of God's plan for Israel."[13] No longer toeing the Baptist's line, which centers on judgment, Jesus focuses on reconciliation, the result of the judgments that restore justice and other practices. But he does not insult or dispute with John; he keeps his challenge mild.

What this pericope shows is that Jesus is remembered as engaging in specific practices that would characterize the coming reign of God. I shall argue below in part 3 that each of the practices of Jesus is a reconciling practice that repairs ruptured community. What Jesus is telling John and his disciples is that the heart of God's reign is reconciliation, the repair of conditions that split communities,

---

12. See Jon Sobrino, *Jesus the Liberator: A Historical-Theological Reading of Jesus of Nazareth*, trans. Paul Burns and Francis McDonagh (Maryknoll, NY: Orbis Books, 1993), 83.

13. Meier, *Mentor, Message, and Miracles*, 135; Fitzmyer (*Gospel According to Luke,* 1:668) recognizes that this is one of the rare beatitudes throughout the Septuagint and the New Testament formulated in the singular rather than the plural. Yet he finds it not directed to John. Dunn (*Jesus Remembered*, 450) agrees with Meier. Fitzmyer wrote before the publication of 4Q521 and the linking of this pericope with Qumran. Hence, he would not have had as much reason to see John as the addressee as did Dunn and Meier, and as do I, following them.

the healing of sickness, and the overcoming of the alienation from God that is sin. Each of the practices undertaken when and where God reigns, as we shall see below, is a reconciling practice. The center of God's rule is not judgment as much as it is reconciliation and restoration, and insofar as God was acting in and through Jesus to reconcile and restore, the reign of God is present.

Conclusion

This brief account of the interrogation of Jesus by John's disciples sets the stage for the next section of this book. If it has not become clear already, it should be clear now that practices of a community, what a community typically does, mark it for what it is. Recognizing what Jesus and the Jesus-movement typically do is crucial to recognizing the reality of God's reign. Peter's confession at Caesarea Philippi is bound up with Peter's success at getting the word right—Jesus is *ho christos*— but getting the story wrong: the messiah would not be engaging in a military battle or seeking to be a political conqueror who overthrew the Roman occupation and the indigenous elite who cooperated with them. Martha's confession and Mary's anointing are also, in their contexts, indicators of getting their "minds" right. Whether Mary's anointing symbolizes that Jesus is *ho christos*, or prepares him for his death, or teaches him the practice of service represented later in the foot washing, it is clear that the actions and words fit together. And Paul's exhortation to the Philippians shows them that even the Christ to whom they sang became a slave to and for others in service—so how could they not live in and live out the faith in practice, even to the point of death? Finally, Jesus' response to John's disciples shows that these are the practices, quite practical in nature, of the one who is to come.

The ancient church father Origen called Jesus the *autobasileia*, the reign of God in person. While many theologians focus almost exclusively on the death and resurrection of Jesus as the points that reveal the reign of God,[14] others, such as Benedict XVI, focus on Jesus' words as the key for understanding Origen.[15] Jon Sobrino writes that Jesus is the reign of God in person, "important words that well describe the finality of the personal mediator of the Kingdom, but dangerous if they equate Christ with the reality of the Kingdom."[16] But what made Jesus the presence of the kingdom of God is not merely what he was in himself and his relationships that empowered others to engage in the practices that constitute reconciliation, the characteristic of the reign of God. Just as a king is no king without a kingdom, so the reign of God is no reign without people living in it and living it out. The *autobasileia* may be the first to understand how to live in and live out God's reign, but he cannot do so alone. What would be a kingdom

---

14. For a classic example, see Reginald H. Fuller, *The Mission and Achievement of Jesus* (Chicago: Alec R. Allenson, 1954).

15. Joseph Ratzinger [Pope Benedict XVI], *Jesus of Nazareth: From the Baptism in the Jordan to the Transfiguration*, trans. Adrian J. Walker (New York: Doubleday, 2007), 49, 60, 146-47.

16. Sobrino, *Jesus the Liberator*, 108.

or commonwealth, a *basileia*, of one? When Jesus responds to John's disciples with the unexpected words from Qumran, he is telling John that indeed the reign of God is here. We recognize it because he realized it in the reconciling practices that constitute God's reign. The imperative, then, is for Jesus' disciples to carry on the practice of living in and living out the reign of God. In so doing they form the body of Christ, the church.

Hence, the claim I am making is this: christology, understanding who Christ is, is not a matter of the intellect alone. Rather, it is a matter that begins in the active imagination of disciples. The disciples' proper imagination required walking in God's ways, not human ways; letting Christ's mind be in one; realizing with God's grace what it means to live under God's reign in each time and place. In engaging in those practices in the company of Jesus, in the Jesus-movement, disciples have their imaginations corrected by the others who walk in those ways. As Peter had his imagination of the *ho christos* directed properly by the first among equals, so we also must have our imaginations corrected by the Jesus-movement, which carries on Jesus' work in the world. It is never finished. In sum, christology is engaging in reconciling practice.

If the Jesus-movement was a discipleship of equals, if Jesus was the first among equals humanly speaking, and if he is perceived as the empowering divine agent, then the question must be asked: Empowering them to do what? The answer is to do God's will, to realize the reign of God—in limited places and perhaps only for limited times. The reign of God is instantiated when the blind regain their sight, the lame walk, lepers are cleansed, the deaf hear, the dead are raised, the poor have the good news proclaimed to them, and people are reconciled to themselves, each other, and God.

How does that happen? That is the politics of God's reign, and politics is always at least the art and the practice of the best practical solutions to problems. Some problems are beyond our solution—death, after all, awaits us all; we may postpone it, but we cannot conquer it. Yet in living in and living out the reign of God there is enkindled the hope that in the end, God will redeem us even in death, as God once exalted a man who was slave to all, who taught all, and who was executed for it. The place of that hope in a practical christology is discussed later in chapter 19.

Part Three

GOD'S REIGN
IN PRACTICE

Twelve

REMEMBERING THE POLITICS
OF THE JESUS-MOVEMENT

*A disciple is not above his teacher, but everyone when he is fully taught will
be like his teacher.*   —Luke 6:40 RSV

Polity and Practice

The practices of the Jesus-movement form the heart of the polity of the reign
of God. Hence, to understand how to engage in the practices of that movement
is to remember in practice and to carry on the politics[1] of the Jesus-movement.
A *practical* remembering, an authentic anamnesis, is not merely understanding
conceptually what those practices were. Nor is anamnesis merely to learn what
Jesus taught about the reign of God. To understand the politics of the movement,
we have to understand how to be disciples who carry on the movement by carrying
out the practices that give the movement its political and practical identity. For
understanding how to live in and live out a faith tradition is a practical, even
political, understanding, not a theoretical one.

The "we" in the previous paragraph is important. Neither memory nor
discipleship is either private or individual. We become individual persons only
in the context of a community. The "we" precedes the "I." We learn how to be
authentically human only by participating in a community with patterns of good
practice. We can recognize whether we are authentic disciples only in such a
community that has models of good practice.[2]

---

1. This phrase echoes the classic text of John Howard Yoder, *The Politics of Jesus: Vincit Agnus
Noster,* 2nd ed. (Grand Rapids: Eerdmans, 1994; 1st ed., 1972). In the preface to the second edition,
Yoder described his field as "ethical methodology" (as distinguished from exegesis). His point is to
argue for a sort of politics displayed in the New Testament witness as Jesus' practical politics (vii).
Such practices, Yoder claimed, are appropriate for the company of Jesus' followers. Yoder developed his position explicitly in contrast to those who portrayed Jesus as "apolitical" and implicitly
in contrast to those who would later construe Jesus as a violent revolutionary. My debt to Yoder's
vision should be clear in the following, even though my approach and focus differ.

2. This is the key point of the argument made by philosopher Charles Taylor in *The Ethics of
Authenticity* (Cambridge, MA: Harvard University Press, 1991). Taylor notes the pervasiveness of
and the difficulties in understanding the injunction to authenticity, "Be true to yourself." He argues

Discipleship is not reserved to individual virtuosi. Of course, we can and do recognize excellence in performance—"saintliness" characterizes those exemplars. However, for one to engage in the practices of discipleship, one does not have to express brilliantly her or his own experience of the empowerment received through Jesus. One needs only to be an active participant in a community of practitioners. Great performers—saints—grow out of and help sustain the life of the community. All in the community—given their abilities—share in the practices of the community. All in the community form the ground from which particular saints grow. Discipleship, then, is living out and living in a pattern of practices in and of a community of disciples who form the ongoing Jesus-movement.

These shared practices both anticipate the coming and show the presence of the reign of God. Luise Schottroff has argued that the interpretive scheme that construes the tension between present and future eschatology in the Gospels is "an invention of biblical scholarship that is urgently in need of hermeneutical critique."[3] It results from a dualism that separates this world from God's world, the reign of God from the time of the present. It construes "eschatological time" as in some sense "after" rather than "with" ordinary time. But such a contrast was not the basis of Christian practice. As she put it, "The early Christian's relationship was to a God who was already near, whose kingdom had come close, to use the language of the Synoptic Gospels. Therefore—then as now—speaking of God means speaking eschatologically."[4] But her approach is nondualistic. She highlights the hope for the coming of God's reign and the justice that constitutes living in and living out the reign of God. She refuses to separate image and narrative from substance. She also is cognizant that the Gospels record oral tradition—and sometimes the responses by disciples to the teaching proclaimed. The parables "really talk about people's lives in the time of the Roman empire, and these depictions contain their own immediate message that needs to be heard."[5] The parables of Jesus are part of the communicative practice that proclaims in deed and word the reign of God.

As with the parables, so with the other practices of the Jesus-movement. They are not clues to what a future reign of God will be like. Rather, they are practices that live in and live out that reign in the present in the hope that the full range of practices that constitute living under God will be realized by all eventually. This is neither the dualism of "proleptically realized eschatology" nor the deferral of hope until some distant future time. The eschatological time is not so much in the future as it is the graced times and places of the past, present, and future. For God does rule, even if that rule is truly effective only at those times and places when

---

against an individualistic view of "authenticity" as an ethical practice or goal and notes that authenticity requires community norms or models. I adapt his insight specifically for Christianity.

3. Luise Schottroff, *The Parables of Jesus,* trans. Linda Maloney (Minneapolis: Fortress, 2006), 2. Her work recognizes that a community both afflicted with sins and blessed in forgiveness and grace (cf. 11, 17, 145-48) both anticipates and realizes God's reign.

4. Ibid., 2.

5. Ibid.

members of the Jesus-movement realize God's reign by living in and living out the reconciling practices of discipleship.

As it was in Jesus' day, so it is in every day. The practices of Christians in every age are to embody the politics of the Jesus-movement. Carrying on the practices of the Jesus-movement means that its members must show forth the politics of the Jesus-movement at their particular times and places. Engaging in these practices constitutes living in and living out God's reign—wherever and whenever the community is doing what it should. Living out and living in a community that has these practices as its polity is to be saved from the powers that would and do oppose God's reign.[6]

Memories are carried by a community. To remember who Jesus was and what he did is a practice of discipleship. The practices of discipleship are public and social. They are *shared* by a group of committed practitioners who have learned how to engage in the practices and how to pass them on. Even private prayer is something one learns how to do from others who teach each of us how to pray.

That living a disciple's life is fraught with difficulties seems obvious. Especially when the members of the community are also deeply shaped by practices that have no place in God's reign, it becomes difficult to live a life of true discipleship. Few Christians have fully embodied the mind of Christ. Indeed, it is highly unlikely that there ever was a time and place in which the perfect community was instantiated. Even the Twelve had two who fought over sitting at the Lord's right hand when he reigned, another who betrayed him verbally, and another who handed him over to his enemies—hardly a community without significant defects or confusions. A perfect community would be one "without sin," and even the original members of the movement—save Jesus, who "became sin for us" (2 Cor. 5:21)—were sinners. What James Wm. McClendon, Jr., wrote about contemporary Christians in particular seems to apply to all: the "line between the church and the world passes right through each Christian heart."[7] We cannot avoid the pull of "the world" because the world is in us, all of us, as we cannot avoid being in the world. All of us have our minds on *ta tōn anthrōpōn* rather than *ta tou theou*.

Hence, communities and individuals all too often fail to do what they should do and be what they should be. Structural sins such as sexism, xenophobia, and hedonism distort communities. Individuals' sins such as lusts, especially the lust for power, prejudice, and pride, distort Christian (and other) communities. These sins and patterns may well change from time to time—lust for power in a big corporation in New York may be quite different from lust for power in a Christian

---

6. Roberto S. Goizueta contrasts the liberal, individualistic, voluntary community with the "constitutive community," which is the birthplace of a self. While we cannot avoid "choosing" a community or way of life when multiple options are available, as in a pluralist society, Goizueta's point that communities constitute individuals in their relationships is crucial to understanding the significance of community: "Each person (precisely *as a* person) is defined and constituted by his or her relationships, both personal and impersonal, natural and supernatural, material and spiritual." See his *Caminemos con Jesús: Toward a Hispanic/Latino Theology of Accompaniment* (Maryknoll, NY: Orbis Books, 1995), 47-65, at 50.

7. James Wm. McClendon, Jr., *Systematic Theology*, vol. 1, *Ethics* (Nashville: Abingdon, 1986), 17.

base community in Brazil. But sins, social and personal, nonetheless distort individual people and communities.

The point is this: No community is untouched by sinful practice, even the community that first formed the Jesus-movement.[8] The implication is this: Criticism (both deconstructive and reconstructive) of communal practices and individual actions is necessarily one of the practices of a vibrant ongoing community.

What are the practices of discipleship? How can we understand the graceful and saving practices of living in and living out the *basileia tou theou*? This politics is embodied in a "community which seeks above all else God's priorities, in which forgiveness is experienced, which is often surprised by grace, and which knows well how to celebrate God's goodness in the openness of table-fellowship and love of neighbor."[9] These generalizations are helpful guides to the community's vision, but they need to be spelled out in practice (so to speak) in order to characterize the practices that give the community its identity. We want to ask what those divine priorities are. How is grace instantiated? What is forgiven? And how did Jesus' disciples and should we, who would carry on those practices, engage in practices that can make real that table fellowship and love of neighbor?

In one sense, there is no definitive answer to these questions. The Gospels, as argued above, are scripts. Scripts require different performances in different contexts. Translating a script from one time and place to another may even require seemingly radical changes—*West Side Story* is another version of the story of Romeo and Juliet, as noted above; the Broadway musical *Rent* is another version of Puccini's opera *La Bohème*, which is another version of Henri Murger's play *Scènes de la vie de Bohème*. Any great classic text has a "surplus of meaning" so that its significance is never exhausted. This insight applies to practices as well as to texts, persons, events, and symbols.[10] So do practices have a surplus of meaning. Just as interpretations of classic scripts like the Gospels may shift in unexpected ways, so may Christians live in and live out the reign of God in different ways.

As the community that carries on the Jesus-movement has developed and diverged over millennia, the community's practices have had to change as the context in which the community lives has changed. Forms of practice are abandoned and new ones develop. This is the ongoing process or deconstruction and abandonment, on the one hand, and reconstruction and novel expression, on the other. Indeed, these kinds of adjustments are necessary if a tradition is not to suffer death by irrelevance, but to live on in new contexts. Creative fidelity, not slavish imitation, is a mark of a vibrant community.

---

8. This point is often neglected in critiques of Elisabeth Schüssler Fiorenza's work. Her feminist interpretation is alleged to presume that there was a primitive perfection in the Jesus-movement from which the movement somehow fell away. For Schüssler Fiorenza's response to this point, see *Jesus and the Politics of Interpretation* (New York: Continuum, 2000), 128-44.

9. James D. G. Dunn, *Jesus Remembered*, vol. 1 of *Christianity in the Making* (Grand Rapids: Eerdmans, 2003), 610.

10. See David Tracy, *The Analogical Imagination: Christian Theology and the Culture of Pluralism* (New York: Crossroad, 1981), 108.

Yet inertia can keep some outmoded practices alive and allow some good practices to degenerate into formalism. Limitation of the priesthood to celibate males (as if all priests were also always called to be monks or members of religious orders) exemplifies the former problem; infant baptism may have become an example of the latter at some times and places. Some practices are controversial, especially those involving order and authority in the community. In short, a community must examine its current practices to see if they are faithful to the classic practices. Creative fidelity to, not slavish imitation of, these practices gives the community both its identity and its ability to respond to the challenges of the present context—of the specific ways in which hearts are split between the community that is and carries the *basilieia tou theou* and the world.

This does not imply a hard and fast distinction of the ways of the Jesus-movement and the ways of other movements. Clearly, members of other faith traditions or no faith tradition at all can engage in reconciling practices. As agents of reconciliation empowered by God's agent, Jesus, we should both applaud and learn from those whose practices are truly reconciling. Jesus rebuked Peter for considering practices opposed to the Jesus-movement. But the issue is not whose practices earned such rebuke, but that those practices did not fit those of the Jesus-movement. The issue is whether their—and our—practices are practices of reconciliation and peace or practices of domination and division. Both forms of practice have power. The question is what the power is used to realize.

To discern the practices of discipleship, we can begin with the obvious: the practices of those who first formed the community. These practices are not archetypes to be instantiated exactly no matter what the conditions, but prototypes—that is, touchstones against which we can understand and test the practices of today's communities.[11] We remember those practices and they can thus guide us, but we do not live in first-century Palestine. We cannot simply replicate the practices of the first disciples. But these practices must be a touchstone for our understanding, evaluating, and transforming when necessary the practices of the community in every age.

The first pattern of practices can be found in the missions of the disciples. The missions embody in practice what Jesus had led the disciples to understand and do. The Gospels record Jesus as sending his disciples out on missions to carry on the practices of the movement. Hence, the Gospels, in inscribing the practices of the Jesus-movement, provide us with what evidence we have for understanding the prototypical practices of the Christian community. They recorded, adapted, and edited the stories and sayings that they had heard so that they would not be lost when the generation of eyewitnesses had gone. The practice of Gospel writing is one of the practices of the Jesus-movement undertaken to ensure that the memory of Jesus' reconciling practices, including his teaching practice, would

---

11. Controversies abound regarding proper adaptation—this seems inevitable. For one view of how to understand and evaluate such adaptations, see my *Inventing Catholic Tradition* (Maryknoll, NY: Orbis Books, 2000).

not be lost as time went by. Like other theologians through the ages, I gratefully use what they have given us.[12]

Jesus' Mission and the Disciples' Missions

The earliest members of the Jesus-movement must have told and retold tales of the disciples on mission. Such stories testify to the connection of Jesus (who is remembered as commissioning) to the other members of the Jesus-movement (who are remembered as sent by him). Given the "practical" approach we are taking here, we can say that the disciples were then and are now those empowered by God in and through the Spirit to act to bring the practices of God's reign wherever they live and travel—a point developed in chapter 19 below, especially with regard to the church's *missio inter gentes* ("mission among the peoples"). The missionary stories in the Gospels show what the first members of the Jesus-movement did on behalf of the reign of God. Hence, these "mission tales" narrate clear instances of the prototypical practices of the Jesus-movement.

The major story of the mission(s) of the disciples was inscribed in at least two different versions which Luke distinguishes as the mission of the Twelve (Luke 9:1ff. and parallels) and the mission of the seventy (Luke 10:1ff.). Standing behind these written records is a cadre of storytellers who repeated the stories of Jesus' sending the disciples out on mission, and the disciples' returning and reporting. As James D. G. Dunn put it:

> It is evident from Mark 6.7-13 and the parallels in Matt. 9.37-10.1, 7-16 and Luke 9.1-5, 10.1-12 that there were at least two variations, one used by Mark and another oral (Q?) version. The variations make it probable that the material was used and re-used, probably beginning with Jesus' own instructions for missions, but developed and elaborated in terms of subsequent experience of early Christian mission.[13]

Although the stories of the disciples carrying on the mission of the Jesus-movement were remembered variously, they display a pattern of practices that constitute the central work of the movement—not surprisingly the central practices attributed to Jesus.

The present work, following Dunn, presupposes that the practices and actions

---

12. The earliest written records that we have of the practices of the movement, of course, are the Pauline letters. However, extending Dunn's methodology by applying the "default position" of orality not only to the deeds and words of Jesus but to the practices of the earliest Christians, we can recognize the Gospels as written records based on the communal practice of remembering how to be part of the Jesus-movement as well. That some of these practices, for example, the reenactment of the Last Supper, are corroborated by both Paul and the Gospels reinforces the importance of those anamnestic practices to carry on the work of the Jesus-movement.

13. Dunn, *Jesus Remembered*, 247. Interestingly, Dunn's focus on orality and memory extends to Jesus' practices, but he does not draw out the implications for understanding how disciples remember Jesus in the practices of the Jesus-movement.

of Jesus are *actively* remembered by his disciples. This view, however, is in tension with one of the basic presumptions of much christology and historical-Jesus research: that there is a profound shift from the practices and teaching of Jesus to the practices and teaching of the other members of the Jesus-movement. Bultmann's dictum, that in the New Testament "the proclaimer became the proclaimed," has become a slogan for this presumption.

Martin Hengel's work provides a clear example of the way this presumption has affected much historical and theological scholarship about discipleship and the practices of the community. Hengel was heavily influenced by Max Weber's understanding of the charismatic individual who attracts other individuals who, in turn, then "institutionalize" (and thus often distort) the "charisma" to which they had responded when the charismatic figure has passed from the scene.[14] Weber's theory is a sociological (that is, it has the cachet of being "scientific") iteration of the "Great Man" view of history mentioned in chapter 4. Hengel took this Weberian construct as axiomatic. This led him to this claim:

> "Following" Jesus concretely as his μαθητής, as one called quite personally by him, and the related abandonment of family and possessions, cannot therefore have been the condition of participation in the approaching Kingdom of God for all. It applied only to those individuals in specific situations. . . . It was not from everyone who heard him that Jesus demanded this unique attachment to his person and his way, the expression of which attachment was "following after" him.[15]

Hengel's claim that not all who participated in the kingdom were to be disciples needs to be unpacked.

Many distinguish an "inner group" of disciples from other followers.[16] It seems obvious that any movement will have members with different levels of commitment and activity. The distinction is not a problem. However, that inner group, sometimes denominated as "the Twelve," may have been somewhat fluid, rather than exactly fixed in membership. While some try to harmonize the divergent lists in the Gospels, recognizing that different memories may reflect different membership seems a more likely way to take this divergence. Nor is it clear that the Twelve were an exclusive group. For instance, the fact that ten were indignant when James and John sought positions of privilege in the reign of God (Mark 10:41) suggests that privilege was not to be sought. Moreover, the missions of the Twelve and of the seventy are so similar that exclusivity seems ruled out, at least with regard to enacting the reign of God.

---

14. See Max Weber, *On Charisma and Institution Building: Selected Papers*, ed. S. N. Eisenstadt (Chicago: University of Chicago Press, 1968).

15. Martin Hengel, *The Charismatic Leader and His Followers*, ed. John Riches, trans. James C. G. Greig, Studies of the New Testament and Its World (Edinburgh: T&T Clark, 1996 [1st German ed., 1968]), 60.

16. See, e.g., Bruce Chilton and J. I. H. Mc Donald, *Jesus and the Ethics of the Kingdom,* Biblical Foundations in Theology (London: SPCK, 1987), 42, 96-99.

Hengel especially, however, despite his protests, reduced discipleship to an elite status. But the disciples were not necessarily a small, elite group. To limit the disciples in this way conflicts with the variety of those who were in the Jesus-movement. Could the seventy all be homeless wanderers? Can we even claim that Jesus was a homeless wanderer, when Mark reports that he "sat at table in his house [with] many toll collectors and sinners . . . for there were many who followed him" (2:15). Could Mary and Martha along with Simon the Leper provide him with something like a Judean home base in the village of Bethany? Hengel simply assumed that the only way to be a disciple was abandoning possessions and family—but it is not entirely certain that even Jesus did that! Surely some must have left all to become itinerant members of the Jesus-movement. But to assume that *all* had to abandon home and family creates the perception of discipleship as limited to an elite. In effect, Hengel excludes many of the women who were disciples by defining discipleship so narrowly.

The existence of such an elite would then consign some key members of the movement to a marginal status in the movement. Why accept that conclusion? Why assume that everyone had to be in the movement in the same way? Moreover, why accept Hengel's claim that Jesus did not want all who heard him to become his followers?[17] In short, Hengel's work offers a perspective that is derived more from presumptions brought to reading the texts than from analyzing the texts. There is nothing wrong, of course, with bringing presumptions to a text—all scholars do that. The problem is allowing these presumptions to answer the questions we might ask of the text. When the question is, Was there an elite among Jesus' followers? the answer needs to come from the text, not from the presumptions we bring to it. What Elisabeth Schüssler Fiorenza has shown us is that some of the "evidence" from the text can be explained as a function of such presumptions crossed with the kyriarchal character of ancient societies.

Hengel's view simply presumed that the invitation to discipleship was an extremely literal call for individuals to abandon all earthly duties and relationships to work for the coming of the reign of God by following Jesus. But why assume that "earthly duties" and working for the reign of God are in conflict? Whatever the reasons for doing so, these presumptions seem part of the interpreter's view, not part of the texts being interpreted.

Hengel also explicitly attributed the identification of "faith" and "discipleship" to a time when "the 'proclaimer' had become the 'proclaimed.'" This inclined him to read the text as if the followers of Jesus invented the identification of faith and discipleship. I find no convincing argument that the text shows this to be the case; this identification, too, is a function of Hengel's Weberian presumptions rather than of the texts under consideration.

Schüssler Fiorenza approaches the text by presuming a continuity between Jesus and the other members of the Jesus-movement.[18] She has provided a perspective

---

17. Hengel, *Charismatic Leader*, 62.

18. Obviously, Dunn (*Jesus Remembered*) has a similar presumption. In a rather different way, Pope Benedict XVI finds a continuity. He claims that "the deepest theme of Jesus' preaching was his own mystery, the mystery of the Son in whom God is among us and keeps his word; he announc-

that avoids both separating the charismatic individual from his followers and portraying the followers as inferior dependents. Hengel's explanation that the disciples' words and deeds "fall into the background"[19] in the Gospels assumes a radical separation between the charismatic leader and his followers. Why not assume that the mission deeds of the disciples begin already during Jesus' ministry as the stories of the sending of the Twelve and seventy say? Why not assume that their practices are simply more of the same once the first among equals, the first empowering agent, has shown them how to walk in the ways that are the reign of God? Why assume that they have no soteriological value, as Hengel does? Why not assume that the "almost inseparable fusion of the 'Jesus tradition' and community formation"[20] and the freedom of the disciples in adapting, rather than repeating by rote memory, are the ways that memory and discipleship function? The active memory of Jesus' practice, including teaching, is the key for unity between Jesus and his disciples, not an indicator of the distance between a charismatic leader and his followers.

Hengel acknowledges obliquely the creativity of the community. But such creativity is essential if a movement is to carry on a tradition it has received.[21] The disciples perceived Jesus as God's agent in that he showed them how to follow the way. However, that Jesus is God's agent does not necessarily make him a man so superior to the others in the movement that he is nearly superhuman. Nor does the fact that he is God's agent preclude disciples from being God's agents as well. Like his mother, Jesus accepted God's call to be God's agent despite the consequences (compare the attitudes in Luke 1:28 and 22:42). Do not all who are called to be disciples also have, in some sense, both the call to be God's agents in practice and the ability to respond to that call?

Like the eschatological dualism that Schottroff found to be a product of the Gospels' interpreters rather than of the Gospels (see n. 3 above), so the dualism

---

es the Kingdom of God as coming and as having come in his person" (*Jesus of Nazareth: From the Baptism in the Jordan to the Transfiguration*, trans. Adrian J. Walker [New York: Doubleday, 2007], 188). The present approach agrees with Benedict that the reign of God is both present where Jesus is and not yet complete. However, it differs from him in its focus on the movement brought into being by and through Jesus; his focus is more on the Jesus who inaugurates the movement. But it seems clear that the Bultmannian separation of the proclaimer from the proclaimed is no longer a tenable presumption for historical investigation or theological reflection, at least in its strong form. That the Jesus movement went further than Jesus did in proclaiming his significance, however, is obvious, but that is a development in continuity, not discontinuity.

19. Hengel, *Charismatic Leader*, 79.

20. Ibid., 83.

21. This is a generalization of the point of the argument of my *Inventing Catholic Tradition*. John E. Thiel makes an analogous point in *Senses of Tradition: Continuity and Development in Catholic Faith* (New York: Oxford University Press, 2000). The issue is to distinguish constructive from perverting creativity. Dunn is quite conscious of perverse creativity. His methodological comments on prophecy (perverse creativity that is not in continuity with the tradition) show, however, that false prophecy and excessive creativity are prime candidates for rejection as constituents of the community's tradition just because they do not fit with the community's memory of Jesus. See Dunn, *Jesus Remembered*, 186-92, for his argument for this very important insight about the communal power of memory and the consequent communal sifting of creative insights for authenticity.

between Jesus and the Jesus-movement is analogously much the product of the conceptual framework of modern biblical interpretation, exemplified especially by the Weberian orientation that shaped Hengel's view. In sum, there is no good reason not to presume a fundamental connection between the practices of Jesus and the practices of the members of the Jesus-movement.

Given this fundamental connection, we can recognize the practices of the mission as both rooted in Jesus' work and remembered and enacted by the whole Jesus-movement.

The pattern of being sent and returning goes like this: "And he called the twelve together and gave them power and authority over all demons and to cure diseases, and he sent them out to preach the kingdom of God and to heal. . . . On their return the apostles told him what they had done" (Luke 9:1-2, 10 RSV). The early communities remembered the disciples as doing three crucial things: they exorcised, they healed, and they preached—just as Jesus famously was remembered as doing and empowering them to do.[22] Here are the practices that the tradition inscribed in the texts as the remembered practices of the Jesus-movement. These are not, of course, the only practices, but they are a place to begin seeing what it means to have, in practice, the imaginative, faithful *phronēsis* that characterizes discipleship.

---

22. Interestingly, Yoder's ground-breaking work refers only in passing to these missionary practices (*Politics of Jesus*). While Yoder sees the text as offering a way for the church to be church as disciples, he evinces little interest in the early church's distinctive practices in discipleship. His focus is on Jesus, not on the disciples. Hengel seems primarily interested in separating the work of Jesus from that of the other members of the Jesus-movement, so that he also simply passes over the content of the disciples' work. He highlights the curing and exorcising, but says little about their prophecy and teaching.

Thirteen

EXORCISING AND HEALING

If I cast out demons by Beelzebul, by whom do your sons cast them out?
—Luke 11:19

*J*esus' exorcisms and other healings were remembered in multiple ways. As James D. G. Dunn put it, "One of the most compelling features of the whole sweep of ancient opinion regarding Jesus is his reputation as an exorcist and healer."[1] J. Ramsey Michaels noted, "Exorcism is clearly an integral and essential part of Jesus' ministry. References to demon possession and exorcism are embedded in every stratum of the gospel tradition."[2] Elaine Wainwright has shown that healing is a key characteristic in the Gospel of Mark, taking the forms of "the healing of named and or described physical illnesses and the casting out of demons or unclean spirits."[3] Paul Hollenbach claims that "Jesus not only explicitly stated that exorcisms are the central act of God in the world (Lk 11:20), but he also sent out his followers on an exorcising mission . . . which also indicates the central importance he attached to exorcisms."[4] A wide range of healings "were credited to Jesus during his mission, no doubt in marketplace gossip as well as disciple gatherings."[5] Exorcism and other healings were well-remembered practices of Jesus and the Jesus-movement.[6]

---

1. James D. G. Dunn, *Jesus Remembered*, vol. 1 of *Christianity in the Making* (Grand Rapids: Eerdmans, 2003), 670.

2. J. Ramsey Michaels, *Servant and Son: Jesus in Parable and Gospel* (Atlanta: John Knox, 1981), 154.

3. Elaine Wainwright, *Healing Women/Women Healing: The Genderization of Healing in Early Christianity* (London: Equinox, 2006), 100. Wainwright uses multiple hermeneutical tools, including feminist and postcolonial theory in her literary, historical, and sociocultural analysis. She reconstructs the placing of women in the early Christian health-care systems.

4. Paul W. Hollenbach, "Jesus, Demoniacs, and Public Authorities: A Socio-Historical Study," *Journal of the American Academy of Religion* 49, no. 4 (1981): 582.

5. Dunn, *Jesus Remembered*, 677.

6. John P. Meier, *A Marginal Jew: Rethinking the Historical Jesus*, vol. 2, *Mentor, Message, and Miracles*, Anchor Bible Reference Library (New York: Doubleday, 1994), 509-1038, is an exhaustive survey and analysis of Jesus' healings, exorcisms, and raising people from the dead. Meier finds that at least most of the stories can be reliably traced back to Jesus' lifetime. Meier also notes that the so-called nature miracles, with the exception of the stories of the feeding of a multitude, seem to belong to later tradition (970).

Remembering Jesus' Healing as Reconciling

Exorcism is one of a set of healing practices.[7] Demons were seen as the causes of some illnesses, evidently what we would call both mental and physical illnesses. However, because we no longer attribute illnesses to demons, we have to reinterpret the exorcising practices of the Jesus-movement if we are to carry on the practice.[8] Whether or not there were demons that the members of the Jesus-movement were actually successful in casting out is not the point here. The point is that whatever such exorcism meant in that society at that time—and the views are varied—members of the Jesus-movement were remembered as healers. However we interpret exorcism, it remains a healing practice.

The practices of healing were not limited to Jesus. Luke has Jesus respond to a challenge from unnamed onlookers who accused him of casting out demons by the power of the prince of demons. In turn, Jesus is remembered as challenging them with a counter-question: "If I cast out demons by Beelzebul, by whom do your sons cast them out?" (Luke 11:19).[9] This response confirms the point that exorcism was an established healing practice at the time. Apparently many engaged in it.

It should also be noted that Jesus did not oppose or condemn "their sons'" practice of exorcism. He merely used practitioners whom his interlocutors could not repudiate to counter their charge. These healers might have been fellow travelers who practically lived in and lived out the reign of God. While they may not have been members of the Jesus-movement, they also may have engaged in reconciling practices and made present the reconciliation of the reign of God.

Jesus did not claim authorization for his practice. Hence, Jesus was challenged to defend his—and, by extension, the disciples'—extraordinary practice. When he was accused of using demonic power, Jesus challenged his accusers. His rhetorical question functions to challenge the pattern of authorization. Jesus is claiming no less authority (and some more) than the "official" exorcists recognized by his

---

7. New Testament scholars divide and subdivide the exorcism and healing stories into multiple forms or patterns, each with a distinctive shape and purpose. This level of detail is generally more than we need here. For a thorough study of such detailed distinctions, see Meier, *Mentor, Message, and Miracles*, 509-970.

8. Today we have to adapt, rather than merely adopt, the exorcising ministry to confront whatever "demons" haunt us and to care for those who are afflicted, whatever the etiology of the affliction. That some still engage in explicit forms of exorcism does not mean that this is a necessary or sufficient way to understand how to carry on Jesus' exorcising and healing practices today. For a useful survey of some contemporary exorcising and deliverance practices, see Michael W. Cuneo, *American Exorcism: Expelling Demons in the Land of Plenty* (New York: Doubleday, 2001).

9. Martin Hengel (*The Charismatic Leader and His Followers*, ed. John Riches, trans. James C. G. Greig, Studies of the New Testament and Its World [Edinburgh: T&T Clark, 1996 (1st German ed., 1968)]) notes this (40). What he also notes is that the polemical claims about being a sorcerer and seducing the people that are found in Josephus and reported (independently?) by Hegesippus in a "legendary" form also are applied to the execution of James, Jesus' brother (Hengel, 41-42). What Hengel does not explore is the possibility that James is simply replicating the practice of Jesus, that James is not a dependent follower of Jesus but, like Jesus, is an observant Jew who is a central member of the Jesus-movement.

interlocutors. "If it is by the finger of God that I cast out demons," Jesus says, "then the reign of God has come upon you" (Luke 11:20). And—we can add—if it is by the finger of God in the name of Jesus that his disciples cast out demons, then the reign of God has also come upon those with whom they have worked.

The claim is clear: the practice of exorcising by the power of God realizes the reign of God. It is a practice of God's reign. In sum, Jesus was certainly not the only exorcist working at that time, and the members of the Jesus-movement were also, like Jesus, exorcising demons as agents of the reign of God and not by any authority granted by community officials.

The Gospels portray various conflicts between Jesus and his critics, especially the Pharisees, over his exorcising and curing practices. Paul Hollenbach has argued that Jesus acted in a way that was not merely "unauthorized"; rather, Jesus, by engaging in exorcism, severely challenged some social structures of his time.[10] Some of the verbal conflicts between Jesus and those who questioned his practice may have been embellished in light of later disputes when the Jesus-movement was working to establish its identity as a group both before and after the destruction of the Second Temple. Hence, this challenge may have been shaped by the developments of memories of Jesus.

"Sibling disputes" are part of establishing a social identity in a context of social difference or conflict. Once the "parent" of the Second Temple had been destroyed, the need to establish an identity independent of the temple must have been acutely felt by all of the movements in Judaism. The "rising" of Jesus and the "diminishing" of John may be at least partly, as noted in chapter 11, rhetorical moves to help establish the superiority of the Jesus-movement and thus preserve its identity. Nonetheless, the tradition evidently remembers a distinction between the practices of the Jesus-movement and other groups. In claiming to have direct authorization from God in both teaching and healing, Jesus is remembered as distinguishing his practice—and those of his disciples—from those who had other patterns of authorization from official political and religious authorities.

---

10. "Social structure" is admittedly vague. It includes the integrated religious, economic, and political systems that constituted a society that benefitted some and oppressed others. In the context of the Gospels, "social structure" presumes the sanctioning of specific exorcists by authorities in the community. The contemporary analogue to such sanctioning is the licensing of medical professionals. That licensing is a practice of social control by (sometimes extremely interested) parties with power is demonstrated for recent history in Paul Starr, *The Social Transformation of American Medicine* (New York: Basic Books, 1982). Those who engaged in "medical" practices that did not come to be recognized by the American Medical Association (e.g., chiropractors, naturopaths) were systematically excluded from the practices of healing available in hospitals and clinics. These unauthorized healing practices were excluded from support by government, the medical establishment, and insurance carriers. By limiting the number of students who could study medicine as well, the AMA and its allies also kept a hegemony of medical practice, thus keeping qualified practitioners relatively scarce and creating an economic situation in which demand exceeded supply—ensuring high profits for physicians, whose services were in short supply. High medical costs are not the result of "natural" factors alone but also of political and social interventions that create a scarcity of resources. Whether analogous restrictions were part of Second Temple Judaism remains speculative, but clearly there were competing exorcists and healers and, then and now, the elites who hold authority in the community can often successfully control practices by licensing practitioners.

As noted above, the healing ministries of Jesus and his disciples were not unique to them. There is no reason to think that this was the *only* alternative pattern of healing, or, as Elisabeth Schüssler Fiorenza has put it more generally, the "only reform movement at the time." Rather, it was "*one among several prophetic movements* of Jewish wo/men who struggled for the liberation of Israel."[11] The question of whether there were generally friendly or unfriendly relationships between these movements seems not answerable, simply because of the lack of historical data to support an answer.

Both the Pharisees and Herod, tetrarch of Galilee, are remembered as being hostile to Jesus. Hollenbach's thesis is that the opposition is at least in part due to Jesus' healing practice, which released the demoniacs from their outcast place in the social structure. The Jesus-movement clearly identified its healing not merely as a medical practice but as an indicator of God's reign.[12] Hollenbach found that the movement challenged "the prevailing social system and its underlying value system. . . . Jesus as an exorcist struck out directly into the vortex of the social turmoil of his day."[13] Again, this is not to say that *only* the Jesus-movement exorcised in an "unauthorized" manner or was the only group that was an emancipatory movement (which Hollenbach may have presumed). But it is clear that the Jesus-movement, which was remembered and endured, did engage in these practices.

The involved and elaborate story of the exorcism of the Gerasene demoniac offers some instructive notes.[14]

> They came to the other side of the sea, to the country of the Gerasenes. And when he had come out of the boat, there met him out of the tombs a man with an unclean spirit, who lived among the tombs; and no one could bind him any more, even with a chain; for he had often been bound with fetters and chains, but the chains he wrenched apart, and the fetters he broke to pieces; and no one had the strength to subdue him. Night and day among the tombs and on the mountains he was always crying out, and bruising himself with stones.
>
> And when he saw Jesus from afar, he ran and worshiped him, and crying out with a loud voice, he said, "What have you to do with me, Jesus, Son of the Most High God? I adjure you by God, do not torment me." For he had said to him, "Come out of the man, you unclean spirit!" And Jesus asked

---

11. Elisabeth Schüssler Fiorenza, *Jesus and the Politics of Interpretation* (New York: Continuum, 2000), 168; emphasis in original.

12. Compare Hollenbach, "Jesus, Demoniacs, and Public Authorities," 583.

13. Ibid., 580. It would be easy to imagine that this practice was unique to the Jesus-movement or that it was meant to replace existing exorcising practices. Such a supersessionist reading is unwarranted. More likely would be a view that the Jesus-movement extended the range of healing practices even though it was not authorized to do so.

14. See Meier, *Mentor, Message, and Miracles*, 650-53; Dunn, *Jesus Remembered*, 673-77; Amy-Jill Levine, *The Misunderstood Jew: The Church and the Scandal of the Jewish Jesus* (San Francisco: HarperSanFrancisco, 2006), 26; the translation here is adapted from Dunn's.

him, "What is your name?" He replied, "My name is Legion; for we are many." And he begged him eagerly not to send them out of the country.

Now a great herd of swine was feeding on the hillside; and they begged him, "Send us to the swine, let us enter them." So he gave them leave. And the unclean spirits came out, and entered the swine; and the herd, numbering about two thousand, rushed down the steep bank into the sea, and was drowned in the sea. The herdsman fled, and told it in the city and in the country.

And the people came to see what it was that had happened. And they came to Jesus, and saw the demoniac sitting there, clothed and in his right mind, the man who had had the legion; and they were afraid. And those who had seen it told what had happened to the demoniac and to the swine. And they began to beg Jesus to depart from their neighborhood. And as he was getting into the boat, the man who had been possessed with demons begged him that he might be with him. But he refused, and said to him, "Go home to your friends and tell them how much the Lord has done for you, and how he has had mercy on you." And he went away and began to proclaim in the Decapolis how much Jesus had done for him; and all men marveled. (Mark 5:1-20)

This complex story, first, is a composite. The story of the swine running into the sea after they were infected by the demons was probably inserted into the story of the cure of the demoniac by a storyteller in the tradition. Alone, either of the stories is possibly a recollection of actual events. Considered as a single story, however, there are lapses in continuity; the nearest sea, for example, is over thirty miles away from the site of the exorcism as portrayed in the story.[15] Hence, the compositeness of the story seems quite likely.

Second, the story is theologically inflected. As Meier notes:

The gruesome description of the demoniac's alienation from self, neighbor, and God is truly gripping (Mark 5:2-10), but for that very reason one must reckon with the possibility of a powerful imagination making a powerful theological as well as narrative point. Certainly, as the story stands in Mark, it serves the theological purpose of symbolizing the bringing of the healing, liberating message of the Christian gospel to the unclean Gentiles, a mission undertaken proleptically by Jesus himself.[16]

Mark's description, however gruesome, is entirely credible. Anyone who has worked with seriously and acutely mentally disturbed people can testify that they can have incredible strength as they resist, screaming, any attempts to prevent them from harming themselves and others. Mark depicts accurately the behavior

---

15. This explains, perhaps, why Matthew re-placed the story from Gerasa to Gadara on the southeastern shore of the Sea of Galilee; see Dunn, *Jesus Remembered*, 675 n. 281.

16. Meier, *Mentor, Message, and Miracles*, 652.

patterns of some people trapped in an acute psychotic breakdown (whatever one may think of psychosis or demon possession). The demoniac here fights with the exorcist, attempts to bind Jesus into his possession, and (mockingly?) worships Jesus. Clearly, this man is sick, has broken off from friends, family, and God, and needs reconciliation with God, himself, and his family and friends.

And it happens! The healing effects reconciliation. Evidently, the man goes home cured and proclaims the one who cured him. Like the Samaritan woman, he proclaims Jesus to those who were not Jews.

Although the location of this story is not entirely clear, Meier opines that this is set in the midst of an area where gentiles were found. Hence he construes it as Mark places the story, so that Jesus reaching out to cure a person, who, if he was not a gentile, was cured where gentiles could hear of it. And according to the story, they did hear of it: the cured man proclaimed in the Decapolis what had happened to him.

Amy-Jill Levine points out that the pigs are a "clue" to the presence of numerous gentiles and that the Jews would not have "mourned the loss of a herd of hogs, animals that are not kosher and that represent conspicuous consumption, in that they cost more to raise than they produce in meat."[17] Now Jesus was not against eating and drinking—a point made in chapter 16 below. Yet here is animal husbandry that may reduce the amount of food available for people. Letting the demons occupy and destroy the bodies of the swine may have helped create the more just conditions typical of the *basileia tou theou,* where all could eat together.

Finally, there is real subversion here. When Jesus asks the demons their name, "Legion" is the response. Christian exegetes do not want to make too much of this. Levine calls this "a nice political dig against Rome."[18] But this minimization seems confused. The general consensus among biblical scholars is that the Romans were finally responsible for Jesus' execution and that the passion narratives attempted to minimize that involvement because the Jesus-movement was distinguishing itself from Judaism and seeking to become more politically acceptable in Greco-Roman circles decades after Jesus' death. Hence, this "dig" is likely an early part of the tradition, suggesting that Jesus' opposition to the powers of evil could also be seen as opposition to the power of the occupying forces of the Roman Empire. It is unlikely to be a late addition.

Exorcisms, however understood, may be performed, at least by Jesus, by calling demons out of people. However, these are not just cures of individuals but healings that enable a community to be reconciled—the Gerasene demoniac was restored into his circle of friends and family. If we were interested in "what the actual man Jesus did," we would be interested in whether the miracle occurred. But as we are interested in the reconciling practices of the Jesus-movement (including Jesus, of course), the key is what the exorcism of the afflicted person did for the community. It was a means of reconciliation. It was a practice of the

---

17. Levine, *Misunderstood Jew*, 25.
18. Ibid.

Jesus-movement realizing the *basileia tou theou*, not a trick of a wonder-worker or magician.[19]

The other form of healing is the healing of specific diseases. A vignette in the Gospel of Mark tells of one interesting example:

> And immediately he left the synagogue, and entered the house of Simon and Andrew, with James and John. Now Simon's mother-in-law lay sick with a fever, and immediately they told him of her. And he came and took her by the hand and lifted her up, and the fever left her; and she served them. (Mark 1:29-31 RSV)

This brief story is the first physical healing in the Gospel of Mark. Like the last physical-healing story, that of the cure of the blindness of Bartimaeus (Mark 10:46-52), this story does not end with the healing. As Wainwright put it, "It goes on to describe the woman's ongoing healed state: she was serving them (διηκόνει)."[20] The story of Bartimaeus's healing has him following Jesus to Jerusalem. "Healing is about transformation, a transformation that opens into participation in the *basileia* which Jesus is preaching and enabling."[21] Jesus enables both of them to do good.

But was Simon's mother-in-law enabled only to serve them as a housewife might? Wainwright argues otherwise. She notes that hearers would have heard this story often in the context of Mark's Gospel. The multiple hearings meant that "they could understand the woman's service, like Bartimaeus' following, in light of the closing of the Gospel when the faithful female disciples follow Jesus to the foot of the cross, ministering to him."[22] The hearers could take the service of the healed mother-in-law as the service, the *diakonia*, of a disciple. Like Bartimaeus, she could be heard to follow Jesus after she was cured. "Healing could open into discipleship in the Markan world of healing for women as well as men, and that discipleship meant participation in the community of healers that was the *basileia* movement."[23] The healed became the healers who engaged in the reconciling practice that restored the ill and possessed to their lives in community. The Jesus-movement carried on the reconciling practice of healing.

The Jesus-Movement as Healing and Reconciling

Jesus' disciples also are remembered as having had some success in carrying out his pattern of exorcising and healing. Luke reports the mission of the seventy:

---

19. Jon Sobrino (*Jesus the Liberator: A Historical-Theological Reading of Jesus of Nazareth*, trans. Paul Burns and Francis McDonagh [Maryknoll, NY: Orbis Books, 1993], 94) makes this last point by examining the verbs used in the New Testament, contrasting them with those used in the narrations of other exorcisms; unfortunately, the textual sources for the other verbs are not cited.

20. Wainwright, *Healing Women/Women Healing*, 110.

21. Ibid., 110.

22. Ibid., 111.

23. Ibid.

After this, the Lord appointed seventy others, and sent them on ahead of him, two by two, into every town and place where he himself was about to come. And he said to them, "The harvest is plentiful, but the laborers are few; pray therefore the lord of the harvest to send out laborers into his harvest. Go your way; behold, I send you as lambs in the midst of wolves. Carry no purse, no bag, no sandals; and salute no one on the road. Whatever house you enter, first say, 'Peace be to this house.' And if a son of peace is there, your peace shall rest upon him; but if not, it shall return to you. And remain in the same house, eating and drinking whatever they provide, for the laborer deserves his wages; do not go from house to house. Whenever you enter a town and they receive you, eat what is set before you; heal the sick in it and say to them, 'The reign of God has come near to you.' . . . He who hears you, hears me and he who rejects you rejects me, and he who rejects me rejects him who sent me." The seventy returned with joy, saying, "Lord, even the demons are subject to us in your name." He said to them, "I watched Satan fall from heaven like a flash of lightning." (Luke 10:1-9, 16-18 RSV adapted).

Luke 10:17 suggests that the disciples were participating in an unauthorized practice—for the demons were subject to them in *Jesus'* name. Like Jesus, the disciples' practice was extraordinary. Their authority had a remarkable source—Jesus, and evidently Jesus claimed to have divine authority in casting out demons. In sending the disciples out, Jesus the teacher was sending out students who were ready to show that they had the "know-how" to exorcise. They learned that ability from Jesus, who empowered them. They went out, returned to him, and reported. Thus, exorcising is a ministry remembered as a practice that the disciples had learned and then engaged in, even when Jesus was alive.

Exorcising in the reign of God could liberate the demoniacs from their despised place and reconcile them into the community, if not the *basileia tou theou* (remember, the Gadarene demoniac was sent back to his friends and family; though an evangelist, as Mark puts it, he does not join Jesus in his travels).

Reconciliation is the key to the exorcising practice of the Jesus-movement. Their exorcising practice is a key to realizing "the emancipatory Divine Wisdom movement of which [Jesus] was a part. . . ."[24] The point is to note that not only Jesus, but also the Jesus-movement, exorcised demons. Jesus exorcised and cured the rich and the poor, Jews and gentiles, males and females. He exorcised a man in the synagogue (Mark 1:23-28), the Gerasene demoniac (Mark 5:1-20), a possessed boy (Mark 9:14-27), and, according to Luke 8:2, Mary Magdalene (although there is no narrative of this). He heals Simon Peter's mother-in-law (Mark 1:29-31), a

---

24. Schüssler Fiorenza, *Jesus and the Politics of Interpretation*, 21. Like Schüssler Fiorenza, I do not take this to imply a supersessionism. It is not that the Jesus-movement was in some way "better" than other movements for equality in the community and fidelity to the convenant in Jesus' time, and thus "better than" Pharisaic Judaism (also a reform movement) or the instantiation of a final, new covenant that supplanted and invalidated the covenants God made with all humanity or Judaism. Even a full-fledged incarnational theology does not require that religious supersessionism.

leper (Mark 1:40-45), a paralytic man (Mark 2:1-12), the daughter of Jairus, a leader of the synagogue, and, along the way to Jairus's house, a woman with a hemorrhage (Mark 5:21-43), a deaf and dumb man (Mark 7:31-37), and the blind man at Bethsaida (Mark 8:22-27), among others. Dunn summarizes clearly the historical significance of the healings and exorcisms: "Whatever we now may think of the events which might have occasioned these stories, the most obvious conclusion to draw is that there were various incidents during Jesus' mission which were experienced/witnessed as miracles, understood as healings brought about by divine power flowing through Jesus."[25] And we would have to add to Dunn's point, "brought about by the divine power flowing through the Jesus-movement" as well because the disciples also exorcised in Jesus' name.

This practice, however, evoked a struggle. Sobrino suggests that the powers that opposed the *basileia tou theou* and the Jesus-movement that sought to realize it were the powers of the Evil One.[26] When, on the return of the seventy, Jesus responded that he had seen Satan fall from the sky, the significance is clear: opposition to the reign of God is the work of the power for evil in the universe, the power that divides rather than reconciles, accuses rather than forgives, and makes people mad rather than whole. When the reign of God is realized, Satan is dethroned.

As with the authority and ability to exorcise, the Jesus-movement heals by the authority of God. This authority can be seen with the curing of the paralytic. The scene (Mark 2:1-12 and parallels) connects Jesus' forgiving the man's sins with his curing of the man's paralysis—a point to which we shall return. But what is often neglected is that Peter also cured a paralytic who was lame from birth. The man lay at the gate of the temple "which is called Beautiful" to ask alms. Peter, who had no money to give him, said "'but I give you what I have; in the name of Jesus Christ of Nazareth, walk.' And he took him by the right hand and raised him up, and immediately his feet and ankles were made strong. And leaping up he stood and walked and entered the temple with them, walking and leaping and praising God" (Acts 3:6-10). What is remarkable about this scene (however much telling and retelling the story has embellished it) is not merely that Peter replicated a cure performed by Jesus, but rather that in doing so he freed a man from the disability that kept him in his place as a cripple at the gate and out of his place as a Jew in the temple. The story portrays Peter not as forgiving the man's sins but as launching into a proclamation witnessing to the power of God in Jesus, "and the faith which is through Jesus has given this man perfect health in the presence of you all" (Acts 6:16 RSV), for which Peter is later imprisoned (a consequence, alas, of acting so that the reign of God—for however brief a time and place—has come in power).

The cures of the Jesus movement removed people from positions of dependence and marginalization. Jesus' curing of lepers, the blind, the hemorrhaging, and others frees them not only from bodily misery but also from the social stigmas

---

25. Dunn, *Jesus Remembered*, 683.
26. Sobrino, *Jesus the Liberator*, 95.

that ostracized them. Peter's cure similarly transformed a mere beggar lying at the gate of the temple into a temple-goer, a man who could walk into the temple like a good Jew at the time of prayer. He could take his proper place as a Jew, not a place assigned him by his disability.

The pattern is clear: the exorcising and healing practices of Jesus and the Jesus-movement challenged in particular the divisions created in and by a cultural system that marginalized the ill. Isolating contagious diseases makes sense, but when one does that one also isolates the diseased person. No longer a full part of the community, the isolated one needs healing in order to be reconciled.

Possession by demons represented physical or mental illness in a society less developed than ours in its medical understanding and practices. Calling someone "possessed" by a demon could also serve "not only as a means for the oppressed to express their degradation, but also . . . as a means for the dominant classes to subdue those who protested against their oppression."[27] What better way to silence and subjugate people than by accusing them of being possessed by demons! So is it surprising that Jesus was challenged about the source of his own ability? The Jesus-movement cured people of demonic possession with the result that they could speak out about their subjugation and rejoin the society that had marginalized them because they were no longer possessed. The Jesus-movement freed people not only from their mental or physical illnesses as a result of their exorcising practice, but also from having to participate in a sociopolitical system that marginalized them by construing them as dirty and dangerous. In sum, healing in general and exorcism in particular reestablished the relationship of those who had been excluded by the larger community; it was a reconciling practice.

According to the Acts of the Apostles, after Stephen was killed and the persecution began, Philip went to a city in Samaria, preaching, healing, and exorcising. "For unclean spirits came out of many who were possessed, crying with a loud voice; and many who were paralyzed or lame were healed. So there was much joy in that city" (Acts 8:7-8). The practice of exorcism was one undertaken by the Jesus-movement before and after Jesus' death and resurrection. The practice created controversy (in Acts, at least with Simon Magus, and evidently with at least part of the established exorcising and healing authority structures that continued to persecute the movement as sorcerers and seducers of the people to revolution[28]). But notice the results of the healing: it brought much joy to the city. The point of the exorcisms and healings was not to amaze or prosper but to bring joy—I would think of reunion—to those who had been forced to isolate the ill and to those who were isolated.

What made the Jesus-movement distinctive was not that it cast out demons, as Jesus did, by the will of God. Rather, it exorcised and healed by the will of God shown through the use of the name of Jesus—such is the inference from the missions of the disciples reported in Luke 10. The warning to beware of false prophets in Matthew includes a reference to exorcism:

---

27. Hollenbach, "Jesus, Demoniacs, and Public Authorities," 581.
28. Hengel (*Charismatic Leader*, 40-42) discusses the evidence for this ongoing opposition.

"Not every one who says to me, 'Lord, Lord,' shall enter the kingdom of heaven, but he who does the will of my Father who is in heaven. On that day many will say to me, 'Lord, Lord, did we not prophesy in your name, and cast out demons in your name, and do many mighty works in your name? And then will I declare to them, 'I never knew you: depart from me, you evildoers.'" (Matt. 7:21-23 RSV)

The will of the Father is the advent of the reign. Some might appear to do what Jesus did, and even use his name, but unless those practices of healing and exorcising were performed as part of realizing the *basileia tou theou*, then those actions would be "false" to the Jesus-movement. They engaged in another political practice that was not pointed to realizing *basileia tou theou*. Perhaps their healing practice was not "nested" with the other practices of the reign of God.

The point of the practice of exorcising and healing is not the doing of good deeds—or deeds of power—alone. The point of the practice is the reconciliation of people with and in the community. Healing does not simply restore the physical or mental health of the individual involved; rather, it restores that person to the community. In healing the sick or sinful or possessed person, the Jesus movement reconciled the afflicted with the community from which he or she had been separated.

But healers can heal the first among equals as well. In Wainwright's skilled interpretive hands, the anointing of Jesus by an unnamed woman (Matt. 26:6-13) shows the circle of healing. She writes:

As for this woman at this time (26.11), it is not the needy who stand in the place of Jesus but it is he himself who is the most needy. . . . [T]he parabling healer becomes the one in need of healing. Over the head and body of the healer she pours out the gift that she has received from the earth, the ointment in the alabaster jar. And, as the story indicates, Jesus is healed and strengthened to go into what lies ahead. It is this that will be told to her memory.[29]

While it is not clear that Jesus needed to be reconciled with the members of the Jesus-movement or even with the will of his Father, he is prepared for his death by the ministry of the unnamed woman. This anointing does not reconcile people as much as it empowers Jesus to face his future—a truly imminent future, for the next episode in Matthew's Gospel begins the passion with Judas's betrayal.

Healing Today?

For many centuries Christians have cared for the sick, the injured, the wounded, and the infirm aged as a way of continuing the healing practices of the Jesus-

---

29. Wainwright, *Healing Women/Women Healing*, 158.

movement. Is contemporary medical practice, in our commodified society with its "for-profit" paradigm of medical practice, a way to engage in the healing practices portrayed in the New Testament today? I would argue not.

We have come to take the practice of medicine as "curing diseases" and "beating death" rather than "caring for people." Even more important, our capitalist, market-driven paradigm has spawned "for profit" hospitals and created the conditions in which insurance companies deny patients, as often as possible, access to care that is expensive because the insurers call the treatments "experimental." The goal of the practices of healing as reconciliation has been overwhelmed by the corporate goals of maximizing shareholders' return.

This is not to deny that caring for people so as to enable them to live as full members of the community is still possible. For over a decade, beginning some forty years ago, I worked as a hospital nursing orderly, caring for literally thousands of men, women, and children who came to us doubled over by back pain, bleeding from wounds, comatose from the low blood sugar of an undiagnosed diabetic condition, crippled with arthritis, infected with virulent diseases from septicemia to leprosy, screaming and violent from psychotic breakdowns that made them intent on harming themselves and others, or afflicted by a variety of conditions. Some of them we could not "cure," since their diseases were incurable or their injuries too severe.

One of the most remarkable patients we encountered was a young man who was comatose for weeks due to a brain injury. He had also lost his foot in a motorcycle crash—that could not be "cured." We cared for him those weeks, nourishing him, cleaning his body, talking to him, stretching his joints—and all the other things nurses did, although he didn't respond. Yet strange things happen. After two days off, I entered his room in the morning with the registered nurse on duty. When out of the blue he greeted me with, "Hi, Terry," we both wept with wonder and joy. We wept again when he returned a few months later, striding onto the neurosurgical ward on his prosthesis and smiling to thank us for his care, to tell us he was back in school, and to show off his gait. And I remember laughing hysterically when a classic "little old lady" severely crippled with arthritis joked that the surgery for her rectal cancer that left her with a colostomy made it possible for her to clean herself again since her arthritis meant that she could "no longer reach her asshole." Over others, though, we neither wept nor laughed for joy, but grieved in sorrow that we had "lost" her or him—the patient was no longer part of our community even if we could believe that all of God's people were united in the communion of saints. I prayed over all of the hundreds I "took down to the morgue." Like all the dead, their presence for us was in the mode of memory and of absence.

How can we exercise the healing practices of the Jesus-movement today? Alas, our national standard of care is captured in banners that proclaim our real values—banners flying in the women's cosmetics department of Macy's department store in Manhattan: "Stem cells . . . the future of skin regeneration." To proclaim that the morally problematic and medically costly practices of harvesting stem cells is to be used to preserve our skin from aging lines is, at best having a mind *ta tōn anthrōpōn.*[30] These ways "are not God's ways, but humans'," to borrow a phrase explored in chapter 8.

The economics of contemporary medical care seem not greatly unlike the economics of ancient pig farming: spending money to feed pigs cost more than it returned and set the conditions for increasing hunger among the impoverished. Spending money on cosmetic care for the rich rather than seeing how best to develop and distribute our resources is not caring for the sick in a way appropriate to the reign of God. Denying benefits to those who need them simply because they are poor is inappropriate to the reign of God.

Some have abandoned—at least for part of the year—the hurly-burly of American medicine. Many donate weeks or months of their time to serve poorly served populations. For example, emergency physician Patrick N. Connell, M.D., spends about half of each year on the island of Roatan off the coast of Honduras. He contributes his time and substantial amounts of his own money so that he can drive around the island in a battered Nissan pick-up truck and treat "everything from diabetes to dengue fever for a free-standing clinic that was started out of an American nurse's kitchen."[31] There are no hassles about insurance and there are no profits. As Connell put it, "practicing medicine is a gift, not a right . . . and I'm finding a way to share it."[32] Connell is one of many who engage in an "alternative practice" to commodified, profit-driven medicine.

Some suspect that the time has come for religious orders to leave the apostolate of hospitals and hospices and to find other ways to instantiate the healing ministry of Jesus, as in L'Arche and the Sant'Egidio movement. Others are convinced that they should stay to provide an alternative to for-profit medicine and live out an ongoing, effective witness of another form of healing practice—one that is not about cures and profits but about caring and reconciling people with their community and the communities with their sick and injured members.

Today's burning questions should not be seen as *whether* some or many of us should engage in medical practices, but *how* at least some of us can engage in the practice of healing in a way that continues the practices that began with the first members of the Jesus-movement and were continued by women and men who cared for the sick and injured throughout history as part of their own calling to lives of reconciliation. Some disciples have always been healers. The issue is not whether we should be healers but how to carry on that practice so that it is a practice of God's reign today. These questions admit of no easy answers, but the contrast of the goals of much contemporary healing practice and those of the Jesus-movement's practices of healing means that they must be asked.

---

30. Banners observed August 1, 2007; of course, someone might say that these banners could mean "adult stem cells," rather than embryonic stem cells; but then the moral repugnance shifts from both harvesting the stem cells and production of the cosmetics to the misuse of productive resources. Even if no one were denied medical care because their care would be a "medical loss" for their insurance companies, this cosmetic medical practice would still stink to heaven.

31. "Docs Abroad," *Phoenix Magazine,* April, 2008, 221.

32. Ibid.

Fourteen

TEACHING

He was praying in a certain place, and when he had finished, one of his disciples said to him, "Lord, teach us how to pray just as John taught his disciples."   —Luke 11:1

$\mathcal{T}$hose who have engaged in quests for the historical Jesus have debated what Jesus "really" taught, especially about the reign of God, since the beginning of the quests over two hundred years ago. The present chapter recognizes that Jesus was an observant Jew attempting to live in and live out God's reign. As such, he was fundamentally a teacher of Torah, of the rule of the reign of God. The present chapter places the content of his teaching in the context of his teaching practice.

Many analyses or syntheses of Jesus' teaching focus on interpreting what Jesus taught.[1] The general rubric is to explore the heart of Jesus' teaching: the coming/ present reign of God.[2] Partisans of the view that Jesus taught that the reign of God is present or imminent have debated with partisans of the view that he taught that the reign of God is distant. Compromise positions, for example, that the New Testament displays a "proleptically realized eschatology" in texts about the

---

1. Any attempt to list the more significant volumes would take up at least as much space as the present chapter. In addition to the numerous "historical-Jesus" books mentioned and discussed in other places in this text, three recent additions to the literature are significant. Luise Schottroff (*The Parables of Jesus*, trans. Linda M. Maloney [Minneapolis: Fortress, 2006]) reviews much of the literature on Jesus' parables and proposes a new "eschatological" approach that is rather consonant with the position taken in this book. Robert Barron (*The Priority of Christ: Toward a Postliberal Catholicism* [Grand Rapids: Brazos, 2007]) bases a theological approach on an "iconic" christology with a grid of "Gatherer, Warrior, King" to summarize the teaching and practices of Jesus. Joseph Ratzinger [Pope Benedict XVI] (*Jesus of Nazareth: From the Baptism in the Jordan to the Transfiguration*, trans. Adrian J. Walker [New York: Doubleday, 2007]) offers a "personal" theological reflection that proffers insights built up over decades of reflection and teaching. Although he recognizes the legitimacy of historical-critical methods (xvi), his work makes little direct use of historians' contributions. Schottroff is excellent on Jesus' parables, while Ratzinger is insightful on Jesus' aphorisms, which represent the ways in which Jesus was a teacher of Torah.

2. "The centrality of the kingdom of God (*basileia tou theou*) in Jesus' preaching is one of the least disputable, or disputed, facts about Jesus" (James D. G. Dunn, *Jesus Remembered*, vol. 1 of *Christianity in the Making* [Grand Rapids: Eerdmans, 2003], 383). In different ways various authors discuss this message. See, e.g., John P. Meier, vol. 2, *Mentor, Message, and Miracles*, Anchor Bible Reference Library (New York: Doubleday, 1994), 237-506; or Terrence W. Tilley, *Story Theology* (Wilmington, DE: Michael Glazier, 1985), 78-100.

coming of God's reign have also been proposed. The debates have not resolved the problem of being able to warrant historically just what Jesus did teach.

However, Jesus did teach his disciples how to pray. The Lord's Prayer compiles petitions that fill out the prayer that the reign of God come soon.[3] Living in and living out the reign of God is hallowing God's name. The reign of God is the time and the place that we each and all receive the basics of life—our daily bread. The reign of God is the time and place in which we forgive and are forgiven our debts and trespasses. We pray not to be tempted to abandon the ways of God for the ways of the Evil One. In the present approach, the crucial thing is not learning what Jesus taught but learning how to engage in the practices of God's reign.[4]

In changing the default settings from orality to literacy, from interpreting texts to responding to acts, and from a focus on christological doctrine to christology as practice, the present text cannot avoid a different approach to the question of Jesus' teaching from the usual one about what he taught. If engaging in the practices of the reign of God is what discipleship is all about, then the reign of God is realized whenever and wherever the disciples practice their faith. The "ontological" questions about God's reign are, bluntly, irrelevant. The issue is practical. God reigns wherever and whenever the disciples live in and live out God's reign. That God does not reign everywhere is due neither to an eschatological deferral nor to the reign not arriving when Jesus expected, but to the fact that not many communities, Christian or other, truly engage in the practices of reconciliation that constitute God's reign in practice, at least in this world.

If Jesus is indeed God's agent who empowers people to engage in such practices when they are his disciples, then that empowerment consists in his teaching the disciples *how* to engage in these practices. What is crucial about Jesus' teaching is not *what content* he teaches but what he teaches the disciples *to do* and what attitudes Jesus is remembered as finding to be proper for disciples. Jesus is remembered as a teacher, of course, and we cannot avoid examining content. But, as in the epigraph for this chapter, the question is how. That question always lingers, if sometimes in the background, for it is crucial to understanding the teaching of the disciples' Jesus.

Michael Amaladoss has offered a perceptive, practical account of Jesus' teaching practice. He wrote:

> The teaching of Jesus does not give us information about heavenly realities. He does not speak about God's inner being or life. He does not describe life in heaven. He does not set up a ritual organization focused on the sacred.

---

3. Analyses of the Lord's Prayer abound. Yet perhaps the better approach is through meditative reflection, prayerful reflection on the practice of prayer. This is beyond the scope of this book, but is at the heart of Cardinal Carlo Maria Martini's book *Praying as Jesus Taught Us: Meditations on the Our Father*, trans. John Belmonte, S.J. (Lanham, MD: Sheed & Ward, 2001). Ratzinger, *Jesus of Nazareth*, 128-68, is another source for such reflection on the Lord's Prayer.

4. Georges M. Soares-Prabhu, writing in the context of Catholicism in India, also has a fundamentally "how" rather than "what" approach to Jesus' teaching. See his *The Dharma of Jesus*, ed. Francis Xavier D'Sa (Maryknoll, NY: Orbis Books, 2003), 175-243.

When he finally leaves a sign for his disciples to remember him by, it is the common gesture of sharing a meal in community, eating and drinking together in his memory. He tells us *how* to live and *how* to relate to one another and to God. He talks in the context of life in this world. He uses ordinary examples with which everyone is familiar: the lilies in the field, the sower going out to sow, the growing corn, the trees and the birds of the air that come to rest on them, the sea and those whose living depends on it, the suffering and the marginalized poor, unjust rulers, the loving and forgiving parent. That is why his teaching has universal resonance.[5]

Jesus also should, of course, be understood as an interpreter of Torah, but Amaladoss brings out the availability of his teaching and its focus on *how* to live.

Jesus' teaching practice is preserved in the memories of the disciples. While the Gospels preserve memories of the disciples' healing and exorcising practice before the death and resurrection of Jesus, there are no recorded memories of the disciples' teaching before Jesus' death. What remains is only an injunction of Jesus to the Twelve: "And he called the twelve together and gave them power and authority over all demons and to cure diseases, and he sent them out to preach the reign of God and to heal" (Luke 9:1-2 RSV adapted). After his death and resurrection, of course, there are numerous examples of the disciples preaching—indeed the Gospels are just that, if we are to believe their roots in orality. The stories told and recorded of Jesus' teaching are the disciples' preaching what they remembered Jesus teaching.

Beyond the remarkable narration of salvation history from the perspective of Jesus' disciples, recorded as the preaching that got Stephen martyred (Acts 7:2-53), numerous examples of preaching about Jesus and his significance are preserved, including Peter's, mentioned in the previous chapter, regarding the faith that brought the lame man to health. That the disciples proclaimed and preached Jesus in a way that goes beyond Jesus' claims for himself is clear. Paul, for example, says things about Jesus that we have no reason to think Jesus could have or would have said about himself. However, in the process of remembering and narrating the stories of Jesus' life and work, the disciples also proclaimed what they had learned and remembered about him and his fundamental work—the coming of the reign of God. There is not a huge gulf between his preaching and theirs. Rather, his preaching effectively became theirs as they recapitulated his aphorisms and parables.[6]

The Bultmannian slogan that "the proclaimer became the proclaimed" implies a real discontinuity between what Jesus did and preached and what his disciples did and preached. It is unfortunate that its appropriate use, e.g., regarding the placing of most, if not all, of the titles of honor into Jesus' sayings as a retrojection,

---

5. Michael Amaladoss, S.J., *The Asian Jesus* (Maryknoll, NY: Orbis Books, 2006), 33; emphasis added. Not everything Jesus taught resonates universally. Understanding some aspects of his teaching requires understanding the very particular context in which he practiced.

6. Martin Hengel (*The Charismatic Leader and His Followers*, ed. John Riches, trans. James C. G. Greig [Edinburgh: T&T Clark, 1996 (1st German ed., 1968)], 80-83) notes this.

has been overextended.[7] The disciples were as much participants in the Jesus-movement as was the man Jesus. As a human being, Jesus was the first among equals[8] in the movement. As God's prime incarnate agent, Jesus was and is the presence of God empowering them.[9] Of course, there was some difference between Jesus' preaching and that of the other members of the Jesus-movement—after all, whatever they preached that is recorded in the scripts of the Gospels was colored by Jesus' death and resurrection as his own teaching could not be. But once we change the default setting to the primacy of orality, as Dunn shows, we can presume that continuity—although continuity creatively adapted, not slavishly replicated—is to be taken for granted, rather than discontinuity. We can presume continuity unless there is reason to prefer a finding of discontinuity. The burden of proof is on those who would find the discontinuity.

The Bultmannian slogan can obscure our vision of how the disciples could carry on the work that they identified as Jesus' work. It was not that they proclaimed him (though they did) as much as that they remembered him by doing what he had done as he had done it, teaching what he had taught as he taught it, and even dying as he did—martyred prophets of the *basileia tou theou*. When Schüssler Fiorenza calls Jesus "the first among equals," she recognizes that the disciples have learned, with him and from him, to be healers and teachers *as he was*. They share with him the political practice of challenging established boundaries by reconciling the outcast, healing the injured, and proclaiming that such reconciliation was the presence of the *basileia*.

The disciples clearly spoke in Jesus' name. Since he was sent by God, and he sent them, they, too, were sent by God. That they were sent to speak and heal in Jesus' name has long been recognized. However, historical criticism made this practice into a problem that historical critics could then try to solve: how do we distinguish in these written texts what is attributable to the historical Jesus and what belongs to the early church. But once we change the default settings not only to "orality" but also to the historic, remembered Jesus, this problem changes its

---

7. See Ratzinger, *Jesus of Nazareth*, which criticizes this approach on a somewhat different basis. However, he attributes Jesus' deepest teaching to be about who he is as God's son (188). In doing so, however, he ignores the regnant historical claim that the christological images in the New Testament are shaped in large part by *responses* to Jesus' teaching and the concerns of the authors of the Gospels. Ratzinger writes, "Jesus understands himself as Torah—as the Word of God in person" (110) on the basis of an uncritical reading of the Gospel of John and of the Sermon on the Mount as an actual event, rather than as a creative compilation and setting by Matthew. While one can take such contrarian positions, to do so without argument for them in the face of the consensus of biblical scholars opposing one's view undermines this important part of his interpretation. A recent useful text that includes articles on the christological images and portraits of the New Testament is *Who Do You Say That I Am? Essays on Christology*, ed. Mark Allan Powell and David R. Bauer (Louisville: Westminster John Knox, 1999).

8. Elisabeth Schüssler Fiorenza, *Jesus and the Politics of Interpretation* (New York: Continuum, 2000), 167.

9. Of course, this is fundamentally a religious and theological claim, not a fundamentally historical one like the claim that Jesus was "first among equals." The work of Larry Hurtado, discussed in chap. 6, shows how early this sort of claim arose in the life of the movement. What historical work cannot warrant is the actual truth status of the claim.

shape. No longer is the goal to strip the husk of commentary from the kernel of Jesus' very teaching (as Adolf Harnack put it over a century ago), but to understand how the community's memory both transmits and distorts Jesus' teaching in the context of both his physical absence and his real presence as resurrected in and to the community.

The frequency with which "Jesus" explains or applies the parables in the Synoptic Gospels, for example, is very likely a development in the oral traditioning process.[10] As they passed on the stories they had learned, explanations and interpretations that the storytellers gave became part of the story. As the stories were retold, Jesus' disciples included those explanations and interpretations when they retold the stories. This is not necessarily a distortion of the teaching that the disciples remembered as from Jesus, but rather a refraction of that teaching in different circumstances. The first disciples might have gotten the point without being told, but later tellings sometimes may have had to make the point explicit. In short, as stories are retold, some items that may have once been a narrator's interpretation become retold as a character's explication. This point can be illustrated as we examine the parable of the rescue of the man in the ditch. We can examine the parable to show just what Jesus' practice was and how the tradition that remembered his teaching shaped it.[11]

The Parable of the Traveler in the Ditch

Luke's script is an amalgam of "forms." This script—as composed by Luke or earlier, even in the oral tradition—incorporates narratives from different genres to give a place to telling a story of Jesus. The text runs as follows:

> Just then a lawyer stood up to test Jesus. "Teacher," he said, "what must I do to inherit eternal life?" He said to him, "What is written in the law? What do you read there?" He answered, "You shall love the Lord your God with all your heart, and with all your soul, and with all your mind; and your neighbor as yourself." And he said to him, "You have given the right answer; do this, and you will live."
>
> But wanting to justify himself, he asked Jesus, "And who is my neighbor?"
>
> Jesus replied, "A man was going down from Jerusalem to Jericho, and fell into the hands of robbers who stripped him, beat him, and went away, leaving him half dead. Now by chance a priest was going down that road;

---

10. See Schottroff, *Parables of Jesus*, 3, and passim.

11. It is well beyond the scope of this book to examine all the parables of Jesus as Schottroff does in *The Parables of Jesus* or to explore the aphorisms as Ratzinger does in *Jesus of Nazareth*. For comprehensive analyses of Jesus' teaching, consult these two texts, supplemented by Meier's *Mentor, Message, and Miracles,* and Dunn's *Jesus Remembered*. I do not agree with all of their interpretations, but these works represent, so far as I know, the current "state of the art"—but this field is always evolving.

and when he saw him, he passed by on the other side. So likewise a Levite, when he came to the place and saw him, passed by on the other side. But a Samaritan while traveling came hear him, and when he saw him, he was moved with pity. He went to him and bandaged his wounds, having poured oil and wine on them. Then he put him on his own animal, brought him to an inn, and took care of him. The next day he took out two denarii, gave them to the innkeeper, and said, 'Take care of him; and when I come back, I will repay you whatever more you spend.'

"Which of these three, do you think, was a neighbor to the man who fell into the hands of the robbers?" He said, "the one who showed him mercy." Jesus said to him, "Go and do likewise." (Luke 10:25-37 NRSV)

The storyteller—whether an oral transmitter or the editor of Luke is no longer discernible—used a verse (10:29; second paragraph in the quotation) to connect the parable to a story of a dispute (10:25-28; first paragraph above). Luke (or his source) narrated the central story (10:29-35; third paragraph above) and inserted a question (10:36 fourth paragraph above) to connect an explanatory moral to the story that makes the story into an exemplary tale: "Go and do likewise" (10:37). The structure of the complex story (10:25-37), dispute–connection–parable–question–admonition, is frequently portrayed as a product of Lukan redaction of disparate elements into a unity. However, it is also possible that this linkage occurred earlier—in the oral tradition that Luke's Gospel alone preserves—and it is not impossible that the linkage reflects or refracts an incident that an early narrator remembered from the time of Jesus' ministry. What likely triggered the assembling of these parts into this whole is the keyword "neighbor." What links Jesus' Torah teaching, the scribe's query, the parable itself, and the "moral" of the story is "neighbor."[12]

The story begins with Jesus endorsing the lawyer's reading of the law. The slightly varied quotation of the Shema (Dt 6:4-5) and the often-associated Leviticus 19:18 is the summary of the Torah. In similar disputations, Matthew (22:34-40) and Mark (12:28-34) have Jesus give the answer and the scribe or lawyer affirm Jesus' reading. Rabbi Akiva a century later affirmed that love of neighbor was a key principle of the Torah.[13] The key—often obscured—point is that Jesus is an observant Jew. He wears "fringes" that people touch, and he keeps kosher. Here

---

12. It seems quite likely that this linkage occurred in the oral tradition behind Luke. A key term can trigger a memory, even a cascade of memories. It is not far-fetched to suggest that Luke's community had a storyteller who could have assembled this material. In the present approach, however, it probably makes little, if any, difference whether the assemblage happened in the oral traditioning process or in a written redaction by the Gospel's final author.

13. Amy-Jill Levine, *The Misunderstood Jew: The Church and the Scandal of the Jewish Jesus* (San Francisco: HarperSanFrancisco, 2006), 22-25. Levine notes that other Jewish texts make the same linkage. Her comment is that "Jesus does not have to be unique in all cases in order to be profound" (24). When Christians read Jesus as unique, they tend to abstract him from his Jewish context. Often, we don't even notice the abstraction—a case of (at least sometimes) unwitting supersessionism or anti-Judaism.

he advocates observance of the Torah. As Jesus is remembered as saying (Matt. 5:17), "'Do not think that I have come to abolish the law or the prophets. I have come not to abolish but to fulfill.'" He is teaching his disciples *how* to fulfill the law in a way that was evidently rather distinctive. He is a teacher of Torah, the rule of the reign of God.

The admonition to the lawyer to go and do likewise (10:37) occludes—at least for most modern readers—the identity of the one who does the rescuing, the "Samaritan," and the significance of his act. When the Samaritan sees the man in the ditch, his first response is to "have pity" on him. The use of this verb for the action of the Samaritan is significant. The verb used here, *splanchnizomai,* occurs in the New Testament only in the Synoptic Gospels. Its meaning is associated with a feeling in one's gut (the splanchnic artery is the blood vessel that leads to the spleen). The idiom in English might be something like "his heart went out to him." One can imagine someone coming up to the man in the ditch and gasping for breath as if kicked in the gut and having almost no choice but to help, as if one were a swimmer standing beside a river hearing a child's voice calling out for help. Eight times Jesus is said to "have compassion." One time Jesus is asked to "have pity" on the crowds. One time the king in a parable of the kingdom "has pity." The father in the parable of the man with two sons (the prodigal son) "has pity" on his wayward son as soon as he espies him returning. In sum, if only God or God's empowering and empowered agent is the only subject of this particular verb in the New Testament, *the power of such compassion must be divine.*

The parable ascribes this response to a Samaritan and denies it to the priest and the Levite! Why? Because they failed to have pity on the man in the ditch and to respond with a *mitzvah,* a good deed.[14] Luke has Jesus instructing the good Jewish "lawyer" to be like a Samaritan, a people not favored by the Jews of Judea or Galilee because, in their view, Samaritans did not worship or observe Torah properly. This divine compassion is attributed to one of "them" because they did better than we what "we" are pledged to do. Jesus is teaching that the Samaritan knew how to act because he was moved with a divine pity when he saw the man in the ditch. Moreover, this Samaritan then took it on himself to get the man to a place where he could get the healing care he needed.

Luise Schottroff and Amy-Jill Levine independently have noted that the story as we have it does *not* identify the person in the ditch; the hearer or reader has no idea who this person is, what he deserves, or where he stands in relation to the three who pass him by. Moreover, it is not the case that the priest and Levite were following purity rules that prohibit the touching of a corpse, as many Christians have interpreted the story.[15] Rather, they were *not* living up to Torah demands; *they* were not properly observant Jews. It is not that they were in some sense inferior (or superior) to the Samaritan simply because they were Jews. Rather, the

---

14. See Schottroff, *Parables of Jesus,* 132-36; and Levine, *Misunderstood Jew,* 144-49.

15. Levine (*Misunderstood Jew,* 145) suggests that this interpretation is an anti-Jewish one that sees the parable as breaking through "the Jewish system that would prioritize purity over compassion, ritual over responsibility. The impression given of Judaism is appalling."

Samaritan is the one who properly observed Torah and the supposedly observant Jews did not.

The issue is not the status of the people in the story. The issue is whether one has compassion and is moved to engage in the deeds of love required by proper Torah observance.[16] If there is a pointed accusation in the story, it is against the priest and the Levite not as *Jews* but as Jews who should have followed Torah observance and did not.

While most exegetes see Luke 10:37 as an addition to the parable in 10:30-35, the significance of the addition is not simply a moral exhortation, but it may be more provocative than that. Those who heard the parable without the explanation in vv. 36-37 may well have had difficulty understanding with whom in the story they should identify themselves.[17] Perhaps they should see themselves as the man in the ditch needing rescue.[18] Perhaps they should see themselves as a rescuer—a point reinforced by the tradition's (or Luke's) comment on the parable urging the hearers to "go and do likewise." Perhaps they should see the parable as a commentary on the need to do justice.[19]

But perhaps this story is about how to recognize Jesus. If so, it also inscribes an identity for his followers. Following John Dominic Crossan, Norman Perrin wrote:

> [A]t the time of Jesus a Samaritan was a "socio-religious outcast." But the story has the Samaritan help the traveler, so that "the internal structure of the story and the historical setting of Jesus' time agree that the literal point of the story challenges the hearer to put together two impossible and contradictory words for the same person: "Samaritan" (10:33) and "neighbor" (10:36)." As told by a Jewish Jesus to a Jewish audience, "the whole thrust of the story demands that one say what cannot be said, what is a contradiction in terms."[20]

But given the context of the other stories told about "having pity," it is not merely the putting together of the contradiction between "neighbor" and "Samaritan," nor combining "Jesus" and "God" and "neighbor" and "Samaritan" and "socioreligious other," but saying that a Samaritan knew how to interpret Torah. And if he is one of the rare subjects of *splanchnizomai* in the Synoptic Gospels, as Jesus is in many other places, then the implied claim is that Jesus = Samaritan = Torah interpreter (but one who is not a typical interpreter). Jesus, the aberrant Torah interpreter,

---

16. See Schottroff, *Parables of Jesus*, 135.

17. Norman Perrin, *Jesus and the Language of the Kingdom* (Philadelphia: Fortress, 1976), 177-79.

18. See Robert W. Funk, "The Good Samaritan as Metaphor," *Semeia* 2 (1974): 74-81, for an example of this interpretation.

19. Ratzinger, *Jesus of Nazareth*, 198-99. Ratzinger's interpretation of the great parables in Luke (194-217) reflects the history of interpretation of the parable in patristic and medieval exegesis. What the present view sees as hinted at in the parables, he finds all too obvious: that this parable, as well as those of Dives and Lazarus and the man with two sons (the Prodigal Son), is christological.

20. Perrin, *Jesus and the Language of the Kingdom*, 164, following Crossan.

was like a Samaritan. His interpretation of how to live in and live out the *mitzvot* (commandments) of God was not one that priests and Levites might accept. His interpretation is different. Hence, the "moral exhortation" typically analyzed as Luke's addition to the story in 10:37 can be heard as a counsel not only to behave as Jesus—the outcast who was crucified—did but also to realize that Jesus is a true interpreter of what Torah requires. If such is the case, then the "moral interpretation" is "Go and do like the Samaritan = Jesus = Torah interpreter has shown you; you have been enabled to see how to live well."

Schottroff has reflected brilliantly on the point of this parable—its point both then and now. She wrote:

> The parable of the merciful Samaritan is often accused of banality: It is only an ethical example story without any deeper dimension. But if the hearers of this story begin to reflect on it and to talk with one another about what each needs to do here and now, the specter of supposed superficiality vanishes. . . . And if the deed of love is even a tiny one, if it really helps to protect the life of the victim, it is a miracle. This, hopefully, makes it unnecessary to discuss whether the Samaritan's idea, binding up wounds, does not represent something that remains on the surface and tends to sustain the structures of injustice than to change them. As long as the soup kitchens cause us not to make light of the structural injustice of violence to the poor, they are a necessary first step.[21]

The deed of love is a miracle—an act of God—as well as a deed of the human who acts. It is a fulfillment of Torah and a living in and living out of God's reign. Here the eternal and temporal are united, the power of human secondary agency is perfectly transparent to divine primary agency, and the *basileia tou theou* is realized, even if only in a little way, in a healing practice.

The story links "Samaritan" with "God," "Jesus," or a character who acts as Jesus or God would act because these are the only subjects of the verb *splanchnizomai*. Each use of the verb *splanchnizomai* occurs in a situation of need. It is the response that makes possible agents to perform the deeds of healing, reconciliation, wound-binding, and feeding.[22] The stories show that agents act as an outgrowth of this feeling. In each case, it is an act of restoration—of reconciliation of father and prodigal, the return of the man in the ditch to health, the relief of the crowds' hunger, the curing of the possessed and the ill. Having compassion is the exemplary, and perhaps necessary, initial response to the situation in which reconciliation, restoration, and relief are the proper practices. For when people respond well, the life of the community is restored, and God is reigning.

This approach also throws the Bultmannian slogan "the proclaimer became the proclaimed" into a different shape. While few, if any, New Testament scholars

---

21. Schottroff, *Parables of Jesus*, 136.

22. For further discussion of the significance of this verb in the context of the Samaritan parable, see my *Story Theology*, 89-96.

would claim that Jesus said that he was the presence of transcendent God in the midst of the people, nonetheless his practices show what it means for God to reign in person. Again, the use of *splanchnizomai* for actions of compassion that respond to real needs indicates the agents who are making God's present reign a reality. It is not Jesus alone who is the "kingdom of God in person,"[23] but the one who incarnates the agency of God makes the reign of God real. As Hurtado noted, the early Christians could not but see Jesus as God present—they indeed were binitarian Jews. It was not because of what Jesus said, but because of what they perceived him to be empowering them to do—to live, even if only for a time, in and to try to live out the *basileia tou theou*. As he released and revealed the power of the reign of God, he became recognized as incarnating God's power. He did not say "who he was" but showed it in his deeds—including his deeds of teaching.

What is the theological significance of this part of the teaching? Levine put it clearly:

> To understand the parable in theological terms, we need to be able to see the image of God in everyone, not just members of our group. To hear this parable in contemporary terms, we should think of ourselves as the person in the ditch, and then ask, "Is there anyone, from any group, about whom we'd rather die than acknowledge, 'She offered help' or 'He showed compassion'?" More, is there any group whose members might rather die than help us? If so, then we know how to find the modern equivalent for the Samaritan. To recognize the shock and the possibility of the parable in practical, political, and pastoral terms, we might translate its first-century geographical and religious concerns into our modern idiom. The ancient kingdom of Samaria is, today, the West Bank. Thus, translated across the centuries, the parable retains the same meaning. The man in the ditch is an Israeli Jew; a rabbi and a Jewish member of the Israeli Knesset fail to help the wounded man, but a member of Hamas shows him compassion. If that scenario could be imagined by anyone in the Middle East, perhaps there might be more hope for peace.[24]

But the political and practical issues are not simply to imagine this but to engage in the practice characterized as compassionate, and I would say, divinely compassionate. Were we to learn how to have compassion and not to pass by the other (religious, political, ethnic "other") in the ditch, then the reconciliation that is authentic peace, the *basileia tou theou*, would be—at least for a time and at a place—realized.

The missions of the disciples, then and now, are the missions of compassion and reconciliation. As the Samaritan was, so would they be. As he had compassion and responded to needs, so would they. The missions of the disciples, then, are the Jesus-movement in action. The members of the Jesus-movement have compassion

---

23. Ratzinger, *Jesus of Nazareth*, 188.
24. Levine, *Misunderstood Jew*, 148-49.

with those in need of healing and understanding. Compassion—care for and with an other—is a key to recognizing those who live in the *basileia tou theou.* They engage in the reconciling practices of healing the sick, exorcising the possessed and returning them to society, and preaching the *basileia.* They can use Jesus' parables of God's reign as he had done—to provide insight into compassion and reconciliation.

Jesus' parables were vivid. They were remembered because they were *used.* The variations in the parables, such as the various versions of parables of the banquet and the talents, suggest that these were preserved in multiple forms in the oral tradition as stories told in various ways and preserved when the performances were transcribed. Those stories are still told, retold, analyzed, and homilized today. Comics can even joke about a Good Samaritan Hospital dunning one to pay one's bills. The stories the movement remembered live still and challenge us today.

Too often we domesticate the parables or other teaching attributed to Jesus. Likely we cannot avoid doing so if we are to understand them as touchstones by which to understand and judge our own practices. We all too easily shape their interpretations for our comfort. We especially read them as if they valorize the non-Jew over the Jewish leaders. But, as Levine notes repeatedly, this is a product of a tradition of anti-Judaism. Rather, the parables have to challenge our complacency and call us to compassion, that active moving in the pit of one's stomach that reaches out to others in need and to accept those who reach out to us.

The Aphorisms

It is clear that Jesus taught in aphorisms. While these may be distinctive to Jesus, many of them can be found paralleled in Jewish writings as well. That these aphorisms were remembered and collected is not at all surprising. They are especially memorable because of their communicative effectiveness. He may have taught many other things, not so memorable and therefore now lost. Because many of the aphorisms were evidently collected without much regard to their context, little can be claimed about what Jesus' teaching responded to. Nor does the disciples' claim that he taught with authority, in contrast to the practice of the scribes and Pharisees, tell us much about his teaching—theirs is clearly an *ex parte* judgment, not an objective report.

Yet it is not so much *what* Jesus' aphorisms communicate as what they say and show about *how* to be a disciple that is crucial. They convey the gracious style of life that constitutes discipleship. The beatitudes are not prescriptive but descriptive of discipleship. Joseph Ratzinger (Pope Benedict XVI) put the connection to discipleship this way:

> The disciple is bound to the mystery of Christ. His life is immersed in communion with Christ: "It is no longer I who live, but Christ who lives in me" (Gal 2:20). The Beatitudes are the transposition of Cross and

Resurrection into discipleship. But they apply to the disciples because they were first paradigmatically lived by Christ himself.[25]

I would only add to this that the beatitudes say what Jesus showed: how to live in and live out the reign of God, not only in death, but in living a life in God's polity, in practices that mark God's reign. And if living in God's reign led to his execution, then his practices are inevitably connected with this "transposition," for without living in and living out God's reign, why would Jesus be executed?
The text runs like this:[26]

Matthew 5:3-6, 11-12 (RSV adapted)	Luke 6:20-23 (RSV adapted)
Blessed are the poor in spirit, for theirs is the reign of heaven.	Blessed are the poor, for yours is the reign of God.
Blessed are those who mourn, for they shall be comforted.	
Blessed are the meek, for they will inherit the earth.	
Blessed are those who hunger and thirst for justice, for they will be filled.	Blessed are you who are hungry now, for you shall be filled.
	Blessed are you who weep now, for you will laugh.
Blessed are the merciful, for they shall receive mercy.	(Be merciful as your father is merciful [Luke 6:36]).
Blessed are the pure in heart, for they shall see God.	
Blessed are the peacemakers, for they will be called children of God.	
Blessed are those who are persecuted for the sake of justice, for theirs is the reign of heaven.	
Blessed are you when people revile you and persecute you and utter all kinds of evil against you falsely on my account. Rejoice and be glad, for your reward is great in heaven for in the same way they persecuted the prophets who were before you.	Blessed are you when people hate you, and when they exclude you, revile you, and defame you on account of the Son of Man. Rejoice in that day and leap for joy, for surely your reward is great in heaven, for that is what the ancestors did to the prophets.

---

25. Ratzinger, *Jesus of Nazareth*, 74. He focuses only on the Matthean version (70-127), not on the Lukan account.

26. Adapted from Dunn, *Jesus Remembered*, 412.

The disciples are those who are poor or poor in spirit. The debate about which is "original" is, of course, insoluble. In this example of "informally controlled tradition," both may be original oral performances. Commentators have distinguished Luke's and Matthew's renditions of the beatitudes, especially this difference about the poor. The poor are blessed because in the reign of God they will not be impoverished but full participants. The poor in sprit are blessed because they live in opposition to the impoverishment of others. In either case, the disciples, those who live in and live out the reign of God, are not acquisitive of wealth and position.[27] When we take the beatitudes as indicators of the sort of people who live in and live out the reign of God, the difference in the ways of talking about the poor becomes less important.

The disciples are the peacemakers, the merciful, the pure of heart. They are comforters, for the Jesus-movement comforts mourners and attempts to reconcile them with the absence of the beloved and with God. Those who mourn can find comfort in the movement. The disciples are not proud; they hunger for justice and righteousness and may even be persecuted for it. In the reign of God, the hungry eat, the weeping laugh, and all receive their reward even if others revile them, for they are at peace, reconciled with each other. The reconciling practices that constitute the christology of the Jesus-movement require appropriate attitudes. If one fails to have the right disposition, one cannot truly be part of the movement of reconciliation that is justice, peace, righteousness—living under the reign of God.

It should be noted that the word "blessed" of the beatitudes can also be appropriately translated as "happy." In Greek, those who are blessed are *makarioi.* In Aristotle's *Nicomachean Ethics,* the person who is happy (*makarios*) enjoys a life that is divine (see 1178b26-27). That Matthew could have had this in mind as he compiled the beatitudes is at best a rather wild speculation; there is no evidence to support such a claim. However, some who would have *heard* the Sermon on the Mount in subsequent Greco-Roman contexts could have easily "heard" that to live under the reign of God was to participate in the blessing of God or to live a satisfying life. God's blessing could be understood as living a happy life.

Luke also included "woes" along with beatitudes, following them with injunctions to those who would be his disciples, living in and living out God's reign:

Woe to you who are rich, you have received your consolation.

Woe to you who are full now, for you shall be hungry.

---

27. Roberto Goizueta (*Caminemos con Jesús: Toward a Hispanic/Latino Theology of Accompaniment* [Maryknoll, NY: Orbis Books, 1995] 185-89), following Gustavo Gutiérrez, identifies three forms of poverty: material (deprivation), spiritual (humility in being at Jesus' disposal), and voluntary (in solidarity with the deprived and in protest against oppression). Goizueta notes that material poverty is not *only* economic. It is often connected with racial, sexual, ageist, and cultural forms of discrimination and oppression. In this view, voluntary poverty would be blessed as a practice, but other forms of poverty would vanish in the realization of the *basileia tou theou.*

Woe to you who are laughing now, for you shall mourn and weep.

Woe to you when all speak well of you, for that is what their ancestors did to the false prophets.

But I say to *you that listen*: Love your enemies, do good to those who hate you, bless those who curse you, pray for those who abuse you. If anyone strikes you on the cheek, offer the other also; and from anyone who takes your coat do not withhold even your shirt. Give to everyone who begs from you; and if anyone takes away your goods, do not ask for them again. Do to others as you would have them do to you. (Luke 6:24-31 NRSV adapted, italics added)

The woes apply to those who do not live in God's reign. The practices that made some rich while others were oppressed, some full while others hungered, some able to laugh while others were weeping are not the practices of reconciliation that exhibit and realize the reign of God. Those who do not live in God's reign can admire the rich and full, those who rejoice while others have too little. But "those who listen" do otherwise.

Those who listen and act are those who are members of the Jesus-movement. Disciples listen. Each of the injunctions that follows leads to reconciliation, not vengeance. The parables and the sayings—two of the main remembered patterns of Jesus' teaching—show that the practices of the reign of God are the practices of reconciliation. Of course, Jesus' example is the primary teaching about how reconciliation works and what its cost is. He was executed for bringing reconciliation, a reign of God that was incompatible in its practice with the reign of Rome. As Baptist theologian James Wm. McClendon once put it: "There is costliness in the work of at-one-ment, the fact that no reconciliation of radically separate persons is effortlessly achieved."[28]

True reconciliation is not merely a human work, as "the deepest element in at-one-ment is the costly act of God, restoring us to himself. Indeed, the historic doctrine allows no final separation, but holds that the reconciliation Christ brings about between man and man [*sic*] is none other than the work of God, reconciling us to himself."[29] That work of God is truly costly even for God, as Christians regard Jesus as truly human and truly divine (see chapter 18 below). The key is this: Jesus gave his life both to and for reconciliation, for the reign of God. Engaging in the work of reconciliation is doing God's work. That reconciliation in practice is the focus of this third part of the present book, as well as of chapter 19.

Far more could be said—and has been said by many commentators—about how Jesus taught and about how he showed and said what living in and living out the reign of God was like. Jesus' teaching was not, of course, merely moral

---

28. James Wm. McClendon, Jr., *Biography as Theology: How Life-Stories Can Remake Today's Theology* (Nashville: Abingdon, 1974), 99.

29. Ibid., 108-9.

injunction. Rather, when Jesus taught and if one listened as a disciple, one could learn not merely how to live but how to receive the ability to act in the ways that God would be present in and to the world in reconciling practices. If God's ultimate work is reconciliation, then our proximate work participates in that work, if we but know how to be the sorts of persons who can engage fully in the practices of God's reign.

Obviously, the attitudes that the Jesus-movement remembered and presumably sought to embody were generated in a culture far from ours. The point is not simply to replicate these attitudes, but to learn and teach attitudes that shape character in our culture as those attitudes did in late Second Temple Judaism. Any commentary on these attitudes—certainly including the present one—is a present-day effort to interpret ways of incarnating such attitudes in the present. Christians will dispute about this, but the key is not merely to be "meek" or "pure in heart," but to work out what it means to have analogous attitudes today. These attitudes are touchstones for our understanding; they are neither models to be slavishly imitated nor criteria for contemporary practice.

Fifteen

FORGIVING AS
A RECONCILING PRACTICE

*And then they brought him a paralytic lying on a stretcher. and having
seen their faith, Jesus said to the paralytic, "Cheer up, child! Your sins are
forgiven"* —Matthew 2:4

*S*in is essentially the creation of separation, of fissure, between sinner and
sinned against. One can sin against oneself, one's relatives and friends,
one's community, strangers, the environment. In any and all of these, one also sins
against God. The forgiveness of sins is the restoration of right relationships. It is
a crucial practice of reconciliation.

Matthew 9:2-8 (and parallels) portrays Jesus' forgiving sin—and the accusation
of blasphemy by some scribes.[1] To show that he has the authority to forgive sin or
at least to mediate or announce the forgiveness of sin, Jesus tells the paralytic to
rise and walk, as if to say, "That'll show 'em." And the paralytic walks home.

This story, however, doesn't quite "work." The story doesn't spend time saying
why Jesus first forgave sins before healing the paralytic. The situation seems to
call for a practice of healing, not of forgiveness. After all, the obvious problem
was paralysis. Nor does the Gospel spend time discussing why the newly healed
person could go home; most of us assume that it is simply because the paralysis
was cured and the sufferer could now walk. But if that was all the paralytic needed,

---

1. For a survey of forgiveness in Jesus' sayings, see Vincent Taylor, *Forgiveness and Reconciliation: A Study in New Testament Theology* (London: Macmillan; New York: St. Martin's Press,
1960), 8-23. Taylor sees the practice of forgiveness and reconciliation as at the center of the Christian experience (223-26). His task, however, is different from the present one as he wants to show
how these lead to justification and sanctification on the basis of a mediatorial account of the doctrine
of the atonement. For a practical theology of atonement, see James Wm. McClendon, Jr., *Biography
as Theology: How Life Stories Can Remake Today's Theology* (Nashville: Abingdon, 1974). James
D. G. Dunn (*Jesus Remembered*, vol. 1 of *Christianity in the Making* [Grand Rapids: Eerdmans,
2003], 590) suggests that the problem is not Jesus' claim to forgive sins per se, but that he (like the
Baptist) was usurping the place of the appropriate cultic intermediary, the temple priesthood. The
priests (perhaps unlike Jesus) did not forgive sins, but offered the prescribed sin offerings so that
God would forgive sins. Jesus' practice short-circuits that mediation. Robert Schreiter (*The Ministry of Reconciliation: Spirituality and Strategies* [Maryknoll, NY: Orbis Books, 1998]) highlights
the significance of forgiveness in reconciliation.

why should Jesus forgive the paralytic's sins? Perhaps the healing practice was not sufficient. Perhaps it had to be connected with forgiveness of sin so the paralytic could return *home*. The unexpected action of Jesus and the unexamined action of the paralytic make for a good confrontation story. However, the odd order of events suggests that more is at play than first meets the hearers' ears.

Forgiveness of sin is one of a set of compassionate reconciling practices. Jesus heals both sin and paralysis. His compassion is for both a sufferer and a sinner. Here the healing practice is nested with another reconciling practice of the reign of God, forgiveness. Forgiveness and healing have a real connection. And when God reigns, fissures of sin do not open up and swallow the community into the fiery depths. Sin is not merely a separation; it is also a social (or psychological) disease that needs healing; sins are not only offenses, but causes of ruptures.

It is clear that Jesus was remembered as forgiving sins. That he may have claimed divine power in doing so is possible. However, the Gospels never report the disciples' forgiving sin. While the Gospels report preaching, exorcising, healing, and other reconciling practices of the disciples, forgiveness is omitted. If forgiveness is so essential as a practice of reconciliation, if it is a practice of those who live in and live out the reign of God, how could Jesus not have taught them *how* to engage in the practice of forgiving? We can look at four texts to show that forgiveness is a distinctive practice not only of Jesus but also of the Jesus-movement.

Practicing Forgiveness

First, forgiveness is mutual. The Lord's Prayer implores God to forgive us our debts as we forgive our debtors (Matt. 6:12; Luke 11:4). Mark has a similar injunction, "And whenever you stand praying, forgive, if you have anything against any one; so that your Father also who is in heaven may forgive you your trespasses" (Mark 11:25). Those searching for historical-Jesus material could argue that this multiple attestation (the Lord's Prayer in Q, Mark) at least suggests that Jesus himself was remembered as urging his followers to engage in the practice of forgiveness as well as of prayer. The centrality of the Lord's Prayer in the life of the community meant that this injunction would often be repeated. Praying for forgiveness, as one forgave others, would be reinforced repeatedly. The Jesus-movement certainly remembers mutual forgiveness as a key practice.[2]

Second, forgiveness is not a one-time thing but an ongoing practice. The Q material preserves sayings of Jesus urging repeated forgiveness (Luke 17:3-4; Matt. 18:15, 21-22). In the Matthean version of the saying, the sinner is to be rebuked until the sinner "hears" it. Matthew then introduces Peter to ask how often he must forgive—seven times? No, Jesus replies, "seventy times seven"

---

2. The connection of forgiveness or nonforgiveness with blasphemy and the sin against the Holy Spirit (e.g., Mark 3:28-29) admits of many interpretations. In some instances, the point may be to deflect accusations of blasphemy against Jesus and or the disciples. Identifying the sin against the Holy Spirit has vexed Christians for millennia; I see no reason to think any probable solution can be found to the problem of identifying that act or practice.

times. In the Lukan version, Jesus instructs the one sinned against to rebuke the sinner. But then he adds that if the sinner repents, the one sinned against is to forgive him—even seven times a day!

Interestingly, only the Lukan context notes that repentance is a condition of forgiveness. This fact, along with the other differences, leads James D. G. Dunn to note that the tradition is fluid and that the tradition frozen in Q is just one stage of that fluid tradition, a tradition Matthew and Luke did not simply copy. Dunn also suggests that the Matthean version, at least, is shaped by consideration of tensions in the emerging community at the time Matthew was writing.[3] This concern, with repeated attempts to forgive, at least makes clear that the evolving tradition remembered Jesus' practice and urging of forgiveness as central to his work.

Moreover, in his teaching *how* to forgive, Jesus is remembered as urging repeated forgiveness. The members of the Jesus-movement should not be stinting in forgiving. Forgiveness is an ongoing practice of reconciliation, repeated again and again. Nor is repentance merely an apology and a firm purpose to mend one's ways; repentance is reorienting one's life by shifting away from the woeful practices noted in the previous chapter to engage in the blessed practices taught by Jesus. Both repentance and forgiveness are ongoing practices.

Third, Luke's Gospel puts a saying about forgiveness at a most crucial moment. In doing so, the evangelist highlights the significance of forgiveness in Jesus' work, and hence in the work of the Jesus-movement. Jesus' final words on the cross are, "Father, forgive them; they do not know what they are doing" (22:34). What they were doing, of course, was executing a criminal, guilty of rebellion. Or so they thought.[4]

Luke's Jesus pled for forgiveness of the perpetrators without their confession or repentance. This powerful remembrance is another piece of the memory of Jesus' teaching how to forgive: forgive freely! L. Gregory Jones has noted that this pattern of forgiveness without repentance is a motif in Luke's work. He also noted that this form of forgiveness of "those who know not what they do" is remembered later by the Jesus-movement (Acts 3:17).[5] Forgiving freely, however, is not a call to masochism, that is, a demand that victims repeatedly forgive repeating victimizers. The Jesus-movement is not a haven for abusive relationships. However, forgiving freely reminds us that in some cases the overwhelming grace of being forgiven can bring even compulsive sinners, especially unwitting ones who know not what they do, to repentance and reconciliation with those who forgive them again and again.

---

3. Dunn, *Jesus Remembered*, 235, 590.

4. Like Mark's crucifixion scene, Luke's crucifixion quotes Psalm 22. Unlike Mark, however, Luke does not place Ps. 22:1 in Jesus' mouth ("My God, my God, why have you abandoned me?"). Rather, Luke uses a quotation from Ps. 22:18 to describe what others did immediately after the plea for forgiveness in 22:34: "they divide my garments among them and for my raiment they cast lots." Psalm 22 is not lost, but is given a place in the narrative that makes it less significant.

5. L. Gregory Jones, *Embodying Forgiveness: A Theological Analysis* (Grand Rapids: Eerdmans, 1995), 101-3, citing the cure of the paralytic (5:17-26) and the calling of Zacchaeus from his tree (19:1-10).

Fourth, John's Gospel records the risen Jesus appearing to the disciples and instructing them to forgive sins. Jesus says, "Receive the Holy Spirit. If you forgive the sins of any, they are forgiven; if you retain the sins of any, they are retained" (John 20:22b-23). Luke's postresurrection narrative also mentions forgiveness: "*Metanoia* to the forgiveness of sins should be preached in his name to all peoples, beginning from Jerusalem" (Luke 24:47). The interpretations of these texts vary widely. Few, if any, would ascribe them to historical-Jesus material if for no other reason than that they are remembered as a postmortem, postresurrection communication. However, just as the narrative of the transfiguration is thought by many scholars to be a "retrojection" of a postresurrection appearance to an earlier point in the story, so the postresurrection sayings of Jesus may be memories of something Jesus taught, however adapted, that are "projected" to a time after the resurrection.[6]

Some see John's Gospel as authorizing the disciples to be agents of forgiveness—and withholding of forgiveness. But it is also possible to read this verse not merely as a commissioning but as a warning: the disciples' refusal to forgive sin is a terrible thing, for they indeed may not be forgiven.[7] On this reading, the notion of mutual forgiveness can be seen as the form of forgiveness that is a constitutive practice of living in and living out God's reign.

Some suggest that Luke has arranged his material specifically for use in preaching. First is forgiveness and then repentance is to follow. But it is also possible to see in Luke a preaching not to the sinners but to those "sinned against" to "repent" to (*eis*) the forgiveness of sins. In harmony with the words from the cross in Luke, it is not necessary to read a sinner's "repentance" as a condition for forgiveness. It may be the sort of change in the injured party and the injured's relationship to the injurer that leads to forgiveness. One has to learn how to accept forgiveness as well as give it.

Despite the fact that the other members of the Jesus-movement are not portrayed as forgiving sin, the centrality of this practice in Jesus' reconciling work is obvious. That the movement is to carry on his work is also obvious. Hence, these texts imply that the disciples were to engage in this reconciling practice—not merely forgiving but freely and repeatedly forgiving.

Forgiveness and the Reconciled Life

Forgiveness is a key practice in living a reconciled life, a life that is living in and living out the reign of God. Forgiveness is also immensely difficult. Miroslav Volf writes eloquently:

---

6. Taylor (*Forgiveness and Reconciliation*) suggests this is a "secondary version of the saying on binding and loosing in Mt. xvi. 19, xviii. 18." If so, these sayings may be an example of informally controlled oral tradition, witnessing to an early memory of Jesus' teaching on forgiveness being reciprocal or, better, fundamentally reconciling.

7. Dunn (*Jesus Remembered*, 590-91) discusses this understanding of warning or urging of forgiveness in relation to Luke 6:37; Mark 6:14-15; and Matt. 11:25.

If perpetrators were repentant, forgiveness would come more easily. But too often they are not. And so both victim and perpetrator are imprisoned in the automatism of mutual exclusion, unable to forgive or repent and united in a perverse communion of mutual hate.

Instead of wanting to forgive, we instinctively seek revenge. An evil deed will not be owed for long; it demands instant repayment in kind. The trouble with revenge, however, is that it enslaves us . . . [in the] endless turning of the spiral of violence. . . ."[8]

To take an eye for an eye, a tooth for a tooth, a life for a life to "rebalance" the scales of justice seems a common "default position" in many of our agonized relationships. The prospect of satisfaction by "getting justice" from those who have injured us lures us into vengeance. But justice must be something other than either balancing injuries or vengeance.

Justice involves the repair of relationships. "Rebalancing" by retribution, however, fails to lead to renewed relationships. It returns to the situation in which the injustice took place, paving the way for an endless cycle of offense and rebalancing. The only way out of the cycle of vengeance is forgiveness. "[F]orgiveness breaks the power of the remembered past and transcends the claims of affirmed justice and so makes the spiral of vengeance grind to a halt. This is the social import of forgiveness."[9] Volf puts it this way:

In the presence of God our rage over injustice may give way to forgiveness, which in turn will make the search for justice for all possible. . . . If forgiveness does take place, it will be but an echo of the forgiveness granted by the just and loving God—the only forgiveness that ultimately matters, because, though we must forgive, in a very real sense no one can either forgive or retain sins "but God alone." (Mark 2:7)[10]

But has the quotation from the scribe in Mark ("Who can forgive sins but God alone?") misled Volf here? Has he forgotten the empowering tradition of John 20? And has he not noted that it is not only sins that are the object of forgiveness, but also debts?[11] And, as Robert Schreiter asks, how does one even begin to forgive "the genocides of Armenia and Cambodia, the Holocaust, the tyranny of Communist governments, the effects of imperialism on colonized peoples, the

---

8. Miroslav Volf, *Exclusion and Embrace: A Theological Exploration of Identity, Otherness, and Reconciliation* (Nashville: Abingdon, 1996), 120-21.

9. Ibid., 121.

10. Ibid., 124-25.

11. Volf does reflect on Matt. 6:12, but uses that verse about forgiveness of debts to introduce the connection of justice with forgiveness. However, the notion that in praying for forgiveness we owe God something in the way that we owe other people something is unpersuasive. The difference is too vast. We are indebted to God for all there is; our debt is infinite and unpayable; I owe my friend fifty dollars because I borrowed it from her. Volf underplays the significance of the forgiveness of debts. See *Exclusion and Embrace*, 122.

global wars and the ethnic conflicts? The list goes on and on."[12] And as I am neither an Armenian, a Cambodian, a victim of the Shoah, a tyrannical regime, or a colonialist, a supporter of global wars or ethnic cleansing (except in the social complicity of all of us due in part to globalization), what good is my forgiveness? *Who* is to forgive in practice is an issue that needs to be explored.

The practice of forgiveness does not play on distributive or retributive justice. Forgiveness in the *basileia tou theou* does not require repentance (in the English-language sense) or confession. Rather, the practice of the Jesus-movement is the mutual, free forgiveness of all that stands in the way of reconciliation. To forgive is to abandon obsession with getting back what was lost, given away, or destroyed. Forgiveness is not retribution.

To forgive is also to give up on what is "owed."[13] Commenting on Luke 14, Luise Schottroff writes:

> The Gospel of Luke proposes a radical social politics for Israel and for Christianity drawn from among the nations. People who are in a position to forgive debts should forgive debts and thus be prepared not only—as the Torah demands—to renounce interest, but even to renounce the payment of principal (Luke 6:34, 35). The gulf between rich and poor is described in the Gospel of Luke as a catastrophe for the rich, who are referred to the Torah for guidance (Luke 16:31).[14]

Forgiveness is oriented not to the past but to reconciliation in the present and life together in our shared future. Forgiveness is a condition for present and future life together. It is the practice of creating justice not by repairing the injustices of the past, by balancing the scales, or by collecting what one is owed, but by letting the past be *past* so that we can live together now and in the future. It is not about the evil acts and conditions that can never be undone but about the relationships among those who—both perpetrators and victims—remember those who are gone and have come to survive together.[15] For to be able to survive together requires a

---

12. Schreiter, *Ministry of Reconciliation*, 56.

13. The practices of borrowing and lending today are not generally comparable to those of the ancient world. A capitalist economy is built on investment and indebtedness. Certainly, the forgiveness of debts in the Lord's Prayer is the forgiveness of those debts that oppress communities and individuals, those debts that would allow the lender to have debtors thrown into slavery or prisons because they could not pay their debts. These debts fracture the community. The indebtedness that is a constituent of our contemporary capitalist system is, at least occasionally, different. Many of our debts are incurred not to rescue us from disaster but to facilitate profits sufficient to pay off the debt and increase the wealth of the debtors. However, the effects of those debts that destroy the community of nations, such as the indebtedness of developing countries to developed countries, may well make them candidates for the Christian practice of forgiveness.

14. Luise Schottroff, *The Parables of Jesus*, trans. Linda Maloney (Minneapolis: Fortress, 2006), 50.

15. See Schreiter, *Ministry of Reconciliation*, 59. Schreiter distinguishes between "social" and more "face-to-face" reconciliation. The former moves from repentance to forgiveness to reconciliation, the latter from reconciliation to forgiveness to repentance (64). In either case, true reconcili-

profound change of mind in both victims and victimizers. To walk in God's ways, not humans', to become practitioners of reconciliation requires a change of heart that can lead not merely to surviving together (rather than apart) but thriving together in this world and being able to hope that such thriving is eternal.

Forgiveness is a practice that is central to living out and living in the reign of God. As such, it is not that "God alone" forgives sin but that we who live in God and God who lives in us forgive debts, sins, slights, and even the execution of the one who preached forgiveness. As God is the primary agent forgiving sin, whether social or more personal, that primary agency is exercised in and through secondary agents—the members of the Jesus-movement. To quote Volf again— and to show that, appearances aside, in the end the Markan scribe has not misled him about "God alone" forgiving sin:

> Assured of God's justice and undergirded by God's presence, they are to break the cycle of violence by refusing to be caught in the automatism of revenge. It cannot be denied that the prospects are good that by trying to love their enemies they may end up hanging on a cross. Yet often enough, the costly acts of nonretaliation become a seed from which the fragile fruit of Pentecostal peace grows—a peace between people from different cultural spaces gathered in one place who understand each other's languages and share in each other's goods.[16]

In a world of violence, avoiding retaliation and violence may seem impossible.

Christians have often not avoided retaliation and violence. When Christian traditions have not been oppressed by state power, Christians have justified wars in the name of Christ (Crusades) or political necessity (just war theory). Volf calls on Christians not to try to justify the violence they do by appealing to their Christian faith. If Christians fight instead of forgive, they neglect the crucial practice of living in and living out God's reign: forgiveness and reconciliation.

It may be that the world is so disfigured by evil that Christians cannot avoid doing violence.[17] But the tradition of the reconciling practices inscribed in the Jesus-movement cannot *justify* doing violence. At particular times and places living in and living out the reign of God by participating in the practices of reconciliation may not be politically possible. But the community of forgiveness that holds all things in common (Acts 4:32) instantiates a polity so different from

---

ation is an occasion of grace, a decision and a process that are transparent to and empowered by the divine.

16. Volf, *Exclusion and Embrace*, 306.

17. Following Daan Bronkhorst, *Truth and Reconciliation: Obstacles and Opportunities for Human Rights* (Amsterdam: Amnesty International, 1995), 31-32. Schreiter (*Ministry of Reconciliation*, 6-13) describes a set of stages through which a society passes on its way to reconciliation. But before the first stage, before the reconciling process begins, it is not clear how anyone can avoid participation in violence. Sometimes our "sins of omission" in such circumstances may be as violently destructive as our "sins of commission"; as the old saw has it, "damned if you do, damned if you don't."

the norm as to seem unworldly.[18] It is a different form of *phronēsis*. It is not clear to what extent the earliest Christian communities practiced such forgiveness. But *metanoia* to forgiveness and compassion for those who have done wrong are constitutive practices of the Jesus-movement.[19] Perhaps that is why Luke's use of Psalm 22 in the crucifixion scene is so different from Mark's and Matthew's use of the psalm and why Luke narrates Jesus' plea: "Father, forgive them; they know not what they do" (Luke 23:34).

The practice of forgiveness is difficult and does not come naturally to most of us, especially those of us who live in a litigious society.[20] But the practice is possible even in the present. A recent story can help make the point. Late in his life, Joseph Cardinal Bernardin was accused out of the blue of sexual molestation of a seminarian. Bernardin narrated the story in his book, *The Gift of Peace*.

Therese Lysaught noted the profound christological connection in Bernardin's narration: The section relating the incident begins with a meditation on the *kenōsis* hymn, focusing on the practice of emptying oneself. As Lysaught noted, Bernardin was shaken by the accusation:

> His world was, in many ways, turned upside down. The accusation struck at one of the key centers of his identity—his chastity. . . . He was angry, bewildered at who could possibly launch such a false charge against him, and deeply humiliated. . . . Here a destructive power was at work, bearing down on him, threatening . . . his life's work, his deepest convictions, his personal reputation, his position as Cardinal of Chicago.[21]

Yet he knew that the truth would ultimately set him free, and he was sustained by his prayerful awareness of God's presence in his life. Though distraught, he was "overwhelmed with a sense of compassion for his accuser. . . . He almost

---

18. In a series of hard sayings about the demands of discipleship, Luke also has Jesus say, "none of you can become my disciple if you do not give up all your possessions" (14:34). That possessions, or perhaps attachment to them when they could be shared with others in the movement, could obstruct the practices of reconciliation that are the coming of the *basileia tou theou* is an undercurrent in Luke's writings.

19. Like Elisabeth Schüssler Fiorenza (*Jesus and the Politics of Interpretation* [New York: Continuum, 2000], 133), I do not "work with a model of 'decline' from pristine egalitarian beginnings to kyriarchal institutionalization" but suspect that the New Testament records an ongoing struggle in the community between the practices of the free forgiveness of sins and debts, on the one hand, with the demand for repentance before forgiveness, on the other. While Matthew recognizes that repeated sin really does require repentance before forgiveness, the generalized demand for repentance before forgiveness or admission into table fellowship may well trap the community in the spiral of violence. That some within the community might use free forgiveness to exploit others is an abuse of the community's practice that needs correction, not an excuse for abandoning the practice or replacing it with a penal system.

20. These three paragraphs are based on a profound paper of M. Therese Lysaught, "Love Your Enemies: Toward a Christoform Bioethic," in *Gathered for the Journey: Moral Theology in Catholic Perspective*," ed. David Matzko McCarthy and M. Therese Lysaught (Grand Rapids: Eerdmans, 2007), 307-28.

21. Ibid., 320.

immediately [wrote] a letter to the man, asking if he might visit him to pray with him."[22] The letter was not delivered by the accuser's lawyers. Bernardin decided not to retaliate, not to stonewall, not to obstruct or resist his accuser, not to do all the things that will keep the accuser from getting his case heard and obtaining a settlement, if successful, from ecclesial coffers. But the case collapsed and Bernardin was exonerated.

Lysaught's analysis gets to the heart of the matter:

> Bernardin could have simply rejoiced in his vindication, or could have brought counter-charges for defamation of character. But this is not the road he chooses. Rather, eleven months after the suit was dropped, he again tried to contact his accuser. This time he was successful. In the end, he meets with him and—beyond what would be wildly imaginable—was reconciled with him. They became friends, such that six months later, when Bernardin is diagnosed with pancreatic cancer, one of the first letters he receives is from his former accuser. It is a powerful story of reconciliation and forgiveness.[23]

Bernardin showed what it means to be open prayerfully to the power and presence of God in one's life. It makes possible the overwhelming response of compassion (as the Samaritan had for the traveler), the ability to forgive a profound injury, almost a demonic assault, and the sharing of life that is a reconciliation—life together under the reign of God. Compassion and forgiveness are inevitably intertwined.

Personal forgiveness can be a component in social forgiveness, but social forgiveness—the forgiveness that restores a fissured society—involves a complex political process of reconciliation. Personal forgiveness and reconciliation are not essentially political, but social forgiveness and reconciliation are part of a political process. Robert Schreiter has clearly highlighted these differences.

Social forgiveness and social reconciliation have characteristics somewhat different from personal, face-to-face forgiveness and reconciliation. 'Social reconciliation "is a process of reconstructing the moral order of a society."[24] As in South Africa, it requires not the action of individuals alone, but the will and action of a society, careful planning and leadership, and a commitment to justice that avoids the ways of retribution and punishment. The better path, one beyond revenge and "rebalancing" and toward reconciliation, remembers fallen victims, recognizes victimized and victimizing victims, and provides ways to redress, at least in part, the tragic effects of past evils. The goal is not "rebalancing" but the creation of a future together that stands a real chance of not replicating the past. Schreiter tells a number of stories about individuals and groups who found alternatives to

---

22. Ibid.
23. Ibid.
24. Schreiter, *Ministry of Reconciliation*, 112, following José Zalaquett, chair of the Truth and Reconciliation Commission in Chile, quoted in *Dealing with the Past: Truth and Reconciliation in South Africa*, ed. Alex Boraine, Janey Levy, and Ronell Scheffer (Capetown: IDASA, 1994), 11.

the power of domination to effect forgiveness and reconciliation. One of them is about the women who formed a "Wall of Peace" in Croatia:

> When Serbs invaded and took over parts of Croatia in the Balkan War in 1991, one of their techniques of terror was the rape of women. When Croatian troops retook the area some years later, Croatian women went ahead of the troops and moved into the homes of the women in Serbian villages. They would not allow the troops to rape the Serbian women in revenge for what had been done to Croatian women. They formed what they called the "wall of peace."[25]

Such action can set the conditions for social reconciliation; when the women form a wall to stop the violence, reconciliation becomes possible. What makes it possible is compassion. The Croatian women knew what would happen to the Serbian women and were moved with pity—remember the verb *splanchnizomai*—to save them. Perhaps those who are sinned against can especially show us what such forgiveness is when they reach out in compassion to prevent more destructive sinfulness.

The power of the reconciling practice of forgiveness is not new. William James captured the power of this reconciling practice in words written over a century ago about a number of late medieval and early modern saints. He wrote, "When [these methods of love] do succeed, they are far more powerfully successful than force or worldly prudence. Force destroys enemies; and the best that can be said for prudence is that it keeps what we already have in safety. But nonresistance, when successful, turns enemies into friends and charity regenerates its objects."[26] Charity, love, and compassion poured out for others is transformative.

Bernardin tried neither force nor "prudence," but the compassionate way of forgiveness and reconciliation. The Croatian women were neither violent nor prudent (according to *ta tōn anthrōpōn*, human wisdom) to move into a war zone, but they helped create conditions in which reconciliation and forgiveness would be possible. This is a reconciling work, a work that instantiates, at a particular time and place, partially and incompletely, the reign of God.

Forgiveness is a reconciling practice of discipleship, a living christology incarnated in the members of the Jesus-movement past and present. It shows how to live in the reign of God now and to hope for the time when all may live in the *basileia tou theou*, in the power of God. Forgiveness is a practice of hope, oriented to the future in which we can live a reconciled life together.

---

25. Schreiter, *Ministry of Reconciliation*, 28.

26. William James, *The Varieties of Religious Experience: A Study in Human Nature* (New York: Collier Books, 1961; first published, 1902), 284-85; we will return to this passage in its context in chap. 19.

Sixteen

KEEPING AND REJOICING IN TABLE FELLOWSHIP

And as he reclined at table in his [Levi's] house, many toll collectors and sinners were sitting with Jesus and his disciples; for there were many who followed him. And the scribes of the Pharisees, when they saw that he was eating with the sinners and tax collectors, said to his disciples, "Why does he eat with tax collectors and sinners? And when Jesus heard it, he said to them, "Those who are well have no need of a physician, but those who are sick; I came not to call the righteous, but sinners" —Mark 2:15-17 RSV

he table fellowship characteristic of the Jesus-movement is another reconciling practice that both realizes and anticipates God's reign. It takes multiple versions, from the miracle stories to the Last Supper to the supper on the road to Emmaus. Eating and drinking are a key and controversial element in distinguishing the Jesus-movement and its leader from the other groups in Judaism.

The Controversial Practice of Inclusive Table Fellowship

Mark's version of the key controversial meal in 2:15-17 tells of a meal given just after Jesus calls Levi to follow him. Levi, of course, responds by following Jesus. And the meal is evidently held in Levi's house (although the Greek text does not name Levi; the text is so ambiguous that it might be Jesus' house). Mark's telling of the story highlights the inclusivity of the table fellowship.

As with many stories in the New Testament, this story appears woven together either by Mark or in the tradition before Mark. Jesus' response is odd. The question was addressed to the disciples, but the story has Jesus answer it. Moreover, the response is indirect, at best. The "scribes of the Pharisees" (another odd combination) asked about those Jesus ate with. Jesus responded not by answering the question but by deflecting it. His answer addressed not his table companions, but those whom he called. The story combines a story of table fellowship with a story of a disputation and frames it with the call of Levi and the call to others.

The choppiness of the narrative suggests that it was woven together from multiple earlier traditions.

It is immediately followed by another challenge about food and drink (Mark 2:18-20). The Pharisees and John's disciples were fasting, but Jesus and his disciples were not. His reply adverts to a wedding feast—one cannot fast when the bridegroom is present. The time for fasting is when the bridegroom is gone. The joy of a wedding celebration is the joy of the presence of the leader of the Jesus-movement and the joy of living in the reign of God. This second pericope shows Jesus and his followers failing to meet the expectations others had of them. The first story, however, makes what may be a more serious accusation.

The story of Jesus eating in Mark 2:15-17 has Jesus accused of eating with those who are outside the boundaries of "good company." The context is complex. One useful reference work puts it this way:

> The Pharisees regarded their tables at home as surrogates for the Lord's altar in the Temple in Jerusalem and therefore strove to maintain in their households and among their eating companions the state of ritual purity required of priests in Temple service (Neusner). . . . Pharisees prescribed no special prayers or unusual foods for their meals. But they did insist on eating only with those who had "undefiled hands" (Mark 7:2-4), that is, with persons in a state of ritual purity (cf. Ex 30:19-21). The Pharisees longed for the time when all of Israel would live in such a state of holiness.[1]

The boundaries of Jesus' table fellowship were quite different from those typically attributed to Pharisees.

Jesus evidently had quite a reputation. The Q tradition remembered it this way:

> For John the Baptist has come eating no bread and drinking no wine; and you say, "He has a demon." The son of man has come eating and drinking; and you say, "Behold a glutton and a drunkard, a friend of toll collectors and sinners!" Yet wisdom is justified by all her children. (Luke 7:33-34; compare Matt. 11:18-19)[2]

While the point of the disciples' remembering this saying may be to distance themselves from some of the practices of the disciples of the Baptist, it hardly seems likely that disciples would invent such a saying. Evidently, Jesus seems "to

---

1. S. S. Bartchy, "Table Fellowship," in *Dictionary of Jesus and the Gospels*, ed. Joel B. Green and Scott McKnight (Downer's Grove, IL: InterVarsity, 1992), 796-97; the reference is to Jacob Neusner, "Two Pictures of the Pharisees: Philosophical Circle or Eating Club?" *Anglican Theologial Review* 64, no. 4 (October 1982): 525-38.

2. For a thorough discussion and review of the literature, see Mary J. Marshall, "Jesus: Glutton and Drunkard," *Journal for the Study of the Historical Jesus* 3, no. 1 (2005): 47-60; Marshall accepts the identification of some of the people at table as "toll collectors," rather than "tax collectors." Nonetheless, toll collectors had the reputation of gouging travelers and shippers.

have been noteworthy for his presence at festive meals and banquets, a remarkably non-ascetic habit considered scandalous by some."[3]

This little story is profoundly inflected by the scriptures. The accusation may well echo Proverbs: "Hear, my son, and be wise, and direct your mind in the way. Be not among winebibbers, or among gluttonous eaters of meat; for the drunkard and the glutton will come to poverty, and drowsiness will clothe a man with rags" (Prov. 23:19-21). The defense may allude to Sirach 4:11: "Wisdom teaches her children." In Matthew's version, wisdom is justified by her "works."

Whether Matthew or Luke more closely reflects the inherited tradition is undecidable. Again, the choppiness of the story suggests that either the writer of Q or someone earlier in the transmission of the tradition combined different sayings. Here is another example of "informally controlled oral tradition."

Jesus is reported as repeating and responding to the accusation. But if the reference to wisdom is indeed a defense, then the suggestion is that wisdom's children do wisdom's works. If Jesus is wisdom—and as wisdom is one of the appellations of the "second power in heaven"—then this reply might even suggest that Jesus as wisdom incarnate is "justified" by his disciples who carry on this work, his "children" (Matt. 11:19). In effect, he may be remembered as saying, "Wait and see how the movement carries on."

Perhaps this passage about wisdom records a memory of an actual attack on the Jesus-movement. However stylized this passage may be, it reflects something crucial about the memory of Jesus' table fellowship: he not only preached to but ate with "toll collectors and sinners" and was remembered as justifying it "pragmatically." And he had a good time doing it.

Some of the elite evidently did not regard some of Jesus' table companions as quality company to dine at the family tables. J. Ramsey Michaels has identified some of the dinner companions as toll collectors who profited from the Roman occupation; prostitutes who served the occupying armies, violating sexual mores; and gentiles, who were ritually unclean, as they were not even Jews. He also finds it possible that Roman soldiers, shepherds, and Samaritans were involved.[4] Of course, Jesus also is reported as eating with Pharisees, and, presumably, with ordinary people without regard for their social status. But it is important to note that this table fellowship was inclusive and extended far beyond the membership of the Jesus-movement.

John R. Donahue summarized a reading of the significance of the meal recorded in Mark 2:

---

3. John P. Meier, *A Marginal Jew: Rethinking the Historical Jesus,* vol. 2, *Mentor, Message, and Miracles,* Anchor Bible Reference Library (New York: Doubleday, 1994), 965. Whether the accusation of "glutton and drunkard" was responded to by the actual man Jesus is irrelevant. The issue is his reputation as remembered and the response to it. Meier thinks it is attributable to the actual Jesus, and Dunn finds it "a memory of one of Jesus' more vivid attempts to signal his own understanding of the difference between his mission and that of John"; see James D. G. Dunn, *Jesus Remembered,* vol. 1 of *Christianity in the Making* (Grand Rapids: Eerdmans, 2003), 454.

4. J. Ramsey Michaels, *Servant and Son: Jesus in Parable and Gospel* (Atlanta: John Knox, 1981), 207.

By his fellowship with the toll collectors and sinners Jesus makes present the love and saving mercy of God to those whom the social structures of his time would classify as unjust and beyond the pale of God's loving concern. Jesus' association with these groups is a form of symbolic activity which proclaims that those ritual laws which were designed to protect the sanctity and justice of God concealed the revelation of the true God.[5]

This comment needs some unpacking. First, Donahue's point about Jesus' symbolic activity indicting the ritual law may fall into the trap of supersessionism. Second, it ignores the fact that all are ritually impure at some time in their lives. Ritual impurity may be a temporary condition and is not one that puts people outside of "God's loving concern."[6] Third, this meal is not merely a symbolic event or even a parabolic action undertaken to challenge those whose vision of God's care and compassion was limited.[7] Of course, it can be read that way. Such a reading is probably part of what the narrators wanted hearers to get from the story.

Rather, the table fellowship of the Jesus-movement realized for a time the banquet of the *basileia tou theou* and anticipated the eternal banquet of the *basileia tou theou*. When God reigns, all share in the banquet. Conversely, when all share in the banquet, God reigns. Table fellowship is living in and living out God's reign. It is not that the sharing of food is a parable of or an anticipation of God's reign. The many stories of banquets and heavenly banquets simply show what the reign of God is in reality.

Meal imagery pervades the Gospels, especially the Gospel of Luke. This imagery is multifaceted and cannot be reduced to formulaic terms. Regarding the meals in Luke's Gospel, Dennis E. Smith wrote:

[Luke] appears to prefer complex rather than simple images, multiple rather than single meanings. Sometimes Jesus is presented as the host of the meal, sometimes as guest, sometimes as servant. Sometimes he dines with the "righteous" (Pharisees), sometimes with "sinners," sometimes with the "crowd" (Luke 9:19). Similarly, sometimes the reader is to see himself or herself as guest (e.g., 5:27-32), sometimes as host (e.g., 14:12-14), sometimes as servant (e.g., 12:42-46; 22:24-47). Yet the meal imagery is so pervasive that it appears to make a significant contribution not only to

---

5. John R. Donahue, S.J., "Biblical Perspectives on Justice," in *The Faith That Does Justice*, ed. John C. Haughey, S.J. (New York: Paulist, 1977), 87.

6. See Amy-Jill Levine, *The Misunderstood Jew: The Church and the Scandal of the Jewish Jesus* (San Francisco: HarperSanFrancisco, 2006), 147. The Christian tradition of contrasting Jesus' "freedom" with Pharisaic "observance" is a mark of supersessionism and, as Levine argues cogently, a creation of interpreting, not remembering, Jesus' actions.

7. See Terrence W. Tilley, *Story Theology* (Wilmington, DE: Michael Glazier, 1985; reprint Collegeville, MN: Liturgical Press, 1990, 1991, 2002), 110-11; Bartchy, "Table Fellowship," 799-800, for this interpretation of Jesus' table fellowship as parabolic.

the literary organization of Luke's Gospel but also to its central theological themes.[8]

The point to be drawn from Smith's analysis is that Jesus is remembered as not taking a specific role at table. Rather, the practice of table fellowship had this "first among equals" taking various roles at table and other members of the Jesus-movement also taking various roles. This understanding of table fellowship further warrants Elisabeth Schüssler Fiorenza's view of the Jesus-movement as a discipleship of equals without regard to social status, political rank, or gender.

Jesus was an observant Jew. As Amy-Jill Levine notes, he "followed the commandments (*mitzvot*) given to Moses on Mt. Sinai *as he understood them*. Consequently, he necessarily rejected the understanding of those commandments put forth by rival teachers."[9] Hence, he would have observed the kosher regulations regarding food. Levine argues persuasively that if Jesus had indeed declared all foods clean (Mark 7:19), then there would have been no reason for disputes in the early church about what foods could be eaten, disputes that continued to flare up into the third century.[10] If there was opposition with other teachers on this point, it was not about keeping kosher. The table fellowship was carried out not in opposition to the law regarding *what* was to be eaten. If there was any opposition at all, it was a disagreement about *who* should eat together.

The table fellowship of the Jesus-movement enacted the *basileia tou theou*. It showed how a renewed and reconciled community could live and eat together. Whether the harvest was scant or bountiful, all could participate in the meal. None had the rank to hold back what he or she wanted from the others.

Eating together was a reconciling practice. Even those one ordinarily would not eat with are welcome to the table of the banquet when God reigns. And the reconciliation was an enactment of the forgiveness of sin and debt. Wilson C. K. Poon finds that Luke's use of meal imagery shows that the "good news of God's unconditional acceptance of sinners is *materially fulfilled* by Jesus' table fellowship with all kinds of 'undesirables'. . . ."[11] The reconciliation is not only "horizontal" but also "vertical."

Yet the word "undesirables" ought give us pause. Poon's labeling the banqueters as "undesirables" also conceals the fact that they had a place in the society, even if some elites did not want to keep company with them. Prostitutes, for example,

---

8. Dennis E. Smith, "Table Fellowship as a Literary Motif in the Gospel of Luke," *Journal of Biblical Literature* 106, no. 4 (1987): 638.

9. Levine, *Misunderstood Jew*, 26; emphasis added.

10. Ibid., 24-26.

11. William C. K. Poon, "Superabundant Table Fellowship in the Kingdom: The Feeding of the Five Thousand and the Meal Motif in Luke," *Expository Times* 114, no. 7 (April 2001): 226. While Poon contrasts Luke's narrative with the Markan/Matthean narrative(s) in useful ways, I find over-drawn Poon's strong contrast between Luke's account of Jesus "welcoming" the crowds and the note in Mark and Matthew of Jesus "having pity" on them (Luke uses *apodechomai* where Mark and Matthew use *splanchnizomai*). Poon rightly highlights the superabundance, but that is not absent from the powerful compassion in the Synoptic uses of *splanchnizomai*. See pp. 156-59 above.

seem a necessity for an occupying army; in prostituting themselves, they help reduce the likelihood of occupying soldiers using the other indigenous women for their sexual gratification. The elites might find this result desirable, as it would save their own women from the dishonor of pollution by strangers, even though they might not want to own up to the means by which it is achieved (that this presumes a patriarchal culture is, of course, obvious; a woman stained by contact with a stranger was of less value as a commodity). Similarly, tax gatherers and toll collectors might not be sterling gentlemen, but without them, could the governing structures, including temple governance, function in such a society?

The practice of table fellowship anchors a set of food motifs in the Gospels. This motif is most obvious in Luke, but all the Gospels have Jesus eating with others; they include a major feeding story and a final meal. The Synoptics have parables of the kingdom as a banquet. The content and point of the particular meal imagery vary from text to text, but the centrality of meals is constant. The great feeding miracles, the parables of the banquet, the Last Supper, and the meal with the disciples on the road to Emmaus, found only in Luke's Gospel, can all be understood in the context of the reconciling practice of table fellowship.

Understanding the range of fellowship is significant for understanding the feeding miracles. Luke portrays Jesus as inviting thousands of people, the crowds (*hoi ochloi*), in a desert place without water for ritual cleansing, to recline and eat. There is no judgment about who is and who is not worthy to join so long as they would sit in the orderly ranks of fifty.[12]

Moreover, Jesus and the disciples served them—men, women, and children. Jesus is identified, as are the other core members of the Jesus-movement, as waiting on guests at the banquet. This superabundant banquet that Luke places in the middle of nowhere not only anticipates but also instantiates at a particular time and place the divine banquet in which God feeds all. God provides the food and the Jesus-movement ensures that all eat until there are twelve baskets of leftovers!

However, this is not all that is significant in Luke's telling of the story. As Poon notes, Luke connects the feeding story to the Caesarea Philippi narrative, which immediately follows the feeding. A few verses earlier, there is a story of Herod trying to identify Jesus, but it is much shorter and much less complex. If, as I noted in chapter 8, Mark connected the questioning of Jesus' identity to Herod and his minions by the use of terminology, Luke connects the question to the feeding miracles. Also in Luke, Jesus does not ask who the people, *hoi anthropoi*, say that he is, but who the crowds (those who were fed), *hoi ochloi*, say that he is. Poon makes the point: "The answer was not encouraging: even after the Feeding Miracle, they still thought Jesus was John the Baptist or Elijah—the

---

12. Luke has the count in the middle of the story, whereas Mark and Matthew have it at the end. Poon notes that this allows Luke to finish the story with the leftovers—making the point that the feeding was not a marvel because of the number fed but because of the superabundant food God provided (Poon, "Superabundant Table Fellowship," 226). One might also read Matthew's "parenthetical remark" about women and children also being there and being fed (often taken as making women and children an afterthought) as a challenge to those who think male fellowship would be sufficient for real inclusivity in the banquet.

arch-ascetics."[13] Who or what Jesus is, is not a "messianic secret." Not knowing him is not the result of not being in on the secret, but of an inability to recognize what the *basileia tou theou* looks like—it looks like a banquet in which all are fed and there is also an abundance of leftovers.

In Luke, *hoi ochloi* still don't get it: Jesus is not an ascetic. How can they think that even after he fed them extravagantly? Luke construes Jesus' identity not only in opposition to the powers of dominance but also in opposition to those who would identify his movement with an ascetic one. Luke thus suggests that *ho christos* is to be understood as one who lives in and lives out a regime that not only finds a God who gives abundance, but who lives in a movement that lives out that abundance in serving the food that sustains all the people who live—even if only for a miraculous moment—in the *basileia tou theou*.

Parables about Banqueting

The parables centered on eating and drinking are elaborate tales that suggest that we need to respond to the invitation to "come to the banquet" *now*. Yet that is only part of the story. Inclusivity and a pattern of upsetting hierarchies are also important. Luke's version of a banquet story is illuminating.

Luke or Luke's oral source constructs a fascinatingly complex scene to "place" a banquet parable. The scene begins on a specific occasion, a Sabbath, when Jesus was going to eat at the home of a leader of the Pharisees. He first cures a man of dropsy—the Pharisees raise no objection. Nor should they be expected to do so.[14] On coming into the house, he urges guests to take the lowest places and be in position to be told by the host to "come higher." He then urges those who give banquets to invite the poor, the crippled, the lame and the blind because those people cannot repay the hospitality. To invite those who can give a *quid pro quo* is not really a good deed; to invite those who cannot repay the hospitality is a *mitzvah*. Then, as Luke has it, one of the guests responded and Jesus replied with a parable:

> One of the dinner guests, on hearing this, said to him, "Blessed is anyone who will eat bread in the reign of God." Then Jesus said to him, "Someone gave a great dinner and invited many. At the time for the dinner he sent his slave to say to those who had been invited, 'Come; for everything is ready now.' But they all alike began to make excuses. The first said to him, 'I have brought five yoke of oxen, and I am going to try them out; please accept my regrets.' Another said, 'I have just been married, and therefore cannot come.' So the slave returned and reported to his master. Then the master of the house became angry and said to his slave, 'Go out at once into the streets

---

13. Poon, "Superabundant Table Fellowship," 229.

14. Levine (*Misunderstood Jew*, 29-33) makes the point that the Sabbath observance would never appropriately be construed as preventing work if a life were in danger. As Jesus' cures were likely not "work" under the law, they could be appropriate, not forbidden, on the Sabbath.

and the lanes of the town and bring in the poor, the crippled, the blind and the lame.' And the slave said, 'Sir, what you ordered has been done, and there is still room.' Then the master said to the slave, 'Go out into the roads and lanes, and compel people to come in, so that my house may be filled.'" (Luke 14:15-23 NRSV adapted)[15]

The abundance of this banquet is astonishing. In a country where the poor, lame, blind, and crippled might be found in abundance, they still do not fill the table. Travelers, merchants, perhaps even soldiers are welcome at the banquet. It is as if the householder is saying, "Find anyone! Drag them in! We've got so much that we have to share it." Many commentators focus on the moment of *decision*; but perhaps more important is the incredible largesse of the *invitation*. The reconciling table is open to all.

Jesus' parables are multilayered and admit of numerous reasonable interpretations. Luke has suggested that the banquet of the *basileia* is a eucharistic banquet (22:30), and Matthew describes a heavenly banquet (8:11). Maureen Tilley has told me that a Catholic missionary returning from China was asked how he explained heaven and hell to the Chinese. He responded that he taught them with the following image: "Hell is like a great banquet at which everyone is given four-foot-long chopsticks so nobody can feed himself; heaven is like a great banquet at which everyone is given four-foot-long chopsticks and everybody feeds each other."[16] Whatever the banquet in the *basileia tou theou* is, it is abundant and shared.

The Last Supper

The Last Supper is a prime example of another form of table fellowship preserved in the New Testament. The supper is remembered in three distinct versions: (1) in Mark 14:17-25 and Matthew 26:20-29, the institution narrative ends with Jesus' saying he will not drink wine again until he drinks it in the *basileia tou theou*

---

15. The next verse reads, "For I tell you, none of those who were invited will taste my dinner." Luke commonly has Jesus explaining the point of his parables (as above, with the story of the man in the ditch). This verse may well have been added to the story as it was transmitted to explain the meaning of the story—it has overtones that suggest the strife between the later Jesus-movement and other parties of late-first-century Judaism. The present interpretation takes a somewhat different tack. Compare Luise Schottroff, *The Parables of Jesus*, trans. Linda Maloney (Minneapolis: Fortress, 2006), 49-56; she opens up a number of interpretive possibilities, including a suggestion that the angry host is criticized, not valorized, in the parable.

16. Compare my *Story Theology*, 88; I have since learned that this story has multiple versions. Like folktales that have common motifs (inability to feed oneself, feeding the other) and local characteristics (four-foot-long chopsticks, four-foot-long spoons, four-foot-long forks, etc.), this story travels well. What I have called motifs is the heart of Sandra Schneiders's "ideal meaning," while each of the variants is a "valid" interpretation because it refracts in its own way the crucial dynamic of the story. See Sandra Schneiders, *The Revelatory Text: Interpreting the New Testament as Sacred Scripture,* 2nd ed. (Collegeville, MN: Liturgical Press, 1999), xxx-xxxiv.

(ouranou); (2) Luke 22:14-38 and 1 Cor. 11:23-26 include Jesus' instruction to do this in memory of him and additional material particular to Luke and to Paul; and (3) John 13:1-16:33, which has the foot washing but no eucharistic "institution narrative" and includes a long speech of Jesus filled with images and metaphors, typical of John's Gospel. The first two *may* be modeled on a Passover meal, but the third clearly is not.[17] If all were welcome to the abundance of God's banquet as narrated in the stories of the feeding miracles and the open table fellowship without regard to status, the remarkably varied Last Supper stories tell of a more intimate meal, a meal of the active participants in the Jesus-movement.

It is often assumed that because the Synoptic texts have the Twelve participating in this meal that it is Jesus and *only* the Twelve who were there. Why assume this? It is actually a function of how we read the text, rather than the text itself. Matthew says that Jesus would eat the Passover with his disciples and they prepared the meal; in the evening he reclined at table with the Twelve (Matt. 26:17-20). Mark has the householder (and the disciples apparently) preparing the meal and Jesus and the Twelve coming in the evening; who is reclining is somewhat ambiguous (Mark 14:12-18). Luke has Jesus sending the disciples to prepare the meal and reclining at table with the apostles (Luke 22:11-14). Paul has received the institution narrative from the Lord, but does not mention a Last Supper or those who were there (1 Cor. 11:23-26). John's version of the Last Supper has disciples at the dinner (John 13:22; 16:29). Given the disparity of the narratives, there is no good reason to think that only the Twelve were there. Indeed, all the stories, save Paul's, mention the disciples' sharing the meal. The view that the Twelve and only the Twelve were at dinner not only assumes a very strong distinction between those Twelve and the other disciples of Jesus, a distinction that we have argued above may not be tenable,[18] but this idea also has no textual warrant. It is rather a reading into the text of the absence of others. Moreover, a meal without women present seems decidedly odd.

The view that this was a meal of Jesus and the Twelve has been hallowed by sacramental theologies that have assumed that Jesus "instituted" the Eucharist there and in fact "ordained" the Twelve as the agents who would "do this" in his memory, leading to an all-male priesthood and especially an all-male hierarchy. This assumption, however, is not at all well warranted, to say the least. John's text does not mention the Twelve. In Mark's text, the meal is prepared for the teacher and his disciples (*not* the Twelve). In Matthew's text, the disciples are *not* numbered, while in Luke's Gospel the disciples are numbered and named (Peter and John). However, in Luke, the guest room was intended for Jesus to keep the Passover with his *disciples* (Luke 22:7-13), not the Twelve. These variations in the

---

17. Dunn (*Jesus Remembered*, 229-31) uses (a) and (b) to help make the case for his argument about the orality of the tradition and the variability of performances, especially in liturgical contexts. The various inconsistencies in the texts are not amenable to harmonization. See, for example, the literature reviewed and the proposals considered and found wanting in Joseph A. Fitzmyer, S.J., *The Gospel According to Luke: Introduction, Translation, and Notes*, 2 vols., Anchor Bible 28, 28A (Garden City, NY: Doubleday, 1981, 1985), 2:1376-81, 1386-95.

18. See above, pp. 133-36; also see Dunn, *Jesus Remembered*, 540, and the literature he cites.

tradition clearly reflect oral transmission of a basic story performed in different ways by different storytellers. The standard reading is not the only possible one. There is as good a textual reason to think that more than thirteen participated in the meal as there is reason to think that thirteen did.

As Quentin Quesnell argues, naming the Twelve as present at the supper may simply be a way of highlighting their presence, in light of their later importance. Quesnell also notes that Luke occasionally highlights the Twelve among the disciples and that one codex contains a textual variant that has "the disciples" instead of "the Twelve" at the supper.[19] Since the group of disciples includes women, Quesnell draws a credible conclusion:

> Luke did think in terms of a larger group at the Supper than just the Twelve. Specifically, he thought of the Christian community he had been at pains to build up around Jesus through the course of the Gospel, and around which he would develop the church of Acts. Further, Luke thought of the women as part of that community, sharing in all its life and actions. When he showed that community gathered for the Last Supper, he never imagined future readers might doubt that the women were present.[20]

While I am less sanguine about stating what Luke could have imagined or thought, Quesnell's arguments are surely sufficient to dethrone the easy assumption of an all-male *symposium*, perhaps with women who cooked and cleaned and waited in another room while the men had their special dinner. If discipleship is open to all, this is highly unlikely. That Jesus was exclusive rather than inclusive in table fellowship is not warranted in the Gospels. Even if this is a more intimate meal, limiting it to a symposium of thirteen males (on the basis of a patriarchal reading of the text) is unwarranted.

Here we have the movement gathered rather than sent. These are not people on mission, but people gathered. In the Luke-Paul version they are also commissioned to engage in this practice of sharing a meal in memory of him. In the narrations of this supper, crucial liturgical patterns are portrayed to sustain the future life of the community. Luke and John portray Jesus as teaching the disciples, as does John, especially in and through Jesus' actions of washing the disciples' feet. However this gathering of the movement is understood, the centripetal table fellowship of the Jesus-movement is, at best, incomplete, without the centrifugal sending as well.

Unfortunately, the Eucharist has been the focus of Christian fractiousness from the beginning. Paul's admonitions about eucharistic and other food indicate a community that has not learned how to engage in the banquet of the kingdom. The later conflicts over what food was fit to eat and who could properly participate in the Eucharist obscure the focus of Jesus' table fellowship: the key was *who* was invited, not what they ate. All were invited.

---

19. Quentin Quesnell, "The Women at Luke's Supper," *Political Issues in Luke-Acts*, ed. Richard J. Cassidy and Philip J. Sharper (Maryknoll, NY: Orbis Books, 1983), 66-67.
20. Ibid., 71.

The disputes over keeping kosher reflected in Acts and 1 Corinthians are disputes not about the reign of God but about the practices that are necessary for communal identity. What is remarkable about the practice of table fellowship in the early Christian communities is that little is recorded about feeding multitudes, inviting strangers, or dining with outcasts. Jesus is remembered in word about inclusive table fellowship, but not in deed. The earliest Christian communities seem to have abandoned this aspect of the practice of Jesus.

Hospitality as a Reconciling Practice

The practice of hospitality was not lost. The medieval monastic tradition of hospitality, especially among the Benedictines, offers not only food but also shelter and sometimes clothing to strangers. The Catholic Worker houses and other similar establishments in the United States also keep alive this aspect of the practice today. Indeed, just because it is not a major theme of the practice of the Jesus-movement—so much so that the inclusive table fellowship seems almost a practice distinctive of Jesus—does not mean that it was abandoned. In a time of scarcity—the Diaspora churches sent financial support to the Jerusalem church—the focus may have been on remembering internal charity. In a time of dispute and identity formation after the death of Jesus, the earliest communities may have had to focus on internal matters and internal relationships.

What are we to make of the memories of Jesus' table fellowship today? First, it has become a commonplace of scholarship that the biblical and historical records do not warrant the claim that Jesus called only men to "ordination." The concept of ordination has shifted vastly, and there is no reason to think that the instruction "Do this in remembrance of me" could be addressed only to men or that Jesus was "ordaining" them. While arguments are made for ordaining only men to the presbyterate, it is not clear that that practice can be warranted by appeal to the practice of Jesus. Second, it suggests that the table fellowship of the gathered should be matched with the table fellowship of the sent. While one might speculate about the connections between Jesus' inclusive table fellowship and the meals of the disciples such as those depicted as the Last Supper, these seem significantly different enough that collapsing them into a single form of table fellowship is also unwarranted. However, without the balance between the service of those sent and the nourishment of those gathered, something is missing if we as disciples are to carry on the practices of the Jesus-movement. Finally, Jesus' stories and practice of hospitality suggest what "catholic" can and should mean with regard to the variously named Jesus-movement, community, or church.

Walter J. Ong, S.J., has suggested that the use of the Greek term *katholikos* as one of the marks of the church is significant.[21] Using a Greek term when

---

21. Walter J. Ong, S.J., "Realizing Catholicism: Faith, Learning and the Future," in *Faith and the Intellectual Life*, ed. James L. Heft, S.M. (Notre Dame: University of Notre Dame Press, 1996), 31-33.

formulating the marks in Latin, when the Latin form *universalis* was available to complement the other three marks ("one, holy, apostolic"), suggests that "catholic" and "universal" are not quite the same thing. Ong suggests that the catholicity of the church consists not in the extent to which the church has spread, but in its distribution as "the leaven in the lump." *Katholikos* suggests "through and through" rather than "everywhere." The church does not cover the world or own the world, nor is it simply worldwide. Rather, it is to be found everywhere where the breath of the Spirit raises the lump of the world into the bread of life. In this sense, the church may be a sacrament by its catholicity, by its obligation not to be the world but to raise the world into new life in the Spirit.

The image of table fellowship—carried through in the yeasty imagination of Fr. Ong—is one that requires both gathering and sending. The leaven must be gathered and nourished, but if it is only gathered, it begins to die. It must also be kneaded into the "lump of dough." It cannot merely be gathered, but must be sent out to do its work. The limited table fellowship nourishes those who would change the shape of the world.

If this is so, then the best form of evangelization is not proselytizing in word but witnessing in practice. The sorts of practices that characterize the Jesus-movement are a model for living well, for living in and living out God's reign. As James D. G. Dunn notes, the stories in the New Testament are neither a blueprint "nor an instruction manual for a complete social ethic or politically mature society." Rather, such stories indicate "the character of the deep personal relations and priorities, values, and motivations without which any social structure or political manifesto will fail to realize its best ambitions."[22] Witness requires words, of course; but, to paraphrase St. James, mere words without the life and practice of faith are dead.

This practical approach, however, carries an important corollary: the church is an ongoing movement that is also a "sacramental sign, which at any given moment of history may succeed or fail in communicating God's grace. To the extent, therefore, that an individual Christian fails to be an effective sign, he or she turns that sign into a lie."[23] The church is a community of redeemed sinners who, addicted to sin, often backslide into sinfulness even though they are part of the Jesus-movement. If the center of evangelization is witness, then our failure to live in and live out a life together that realizes and anticipates the *basileia tou theou* is a sign of our failures as disciples.

Such failures are not new, as Peter did testify.

God acts in and through the church as God acts in and through the bread and wine of the Eucharist. This action can be understood in a number of ways. Just as the sacrament of baptism classically was construed as having three modes depending on the circumstances (baptism of water as the ordinary way, of blood for those catechumens who were martyred before being baptized, and of desire

---

22. Dunn, *Jesus Remembered*, 893.

23. Michael C. McCarthy, S.J., "Religious Disillusionment in a Land of Illusions," in *Rahner beyond Rahner: A Great Theologian Encounters the Pacific Rim*, ed. Paul G. Crowley, S.J. (Lanham, MD: Rowman & Littlefield, 2005), 106.

for those who were not Christians but were oriented to the Good that is God in their lives), so perhaps we can think of the sacramental presence of the church as multimodal depending on the circumstances.

Recent theological reflection on the church in Asia fits with this image of the community as the ongoing presence of the Jesus movement. Christians are empowered to be the sacrament of—the present instantiation of and the anticipation of the fullness of—God's reign. To paraphrase George E. Griener, S.J., the mission of the church is not first and foremost about the church, nor even about Jesus Christ, but about the reign of God that both the church and Gospel are meant to serve. Borrowing a phrase credited to William Burrows, Jonathan Yun-Ka Tan suggests that the appropriate missiological strategy for serving the reign of God, especially for the church in Asia, is best understood not as *missio ad gentes* ("mission to the peoples") but as *missio inter gentes* ("mission among the peoples").[24] The question is not what the mission is or who is to be doing it, but how to live among people in a way that may be mutually enriching. To make disciples of all nations may not necessarily involve explicit commitment to Jesus and the church, but it may involve showing all nations how to live together.

Yeast feeds off the lumpy dough, and as it develops it raises the dough. The lump can and does nourish the leaven as the leaven works to raise the lump—a point developed later in chapter 19.

Table fellowship is not proselytization. It is treating the stranger as guest, the Other as a friend, the opponent as a colleague who differs, sometimes in important ways, from us. The notion that the Jesus-movement has a mission *inter gentes* fits remarkably well with the practice of table fellowship in the early Jesus-movement. "For the *basileia tou theou* is like a banquet. . . ."

---

24. George E. Griener, S.J., "Rahner and the Pacific Rim: From the *Kulturkampf* to China's Cultural Christians," in *Rahner beyond Rahner*, ed. Crowley, 106. Griener refers to documents of the Federation of Asian Bishops' Conferences: Jonathan Yun-Ka Tan, "*Missio Inter Gentes*: Towards a New Paradigm in the Mission Theology of the Federation of Asian Bishops' Conferences," prepared as a discussion guide for the Eighth Plenary Session of FABC at Taejon, Korea, August 2004, available online at www.ucanews.com/html/fabc-papers/fabc-109.htm (accessed July 15, 2007); and Edmund Chia, "Interreligious Dialogue in Pursuit of Fullness of Life in Asia," *Seventh Plenary Assembly Workshop Discussion Guide,* FABC Paper No. 92k, p. 10; available online at www.ucanews.com/html/fabc-papers/fabc-92k.htm (accessed July 15, 2007). The significance of this insight will emerge in chap. 19.

CONCLUSION TO PART THREE

But there are also many other acts that Jesus performed, which, if they were written one by one, I think the world could not hold all the books written.
—John 21:25

*W*hat the author of the final chapter of John's Gospel said about Jesus' deeds certainly applies to the practices of the Jesus-movement. Part 3 could be expanded almost infinitely. The varieties of reconciling practices, rooted in the practices of the Jesus-movement, have taken a wide range of forms appropriate to different times and places. A sampling of them can be found in any "lives of the saints," although some saints do not seem very edifying or even very interested in reconciling practices. Clearly, healing, teaching, forgiving, and enjoying table fellowship are central practices of the Jesus-movement, touchstones for understanding the validity of new practices.

Some may wonder about omissions from this section. I am conscious of how much has been omitted. Most of the sacraments are not here, and they are practices that grew out of Jesus' practices. Praying and worshiping are not much mentioned either. Much has been left out.

The reasons for the omissions are twofold. First, the book is long enough and the specifically religious practices have legions of books and articles written about them. In many ways it seems almost unnecessary to include them not only because they are covered so extensively elsewhere but also because without a life of communal worship, individual prayer, and sacramental practice, the community of disciples—the Jesus-movement—cannot even exist. But neither can discipleship or spirituality consist only in those practices. The Jesus-movement exists to serve and to realize the reign of God. It does so in and for the world that God has created, as the "leaven in the lump," to use Walter Ong's less than elegant phrase. Christologists sometimes connect spirituality with christology through soteriology. I thought it important that these outgoing reconciling practices that show what it means to live in and live out the reign of God be explicitly connected with christology—indeed, that they practically constitute what it means for the disciples to recognize Jesus as *ho christos*. Second, I have little theological competence in the areas of prayer and worship even as I "keep practicing." It is better that these topics be left to others.

In the preface, I wrote that this volume is only a voice in an ongoing conversation that began nearly two millennia ago. That conversation is a constituent in discerning imaginatively how to participate in the reconciling practices that Jesus' disciples viewed as beginning with him. That conversation will go on long after this book is dust. Much more could be said even now. But now it is for others to chime in about how to live in and live out God's reign inaugurated by the one whose disciples we strive to be.

Part Four

IMPLICATIONS

INTRODUCTION TO PART FOUR

*T*his final section of the book brings this essay in christology to its close. Chapter 17 attempts to clear away some brush regarding christological doctrine. In recent years, the Congregation for the Doctrine of the Faith has issued documents regarding "serious errors" in the work of some contemporary Catholic christologists. The CDF imposed serious penalties on Roger Haight, S.J., but did not impose any on Jon Sobrino, S.J.[1]

Methodologically, Haight is a critical correlationist, an approach that has many characteristics of what has come to be called in the United States the "Chicago school" of narrative theology.[2] His approach works with the paradigm of correlating the tradition with key aspects of contemporary culture, specifically contemporary academic understandings of the practice and results of historical investigation and the situation of religious diversity.[3] While I have similar concerns, the method in the present essay is "constructivist." As noted in chapter 2, it crosses aspects of both critical correlationist and postliberal theologies with both the "praxis" approaches of Latin American liberation theologians and the "practice-oriented" approaches of other U.S. Christian theologians such as James Wm. McClendon,

---

1. That I have great respect for these theologians and have learned much from their mature works is, I hope, clear from what follows. That I also differ with them on specific points in method and content should also be clear. Haight's work is a serious attempt to translate an understanding of Jesus as God's Sacrament from its modern Dutch (Piet Schoonenberg, Edward Schillebeeckx) context to a postmodern, postcritical U.S. context. Sobrino's mature works are among the very best that have emerged from Latin American liberation theology. But as my context is different from each, so is my approach. In chap. 17, I note that the CDF reading of Sobrino's work is widely regarded as seriously defective. The CDF interventions have resolved *quaestiones disputatae* among theologians exploring the significance of Jesus in a pluralistic world by imposing a juridical resolution that has decided in favor of one theological approach over others, rather than by letting theologians continue to dispute and to let those disputes about how to express the faith come to theological resolution.

2. See Gary Comstock, "Two Types of Narrative Theology," *Journal of the American Academy of Religion* 55, no. 4 (1987): 687-717. The two "schools" Comstock finds are the "Chicago correlational" and "Yale postliberal" approach. A third distinctive approach is more eclectic, including theologians from Berkeley at one time or another (James Wm. McClendon, Jr., Michael Goldberg, Theophus Smith, the present author) and others who work similarly, such as John Shea.

3. See Roger Haight, *Jesus Symbol of God,* 2nd ed. (Maryknoll, NY: Orbis Books, 2000), passim. For my views in these areas, views that are reflected in this book, especially in this final part, see my *Inventing Catholic Tradition* (Maryknoll, NY: Orbis Books, 2000); *History, Theology, and Faith: Dissolving the Modern Problematic* (Maryknoll, NY: Orbis Books, 2004); and *Religious Diversity and the American Experience: A Theological Approach* (New York: Continuum, 2007).

Jr., Stanley Hauerwas, and Robert Schreiter, C.Pp.S.[4] Whatever "errors" might be found to infect the present work would thus be of a somewhat different order from the "errors" found in Haight's work because of these methodological differences. Hence, I do not address the concerns that the Congregation raises with Haight.

I do, however, address some of the concerns that the Congregation raised with Sobrino in the first section of chapter 17. Some of the methodological concerns the Congregation raised are clearly relevant to the present approach. I have taken this opportunity to use the Notification to clarify my own position. The second section of the chapter details more precisely the understanding of doctrine presupposed here.

Chapter 18 explores the key christological affirmation of Jesus the Christ as truly human and truly divine. In so doing it reflects on some difficulties with interpreting the classic christological claims of the Council of Chalcedon. One profound misunderstanding has been the notion of what the "two natures" in Christ can mean. I identify the problem as theologians' making syllogistic deductions from tropological language.

The final chapter recaps the heart of the book, that true christology is found in the disciples' engagement in reconciling practice. It suggests a rather different way forward in the light of religious diversity from many of those currently "on offer" in the theological marketplace. In light of the church's mark of "catholicity," I find the suggestion that Christians have a *missio inter gentes* to be most apt. Thus, I sketch the place of faith in the resurrection of Jesus and what atonement, properly at-one-ment, means in practice.

Admittedly, I do not spend a lot of time on these significant doctrines. That is a result, at least in part, of the change in perspective characteristic of the present practice-based approach to doing theology. This change in perspective significantly affects how doctrine is "placed." Consider an illustration: The Chrysler Building in New York City looks quite different when one pictures it from the street, from the Empire State Building, from a helicopter, from northern New Jersey, from an airplane landing at LaGuardia airport, or from a satellite. If one is attempting to figure out how the steam supplied by the power company heats and cools the building, no picture will help, but a schematic of the building's plumbing will be useful. The ways we understand the building differ depending on our perspective and our purposes. The building remains fundamentally the same.

It seems obvious that no picture or schematic "is" the Chrysler Building, but rather, such a plan offers a perspective on the building. Each picture should represent the whole building, but not the whole of the building. No perspective, save God's, is complete. That no doctrinal formula "is" the "idea of Christianity" about Christ seems equally obvious.[5]

---

4. For a more developed sketch of this approach, see my *Religious Diversity and the American Experience*, 4-9. I also have adapted the work of some contemporary Thomistic philosophers and theologians in this part of the work, an approach I have not taken before. My debts to them will be seen in what follows. Whether I have interpreted and used any of the insights others have generated in ways they would find suitable is, of course, another matter.

5. I use "idea" in a manner similar to that of John Henry Newman. For Newman, the idea of

It is difficult to overstate the importance of the distinction between what a thing is and what expresses and shows it. This is not at all the same distinction as the classic philosophical distinction between "appearances" and "reality." Faith is a divine gift that is lived in and lived out—or rejected. The life of faith is a life lived under the guidance of a Christian vision. The articulation of that vision and the practice of the faith vary from time to time and place to place. Christians use *these* expressions and engage in *these* practices and avoid *those* expressions and practices.[6]

The question is not whether a formula captures the whole, but which picture is useful for what purpose at what time. Even though they may be wildly different, our photographs and schematics may each be a good portrayal of the Chrysler Building that does not distort it (unless used ineptly). The question is which formulae are useful for understanding how to live as disciples of Jesus promoting the *basileia tou theou* in particular times and places. Is the present "practical" approach a good sketch of a practical christology appropriate for living in and living out the Catholic Christian tradition in the present?

Two questions must be asked: first, is this approach appropriate to the contemporary community and, second, is it faithful to the practice of the past? Just as we don't fault satellite pictures for not clearly showing the art deco lines of the upper stories of the Chrysler Building, so it is inappropriate to fault contemporary christologies because they don't use terms generated in a perspective from the past. Rather, theological work should be measured by its appropriateness for the contemporary community that seeks to be faithful in the present to the practice of the Jesus-movement.

Christianity *appears in* a succession of historical events, but is not *reducible to* them. The faith *is* what it is; God is what God is. For Newman, the idea of Christianity never changes essentially. What develops is the expression of that idea. "[T]hese expressions [Creeds and dogmas] are never equivalent to" the idea, although those expressions "live in the one idea which they are designed to express, and which alone is substantive. . . . Catholic dogmas are, after all, but symbols of a divine fact, which, far from being compassed by those very propositions, would not be exhausted, not fathomed, by a thousand." Doctrinal formulae do not determine what the faith is, but express and show the faith. The quotation is from Newman, *An Essay on the Development of Christian Doctrine*, 2nd ed. (London: James Toovey, 1846), 56-57; Newman is quoting from his *University Sermons*. The version cited is a reprint of the 1845 edition with a few trivial corrigenda noted on p. xv.

6. See my *Inventing Catholic Tradition*, chap. 5, for further discussion of this point.

Seventeen

THE FORM AND FUNCTION
OF DOCTRINE

*O*ne of the challenges to approaching the disciples' Jesus and construing doing christology as carrying on the reconciling practice of the Jesus-movement is that traditional christological doctrines may be slighted. This is a key issue brought up in the "Notification on the Works of Fr. Jon Sobrino, S.J.," issued by the Congregation for the Doctrine of the Faith in 2007. In the first section of this chapter, I examine a few of the issues that the Congregation raises that could be seen as relevant to the present project, which has affinities with Sobrino's approach. In the second section, I sketch a form of the "rule theory" of doctrine that I have discussed in other writings to clarify the way I use that theory here.

The CDF and Sobrino

The differences between the CDF and Jon Sobrino are emblematic of the tension between theological approaches that are "progressive and conservative . . . daring to the verge of presumption and prudent to the verge of despair."[1] Baron Friedrich von Hügel, author of those words, argued that both approaches were necessary for the life of the church. In the congregation's "conservative" view, Fr. Sobrino, in his "progressive" mature works in christology, *Jesus the Liberator* and *Christ the Liberator*,[2] has not done full justice to traditional christological doctrines.[3] Given the approach to christology taken by the CDF document, seeing

---

1. This quotation is taken from Friedrich von Hügel, "Official Authority and Living Religion," in idem, *Essays and Addresses in the Philosophy of Religion*, 2nd series (London: J. M. Dent, 1926), 16, 17. This essay was delivered as a paper in 1904.

2. Jon Sobrino, *Jesus the Liberator: A Historical-Theological Reading of Jesus of Nazareth*, trans. Paul Burns and Francis McDonagh (Maryknoll, NY: Orbis Books, 1993); idem, *Christ the Liberator: A View from the Victims*, trans. Paul Burns (Maryknoll, NY: Orbis Books, 2001).

3. "The Congregation does not intend to judge the subjective intentions of the Author, but rather has the duty to call to attention to certain propositions which are not in conformity with the doctrine of the Church" (see http://www.vatican.va/roman_curia/congregations/cfaith/documents/rc_con_cfaith_doc_20061126_notification-sobrino_en.html [accessed July 15, 2007]). For present purposes, that the Notification is, at best, an uncharitable reading of Sobrino's works, is not relevant. The Notification highlights some of the points that the CDF finds neuralgic. On the substance

some "inadequacies" in Sobrino's work is practically unavoidable. The CDF's criteria are formulae that were developed in a deductive, neoscholastic approach to christology that centered on explicating the positions of the Councils of Nicaea and Chalcedon, and Sobrino's approach is quite different.[4]

The approach of the CDF fits what most would describe as a "christology from above." Sobrino, in contrast, is doing a "christology from below." Sobrino simply cannot, given his approach, say what the Notification insists that he must say in the way the CDF claims he needs to say it. The CDF, in effect, while pointing out concerns it has regarding Sobrino's work, fails to understand or to accept the significance of the approach Sobrino is taking. Or, if the Congregation does understand Sobrino's method, it may simply reject the possibility of doing christology on the basis of using the results of historical criticism in an approach that does not find doctrine or theory a foundation for, but rather a moment in and of, concrete praxis.

Sobrino's approach, like the present one, presumes the priority of practice or praxis. Both are committed to a theological approach that is thoroughly historical as well as faithful to the tradition. Both also critically adapt recent and contemporary work in New Testament scholarship—for what could one say about Jesus Christ if one did not take seriously what we can affirm about his actual life and work? As theologians of the past used the best historical and theological scholarship available to them, so do theologians today. The CDF is, in effect, attempting to undermine this continuity in the practice of theology in favor of requiring theologians to use the words (and only the words?) that the CDF's neoscholastic approach finds the (only?) right way to signify the faith.

The approaches that begin with practice/praxis work in a different theological style from that of the doctrine-centered approach of the CDF. The CDF approach takes the formulae of the great councils as historically unsurpassable. Because of the status of the Notification regarding Sobrino's works—there are no penalties or censures associated with it—one can legitimately argue that this action is not an abuse of power, which would have occurred if the CDF had offered a definitive finding against a theologian from one school of theologians on the basis of the approach preferred by another school of theologians regarding actively disputed

---

of the Notification, British theologian Nicholas Lash finds it to have "incompetent and possibly malicious misreadings of his theology" ("Letter to the Editor," *The Tablet* [London], March 24, 2007). Other theologians have said similar things; see also "Jon Sobrino—Dossier," *Concilium* no. 3 (2007): 125-34 for some other responses to the Notification; also see the editorial board's support for Sobrino in the same issue of *Concilium*, 7-8.

4. William P. Loewe makes the point that Sobrino's theological work is measured "not only by the faith of the church, but also from the viewpoint of one particular, if rich and valuable theological tradition, namely scholasticism" in "The Sobrino File: How to Read the Vatican's Latest Notification," *Commonweal* 134, no. 10 (March 18, 2007), http://www.commonwealmagazine.org/print_format.php?id_article=1939 (accessed July 19, 2007). Sobrino is one of many contemporary theologians who share the contemporary "disenchantment with the traditional formula of Chalcedon" and who have "sought to relocate the doctrine of Chalcedon in a different frame of reference," as the scene was described over thirty years ago by Dermot A. Lane, *The Reality of Jesus: An Essay in Christology* (New York: Paulist, 1975), 109.

questions, especially in methodology. Preference for a particular approach in theology is not cause for a CDF censure. Entering the theological fray, as the CDF does here, may be another issue, but if the Congregation is entering the fray, it does so from a position of institutional privilege.

The CDF claims that one can deduce historical claims about Jesus of Nazareth from philosophical theses and doctrines developed centuries after Jesus lived. For example, the Notification states, "The filial and messianic consciousness of Jesus is the direct consequence of his ontology as Son of God made man" (§8). If this is intended as a statement about a historical fact, it cannot be warranted by any sort of methodological approach that can pass muster among serious practitioners of the discipline of history today.[5] By contemporary standards, the CDF statement has no historical warrant as a claim about the actual man Jesus. If this is not a statement about the actual man Jesus, it has no force other than the deduction of a claim *about* a person of the past from a premise that is unhistorical. It may be a "faith statement," but, if so, it has no warrant for countering Sobrino's (or others') historically based claims about Jesus of Nazareth. It is of a different status; it is a reflection on history or a theological proposition derived using a hypothetical-deductive method, not a claim based on historical investigation. While one cannot entirely separate theological claims from historical claims, the way each is warranted is different in contemporary practice. It should be obvious that the CDF is working with a methodology that is, by present standards in history and in theology (apart from some forms of neoscholastic theology), insufficiently clear about the work that each of the disciplines, history and theology, can do. Contemporary theologians conscious of the contributions of historical methods treat reflective doctrines as based on, not the basis of, claims about actual, historical events and persons.

This is *not* to say that one cannot make claims about the actual consciousness of Jesus. Rather, it is that such claims are rather difficult to warrant on historical grounds given the evidence we have. Scholars have argued, for example, that Jesus' "Abba-consciousness" indicates a filial awareness.[6] And Jesus calling God "Abba" likely was a hallmark of his teaching. But this usage cannot be developed into an argument about the uniqueness of Jesus or of his "God-consciousness." Not only does the Babylonian Talmud indicate that others whose time antedates Jesus used "Abba" as Jesus did, but God was designated as "Father" throughout the Second Temple period.[7] That Jesus addressed God as "Abba" is historically reliable. But it is not unique and may not be distinctive. The historical evidence neither supports a claim of Jesus' *uniqueness* nor undermines such a claim. Any substantial claim about Jesus' uniqueness or consciousness is a theological, not

---

5. See my *History, Theology, and Faith: Dissolving the Modern Problematic* (Maryknoll, NY: Orbis Books, 2004), 86-141.

6. Joachim Jeremias, *The Prayer of Jesus*, trans. John Bowden (London: SCM, 1967), 11-65, is a classic discussion.

7. See Amy-Jill Levine, *The Misunderstood Jew: The Church and the Scandal of the Jewish Jesus* (San Francisco: HarperSanFrancisco, 2006), 41-47 and the literature she cites.

a historical, claim, based in the faithful response of disciples to Jesus, not in the disciplined practice of historians.

Yet the historic result of Jesus' distinctive, if not unique, consciousness of closeness to God was unique. His disciples remembered that consciousness and the Jesus-movement endured Jesus' death and continues to this day. That particular memory carried by a particular community is evidence of a distinctive, even unique, power that Jesus' disciples found and continue to find in his life and work. Even though one cannot read Jesus' "uniqueness" from the historical record, one can read, from the historic response to him, a remembered particularity about his consciousness and the uniqueness of the memory of him as an, if not the, incarnated divine agent.

One difference between the present work and Sobrino's is that Sobrino generally relies on the research paradigm of the "historical-Jesus," whereas the present work, as articulated in part 1, has presumed the cogency of the "historic Jesus" approach. One can make claims about how the *movement* remembered Jesus and infer how Jesus likely impacted his disciples. That they regarded him as a divine agent is a conclusion of Larry Hurtado's work, reinforced by Daniel Boyarin's analysis. That they remembered his devotion to God as Father is indubitable. As noted above (pp. 61-64), it is possible that early Christians believed he was the incarnation of a second power in heaven and that this belief may have been distinctive to Christians in Second Temple Judaism. But all these are expressions of *responses* to Jesus, the basis of attempts to understand his person and significance. These claims are not deductions from ontological claims, which have little, if any, historically reliable connection to the actual man Jesus of Nazareth. Claims about Jesus' status are developed from the memories of the disciples' responses to Jesus, not from ontological claims of the fourth and fifth centuries. Thus, Jesus' uniqueness looks different in this approach from either Sobrino's or a neoscholastic approach.

As the diagram on p. 36 and the discussion there illustrate, the present approach finds the separation of christology into "from below" and "from above" inadequate. Such a distinction can be helpful shorthand to be used as a tool to analyze the challenges that face particular christological approaches. And in that sense, Sobrino's christology is "from below" and the CDF's "from above." Nonetheless, such labels are useful insofar as they can remind theologians of the dangers of christology "from above" slipping into docetism (or other views that neglect Christ's humanity) or christologies "from below" of slipping into Arianism (or other views that deny Christ's divinity). Yet, finally, christology cannot be simply "from below" or "from above" and properly balance humanity and divinity in Jesus Christ. A different approach is required, especially if one attends to the historic Jesus. And attending to the historic Jesus bypasses the christologies from below that begin with the so-called historical-Jesuses or from above that begin with ontological assertions derived from conciliar definitions or theological concepts.

Unlike the present work, which follows the work of Hurtado and Boyarin,

Sobrino seems to assume that the attribution of divinity to Jesus is a late development. While it is also clear that the New Testament is more binitarian than trinitarian,[8] its claims for Jesus being God's divine agent in human form now seem rather well established on historical grounds, as articulated by Hurtado and reinforced by Boyarin (see chapter 6). That doctrine developed and nuanced understandings of Jesus over centuries is also clear. Would St. Peter and St. Stephen have understood their faith in the terms of the Council of Chalcedon? This seems rather unlikely, as neither had gone through the crucibles of conflict that led to the conciliar formulae.

The point of the difference can be made clear by considering a particular objection to Sobrino's work made by the CDF Notification:

> Father Sobrino does not deny the divinity of Jesus when he proposes that it is found in the New Testament only "in seed" and was formulated dogmatically only after many years of believing reflection. Nevertheless he fails to affirm Jesus' divinity with sufficient clarity. This reticence gives credence to the suspicion that the historical development of dogma, which Sobrino describes as ambiguous, has arrived at the formulation of Jesus' divinity without a clear continuity with the New Testament. (§4)

While this assessment is unfair to Sobrino's work, it serves to highlight a difference between Sobrino's approach and that of the present work. The present work accepts the continuity with the New Testament as does Sobrino (*pace* the CDF), although in a slightly different way than Sobrino.

The New Testament reports that the disciples recognized Jesus as divine very early in the tradition. As James D. G. Dunn notes, "[I]t is hard to see how Easter faith could create such a weighty christological affirmation from the start, had the pre-Easter impact of Jesus not *already been measured in terms of divine authority and power*."[9] Hurtado has claimed that "the really crucial period for the origin of remarkable beliefs about Jesus' significance is 'the first four or five years' of the early Christian movement."[10] High christological affirmations evidently emerged "from below" and quite early in the development of the New Testament. Yet it is a long road from that recognition to the doctrinal formulae of Nicaea and Chalcedon—a point that is undeniable. Sobrino uses the metaphor of "seeds." Perhaps Sobrino emphasizes the novelties in the theological developments more than the CDF finds appropriate, but for the CDF to say that he denies "continuity" is a less-than-charitable reading of his text, especially because novelties *were* introduced into the tradition between the writing of the New Testament and the

---

8. This assumes that the trinitarian baptismal formula, unique to Matt. 28:19, reflects later practice developing the earlier formulae for baptism "in the name of Jesus."

9. James D. G. Dunn, *Jesus Remembered*, vol. 1 of *Christianity in the Making* (Grand Rapids: Eerdmans, 2003), 892; emphasis in original.

10. Larry W. Hurtado, *How on Earth Did Jesus Become a God?: Historical Questions about Earliest Devotion to Jesus* (Grand Rapids: Eerdmans, 2005), 37, quoting Martin Hengel, *Between Jesus and Paul* (London: SCM, 1983), 44.

formulations of the Councils of Nicaea and Chalcedon, such as the use of the term *homoousios*.[11]

These developed doctrinal formulae were forged in the crucible of internal and external debates about the person and work of Christ with gnostics, Arians, and others. The debates were carried on mostly in a Greek language suffused with Platonic, Neoplatonic, Stoic, and Epicurean concepts foreign to the earliest disciples and used in ways foreign to at least most of the New Testament scripts. The debates are situated in a milieu in which Christianity has become in the Roman Empire first politically tolerated and later the official religion, rather than in the context of the Jesus-movement's need to establish its identity in the face of opposition from other Jewish groups mostly in Palestine, both before and after the destruction of the Jerusalem temple in 70 c.e. The developing church needed centuries to develop these doctrinal formulae and to refine the New Testament's claims about Jesus, and its theologians worked in a wildly different linguistic, religious, philosophical, and sociocultural milieu from that in which the New Testament memories of Jesus were transmitted, organized, and scripted.

Neither Sobrino nor I *deny* continuity. However, identifying in what that continuity consists is difficult. It is certainly not simply verbal or conceptual continuity. Nor is the result historically certain—historical events are contingent, and it is possible that things might have gone otherwise in history.[12] The actual shape of the doctrines that emerged is determined, at least in part, by the controversies that the doctrines sought to resolve. Had the controversies been different, so might the resulting doctrines have been different. Nicaea and Chalcedon responded to Arian and monophysite conceptions (among others). One suspects that had there been no Arian controversy, there might have been no need to use *homoousios* in the Nicene Creed.

While the present work may yet have even more "inaccuracies" (as the CDF puts it) than Sobrino's, the shift in emphasis from working with the "historical-Jesus" to the historic Jesus as remembered in practice makes a significant difference in how one construes the shifts over the centuries. Even though the formulae of Nicaea

---

11. John E. Thiel (*Senses of Tradition: Continuity and Development in Catholic Faith* [New York: Oxford University Press, 2000]) notes that one cannot understand the actual history of the Catholic tradition unless one notes that the tradition includes abandonments of accepted truths and novel introductions that become "tradition." One of Thiel's key examples is the novel introduction of the term *homoousios*. Being novel does not mean that it cannot become part of the tradition—since it was a novel term and has been actually used, it must be possible to introduce novelties into the tradition. Whether this can be understood as "continuity" of the New Testament claim is unclear; its primary purpose was to deny subordination of the Son to the Father, which was not an issue, as far as I can tell, for New Testament authors.

12. This is not to say that we need to consider all the questions that begin, "What if . . ." (for example, "What if Mary had said 'no' to the angel at the annunciation?" or "What if George Washington had drowned crossing the Delaware?"). Such counterfactual inquiries can only be answered speculatively. There can be no historical evidence for or against them, as there are no facts that can support or undermine them. Their significance is to alert us to the contingency of history: "it might have gone otherwise." That events went the way they did is historical. That we can uncover what that "way" was and warrant our claims about what we uncover produces "historical facts." However events may appear in other perspectives, historically they are contingent.

and Chalcedon are not found in the New Testament, the recognition of Jesus as a divine agent is clearly part of the earliest perception of him. The disciples' Jesus is recognized as the empowering presence of the divine in the midst of the Jesus-movement. Sobrino's metaphor of "seeds" may well be appropriate to describe the present approach, if the term is read charitably. To adapt von Hügel's terms, I think that Sobrino is not "daring to the verge of presumption," but that the CDF is "prudent to the verge of despair."

Nonetheless, the issue between Sobrino and the CDF is important and enduring. The problem is especially acute for any practice-centered theology: how can this theology deal with the great creedal affirmations and the classic doctrines of the tradition? To begin to answer this question, the present chapter presents my position on the status and function of doctrine. The next chapter turns to the content of that doctrine.

Doctrines as Rules[13]

Lutheran theologian George Lindbeck has developed a theory of doctrine that construes doctrines as rules, adapting the ancient notion that doctrine is the *regula fidei*. Lindbeck calls his a "cultural-linguistic" approach, although many today label it "postliberal." It was developed in contrast to the traditional claim that doctrines are simply propositions people believe. He calls this a cognitive-propositional approach, characteristic of premodern religion. Modernity has rendered such an approach problematic, at best. Modernity discovered, as Gershwin put it, that "the things that you're liable to read in the Bible, they ain't necessarily so." The acids of modern criticism have eaten into our assumptions about the historical reliability of all ancient texts. We can no longer assume that doctrinal formulae can pass tests of historical reliability of or philosophical coherence. But to avoid modern criticism is to fall into an irrational fideism. Doctrines are clearly important, but they are not credible if they are taken to be propositions that in some sense literally and finally state truths. A doctrinal fundamentalism may be a reaction to modernity, as was biblical fundamentalism.[14] But both are disengagements from, rather than engagements with, the issues of the age. Had the fathers of the church refused to

---

13. Material in this section is based in part in claims developed more fully in my *Inventing Catholic Tradition* (Maryknoll, NY: Orbis Books, 2000); and *History, Theology, and Faith*.

14. Fundamentalism erects to an absolute place in modernity a particular premodern understanding of the biblical tradition. Fundamentalism treats the Bible as an unsurpassable foundation on which to build one's theology. It claims to "read," not interpret the biblical text and refuses to accept any claims that explicitly contradict the "statements" revealed in the Bible, even if the best understanding of those sentences and stories is figurative. The first recorded use of the term "fundamentalism" is, according to the *Oxford English Dictionary*, in 1922. While the notion of the "fundamentals" of the faith is a concept that goes back at least to the beginning of the Enlightenment era, it is only in the modern period and only in opposition to "modernism" or "experiential expressivism" that a person could be a "fundamentalist" in the sense in which we now use that term.

engage and adapt the currents of their age, the high christologies using nonbiblical terms might never have developed.

Lindbeck also seeks to avoid what he calls the prototypical modern response to the collapse of the cognitive-propositional approach, a "symbolic" approach he dubbed "experiential expressivism." This dominant, modern, "liberal" position construes religious doctrines as culturally conditioned linguistic expressions of a fundamental "prelinguistic" religious experience (often an experience of the "Sacred" or "Holy" alleged to be "the same" experience underlying many religious traditions). Such expressions may be "true to" experience, but they cannot be "true" or "false" as propositions can be.[15] Experiential expressivism finally gives up on any "truth content" in doctrines of particular faith traditions. Employing the experiential-expressivist view, a person cannot use a doctrine to "say of what is, that it is so, or of what is not, that it is not."[16]

Lindbeck's cultural-linguistic approach construes a faith tradition as being shaped by the doctrinal rules that form its framework.[17] Rules can guide the formation of propositions that express the faith, even if they are not propositions themselves. Lindbeck claims that doctrines are to be understood as "communally authoritative rules of discourse, attitude, and action, specifically with regard to those beliefs and practices that are considered essential to the identity or welfare of the group."[18] Doctrines are not statements of belief but the rules of the grammar of a form of life or the way of life that carries and is carried in and by the practice of the faith.[19] As rules, doctrines do not and cannot state truth claims, but can and do shape both the practical concepts that a tradition uses and the particular faith claims that members of the tradition make.[20]

---

15. See George A. Lindbeck, *The Nature of Doctrine: Religion and Theology in a Postliberal Age* (Philadelphia: Westminster, 1984), 16-17, 47, and passim.

16. While many formulations of epistemological realism are possible, this elegant version is from Susan Haack, "Confessions of an Old-Fashioned Prig," in eadem, *Manifesto of a Passionate Moderate: Unfashionable Essays* (Chicago: University of Chicago Press, 1998), 21. On doctrinal formulae being used to make truth claims, see below.

17. For a sympathetic, but critical, analysis of Lindbeck's approach that informs the present work, see Terrence W. Tilley et al., *Postmodern Theologies: The Challenge of Religious Diversity* (Maryknoll, NY: Orbis Books, 1995), 91-113.

18. Ibid., 94, referring to Lindbeck, *Nature of Doctrine*, 18, 74.

19. The phrase "the grammar of faith" is taken from a book by Lindbeck's late colleague philosopher Paul Holmer, *The Grammar of Faith* (New York: Harper & Row, 1978). See especially Terrence W. Tilley, "Incommensurability, Intratextuality and Fideism," *Modern Theology* 5, no. 2 (1989): 87-111. This paragraph draws on material published in Tilley, *Postmodern Theologies*, 95.

20. For example, a brief comment by Gavin D'Costa might be read as making this error, which arises because sometimes the same words are used in dogmatic declarations, like the Nicene Creed, and in belief expression. He wrote, "I take dogma, like Lindbeck, to provide grammatical rules by which Christian speech is to be ruled and, unlike Lindbeck, I also take dogma to provide substantive ontological claims, which are the grammatical rules being applied in a historical context showing the instantiation of the rule" (D'Costa, "'Christian Orthodoxy and Religious Pluralism': A Further Rejoinder to Terrence Tilley," *Modern Theology* 23, no. 3 [2007]: 458). If D'Costa means that dogma or doctrines *make* theological claims, he is missing the point of Lindbeck's approach and the way rules work; rules do not *say* how things are or are not, but *direct* how we should speak. If he means that statements

Lindbeck's key move is to distinguish doctrinal rules from religious beliefs. Lindbeck's approach does *not* deny that participants in a tradition can say what they believe. Nor does he deny that what believers say are statements that can be either true or false. Participants' statements of their beliefs have the force of "first order speech," that is, ordinary usage in the everyday language of the community, and the doctrinal rules are "second order rules," that is, the grammar of that language of the community that guides good first order speech. Participants' statements may be true or false, testable or untestable, but grammars are neither true nor false, but more or less useful, more or less faithful to the language used in a form of life.

The problem for both cognitive-propositional views and experiential-expressivist views is that they collapse doctrines and faith claims into the same things. Even if they use the same sentences, doctrinal declarations (whether implicit or explicit) function as rules and faith claims as statements. Conflating their forces is the key mistake that traps both cognitive propositionalism and experiential expressivism. The former keeps the truth value of religious beliefs, but at the price of their credibility. The latter keeps the expressions of religious belief, but at the price of their truth value. The distinction of "second order" rules from first-order statements nuances the issue and avoids the traps.[21]

Of course, an ordinary believer can, and perhaps should, *use* a doctrinal formula meant to guide the believer's practice (a rule) to *state* his or her own belief. But this usage has the force not of a declaration of doctrine but of the utterance of a belief. The same sentence can be used in multiple ways with multiple forces. Doctrinal language can be used as creedal language. Focusing on the sentence rather than the force and the use means that theologians may fail to distinguish these two different forces and uses—the regulative function of doctrine and the constative function of saying what one believes. Distinctions need to be made between ordinary statements that believers make ("first order" utterances) and rules that doctrines express. Doctrinal rules regulate believers' ("first order") statements. They are related as imperative ("Talk this way!") and performance in response to the imperative. Whether a sentence is being used to state one's view or to regulate a community's practice depends not on the sentence or proposition itself but on its use in a particular context and for a particular purpose.

"First order" utterances of religious belief can also be assessed as true

---

of belief in accord with those rules make truth claims, saying how we find things to be, then these are not rules ("directives" in speech-act terms), but assertive speech acts. Declaring or discerning rules has a different force and structure from asserting claims. See my *The Evils of Theodicy* (Washington, DC: Georgetown University Press, 1991), 11-15, 34-42, 46-50, 63-66, for discussion of these points in the context of more general theory of speech acts in religious contexts. That religious people make truth claims using dogmatic language is undeniable; to say that dogmatic rules do so is confused.

21. In *The Wisdom of Religious Commitment* (Washington, DC: Georgetown University Press, 1995), 121-54, I argued that theologians as experts have different and more arduous requirements to meet in warranting the wisdom of making religious commitments—and accepting the doctrines of faith traditions—than do ordinary believers in their faith claims.

or false.[22] However, doctrinal rules do not directly represent what is true, but regulate the practice of believing. Rules may be wise or unwise, appropriate or inappropriate, insightfully expressed or obtuse, faithful to the tradition and form of life or unfaithful, but because they are not propositional statements, they cannot be simply true or false. "Talk this way!" doesn't have a truth value. Ordinary believers' "first order" statements of their beliefs are not doctrines. They may be true or false, in line with or in contradiction to the community's doctrines, precise or vague, and so on. The distinction between beliefs and doctrines is important.

Doctrinally, the statement "Jesus is truly human and truly divine" is a directive. It tells the Christian not to minimize either of the "two natures" in the "one person." For a believer to say, unqualifiedly, "Jesus is God" is out of order. For a believer to say, unqualifiedly, "Jesus is human" is equally out of order. Of course, both believer's assertions may be true or false, complete or incomplete, and so on. In certain contexts, each may be both in order and true (as when arguing against Arians or docetists, respectively). Christians believe both are true, but the doctrine effectively instructs Christians that neither alone is complete as an expression of Christian faith. So, if a believer makes either claim and thinks it complete, the believer has failed to follow the doctrinal rule. If the believer makes either claim and recognizes that it is incomplete, such a claim or expression of faith may be in order.

Christian doctrines are the rules that guide the practices, especially the practice of believing, that constitute the Christian tradition. Lindbeck has argued persuasively that there are three fundamental identity principles implicit in the tradition that guide the *development* of the doctrinal rules that emerge from the practices in the tradition. They are not so much doctrinal rules as rules that set the minimum identity conditions for the community. A community or theological position that fails to embody these rules, however loosely, simply fails to be a candidate for being seen as a Christian community or theology:

> First, there is the monotheistic principle: there is only one God, the God of Abraham, Isaac, Jacob, and Jesus. Second, there is the principle of historical specificity: the stories of Jesus refer to a genuine human being who was born, lived, and died in a particular time and place. Third, there is the principle of what may be infelicitously called Christological maximalism: every possible importance is to be ascribed to Jesus that is not inconsistent with the first rule. This last rule, it may be noted, follows from the central Christian conviction that Jesus Christ is the highest possible clue (though an often dim and ambiguous one to creaturely and sinful eyes) within the space-time world of human experience to God, i.e., to what is of maximal importance.[23]

---

22. See my *Inventing Catholic Tradition*, 156-70, for a sketch of how an appraisal account of the truth of religious utterance works.

23. Lindbeck, *Nature of Doctrine*, 94. Some might see these principles as "constitutive rules," that is, those rules that must be followed to make Christianity possible, analogous to the rules of the

These principles are not sufficient to generate or guide the practices that form the Christian tradition, although some expression of them seems necessary to every Christian tradition. Any form of life or tradition that claims to be Christian will incorporate, in some form or other, these identity principles. Each Christian tradition may articulate or formulate them differently, but a tradition without some form of them has difficulty claiming to be Christian.

It is important to note that these principles are not doctrines. Although Lindbeck proposes a "rule theory of doctrine," his primary principles are not official doctrines but identity principles that are necessary if a community is to embody a form of the Christian tradition.[24] Actual Christian doctrines regarding God and Jesus *embody* these principles. Some particular expressions prove to be more suitable than others. Christological and soteriological doctrines, for example, that fail to flesh them out well, such as docetism (which fails to embody the second principle) or Arianism (which sacrifices the third at the expense of the first) can be recognized as failing to be good Christian doctrine because they fail to articulate these principles well. These principles provide the *loci*, the theological "places," in which Christianity comes to have an identity.[25]

The first principle, independently called "creational and covenantal mono- theism" by N. T. Wright, distinguishes the classic versions of the monotheistic traditions from most Eastern religious traditions and from Western dualistic and pantheistic traditions.[26] As a group, these principles also distinguish Christianity from Judaism and Islam, in both of which a version of the first is operative, but for which the second may be held to be true, but is not a principle, and for which the third cannot be a principle or, possibly, even held to be true.

Some caveats are in order. First, further principles besides these distinguish various Christian denominations from each other, such as the Catholic analogical imagination as a principle of the identity of the Catholic intellectual and theological community as opposed to the "dialectical imagination" more characteristic of (some) Protestant groups.[27] Second, these identity principles have a "negative

---

Constitution of the United States that make the U. S. government possible. However, these principles are not *positive* rules but *negative* ones: we cannot imagine how to recognize any community without some form of them as a Christian community. More importantly, these principles are not *sufficient* to constitute any specific Christian community.

24. Ibid., 75; Lindbeck calls them "operational doctrines," but they clearly function as identity principles, the term used here.

25. Historically speaking, the emergence of these principles, like other historical events and pro- cesses, is contingent, not necessary. Once they have emerged, we can claim that they are theologically necessary identity principles for Christian communities. There are two caveats to note in this area. First, it may be that there are other identity principles we have not yet discovered; these principles are not jointly sufficient, as noted above, to generate a Christian tradition. Second, it is arguably an illegitimate retrojection to brand as "heretics" those who worked and wrote before the principles were clear. To claim that those who actively rejected the principles once they were clearly formed were "heretics" is another issue.

26. Marcus J. Borg and N. T. Wright, *The Meaning of Jesus: Two Visions* (San Francisco: Harp- erSanFrancisco, 1999), 158-60.

27. See David Tracy, *The Analogical Imagination: Christian Theology and the Culture of Plural- ism* (New York: Crossroad, 1981), 405-45; Andrew Greeley, "Theology and Sociology: On Validating

normativity": a religious tradition whose set of doctrines fails to have formulae that embody these rules or fails to attend to these places in theological discourse would not be the Christian, or even a Christian, tradition. These rules have a negative, rather than a positive, normative significance because there may be multiple ways of understanding them and living them out.[28] Third, given the "negative normativity" of these identity principles, they cannot in some simple way be said to "generate" doctrines. Whether these principles are finally to be understood as "rules" guiding Christian faith and life or *loci* that must be traversed in understanding Christian identity, particular doctrines tend to emerge from particular practices in particular, often difficult or challenging, circumstances. These rules must not contradict the fundamental orientation given by the "identity principles." Fourth, these principles are not all the principles the Christian tradition needs somehow to embody and are surely not sufficient to be doctrines that are the grammar of any rich faith tradition. Arguably, other principles might include a recognition of God's covenant with Israel, an acceptance of the divine universal salvific will, and a requirement for an ongoing community.

The process of discerning which particular doctrines actually embody the rules of the various practices of the tradition that constitute living in and living out the faith and are in accord with these principles at any given time can be exceedingly difficult. Some forms of trinitarian doctrine, those that are strongly "social," may violate the first principle (indeed, traditional Muslim objections to "Christian tri-theism" may indicate a difference in criteria about what does and does not fit this shared principle). A number of forms of trinitarian doctrine, from a non-sequential modalism that finds our authentic and veridical experience of the one true God in three personal modes to a community of three *hypostaseis* coinhering perichoretically in and as one God, may fit with the principles. These identity principles, as negatively normative, are not narrow. Thus, they do not necessarily pick out "orthodox" doctrines, but unorthodox ones. But discerning whether a doctrinal proposal is orthodox or not requires more than discerning its adherence to these identity principles.[29]

That "more" can be summarized as follows: Doctrines that fit the identity principles *and* are useful and proper guides to Christian practice are proper doctrines. All relevant Christian doctrines claim, in effect, to fit with these principles. If a community failed to have doctrinal formulae that did not at least attempt to express these principles, that community would not be Christian. Logically one could not ask whether the formulae in question were good Christian formulae if

---

David Tracy," *Journal of the American Academy of Religion* 59, no. 4 (1991): 643-52; and Tilley, *Inventing Catholic Tradition*, 125-34.

28. For a helpful discussion of the distinction between negative and positive normativity, see Roger Haight, *Jesus Symbol of God,* 2nd ed. (Maryknoll, NY: Orbis Books, 2000), 409-10.

29. That authorities in various Christian communities may narrow the range of acceptable formulations for their communities is another issue, one not addressed here. Clearly, many Christian communities have developed narrower or more precise formulations of each of these principles for their own communities. The point here is not to pick out particular Christian communities, but to pick out what principles any community has to have to be Christian.

the community that formulated them failed to be a Christian community. These principles are benchmarks for recognizing a community as Christian, not for judging particular formulae.

The tasks of theologians are to discover, critically understand and evaluate, creatively transform when necessary, and proclaim when appropriate the rules that communicate and guide the practices of the tradition. The three identity principles that Lindbeck formulated clearly embody principles that are necessary for a tradition to be Christian. Both additional principles and other doctrinal rules need to be discovered and formulated to flesh out the tradition. This is the work of the theologians who should reflect on Christian practices, including believing, past and present.

It is also clear that these identity principles, as well as other doctrines, can be articulated in various ways. Theologians properly work to discover which articulation is appropriate to communicate the tradition in a particular context. Some formulae need transformation; indeed, the next chapter argues for reformulating the way we talk about the true humanity and true divinity of Jesus. The task of proclaiming is often a task of witness, a task that belongs to all the participants in a tradition.[30]

Particular principles that give identity to a tradition can be found outside that tradition. For example, if the analogical imagination is a particular identity principle of the Roman Catholic Church's tradition (as David Tracy and Andrew Greeley have argued),[31] this does not mean that members of other Christian churches, other religious traditions, or no religious faith at all could not exhibit this principle. Following or formulating a particular principle can be done by people from other traditions. And some traditions would share principles (as do Judaism, Christianity and Islam, at least, for the monotheistic principle considered alone), but would use them differently as identity principles. It is the *nexus* of principles and the rules given in the practices, including believing, of the tradition that distinguish one faith tradition from another, not the individual principles.

I have argued at length in *Inventing Catholic Tradition* that rules are not metaphysical entities, nor rigid algorithms, nor contentless directives. They are shorthand guides derived from good practice with the purpose of guiding those who would wish to learn or understand a practice. They form a "grammar" of Christian talk. A grammar systematizes the speech of a particular linguistic community at a particular time. Once we know how people who know how to practice the faith live and talk, we can formulate a guide for those who wish to learn how to communicate or to understand how speakers and writers of a language communicate. Hence, actual doctrines are shorthand guides derived from good practice with the purpose of guiding those who live in and live out a faith tradition. In the process of learning, we may learn rules before we become good

---

30. For a fuller exploration of the material in this paragraph (in a slightly different formulation), see my *History, Theology, and Faith*, 142-91.

31. See n. 27 above.

at a practice. But it is otherwise when considering the constitution of a practice: *Practice first; rules second.*

A tradition endures through time not by following rules, but by the fact a community of practitioners continues to act in ways that carry on and carry out the distinctive practices of the tradition, such as the practices of reconciliation described in part 3, in ways faithful to the identity principles. These practices express the significance of the principles that give a tradition its identity. Perhaps such practices have changed wildly—consider the differences between modern medical care in a Catholic hospital and the exorcisms of the early Jesus-movement—but the tradition is preserved by a continuity of practices that display identity principles, not by seeking simply to state the identity principles.

Classic dogmatic formulae are important. Baptist theologian D. H. Williams has argued against the pattern of *sola scriptura* in the Baptist context on the basis of the practice of the reformers. In so doing, he articulated a strong position that has not been part of the ongoing heritage of the Baptist communities. His motive for this is clear:

> To introduce the young or a novice to the church of Jesus Christ is to open for them treasures of the central points of the apostolic faith, a faith that is larger than any one denomination's or church's claims upon it, sharpened and transmitted through the ages. We too often assume potential church members already know the fundamentals of their faith, whereas in reality they are usually incapable of explaining the basics of "the pattern of sound teaching" (2 Tim. 1:13).[32]

But why presume, as Williams seems to, that we have access to an apostolic faith and that it is found only or primarily in the ante-Nicene period? Why prefer the pre-Nicene silence to the Nicene novelty *homoousios*? Williams wants to delimit "tradition" to the patristic era. But on what grounds does he privilege Basil and Gregory over Aquinas, Luther, Calvin, Barth, and Rahner? In effect, he uses Luther and Calvin as resources to support his own arguments regarding the inadequacy of "*sola scriptura*." They are part of his (alas, unacknowledged explicitly) operative tradition. Why does he not include them as articulators of the apostolic tradition as well as the patristic writers?

To introduce the novice to creedal symbols is well and good. But the patristic uses of *hypostasis, ousia, physis, prosōpon, persona, substantia,* and so on, are not the same as our uses of "being," "person," or "nature." And "substance" and "essence" are words hard to get anyone, much less a novice or the young, to use, much less to understand.[33] Why privilege the ancients over the medieval

---

32. D. H. Williams, *Retrieving the Tradition and Renewing Evangelicalism: A Primer for Suspicious Protestants* (Grand Rapids: Eerdmanns, 1999), 77.

33. Even the word "transubstantiation" narrowed and changed its meaning from the twelfth century to the sixteenth, as Gary Macy has demonstrated. The affirmations of the Fourth Lateran Council of 1215 that Trent used to support its acceptance of St. Thomas's theology could not have affirmed

and the modern as carrying on tradition? On what *theological* grounds can this be sustained? Williams's motive is clear, and his preferences, like those of the CDF, are clear, but the *rationale* for such delimiting is not. Moreover, it is hard to imagine how these ancient words can communicate clearly today what they communicated when they were formed.

Theologians are obliged to communicate clearly. As the Second Vatican Council put it in the Pastoral Constitution on the Church in the Modern World, *Gaudium et spes*:

> For recent studies and findings of science, history, philosophy raise new questions which influence life and demand new theological investigations.
>
> Furthermore, while adhering to the methods and requirements proper to theology, theologians are invited to seek continually for more suitable ways of communicating doctrine to people of their times. For the deposit or truths of the faith is one thing; the manner in which they are communicated with the same sense and understanding, is another.[34]

The use of words and concepts formed in cultures wildly different from our own in science and philosophy do not communicate today what they did in the past. It is a theological obligation to find better ways to communicate the faith.

Some doctrinal formulae articulate the identity principles of a tradition. In the terminology of Vatican II, these are the *depositum fidei seu veritates*. Following Lindbeck, Avery Dulles espoused an understanding of the articulation of revelation that he called "historical situationism."[35] I would call it "contextualism." To take a lead from John Henry Newman, one could say that the "idea of Christianity" may be unchanging, but the doctrinal formulae that express that idea are ever adapting to the circumstances in which the tradition that carries and is carried by that idea is lived in and lived out. There is no access to the idea except as it is incarnated

---

St. Thomas's view—he hadn't even been born in 1215, when at least three different accounts (at least two non-Aristotelian) were accepted as forms of "transubstantiation." See Gary Macy, "The Doctrine of Transubstantiation in the Middle Ages," in idem, *Treasures from the Storeroom: Medieval Religion and the Eucharist* (Collegeville, MN: Liturgical Press, 1999). For further discussion of this, see my *History, Theology, and Faith*, 96-105.

34. Second Vatican Council, *Gaudium et Spes* §62: "Etenim scientiarum, necnon historiae ac philosophiae recentiora studia et inventa novas suscitant quaestiones, quae sequelas pro vita [1083] quoque secumferunt et etiam a theologis novas investigationes postulant. Praeterea theologi, servatis propriis scientiae theologicae methodis et exigentiis, invitantur ut aptiorem modum doctrinam cum hominibus sui temporis communicandi semper inquirant, quia aliud est ipsum depositum Fidei seu veritates, aliud modus secundum quem enuntiantur, eodem tamen sensu eademque sententia." Translation adapted from *The Documents of Vatican II*, ed. Walter M. Abbott, S.J. (New York: America Press, 1966); Latin text accessed August 17, 2007 at http://stjosef.at/concilium/gaudium_et_spes.htm.

35. Avery Dulles, S.J., "Tradition as a Theological Source," in idem, *The Craft of Theology* (New York: Crossroad, 1996); for a sketch of a way of understanding revelation in the context of a practice-centered theology, see the epilogue.

and articulated in the formulae that our ongoing community generates as contexts for living in and living out the tradition change.

In this view, the classic pattern of sound teaching is a prototypical instantiation of the idea of Christianity in doctrinal formulae. They are not unsurpassable formulae, but they set the pattern and cannot be ignored or forgotten even if the words that form them are not actively used by a theologian. In one sense, we cannot but privilege the scripture in some way. It is an unsurpassable monument of the tradition, the prototype of our heritage. Much the same could be said for the conciliar definitions.[36]

Yet prototypes are not archetypes. They are not the final or only word but the first defining word.[37] Consider airplanes. The prototype Boeing 747 was not *the* 747; no 747 fully realizes what the 747 is. What the 747 *is* is something we *abstract* from the whole model run, from the first to the current (so far) 747-800. If we abstract well, then we articulate well what the 747 is; but we don't and can't articulate an eternal, unchanging idea of the 747 in time. We can only approach it. Each of the models of the 747 articulates what the 747 *is*, but is not what "the 747" is. The analogy with the "idea of Christianity" and its doctrinal formulae should be obvious. No time-bound, language-bound formula can express the Eternal Idea fully, but all the formulae can and do express the idea (in my view "sacramentally") more or less well, given their contexts.

We need to remember an important distinction between principles and their formulation. Historical investigations may bring up facts that "force" theologians to rethink their formulations, but not that force them to reject their faith or its identity principles. (Of course, they may lose their faith, as anyone may, but historical and theological investigations do not force them to do so). Critical scholarship has forced theologians to far greater reticence on the knowledge of Jesus. Historical work has shown that questions such as, Was Jesus conscious that he was divine? are practically impossible to answer on a historical basis, and less than helpful if understood simply as ontological deductions (see pp. 217-21 below).

A historian of ancient Christianity might acknowledge that in the fourth century, the Arians did not accept christological maximalism, at least in the ways that the Athanasians did. That historian might warrant the claim that powerful political and economic motives were at work, that the Athanasian party, in cooperation with imperial wishes, sought to dominate the Arian party by imposing a specific theology on the whole church. A theologian might accept both the factual claim about the

---

36. It is also important to note that some formulations developed in particular contexts can have real significance in other contexts as well. The great affirmations of Nicaea and Chalcedon are two of these. These have significance in their context, but need to be translated for other contexts, as the next chapter argues. This is *not* to say that they do not have "any value except in the cultural milieu in which these formulations were developed," as the CDF says of Sobrino in the Notification §3. Indeed William P. Loewe notes that their saying this is "puzzling because he explicitly affirms the same thing" that the document advocates. See Loewe, "Sobrino File."

37. The present discussion is a reflection on Karl Rahner's question, "Chalcedon: End or Beginning?" (The 1951 German original of "Current Problems in Christology," in idem, *Theological Investigations* I, trans. Cornelius Ernst, O.P. [New York: Herder & Herder, 1961], 149-200).

Arians and the more controversial claim about the Athanasians' motives and the forces at work in the dispute while also finding that the principle of christological maximalism was and is constitutive (in part) of the Christian tradition. That theologian might also find that an understanding of that principle was defective, if not among the Athanasians in the fourth-century controversy, perhaps in a fifth-century controversy between orthodox Christians and Nestorians. Indeed, Pope John Paul II and Mar Dinkha IV, Catholicos-Patriarch of the Assyrian Church in the East, have, in their "Common Christological Declaration" of November 11, 1994, paved the way for rapprochement between their two churches and declared that Nestorians and Catholics have expressed the traditional faith in different formulae.[38] This religious accord is based not merely on historical investigations but on theological analyses of earlier disputes and theological judgments that those disputes were not about the principles of the faith but about their formulations.

My point is this: in what follows, I will not be using classic christological fomulae. Not only are the terms of those formulae historically embedded in the explorations and disputes of the early Christian tradition, but their transliteration into English terms is deceiving. When a theologian talks, for example, of "two natures in one person," what is heard is something like "two apples in one basket" or "two fruits in one pie." Each fruit may be distinct, not separated or confused, but the problem is that the "natures" involved are taken to be "instances" of the same sorts of things, like "human nature," "animal nature," or "the nature of stars," and so on. Elizabeth A. Johnson has made a similar point specifically about "nature" to which we will return in the next chapter. She wrote that in the theological manuals "the two natures had come to be understood as two varieties of the same basic thing, two species of one genus, something like apples and oranges are two kinds of the one category fruit. The point that divine nature is holy mystery, in a class by itself and in no way comparable to human or any other kind of nature, had simply slipped from view."[39] But divine nature is not and cannot be part of the same set or class as human nature. God is simple, humans are composite. God is infinite, humans are finite. God had no beginning, humans began at a particular point in time. The "Englishing" of these terms as transliterations of formulae not only participates in the degeneration of the formulae, as Johnson noted, but also cannot but fail to convey the principles they attempt to formulate. Indeed, it is necessarily misleading to transliterate ancient terms rooted in ancient Greek "philosophy" (a term that itself means something wildly different today from what it meant in the fourth and fifth centuries) and adapted, not adopted, by Christian theologians into almost any modern language: our languages today are inflected or infected by modern scientific understandings of "nature" and "person."

The present approach necessarily views the monuments of the tradition in a

---

38. For the text of this declaration by the pope and the patriarch on November 11, 1994, see http://www.vatican.va/roman_curia/pontifical_councils/chrstuni/documents/rc_pc_chrstuni_doc_11111994_assyrian-church_en.html (accessed July 17, 2007).

39. Elizabeth A. Johnson, *Consider Jesus: Waves of Renewal in Christology* (New York: Crossroad, 1990), 20. I would suggest that God cannot even coherently be said to be in a class, but that is a technical quibble.

different perspective. As suggested in the introductory material to part 4 using the illustration of perspectives on the Chrysler Building, the perspective from which one writes theology changes the appearance of the monuments in ways that are crucial. The next chapter examines the problems caused by oversimplified transliterations of the terms in those monuments, and proposes a different approach. Even though each formula, past and present, may seem wildly different, each may be faithful to the idea formulated prototypically and unforgettably in the Council of Chalcedon, which built on the work of the Council of Nicaea. These are benchmarks for the Christian tradition.

Eighteen

THE HEART OF
CHRISTOLOGICAL DOCTRINE
Truly Human, Truly Divine

*T*he prototypical formulation of christological doctrine that stands as a key theological monument was given by the Council of Chalcedon in 451 C.E.[1] It seeks to incarnate a principle of christology that balances the identity principles of the tradition and also expresses the appropriate way to continue the devotion to Jesus that began even in his lifetime. Earliest devotion recognized him both as the first among equals in the Jesus-movement and as a divine agent. Chalcedon recognized him as "truly human, truly divine." It took over four hundred years for this formulation to emerge as a principle guiding the appropriate way for Christians to talk about Jesus of Nazareth. It took hundreds more years for it to be generally accepted.

Beginning with Chalcedon

The question is how to formulate in the twenty-first century the principle that the Chalcedonian council formulated in the fifth century. As Karl Rahner put it, "The formula is—a formula. Thus we have not only the right but the duty to look at it as end *and* as beginning."[2] The contemporary understanding must be in continuity with the tradition in which Chalcedon is a monument and must also communicate now the principle that Chalcedon formulated then. As we shall see along the way, however useful attempts to formulate the principle have been, they can lead to confusions because they do not adequately translate the concepts. Words and concepts shift in their meaning and significance over time. When they do, the same words may not communicate the same principle as they did in the

---

1. For accessible brief accounts of this history, see William P. Loewe, *The College Student's Introduction to Christology* (Collegeville, MN: Liturgical Press 1996), 5-7, 188-203; Dermot A. Lane, *The Reality of Jesus: An Essay in Christology* (New York: Paulist, 1975), 94-108. A useful compilation of the textual sources is Richard A. Norris, Jr., *The Christological Controversy* (Philadelphia: Fortress, 1980).

2. Karl Rahner, S.J., "Current Problems in Christology," in idem, *Theological Investigations* I, trans. Cornelius Ernst, O.P. (New York: Herder & Herder, 1961), 150; the essay originated in 1951 on the fifteen hundredth anniversary of the council.

past. Some of the problems in the tradition are due to neglecting such shifts in significance.

The key passage from the Council of Chalcedon (451 C.E.) can be translated as follows:

> So, following the holy fathers, we confess one and the same Son, our Lord Jesus Christ, and we all agree in teaching that this very same Son is realized (*teleion*) in his divinity and realized in his humanity, truly God and truly human, composed of a rational soul and a body; of the same being (*homoousios*) with the Father as regards his divinity, and of the same being with us as regards his humanity; like us in all respects except for sin; before the ages, begotten from the Father as regards his divinity, and in the last days the same for us and for our salvation born from Mary, the virgin God-bearer (*theotokos*) as regards his humanity; one and the same Christ, Son, Lord, only-begotten, acknowledged to be in two natures (*physesin*), unconfusedly, unalterably, indivisibly, inseparably; since the difference between the natures was not destroyed through the union, but rather the character (*idiotētos*) of each nature is preserved and meet (*syntrechousēs*) in one person (*prosōpon*) and one *hypostasis*, not divided or torn into two persons, but one and the same only-begotten Son, God, Word, Lord Jesus Christ, just as the prophets in earlier times and as the Lord Jesus Christ taught us and as the representation (*symbolon*) of the fathers was handed over to us.[3]

The technical details of this definition are difficult to understand not only because the ancient technical terms are foreign to our contemporary ways of thinking, but because many of them are borrowed from the scientific philosophical vocabulary of their time. It is an understatement to say that the grammars of our contemporary philosophical and scientific discourses operate quite differently from those of the fifth century.

While it is easy to use transliterations or literalist translations of the words, the concepts they convey are not the same. For example, the council warns against attributing two *prosōpa* or *hypostaseis* to Jesus because Jesus has two *physesin*. Standard translations would say that this warns against construing Jesus as having two persons because he has two natures. But what could that mean today? Can this be understood as a warning against attributing multiple personality disorder to Jesus? Are we to avoid saying he had two bodies or two minds or two sets of memories?[4] Are the two natures that meet in Jesus somehow parts of the person?

---

3. Translation is based on and adapted from Norris, *Christological Controversy*, 159; also see Henricus Denzinger and Adolfus Schönmetzer, S.J., *Enchiridion Symbolorum: Definitionum et Declarationum de Rebus Fidei et Morum*, 36th ed., amended (Freiburg: Herder, 1965), 108 (§§301-2). *Hypostasis* is simply retained; the Latin is *subsistentiam*; the most obvious English literalist rendering of the Greek is "standing under" and of the Latin "being-under"; neither of these nor the more common renderings seem good translations of this difficult and slippery concept.

4. This alludes to contemporary debates regarding the criteria for personal identity. For an ac-

How do natures meet in a person? Unlike grass, granite boulders, stars, dogs, and people, which have one nature, is he the only entity with two natures? Are the "two natures" two of the same sorts of things so that they are comparable to each other?[5] Because divine nature and human nature are not and cannot be in the same class of things, the challenge is how to construe "two natures" without taking them as in the same class.

The point is *not* that the council was silly or wrong or confused or anything like that. The point is simply that the grammar and use of "nature" and "person" in contemporary language are not those of *physis* or *prosōpon* in ancient Greek. We cannot mean what they meant using transliterations or simplistic equivalents in our modern tongues for the words they used in the midst of discussions formed in fourth- and fifth-century Greek and Latin. The concepts in each context are different, perhaps even incommensurable. In order to convey the significance of these doctrines, not only must the words be translated into a different language, but the concepts have to be transformed into a formula that uses a contemporary conceptual paradigm if they are to be understood today.[6] And the philosophical resources that we can adapt for our christological affirmations are as far from fifth-century philosophy as our biological resources (for Jesus is a *person* with a biological body) from fifth-century biology.

The key formulation is that Jesus is truly human, truly divine. As noted in the previous chapter, the key theological purpose is to strike a balance between positions that, despite the best intentions, could slip over into docetism or subordinationism, denying the full humanity or full divinity of Jesus. Hammering out this view literally took centuries—and many more centuries for it to be accepted by the mainstream of the Christian tradition.

According to many commentators, the goal of Chalcedon to present the unity of the two natures in Christ has not been met in the present. On the one hand, piety has denied fundamental human characteristics to Jesus. The Jesus of the church has been seen as truly divine but not very human. On the other hand, popular presentations such as *Jesus Christ Superstar* have shown Jesus as truly human, but hardly divine.[7] I think it obvious that Christians in our era are pulled

---

cessible summary of the current state of the debate, see John R. Searle, "Consciousness and the Philosophers," *New York Review of Books* 44, no. 4 (March 6, 1997), available at http://www.nybooks.com/articles/1258 (accessed January 29, 2007).

5. See Elizabeth A. Johnson, *Consider Jesus: Waves of Renewal in Christology* (New York: Crossroad, 1990), 20.

6. This point is not an argument against theologians using and exploring these concepts. Indeed, the key insight of "critical correlational" theologies is the need to translate such terms into terms that people who are not trained in theology can understand today. Nor is it a call to revise items in the creed, such as "he came down from heaven," even though the concept of "heaven" is radically different in the fifth and the twenty-first centuries. It is an argument that theologians and teachers need to figure out how to communicate the faith in order to hand it on faithfully to subsequent generations of Christians. For a range of theological work in this area, see the articles in *Handing on the Faith: The Church's Mission and Challenge*, ed. Robert Imbelli (New York: Crossroad, 2006).

7. College professors in the United States have gotten into trouble, perhaps even fired, for asking students—as a tactic for getting around pious docetism—if Jesus ever had erotic yearnings (as other humans do). If they say Jesus did not, then they have to deny erotic yearnings as part of what

between contemporary forms of understanding that are essentially docetist and subordinationist, denying either Jesus' true humanity or his true divinity. Many seem to vacillate from one to the other without ever connecting them—in practical terms, denying the Chalcedonian symbol that finds that they meet in the person of Jesus.

In the conceptual framework of the time of Chalcedon, to acknowledge this union of divinity and humanity without splitting the person in two, the church had to use the "two natures" language. But doing this led to a profound confusion in subsequent theology. The confusion is this: the human was swallowed in the divine because the formula seemed to convey that human nature and divine nature were two items of the same kind with the latter overwhelming the former as a glass of wine overwhelms a drop of water dissolved in it.[8]

The root problem is that the two natures could thus be taken as comparable; properties of one could be applied without difficulty to the other. This seems to be a presupposition of one common understanding of the theory of the *communicatio idiomatum*, "communication of properties," so that one can predicate of Christ "attributes of one nature even when he was being named with reference to his other nature: e.g., 'the Son of God died on the cross'; and 'the Son of Mary created the world.'"[9] The language of *communicatio idiomatum* is a theoretical explanation of the points made by the Council of Ephesus (431 c.e.) in affirming that Mary is not only the mother of Christ but the mother of God. This terminology is not found in the content of the text of that council or of other councils. In fact, the first actual use of the term in the Latin West seems to be in the thirteenth century in the school of Alexander of Hales.[10] Scholars tend to see the "doctrine" in earlier writers, such as Cyril of Alexandria, but this seems to be a retrojection of a later theory onto an earlier practice. The problem has numerous aspects.

First, this terminology is not found in the text from the Council of Chalcedon. The council uses *idiotētos*, the character of each. This term is singular, not plural. Chalcedon does not say that the *attributes* or the *properties* or any aspect of

---

it means to be truly human. If they say Jesus did have such yearnings, a point rather uncomfortable for some, then they could say that he is like us in all things save sin, truly human. Even some of the fathers of the church, for example, Cassian, had difficulty with this point (as discussed by Rowan Williams, "'Tempted as We Are': Christology and the Analysis of the Passions," Opening Lecture, Fifteenth International Conference on Patristic Studies," Oxford University, August 6, 2007, not yet published). For the popular reference, see Lane, *Reality of Jesus*, 16.

8. Compare Rahner, "Some Issues in Christology," 156-63.

9. Gerald O'Collins, S.J., *Christology: A Biblical, Historical, and Systematic Study of Jesus* (Oxford: Oxford University Press, 1995), 168, with reference to Denziger §251.

10. Grzegorz Strzelczyk, *Communicatio Idiomatum: Lo scambio delle proprietà: Soria, status questionis e prospettive* (Rome: Pontificia Università Gregoriana, 2004), 162. A search for *communicatio idiomatum* in J.-P. Migne's *Patrologia Latina* finds the term *only* in the footnotes, and never in the texts of documents (see http://pld.chadwyck.com.avoserv.library.fordham.edu/ [accessed August 20, 2007]). Walter Principe (*William of Auxerre's Theology of the Hypostatic Union* [Toronto: Pontifical Institute of Mediaeval Studies, 1963], 230 n. 1) remarks that the first theologian that Artur Landgraf (*Dogmengeschichte der Frühscholastik,* 4 vols. in 9 [Regensburg: Pustet 1952-56], II/1 145) had found who used the expression *communicatio idiomatum* was Odo Rigaldi, a thirteenth-century theologian.

the human and divine nature meet in the one person. Chalcedon rules that we need to say that the *character* (singular) of each is retained when the *physesin* meet in the person of Jesus Christ. Yet some theologians seem to presume that Chalcedonian orthodoxy requires a "communication of attributes or properties," *communicatio idiomatum*, as if the properties of the infinite divine nature could be unproblematically applied to the finite human nature. Yet this formulation of a communication of properties is *not* a doctrine articulated by the Council of Chalcedon. The *communicatio idiomatum* might be one way that the character of each might meet in the person of Christ, but it is not conciliar doctrine.

A dilemma illustrates that the issue is not so simple and that the theory of *communicatio idiomatum* may not be satisfactorily understood if we take the rule of Chalcedon as a monument in christology. The point is that we cannot apply the properties as if there is a simple transfer of properties from the divine to the human. God can be said to have the property of being omniscient. Does the son of Mary have this property? If so, then the portrayal of Jesus' agony in the Garden of Gethsemane would have been a sham. If the agony is not a sham, then he cannot know at that time that he will be resurrected. The dilemma is plain: either it is confused to attribute omniscience to Jesus or Jesus knew all along that it would be all right in the end, clearly in tension (to put it mildly) with the gospel tradition.

Second, many ways of understanding *communicatio idiomatum* as a communication of properties, rather than the Chalcedonian meeting of natures, each retaining its own character, can result in serious confusion. Gerald O'Collins, S.J., thinks such confusion even afflicted Aquinas's christology. As he points out:

> Aquinas encouraged the subsequent Catholic theological tradition to hold that in his human mind the earthly Jesus enjoyed the beatific vision and hence lived by sight, not by faith. Notable difficulties can be brought against this view. For instance, the comprehensive grasp of *all* creatures and *all* they can do (which Aquinas attributed to the beatific vision) would lift Christ's human knowledge so clearly beyond the normal limits as to cast serious doubts on the genuineness of his humanity, at least in one essential aspect.[11]

Some traditional understandings of *communicatio idiomatum* create such confusions. These understandings assume both that an infinite nature can be said to give, in some way, its properties (not its character) to a finite nature or to a finite person, and that infinite nature can do so without obliterating the finite nature. Having infinite knowledge obliterates the limits of finite knowledge, a property of human nature. The problem is not so much the key doctrine of Chalcedon, a doctrine ruling the practice and understanding of the church; rather, the problem is, first, understanding that rule in a world that shares little of the philosophical resources that provided the intellectual *lingua franca* of that time, and, second,

---

11. O'Collins, *Christology*, 207; emphasis in original. For a very accessible sketch of the twentieth-century version of this confusion, see Johnson, *Consider Jesus*, 35-47.

using a notion, *communicatio idiomatum*, in a way that seems to conflate the infinity of divine nature with finite human nature.

The heart of the problem seems to be that theologians presume that the doctrine is ontological when its actual function is rhetorical. In contrast, O'Collins's formulation noted above—that one can predicate of Christ attributes of one nature when he was being named with reference to his other nature—seems to make *communicatio idiomatum* merely nominal. But it is hard to imagine that such an approach would be accurate or fair to the tradition. Rather, the solution is to recognize that the *communicatio idiomatum* is not a "theory" but can be understood as a form of metonymy.

Metonymy is a figure of speech that uses a name of one thing for another of which it is a property, for example, "these lands belong to the crown." To say that Mary is *theotokos*—the key issue in the debate leading up to the Council of Ephesus in 431 finding Mary to be not merely *christotokos* but *theotokos*—was the key problem for which the *communicatio idiomatum* was thought to be the solution. But this attribution is a metonym: "Mary is the mother/bearer of God." She is not the mother of the Father or the Spirit. Hence, the use of *theotokos* is a trope, a use of figurative language. It is good metonymy in that it works to preserve the unity of the *prosōpon* of Jesus Christ by attributing his divine *physis* to his *prosōpon*.

To recognize this language as a rhetorical trope is not to deny or demean its importance. Rather, it helps us avoid the confusions inevitably introduced by assuming that a trope requires a theory to explain its use. To attribute the creation of the world to the fetus in Mary's womb is a mind-boggling use of metonymy. Mary's womb is in the world that the fetus created. Did the world not exist before the fetus did? However, saying that the Word through which the world was created came into the world from Mary's womb can express a profound devotion, and it articulates much more accurately that "the Word became flesh."

The problem occurs when a trope is thought to license syllogistic inferences such as, for example: Mary is the mother of God; God is the creator of the world; therefore, Mary is the mother of the creator of the world. This practice of deducing attributes from a trope has introduced the difficulties noted above about "omniscience" and the "beatific vision" for Jesus. Such deductions are simply bad practice. Tropes convey important insights, but they do not license deductions because they are not propositions. The trope "Mary is *theotokos*" functions as a doctrinal rule, perhaps even an identity principle, but it is not the major premise of a valid deductive syllogism. Tropes are not simply "true" or "false."

While one can make deductions from theories, to deduce an implication from a trope is bad practice. We can show this by reflecting on the balcony scene from Shakespeare's *Romeo and Juliet* mentioned in chapter 2. One cannot take any trope, such as the metaphor "Juliet is the sun," in such a way as to deduce from it, for example, that her internal temperature is six thousand degrees centigrade or that she was some ninety million miles away from earth. To say metonymically that the fetus in Mary's womb is God incarnate and thus has the character of the infinite God as well as the finite character of being human expresses a profound paradox and reveals a deep mystery. To avoid insoluble puzzles, we need to construe *communicatio idiomatum* as naming a form of metonymy, not as a theory that licenses syllogistic deductions. Early Christian leaders may or may not have had a theory for their use of tropes like metonymy and metaphor; Augustine, however, spends significant time detailing rules for dealing with figurative and literal language.[12] If we take *communicatio idiomatum* as an elegant term for a particular trope, we can resolve the problems introduced when we take this term as an assertion. If we take *communicatio idiomatum* as a rule rather than as a theory about the transfer of properties, we can hold on to the mystery of the incarnation and avoid the confusions and problems introduced when we take it as an assertion.[13]

Lest it be thought that I am minimizing this important point by recognizing its rhetorical side and rejecting its ontological point, it should be clear that this move is implied by the theory of doctrine adumbrated in the previous chapter. The rule theory of doctrine works perfectly well with a rhetorical approach. Indeed, if the "truly human, truly divine" is an identity principle, then one rule for articulating it is a rule of metonymical attribution. The refusal of such metonymy by the Nestorians, who would accept *christotokos* but not *theotokos*, arose from a conflict about a rule of doctrine, a denial of the emerging "two natures in one person" rule that formulated the "truly human, truly divine" principle. In retrospect, the language of the debate may have been philosophical and assertive, but the substance was doctrinal and regulative. The rhetorical battle was a crucial battle over the proper practice and the appropriate rule for understanding the one whom the disciples followed.

Given that the term *communicatio idiomatum* is not used by, but inferred from, Chalcedon's definition, and given that its use as a theory can lead to serious problems, as well as distortions and avoidable paradoxes, it is possible to re-understand the term as a name of a particular trope used in a particular context. This brief exploration of the rule as a trope is not exhaustive by any means. However, taking it as the name of a trope resolves problems of perplexing inferences and transfers of properties between incommensurable natures. Thus it preserves the key insights about the principle that Jesus is to be regarded as "truly human, truly

---

12. See Augustine, *De Doctrina Christiana* book 3, chap. 25, online at http://www.newadvent. org/fathers/12023.htm (accessed August 21, 2007).

13. Strzelczyk (*Communicatio idiomatum*) argued that the use (I would say "practice") dates back to the Gospels. His thesis takes the *communicatio idiomatum* to have arisen as a way of speaking about Christ (225), but it is not clear whether he takes it to be a proposition, a rule, an idea, a trope, or merely an intuition, as he suggests at one point (6). The *communicatio idiomatum* is said to have both logical and ontological sense (242). While Strzelczyk offers an elegant theory of the "logic" of this trope, it is not clear why it should have ontological sense. Nor is it clear whether this ontological sense licenses deductions, some of which have been problematical, as noted above. Strzelczyk does not evaluate the appropriateness or offer a cogent way to distinguish valid from invalid uses of the trope, apart from finding that a valid use in some sense corresponds to an author's intention (256). While Strzelczyk's historical survey is a useful and serious contribution, his systematic theological connection is overly formal and schematized. Finally, his work seems to leave unsolved the problems produced when one deduces claims from metonyms.

divine" that doctrinal rules such as "call Mary not only Christ-bearer, but God-bearer" preserve.

Divine Nature, Human Nature: The Problem

What can it mean for two incommmensurable *natures* to be joined in one *person*? The difficulties in understanding this abound. It requires working through an argument that seeks to expose confusions regarding these terms and their application. Recent work by Catholic philosophers and theologians influenced by St. Thomas Aquinas has sought to clarify Christian thinking about God's "nature" and God's relationship to the world.[14] The key distinction is between the Creator and the creature, the infinite and the finite. The key point that they are making—and which they attribute to St. Thomas—is that God is not in competition with the world because God's way of being is not comparable with or in the same category as the ways of being of every person, event, action, thing, or state of affairs in the world. God as Creator brings to be whatever is out of overflowing love. God is not a being like other existents, but the bountiful Creator of each and all there is. God's creative power is not in competition with human powers, but is the primary source of all that is and the power that empowers every secondary agent—that is, every agent in the world, and thus for whatever is done by secondary agents.[15]

Finally, God's love is not properly comparable to human love. God's love is overflowing pure donation, pure gift that loves whatever there is into being. No finite love can create *ex nihilo* or adequately "love back" the gift of infinite love. Nonetheless, properly ordered, a person of sinless, finite love could perfectly accept God's gift of being and be in perfect tune with the infinite. Jesus' finite human nature is perfectly in tune with (meets) his infinite divine nature. Neither God's love nor God's power is in competition with human love and power. To

---

14. For example, Austin Farrer, *Faith and Speculation: An Essay in Philosophical Theology* (London: A. and C. Black, 1967), 62; cf. 65, 82, 154; William R. Stoeger, "Describing God's Action in the World in Light of Scientific Knowledge of Reality," in *Chaos and Complexity: Scientific Perspectives on Divine Action*, ed. Robert John Russell, Nancey Murphy, and Arthur Peacocke (Vatican City: Vatican Observatory; Berkeley: Center for Theology and Natural Science, 1997), 239-61; idem, "Epistemological and Ontological Issues Arising from Quantum Theory," *Quantum Mechanics: Scientific Perspectives on Divine Action*, ed. Robert John Russell, Philip Clayton, Kirk Wegter-McNelly, and John Polkinghorne (Vatican City: Vatican Observatory; Berkeley: Center for Theology and the Natural Sciences, 2002), 81-98; Elizabeth A. Johnson, "Does God Play Dice? Divine Providence and Chance," *Theological Studies* 57, no. 3 (1996): 2-18; Robert Sokolowski, *The God of Faith and Reason: Foundations of Christian Theology* (Notre Dame: University of Notre Dame Press, 1982), 35-37; Robert Barron, *The Priority of Christ: Toward a Postliberal Catholicism* (Grand Rapids: Brazos, 2007), passim; Brian Davies, O.P., *The Reality of God and the Problem of Evil* (New York: Continuum, 2006), among others.

15. This would seem to make God the cause of evil. But Brian Davies (*The Reality of God and the Problem of Evil*, 173-96) shows that such cannot be the case if God is construed noncompetitively. I have taken a similar position in "Towards a Creativity Defense of Belief in God in the Face of Evil," in *Physics and Cosmology: Scientific Perspectives on the Problem of Natural Evil*, ed. Nancey Murphy et al. (Vatican City: Vatican Observatory Press, 2007), 195-215.

be redeemed, then, is to will what God wills for us: abundant, flourishing life together now and forever. Jesus does this perfectly.[16]

We have a great difficulty in even glimpsing what such noncompetitiveness and incomparability could mean. The key problem is that we think of God as the supreme being, the biggest and best being there is. In effect, we have been conditioned to think this way by numerous sources. Religious stories about Israel's God that make God competitive with other gods dispose us to think of God as one among many beings.

Nominalists, such as Duns Scotus in the late medieval era, sought to make God more intelligible by proposing "a univocal conception of existence, according to which God and creatures belong to the same metaphysical category, the genus of being." The problem is that while this approach construes God as "quantitatively superior to any creature or collectivity of creatures, there is nevertheless no qualitative difference, in the metaphysical sense" between Creator and creatures.[17] This nominalism led eventually to the eclipse of the supernatural in the modern, scientific understanding of "the natural world." Since the natural world and its history can be explained scientifically and historically without reference to a creator, God is invoked only to explain remarkable, unnatural events, that is, miracles. But these events are often explained away by natural and human sciences. God, who is presumed to be the being who brings about (as a direct or secondary cause in the world) such miraculous events, disappears. No longer is any divine cause needed to explain these events.[18] God has disappeared from the world: this is the upshot of rendering God and everything else as part of the class of existents.

But contemporary Thomists point out that this disappearance is the result of a serious philosophical error (among other things). We have become nominalists in fact and mistakenly placed God "in" the world (in the class of all existents). The result is that God has disappeared. There is no place in the world for the creator of the world. To think there is, is a philosophical confusion with dire consequences.

This problematical way of thinking of God as the biggest and best being is true not only of ordinary believers, but even of some Christian philosophers.[19] When some contemporary philosophers, for example, attempt to show that God is not responsible for evil in the world, they use a form of "possible worlds metaphysics," asking if there could be a possible world such that God brought it about that it had no moral evil in it; they answer that it is possible there could not be such a world.[20] In so doing, they sometimes debate the possibility of any "possible world" being a

---

16. This point is developed below in a discussion of the monothelite controversy, pp. 225, 230–31..

17. Barron, *Priority of Christ*, 13; also see David Burrell, *Faith and Freedom: An Interfaith Perspective* (Oxford: Blackwell, 2004), 91-112.

18. For the latter point, see my *History, Theology, and Faith: Dissolving the Modern Problematic* (Maryknoll, NY: Orbis Books, 2004), 70-76.

19. For examples, see Burrell, *Faith and Freedom*, 3-19.

20. For example, *inter alia*, Alvin Plantinga, *God Freedom and Evil* (New York: Harper & Row, 1974).

coherent possibility without God in it.[21] But in this way, they assume that, in some sense, God exists in the world. While the world cannot exist without God from a Christian perspective, God is not "in the world" in the same way that quarks, rocks, roses, toads, sneezes, and humans are. "Possible worlds metaphysics," analogous to the "divine middle knowledge" of the nominalists, participates in construing God as an existent, as did the nominalists.[22]

The fundamental problem is that this way of thinking treats both being and power as a "zero-sum game." God always has the controlling power, if God wants to use it, because God is thought to exercise the same kind of power as other entities do. In effect, this makes God the best and biggest denizen of the world rather than its creator. This creates two crucial problems: reconciling human free will with divine omnipotence and construing divine power as interventionist. In christology, it creates a subsidiary problem: if Jesus' human will is always in tune with his divine will, how can he, in any human sense, be free?

Many contemporary Christian philosophers have great difficulty in reconciling divine omnipotence with human freedom. One net result of such comparability and competitiveness with humans is that modern anti-Christian philosophers see God as the enemy of human freedom, rather than the creator, source, and goal of human freedom. Modern freedom is arbitrary liberty to choose, not the virtue that brings our wills in harmony with God's will for abundant life for us. For them, liberty is not a virtue that points us to the ultimate goal of union with God.[23] Thomists avoid the modern problem of pitting divine omnipotence against human freedom not by showing their compatibility, as some contemporary analytical philosophers do, but by finding that God's will for human beings is to thrive and that God's power is not competitive with human freedom; rather, it enables freedom and creativity to flourish. Jesus' human will is fully for human flourishing, as is his divine will. As human, he is free from sin. He flourishes freely and wills flourishing freedom for all.

Many believers construe miracles as interventions in the natural world by divine power from another part of the world, the supernatural world. Indeed, most believers in practice assume this by taking God as an agent who interferes in the world to do things, whether miraculously or not, a position that many contemporary Thomists reject. Thomists find that God's power is not interventionist. God does not exist in a world to intervene in it as a policeman attempting to stop a crime or a mother stopping her child from swallowing a poison. God creates the world and

---

21. See, e.g., Alvin Plantinga, *God and Other Minds: A Study of the Rational Justification of Belief in God* (Ithaca, NY: Cornell University Press, 1990; 1st ed., 1968), 3-94, for a "possible worlds" version of the ontological argument.

22. Some philosophers would respond that this is unfair in that God is the only entity that can be said to exist necessarily, a fact that preserves the divine uniqueness as all other entities exist contingently. This approach, however, does not undermine the point that it makes God one member of a distinct set of existents, the set of entities and events that compose one possible world that happens to be the actual world. God is still in the same super-set of existents as are creatures even if God exists "necessarily"; that is, God exists in all possible worlds.

23. Compare Barron, *Priority of Christ*, 262-64.

all that is in it. God is yet present in the world as the power to be of every being.[24] God is the divine agent who makes human and other agency possible. Hence, God's presence in and through the world is not an alien presence that intervenes but a constant presence that at its most intense creates creative agents.[25]

The root of the problem with the "two natures" doctrine is linguistic slippage. The very words "world" and "nature" have altered their meanings between the time of the classical understanding (before nominalism) and modern understandings of the terms. We have assumed something that is inaccurate, to put it mildly: we have assumed that these terms (or the concepts that they articulate in the different languages) mean the same things in each context. They do not. A "world" before nominalism is God's creation; now it includes God, who creates "the world"—an event that occurs in a "possible world." Before the scientific revolution, "natures" were understood to be like essences that individuals instantiate (sometimes more or less well). In the wake of the scientific revolution to which nominalism contributed, "nature" is what science investigates. "Agency" or "causality" is presumed to be a generic notion, with two species—divine primary and worldly secondary. But this is confused. As Austin Farrer put it regarding agency, "Both the divine and the human actions remain real and therefore free in the union between them; not knowing the modality of the divine action we cannot pose the problem of their mutual relation."[26] Since they are not two species of the same genus "action" or "agency," we cannot say how they are related, as we cannot assume that infinite divine Agent shares any characteristics with finite powers or agents in the world God created. Even when we use similes to talk of God's power and agency, these tropes do not license inferences about what God can and cannot do—and we use similes or metaphors only to talk of God's agency.

Divine Nature, Human Nature: Toward a Solution of the Problem

The resolution of the problem begins by rejecting the notion that divine and human agency are in a "zero-sum game." Thus, we must reject the nominalist claim that God belongs to any class that includes any other thing. God is unique, not a member of any class, including the class of existents. Putting God and other things into the same class (meaning, individual items in a world or two sorts of

---

24. This does not preclude the possibility of miracles, as Davies shows (*Reality of God and the Problem of Evil*, 74-77). However, this is not a modern understanding of "miracle" that many would find to be a point in its favor. Lieven Boeve (*God Interrupts History: Theology in a Time of Upheaval*, trans. Brian Doyle [New York: Continuum, 2007]) has offered an interesting twist on this point in his analysis of the religious situation of contemporary Europe: "People no longer believe in an interventionist God, who rules and controls everything. Hierarchy, monarchy and patriarchy, images of divine omnipotence, divine will and predestination are a hindrance to believing in God because they too easily invoke corresponding faith attitudes of submission, obedience, and guilt. Moreover, they give rise to an image of competition between God and human beings" (143). In other words, the god created by nominalism and scientism is simply incredible in a postsecular culture.

25. I explore this in "Towards a Creativity Defense of Belief in God in the Face of Evil."

26. Farrer, *Faith and Speculation*, 66.

agents with comparable powers) renders the possibility that God, as the greatest existent among many in a possible world, is comparable to other things that exist in that world.

Robert Barron helpfully summarizes the collapse of the medieval understanding of God and the creation in modernity of a framework in which God and other existents can be compared and thus be in competition with each other. He highlights the move made by late medieval nominalists who treated God as "existent":

> Because all created beings participate in God who is *ipsum esse subsistens*, they are unavoidably related to one another by means of that shared participation. It has been central to the intellectual projects of Louis Dupré, Hans Urs von Balthasar, Alisdair MacIntyre, and many others to show how this metaphysical vision fell apart through the introduction of a univocal conception of being, which effectively placed God and creatures side by side under the general heading of existence, and thereby separated them from one another. In a word, the univocal understanding of the concept of existence blinded us to the centrality and the primordiality of co-inherence.[27]

In placing God and creatures "side by side," this univocal understanding of being implicitly made God comparable to creatures, divine power to creaturely power, divine goodness to human goodness, divine willing to human willing. But this is to make the infinite comparable to the finite—and that is just the problem, for God is properly infinite and thus incomparable. What is lost, as Barron notes, is the reality of God not as an individual existent but as that which coinheres with all things and ties them together into a world. God is not one thing among others, but in some sense the heart of everything, the infinite creator who loves all finite things into being. Nothing is or can be unless God brings it into being out of God's own overflowing goodness.

The distinction between finite and infinite, Creator and creature, has significant implications for understanding the claim that Jesus Christ is truly human and truly divine. Barron understands the force of Chalcedon this way:

> [D]ivinity and humanity come together in the most intimate kind of union, yet non-competitively. But such non-competitiveness is possible only in the measure that God is not, himself, a creaturely or finite nature. Due to their metaphysical structure, finite things, despite the numerous ways in which they can find communion with one another, remain, at the most fundamental

---

27. Robert Barron, "The Metaphysics of Co-Inherence: A Meditation on the Essence of the Christian Message," in *Handing on the Faith: The Church's Mission and Challenge*, ed. Robert Imbelli (New York: Crossroad, 2006), 83. Subsequent notes indicate my debt to Barron's work. I do, however, draw some inferences from this that Barron did not; also see his *Priority of Christ* for his own developments, which are different from those adumbrated here. Jean-Luc Marion, although not a Thomist, goes even further in that he finds that construing God as being leads to the modern philosophical problems diagnosed by Martin Heidegger and others. See his *God Without Being: Hors-Texte*, trans. Thomas A. Carlson (Chicago: University of Chicago Press, 1995).

level, mutually exclusive, so that one can "become" another only through ontological surrender or aggression. Thus, a wildebeest becomes a lion only by being devoured; a building turns into rubble only by being destroyed; and you "become" me only through some act of enormous psychological manipulation.[28]

What sort of union is this nonviolent, noncompetitive meeting of finite and infinite? That is what the "two natures" doctrine of Chalcedon requires, if it is not to be rendered so that the two natures are two items of the same kind, two comparable sorts of things that might be in competition with each other (a problem that is highlighted by taking the *communicatio idiomatum* as licensing inferences, as noted above).

To attempt to answer such a question of what a union of finite and infinite is, is to attempt to plumb depths that the greatest minds find difficult, to put it mildly. However, there is a simple way to begin to imagine how this is so. When Peter confronted Jesus at Caesarea Philippi, Jesus told Peter, "Your ways are not God's ways, but humans'," *hoti ou phroneis ta tou theou alla ta tōn anthrōpōn*. Peter failed to understand because the wisdom of the human way alone cannot plumb the depths of God's ways. In contrast to Peter's failure to walk in God's ways, we can say that, for Jesus, his ways and God's ways are the same. This is the key. There is no separation or confusion in Jesus of the true ways of God and the true ways of humanity. To understand this theological claim about Jesus' significance, we can borrow insights from various parts of the tradition.

First, God is always nearer to us than we are to ourselves and completely superior to us (after St. Augustine, *Confessions* 3.6.11). This insight of Augustine is worked out in Barron's understanding "that the world to the very roots of its being exists in God by means of a relationship, and that God can reach most intimately into things, as Aquinas puts it, 'by essence, presence, and power.' The intertwining, the coinherence of God and the universe is a principal metaphysical consequence of the non-contrastive transcendence of God."[29] God is not just an item in a possible world external to every thing in the world. God is the heart of each and all. Hence, being truly human, Jesus would have to realize at least one way of being human truly. He would live in and live out the divine perfection as well as humanly possible at that time and place. In effect, Christians can claim this because they respond to him as a focal point in which divine love reaches out most intimately to all there is because God's love connects all there is. In every way, then, Jesus' ways are *truly God's ways and truly human ways as well*. Chalcedon formulated the principle that stands behind this and other affirmations: truly human, truly divine. The Third Council of Constantinople over two centuries later

---

28. Barron, "Metaphysics of Co-Inherence," 79-80. There are also, of course, nondestructive unions, such as sexual union, but even the most intimate human union, however much a full giving in love, is that of two finite beings, and so also cannot provide an understanding of the communion of the divine and the human, although it may provide a metaphor or simile. As with all tropes and analogies, of course, this one would limp.

29. Barron, "Metaphysics of Co-Inherence," 82.

affirmed that the divine will and the human will of Jesus are in perfect harmony as a way of keeping clear the distinction between the divine and human natures (for monothelitism, "one will," would have collapsed the finite human will into the infinite divine will).

Jesus as truly human and truly divine is seen as having a perfect natural harmony ("natural" in the ancient, not modern, sense). As human, he wants and wills finitely in particular situations what the infinite God wants and wills in those situations. Yet this man, the first among equals, is also the divine agent, unconfusedly, unalterably, indivisibly, inseparably. This is the faith claim that Christians make in practically realizing the Chalcedonian rule.

What the tradition could remember Peter *not* doing—realizing both human and divine ways in practice—Jesus does. Peter may be a saint, but he is not and was not divine. Peter was human, but failed to realize fully what it meant to be fully and properly human in that he sinned. His will was not in tune with God's at every moment. God's nearness to humanity is realized most perfectly, indeed just perfectly from the response of Jesus' disciples, in Jesus. In Jesus, God's ways are human ways and vice versa. So, we can imaginatively "riff" on the Caesarea Philippi scene: when Jesus repudiated Peter, he also pointed the way for us to account in practice what true humanity and true divinity would be: when God's ways and human ways meet perfectly. And the result of that? Those who reject God's reign and God's ways—those who support and seem to thrive under the dominating power of Rome and who reject the reconciling practices that are God's ways and God's reign—crucify Jesus.

Second, if God is not a competitor with humanity, but what/who brings all there is into being through loving them into being, then authentic human flourishing is God's will. Love simply wishes the flourishing of the beloved. God wishes the flourishing of each and all—God's love is total and infinite. Thus, human thriving is acceptance of God's wish for each and all. To thrive, humans require freedom. But then human freedom is not best understood as arbitrary choice, but as doing God's will, even surrendering to God's will. God's will for each and every creature is fulfillment or happiness. As Barron notes, St. Thomas begins the *Summa Theologica*'s section on morality not with rules or duties but with happiness.[30] That God wants human happiness is a disciple's root understanding of God's desire for humanity.

The apparent paradox that runs through much theology since Augustine is that "true freedom is obedience to God." This connection of freedom with obedience is paradoxical only if God's will and human wills can be in competition with each other, as a child's will can be in competition with its parents'. Of course, humans can be seen as resisting God or rebelling against God. We can engage in practices that treat our wills as if they were God's. We commit sins individually and participate in structures of evil, which is social sin. We can and do make choices

---

30. See ibid., 87-89. Of course, there are reasonable disputes about what constitutes human happiness and thus what God wills for humanity. Ultimately God wills human happiness; more proximately, the focus of the practices that constitute discipleship are practices of reconciliation, the reunion of those who had been separated by social or personal sin.

that, wittingly or not, do not comport with God's will for us. However, *we cannot compete with God and God will not compete with us*. If we do what reflects God's will for humanity, then the result will be authentic human freedom and authentic human flourishing. If we fail to do what reflects God's will for humanity, then the result will be attenuated freedom and partial flourishing, at best.[31]

Discerning God's Will

The problem, however, comes in discerning God's will. We are confronted with choices in nearly every significant act we do. The formal point that freedom is doing God's will is not very helpful when in practice we have to figure out how to actualize God's will. We are advised "this is God's will," "that is God's will," "the other is really God's will," whether "this, that, or the other" are choices we have to make about sexual behavior, participating in or opposing a war, or determining how to use and share our goods. The modern obsession with choice correctly understands that conditions of intellectual, political, social, moral, and religious plurality—not to mention the many instances of corrupt authorities in every area—have made discerning God's will—hearing the most truly refracted voice of God in all the voices—subject to endless disputes. And the worst of those disputes—who has the true authority?—can logically never be resolved by appeals to authorities because it is just the authenticity of authority that is in question. In our era, we cannot simply assume that one particular voice is "the" voice of authority. From Catholic bishops covering up sexual abuse by clergy to Muslim imams condoning suicide bombings against fellow Muslims, religious authority is in grave jeopardy.

We can only discover God's will, although perhaps not easily, in practice.[32] As Christians, we discover God's will in the reconciling practices that constitute living in and living out the *basileia tou theou*. For in the practices of the Jesus-movement, we can recognize and display the overflowing love of God as present. We stop committing sins and refuse to give our allegiance to social and

---

31. The total refusal of God's will for human flourishing may be the loss of even being truly human. See my *The Evils of Theodicy* (Washington, DC: Georgetown University Press, 1991), 154-57, commenting on Boethius, *The Consolation of Philosophy* IV pr 3 (book 4, prose section 3).

32. It is also important to note the capaciousness of God. It is possible that God's will is not monolithic, that is, that God could will only one thing in any situation. A systematic account of such is beyond the aims of this text, but a simple version can be rendered clearly (understanding that our terminology is inevitably temporal while God's will is eternal, so that this version, from a systematic perspective, would limp). Given that there is sin in the world, and given that "in Adam," all sinned, then God has to have "contingency plans" to take account of this shift away from the best that the world could be. Some construe the incarnation as one of those contingency plans. But given that the way the world is not and cannot be determined by God (unless God determined Adam and all of us to sin, which Christians cannot believe), then it is possible that God could eternally envision a number of good outcomes for every situation, rather than just one. All of them would fulfill God's will, considered as bountiful rather than monolithic. Such an account fits especially with the picture painted by Johnson, "Does God Play Dice?"

personal sin that blocks the realization of the reign of God. We live in and live out a tradition that seeks to overcome evil and sin not by "overpowering" them but by reconciling sinners and saints, perpetrators and victims, the warriors and the vanquished, the exploiters and the exploited, insofar as that reconciliation is possible for those committed to living in and living out that tradition. That we often fail to do so means that the community is as sinful as, if not more sinful than, the Zebedee brothers fighting over primacy in the *basileia*, Peter denying Jesus, or the disciples falling asleep in the Garden of Gethsemane and then fleeing when Jesus was arrested and executed. Living in God's reign may well put one at odds with earthly reigns—certainly not always or everywhere. But the question is whether we will live in and live out that tradition or fall asleep and run away from it when we see its cost. It is clear that it might be difficult to embody these practices; it is also clear that there are guides to "how to" embody them (see pp. 236-42 below).

That Jesus was the leader of the movement that became Christianity, that he was the first among equally human folk, as Elisabeth Schüssler Fiorenza has argued, seems unexceptionable. It also seems unexceptionable that the movement itself recognized Jesus as God's agent, even in some ways in his lifetime, as Larry Hurtado and James D. G. Dunn have argued in different ways. What Jesus made real was the power of God in practices that became the practices of the Jesus-movement. As God loved the world into being, what made Jesus recognizable as divine was his empowering the saving and reconciling practices that shaped the Jesus-movement when it was what it was supposed to be, when it carried out God's will. Jesus as the agent of God did not exercise a power over or a power against, but a power that empowered people to live in and live out the reign of God. His divine nature can be seen as the power empowering the disciples' missions.

Archbishop Rowan Williams has suggested that Christ's overcoming temptations in the desert was understood in the catechetical tradition rooted in the "New Adam" christology of the New Testament, which informs the work of patristic authors Irenaeus, Evagrius Ponticus, and Cassian. Just as the first Adam succumbed to temptation from the devil in the garden, so the New Adam was victorious in passing the probing tests that the devil gave him in the desert. Whereas the "old Adam" was imperfect in realizing God's will for him, the New Adam was perfect in doing so. And in so doing, Jesus as truly human not only exemplified what humans are to be and do, but as truly divine empowered others to do so. As Williams put it, "The victory over these trials [in the desert] is part of the liberation of humanity."[33] Just as Jesus did not allow these probes of temptation to distort him out of being perfectly human, so we can become empowered by following him to become truly human.[34] Just as Jesus did not give in to the desire

---

33. Williams, "'Tempted as We Are.'" That this tradition might be rather speculative by modern standards does not undermine the points adapted from it.

34. Williams also pointed out that temptation was understood in the ancient world more as a test and probe of virtue and fidelity rather than as a psychological desire for something forbidden or not good for us, the modern conception. Stories of temptation resisted or tests passed or probes met,

to let the cup pass from him in the Garden of Gethesemane, but prayed to do God's will, so we can become faithful to the death because he, being as human as we are, could. Because Jesus is truly human and truly divine, his human behavior is not only exemplary, but also empowering and liberating divine grace for those who carry on the practice of refusing to succumb to the distortions to which one is tempted.

Michael Amaladoss has argued that an image to use for Jesus in Asia is "Jesus the Sage." His rationale for using this image is important, for it helps show the connection of our practices with the redemption wrought in Jesus. He wrote:

> In looking on Jesus as a sage, I am not denying the perspectives of Jesus as Wisdom incarnate. I am simply paying attention to the wisdom of Jesus. Theologians' soteriological concerns make them concentrate on the passion of Jesus who died for the sins of humanity, not on his life and teachings. In evoking the image of Jesus as the sage I am trying [to] understand the significance of Jesus as a teacher and guide for our lives in this world through his own life and preaching.[35]

If Jesus is Wisdom incarnate, then he can be seen as a sage who shows God's ways in life and death, and, I would add, as an *empowering* guide for living God's ways.

We may and do resist living in God's ways. We are not, like Jesus, truly human. Thus, we are imperfect in realizing what God wishes for us. But what God wishes is that we flourish together. It is hard to imagine that any rational person could deny that many people refuse to do what is best for them, however. Yet they do—that is the power of those things that tempt us bodily, and spiritually. That we fail to do what is really best for us means that we are sinners, missing the mark, sometimes so badly that we separate ourselves from the Jesus-movement. But as we are all sinners, we are all called to engage in the practices of reconciliation— overcoming the final temptation to throw away others from our lives. As noted in chapter 19, because Jesus resisted temptation and died for all, we cannot settle for alienation from others.

Third, it is Jesus who perfectly—that is, sinlessly—carried out God's will. However, how Jesus did this is a crucial theological point debated in the seventh century in the "monothelite controversy" mentioned above. While this seems like an obscure dispute, it reveals important points about understanding the true humanity and true divinity Christians are to attribute to Jesus. Barron summarizes this significance of this dispute elegantly:

> Theologians of a more monophysite [one nature in Christ, not two] bent maintained that there was but one divine will in Jesus, but others held that

---

such as Jesus resisting Satan in the desert, are narratives that reveal truth, the truth of God's will for humanity.

35. Michael Amaladoss, S.J., *The Asian Jesus* (Maryknoll, NY: Orbis Books, 2006), 32.

a key implication of the two-natures doctrine of Chalcedon is that there must be two wills, divine and human, in the Lord. After much wrangling, the fathers of the Third Council of Constantinople in 681 determined that Christ possesses two wills and two natural operations, not opposed to one another, but cooperating in such a way that his human freedom finds itself precisely in surrender to his divine freedom. . . . [H]umanity is enhanced rather than diminished when placed in tight co-inherent relationship with the non-competitive God. Divine freedom and human freedom can interlace and overlap as thoroughly as any of the designs in the book of Kells.[36]

What distinguishes Christ from us is that he is "like us in all respects except for sin," as the Epistle to the Hebrews and the Council of Chalcedon put it. But sin is resistance to and refusal of God's will. Therefore, the disciples recognized that in Jesus there was an identity in practice of a human will with the divine will, but not a reduction of one to the other. The infinite nature of God and the finite nature of the human may be incomparable, but in practice there is no reason to say that they could not be perfectly "in synch." In Jesus, God's ways and human ways aligned. Therefore, in us God's ways and human ways can align because by resisting temptation to let the cup pass from him, Jesus has shown us how not to resist God's ways. The great temptation is the temptation to resist God.

Fourth, this "metaphysical" understanding in effect suggests that the ancient recognition of Jesus as God's agent was a recognition that what Jesus did is just what God would do for humanity in the concrete situation. And what God has done for us, as noted above, is love us into being. God creates because it is God's nature to give. "Because it is the nature of the good to give of itself and because God is the supreme good, it is only fitting that God should give himself utterly, superabundantly, and this explains the fittingness of the Incarnation."[37] What Jesus did for the movement was not to lord it over them or to demand recognition—indeed, when others asked who would be first in the *basileia tou theou*, Jesus remonstrated with them. Hence, Christians find that Jesus embodies the truly divine presence and power enabling people to be made whole again, to be in conformity with God's wishes for them, to be free and flourishing, and to share that gift with all who would encounter those who live in and live out the *basileia tou theou*, the Jesus-movement. This is the true gift of reconciliation.

Conclusion

Theologians sometimes forget that Chalcedon did not "settle" christological issues. Behind the developments that led to the monothelite controversy were a number of disagreements about christology. A number of non-Chalcedonian positions

---

36. Barron, "Metaphysics of Co-Inherence," 89.
37. Ibid., 90.

existed for centuries even after Chalcedon. From our perspective, Chalcedon seems to put an end to christological controversies; but it did not do so.

William Harmless has pointed out that the desert monks in early Christianity had a variety of views of Jesus, both Chalcedonian and non-Chalcedonian. In working with the late-fifth-century collection *The Sayings of the Desert Fathers* (*Apophthegmata Patrum*), Harmless noted both the inclusion of sayings from anti-Chalcedonian monks as well as from Chalcedonians, and the collection's lack of christological reflection. He wrote:

> While the *Apophthegmata* is strangely silent about christology, the wider monastic world it came from was not. Christology first moved to the forefront of the theological agenda in the clash between Cyril of Alexandria and Nestorius at the Council of Ephesus in 431. It continued on the front burner for the next century (and beyond) and ended up bitterly dividing segments of the ancient Christian world, most acutely after 451, after the Council of Chalcedon. . . . The Alphabetical Collection [one recension of the *Apophthegmata Patrum*] includes the sayings of Longinus, abbot of the monastery of Enaton outside Alexandria and an outspoken opponent of the Council. Also one of Poemen's sayings speaks of Abba John, who was exiled by the Emperor Marcian, presumably because John opposed the Council. . . .
>
> Given the christological noisiness of the monastic world at the time of the editing of the *Apophthegmata*, its christological silence makes enormous sense. Christology was dividing monk against monk. . . . The editor(s) who created the text of the *Apophthegmata* knew that whereas theology divided monk from monk, *praktikē*, ascetic practice, united them. . . . The *Apopthegmata*, I would argue, is the work of a peacemaker (or a circle of peacemakers).[38]

Rather than speculate theologically when the monks were divided theologically, the editors were ecumenists. They realized that monastic practice, the ascetic practices that make a community of practitioners possible, could still knit the ideologically diverse monks into a community. Monks rooted in both the practices of monastic life at Scetis in Egypt and in the christological battles of fifth-century Palestine sought "to mark out an ecumenical common ground by consciously seeking to remain silent about christology and by focusing instead on what united

---

38. William Harmless, S.J., "Desert Silence: Why Christology Is Missing from the *Apophthegmata Patrum*" (paper presented to the Fifteenth International Patristics Conference, Oxford, August 10, 2007), 15. I am grateful to Professor Harmless for a copy of his not yet published paper and for permission to quote from it here. Harmless follows Lucien Regnault, "Les apophtegmes des pères en Palestine aux Vᵉ-VIᵉ siècles," *Irenikon* 54 (1981): 320-30, which places the written version of the text in the second half of the fifth century, that is, after Chalcedon. Although many of the texts preserved are from the Egyptian monks, the collection, Harmless and Regnault argue, was compiled in and distributed from Palestine.

monks in their common quest for purity of heart."[39] Where ideology divides, shared practice can unite—at least for a particular time and in a particular place.

The very sharing of practice in spite of diverse ideologies is in itself a reconciling practice, a practice of the Jesus-movement. Demanding theological conformity in a situation of diversity is a divisive practice. The christological silence of the *Apophthegmata Patrum* indicates the centrality and efficacy of shared practice, especially in a time of theological or ideological disagreement. Time may work out those theological disagreements, but failure to share practices will destroy the possibility of having time for an enduring community to work out theological difference. Practice, not theory, is the heart of Christian life together; to insist on ideological identity in a time of diversity is not a reconciling practice.

The terms of the ancient doctrine of Chalcedon cannot simply be transliterated if that doctrine is to be a guide to Christian life in the present. Paula Fredricksen has perhaps overstated the point, but she found that the terms of Chalcedon, perhaps paradoxical in the past, are simply nonsense now. As she put it:

> The classic christological formula remains, embalmed by institutional sanction; but both the universe and philosophy are much changed. With the advent of modern science, the world has grown progressively disenchanted. In consequence, Western ideas of godhead have grown more austere, while Western concepts of personhood increasingly focus on issues of identity, memory, and embodiment. To affirm that a human being is god, howsoever moderns might try to do that, is not paradox. Without reworking or redefining the terms, it *is* nonsense.[40]

The central principle that Chalcedon formulates as "truly divine, truly human" must be held by Christians. But merely repeating the formula's words, or transliterations of them, does not guarantee fidelity to the tradition. The idea, to be understood, may well need to be formulated differently now. If the ongoing Jesus-movement embodied in the church wishes to communicate to its fledgling members and to nonmembers what this principle means, Chalcedonian terminology may not be helpful.

In these practices, including belief, the following two principles are identity principles for Christianity, principles that go beyond, but also explicate, Lindbeck's three "operational doctrines," cited on p. 205, above:

1. Don't deny the true finite humanity or true infinite divinity in Jesus.
2. Don't confuse, divide, separate, split, or reverse the unity of humanity and divinity.

---

39. Harmless, "Desert Silence," 18.

40. Paula Fredricksen, "What Does Jesus Have to Do with Christ? What Does Knowledge Have to Do with Faith? What Does History Have to Do with Theology," *Christology: Memory, Inquiry, Practice*, ed. Anne M. Clifford and Anthony J. Godzieba, College Theology Society Annual 48 (Maryknoll, NY: Orbis Books, 2003), 10.

As noted above, contemporary Christians all too often violate the first principle. In their religious practice they are docetists who deny the humanity, or subordinationists (at best) who deny the divinity. If we forget the incomparability and noncompetitiveness of divine and human, a characteristic of much Christian theology since the early modern period and perhaps of most uses of the *communicatio idiomatum*, we confuse the humanity and divinity in and of Jesus, or construe the unity as if it were the unity of two essentially similar things.

There are numerous ways to formulate these principles that are suggested by theologians and by ordinary practitioners of the faith. The point, finally, is to recognize in practice both that Jesus is humanly first among equals and divinely the love of God incarnate. The unity is given in the practice of reconciliation, a practice of realizing what God wishes for humanity in a situation of conflict and sin, a practice that is both human and divine, unconfusedly, unalterably, indivisibly, inseparably, a practice that the disciples remember as Jesus, and Jesus alone, incarnating perfectly because although he was like us in all things including temptation, he was sinless. And as he lived a life of empowerment, so he died a death of empowerment—the empowering of hope even in the face of the grim reality of death—a point developed on pp. 253-54 below.

In one sense, what is being suggested here is a modern version of the "exemplary" theory of at-one-ment associated with Abelard. But this exemplarism is not merely a model but an empowering example. Jesus does not merely show us what to do; Jesus empowers us to practice the faith. Jesus, in showing us *how* to live in and live out the reign of God, empowers us to be (secondary) agents of reconciliation. He shows us how to become transparent to God because we would be in harmony, however imperfectly and partially, with God's will (as Jesus was perfectly and fully). As first among equals, Jesus of Nazareth taught and showed the members of the Jesus-movement how to live; as God's divine agent, he empowered us to do so. If our speculation about Mary of Bethany noted in chapter 9 is accurate, then Jesus, as first among equals, could even learn how to live in and live out God's will from those with whom he had an intense relationship formed by a community of practice. A "practical" christology thus indicates the way to understand in reconciling, at-one-ing practice *how* to follow the one who is truly human, truly divine.

Nineteen

THE HEART OF DISCIPLESHIP

A Christology of Reconciling Practice

*C*onstruing christology as reconciling practice means, among other things, that the previous two chapters felt, perhaps, like a roundabout way to get to this final chapter. However, the noncompetitive, noncomparable power and love of Creator for all creation and each creature, the refusal to deny Jesus either true divinity or true humanity, and the recognition of the harmony (not identity) of divine and human willing in Jesus are important doctrinal guides for our practices. While such doctrines cannot determine what our practices should be, they can help us discern good practice. Good practice will be consistent with such doctrinal rules.

The shift in perspective from a doctrinal to a practical focus means that these doctrinal issues are not at the center of christology. Yet practical disciplines give rise to and need theoretical moments. Praxis without theory can go off blindly; theory without practice can be empty words, clanging gongs, communicating nothing.

This chapter spells out some of the implications this shift in perspective has for living out the tradition. Yet it may all come down to one point that can be summarized as: "Neither are you God nor is God your possession; but you are God's agents of reconciliation."

Reconciling Practice

In 1 Corinthians 12:27, having discussed the gifts of the Spirit at length, Paul writes, "You are the body of Christ and members in part."[1] To get students to

---

1. This section includes material adapted from my *Story Theology* (Wilmington, DE: Michael Glazier, 1985), 60-64, 147-78. There I argue that "saints"—all God's people—are the body of Christ in the world today. A similar approach regarding Christian ethics in the context of christology can be found in Robert Barron, *The Priority of Christ: Toward a Postliberal Catholicism* (Grand Rapids: Brazos, 2007), 298-342. Barron uses Edith Stein as a model of courage, Thérèse of Lisieux as a model of prudence, Katharine Drexel as a model of justice, and Mother Teresa as a model of temperance—all exemplars not merely of natural cardinal virtues but of virtues elevated by divine grace. The similarities in our approaches are likely due in part to the fact that both of us are North Americans who have been influenced in different ways by the work of Baptist theologian James Wm. McClendon, Jr., *Systematic Theology,* vol. 1, *Ethics* (Nashville: Abingdon, 1986), as well as by our Roman Catholic heritage. The differences are due, in part, to the differing use of historical

think about the significance of this, I ask them, "Where would you be without your body?" This question, of course, confuses them. They do not know how to answer it. The suggestions they make inevitably turn out to be flawed. Then I ask, "What could you do without your body?" After struggling with possibilities that inevitably get "shot down" by other students, and occasionally by the teacher, they realize they cannot answer the question. I can then ask effective rhetorical questions about reconciling practices. "Where would Christ be without his body?" "What in the world could Christ do without his body?" If the Jesus-movement is in some metaphorical or metonymical sense the body of Christ, and those who are sent into the world do what he has taught them to do, then when the members of the movement engage in reconciling practices, they continue his work in the world. Jesus, the divine agent, is present, sacramentally and practically, in the movement we call "church," a movement that functions as Christ's body for the healing of the world and wherever communities undertake the reconciliation of the world. The body of Christ, the Jesus-movement, carries on the work by incarnating atonement.

The members of this body are saints. In 1902, William James, the American pragmatist philosopher, described saints and their effects in the following way:

> The saints are authors, *auctores*, increasers of goodness. . . . St. Paul long ago made our ancestors familiar with the idea that every soul is virtually sacred. Since Christ died for us all without exception, St. Paul said, we must despair of no one. This belief in the essential sacredness of every one expresses itself to-day in all sorts of human customs and reformatory institutions, and in a growing aversion to the death penalty and to brutality in punishment. The saints, with their extravagance of human tenderness, are the great torch-bearers of this belief, the tip of the wedge, the clearers of the darkness. . . . [T]hey are impregnators of the world, vivifiers and animaters of potentialities of goodness which but for them would be forever dormant. . . . No one who is not willing to try charity, to try non-resistance as the saint is always willing, can tell when these methods will or will not succeed. When they do succeed, they are far more powerfully successful than force or worldly prudence. Force destroys enemies; and the best that can be said for prudence is that it keeps what we already have in safety. But non resistance, when successful, turns enemies into friends; and charity regenerates its objects.[2]

Many of James's examples of sanctity were canonized Christian saints, although not all were.

---

materials in our work, the differing impacts of liberation theologies on our views, and to my being more influenced by McClendon, *Biography as Theology: How Life Stories Can Remake Today's Theology* (Nashville: Abingdon, 1974); and Robert J. Schreiter, C.Pp.S., *The Ministry of Reconciliation: Spirituality and Strategies* (Maryknoll, NY: Orbis Books, 1998), than is Barron.

2. William James, *The Varieties of Religious Experience: A Study in Human Nature* (New York: Collier Books, 1961), 283-84.

Not all the officially recognized saints may be worth venerating in the present. Some uncanonized saints, including Dorothy Day, Oscar Romero and the other martyrs of El Salvador, including the American churchwomen and the Jesuits and their staff from the University of Central America, Mother Teresa, and others, may be more worthy of veneration and imitation than the canonized ones. James's description of what saints do is crucial: the process of reconciliation turns enemies into friends, and the saints' love is the love of God that regenerates not only those to whom it is directed but also the relationships among people.

What is key in a saint is a certain *sort* of sanctity that must be "displayed to the world and it has a history: canonized saints are the creative models of sanctity who have set a concrete example, each for his own particular age, of a new way to be Christian, creatively and with new understanding."[3] Carrying on the practices of the Jesus-movement does not mean slavish imitation. Times change and familial, social, political, religious, and economic structures and conditions change. Whereas saintly practice in the early modern period might be exemplified in nursing the sick and the injured, perhaps in the present that good work can and should be supplemented by the practice of working for health-care reform. Whereas saintly practice in the medieval period involved hospitality to strangers who came to monasteries, perhaps in the present the work of hospitality, rooted in table fellowship, needs to be carried out in the arena of immigration reform. How saintly practices evolve cannot be predicted, but only recognized by the community as practices of the Jesus-movement.

Saints are saints in a particular time and place. But when Paul greets the Romans, he recognizes "all the saints" (16:15).[4] In one sense, all disciples are "saints," holy ones of God (as well as being sinners, those whose wills are not in harmony with God's). But to be a disciple requires discipline, in Greek, *askēsis*. Although this term is normally used for the practices of the monks and hermits in the desert, all Christians are called to asceticism. The form of that asceticism, that serious spiritual discipline, differs from age to age. But the pattern is set by those ancient ascetics and martyrs. Those who engaged in these practices are the prototypes of sanctity, disciples who carried on the practices of the Jesus-movement as it became a faith-tradition in the Greco-Roman world, eventually independent of the Jewish tradition of Jesus and his first followers (and, alas, its identity established in opposition to Judaism, a painful heritage that still lingers).

Legend has it that all the "Twelve" "apostles" (except St. John) died as martyrs, as did St. Paul and others. The martyrdom of St. Stephen as narrated in the Acts of the Apostles became a model for Christians. To be a martyr was first to be a witness (*martyrion*) to the way of Jesus, living in and living out the reign of God he realized. But later, and permanently, a martyr became a person who exemplified this witness and fidelity even unto execution. To be empowered to

---

3. Karl Rahner and Herbert Vorgrimler, *Theological Dictionary*, trans. R. Strachan (New York: Herder & Herder, 1965), 479.

4. In what follows, the term "saint" is generally used to refer to "recognized models of sanctity," rather than the broader designation. The context will make it clear when the term is used more broadly.

be such a witness—whether one's life is demanded or not—requires discipline, ascetic practice.[5]

The ascetics of early Christianity sought to reconcile in practice sinful humanity with the divine. They made the desert a city and engaged in practices that are often seen as individualistic taming of the body for the sake of individual souls. But they were far more than that. These monks and hermits were sometimes called "white martyrs," witnesses who were not killed for their faithful practice, as were the "red martyrs." Ascetic training prepared people to be martyrs, witnesses. Some became the "red martyrs," those whose blood was shed for their faith. "White martyrdom did not replace red, contrary to widely held beliefs. . . . On the contrary, asceticism flourished within Christianity from its inception. . . . But toward the end of the second century, when the persecution of Christianity became more intense, asceticism provided the theoretical and practical basis for heroic martyrdom."[6] Learning how to be a follower of Christ in particular contexts, that is, learning how to engage in the practices of the Jesus-movement as they are shaped and reshaped in different contexts, is the asceticism of discipleship. There is no single form of this training—although the monks and hermits provide a prototype that always remains informative. Their *askesis* began with working to overcome the temptations of gluttony and lusting for bodily pleasures to that of pursuing pride, the affectation that comforts us as being superior to any other. Each form of training in *askesis* properly is tailored to the needs of particular times and places.

Members of the Christian community can become martyrs only when political authorities persecute them. Christians recognize the rebuke Jesus gave to Peter at Caesarea Philippi. "Your ways are human ways, not God's ways." Specifically, ascetics are well-disciplined Christians who have learned the difference between God's ways and human ways. The martyrs are those Christians who are murdered, assassinated, or executed by political leaders (or their lackeys) for the witness they give to their faith by living in and living out God's ways. It is important to note that, like Jesus, martyrs do not merely die for engaging in the practices of God's reign, but, like Jesus, are executed or assassinated for doing so by political authorities.

The logic of Christian martyrdom is this: Just as Jesus was executed by the Roman procurator for his life and work, so the martyrs are executed for their life and work. Just as Jesus would be exalted into glory by his father in heaven after his death, so the martyrs would be welcomed into eternal life. Jesus and the martyrs died by diabolical state violence.

---

5. "Ascetic practice" is not a univocal term. The practices will vary. For example, walking with Jesus and the community through the Triduum is a powerful ascetic practice in Hispanic communities that places the participants in a different time and place—on the road and on the cross with Jesus. See Roberto S. Goizueta, *Caminemos con Jesús: Toward a Hispanic/Latino Theology of Accompaniment* (Maryknoll, NY: Orbis Books, 1995), 32-37; for a remarkable reflection on the significance of participation, see p. 103.

6. Maureen A. Tilley, "The Ascetic Body and the (Un)Making of the World of the Martyr," *Journal of the American Academy of Religion* 69, no. 3 (September 1991): 468.

Jon Sobrino found that Jesus' execution "presents two related but distinct problems: 'Why was Jesus killed?' (a historical question about the causes of his death), and 'Why did Jesus die?' (a theological question about the meaning of his death). Both are given an answer in the New Testament. The first is explained in terms of Jesus' history, and the second is not, strictly speaking, answered, but referred to the mystery of God."[7] And so with martyrs: they are killed for the way they lived, but why they had to die is a mystery.

Alas, we have often watered down martyrdom. We have treated faithful Christians who resist political and religious coercion as if they were martyrs. We have treated holy women, like St. Maria Goretti, who was killed resisting rape, as if they were martyrs. Such holy men and women are heroic saints worthy of veneration. But they are not properly said to be martyrs. To be a martyr is to be *executed* for the practice of one's faith, not to give one's life to protect one's virtue. Whether killed by persecuting governments, by peoples resistant to colonization, or even by fellow Christians, martyrdom is not merely a religious act. Martyrdom is a political act that witnesses to faith in Jesus, also executed for the way he lived. Martyrs do not die in hospital, hospice, or home. Nor do they simply *die* for the faith. Nor are they killed for their faith. They are *killed by political leaders or their minions* for their living in and living out the *basileia tou theou.*

It is all too convenient to forget the political constituent of Christian martyrdom. The martyrs of El Salvador were executed, assassinated, or murdered because their ways were not the government's ways. Properly understood, being a martyr is being a "political saint," for the martyr is one who lives out the faith in practice and is killed for doing so.[8]

Not all saints are martyrs. Nor can they be. Whoever lives a heroic life of Christian virtue may be recognized as a saint. Whoever gives her or his life for the greater honor and glory of God in the face of opposition or even torture may be recognized as a saint. Whoever is killed to avoid cooperating in a sinful act may be recognized as a saint. True disciples are saints, but not all saintly disciples are martyrs. Not all who live and die for Christ are martyrs. Martyrs stand up to authorities who seek to kill them for political reasons—and succeed.

The "opposites" of martyrdom may help us see the limits of the practices of the reign of God, just as the contrast with the vices of "despair" and "overconfidence" helps us to understand the virtue of hope. Because martyrdom is the possibility that all Christians ought to prepare for, it provides an important guide. If the practices of the reign of God are good enough to give one's life *to*, then they ought be good enough to give one's life *for*. Because martyrs go the full distance and have their lives taken from them for their fidelity, their "opposites" can be instructive for discipleship.

The first opposite of a martyr is a traitor. In the sporadic persecutions of

---

7. Jon Sobrino, *Christ the Liberator: A View from the Victims,* trans. Paul Burns (Maryknoll, NY: Orbis Books, 2001), 195.

8. For the story of one ordinary priest, Fr. Hector Gallego, whose life work, which included helping peasants in Panama form a *communidad de base,* led to his (presumed) execution, see my *Story Theology,* 166-74.

Christianity before Constantine, some members of the community—layfolk, deacons, presbyters, bishops—did not pass the test. They confessed the faith but then recanted under torture or threat of torture. They could not give their lives *for* their faith. Some worshiped gods or emperors. They sometimes "turned over" the scriptures to the authorities rather than keep them inviolate. Hence, they were called *traditores*, traitors who turned themselves or their scriptures over to the authorities to save their necks. When faced with death for practicing the faith, they buckled. While they had flourished in the faith, they could not face public execution for it. They had passed their tests, but when the final probe came, they wilted. The early Christian communities often forgave them—at least once—and welcomed them back as women and men who would again live in the faith and who would also pledge to die for it, if necessary.

There was precedent for such reconciliation and forgiveness. Peter had denied Christ. He was forgiven for his betrayal and eventually proved his worth by being martyred in Rome. The other Synoptic Gospels tend to follow Mark, who presents all the disciples as dim during Jesus' life and cowardly at his arrest, but the other Gospels also "unambiguously present the body of Jesus' disciples as restored and validated."[9] As the first members of the Jesus-movement were faithless, and yet forgiven, so some later traitors could be forgiven, too.

The circumstances under which such forgiveness could be granted and traitors reconciled with the communities they had betrayed were hotly debated in early Christianity. Some did not find reconciled traitors worthy of leadership. Yet in some communities, former traitors even became presbyters or bishops. The key point is that forgiveness and reconciliation were possible; even traitors could be reconciled.

But most Christians are never put to the test. Most Christians do not have to choose between martyrdom and betrayal. Most Christians can be disciples without being martyrs. But if the authorities wanted to root out the religion or punish the disciples for their actions, then some Christians would face the choice of martyrdom or betrayal.

A *traditor* is one who puts other practices ahead of the practices of the reign of God. Rather than reconciling practices, these are dominating practices, controlling practices. When we try to have it all, to live in luxury while others starve, or to control others' lives rather than empowering them, we engage in the practices that destroy the community and oppose the *basileia tou theou*. These practices are patterns of behavior that alienate individuals from who they are and should be, split communities into quarreling factions, and distance all from God.

The *traditores* perhaps rarely really wanted to take up practices of domination. But in turning themselves or the scriptures over to the authorities who demanded their death if they would not capitulate, they acknowledged the power and authority of those who would rule by such practices. To worship the emperor or the gods of the cities was to acknowledge the validity of the violence of conquest

---

9. Larry Hurtado, *Lord Jesus Christ: Devotion to Jesus in Earliest Christianity* (Grand Rapids: Eerdmans, 2003), 587.

and/or successful military resistance to conquest. Rather than give their lives, they at least paid lip-service to ways that were humans', not God's.

Another opposite of a martyr is a killer. Christian martyrs are neither suicides nor murderers. Of course, some early Christians sought the glory of martyrdom. But they did not kill themselves (unless they helped a faltering executioner, as some stories say). Nor did they kill others, as some of the violent "martyrs" glorified by terrorists do today. Martyrdom signifies a way of life that one would die for. But martyrs also showed that no way of life was worth killing for. Even William James, in the quotation above, noted the power of nonresistance, of refusing to destroy enemies.

Some terrorists call suicide bombers "martyrs." But killing for the faith is not martyrdom as Christians understand it. Jesus was not a killer but a healer. He did not resist his execution, but Christians do not believe he sought it either. Otherwise, why the scene in the Gospels in which Jesus prays alone in the Garden of Gethsemane that "this cup" may pass from him? His execution tested him, and he passed. Whether the scene in Gethsemane has a historical core is irrelevant here. The historic point it makes is that Jesus' followers did not believe he sought his death as suicides do. Nor did he ever seek the death of others, as suicide bombers do. Martyrs follow in his path—they do not take up the sword or don vests filled with explosives to kill in defense of their lives or in support of their faith.

Admittedly, many Christians find violence, and even killing, justified at times. Chapter 15 touched on these issues. But violence is, at best, a dangerous means to the true goal of Christian life: living in and living out the reign of God. Whether violence in general and war in particular is ever justified as a means to Christian ends is vigorously debated among Christians. To resolve these issues is far beyond the scope of this text. Yet William James reminds us correctly in the quotation above, "Force destroys enemies; and the best that can be said for prudence is that it keeps what we already have in safety. But non resistance, when successful, turns enemies into friends; and charity regenerates its objects." Active nonviolence is a practice of the reign of God, a practice in and of reconciliation. To engage in a violent practice cuts against the grain of living in and living out God's reign and suggests that instead of giving our lives over to God's hands—the God who raised Jesus from the dead, the firstborn of the new creation—we would rather take matters into our own hands.

To be a traitor is to convert to "humans' ways, not God's." It is to place other practices "in front of" the practices of the Jesus-movement; it is to accept the authority of others above the authority of Christ. To kill is to deny the possibility of reconciliation. In effect, we "play God" with others' lives, cutting them off when *we* give up on them. We deny the insight so clearly formulated by William James: "Since Christ died for us all without exception, St. Paul said, we must despair of no one." To kill is to despair of reconciliation with another. Betraying the Jesus-movement and killing the other remain two "opposites" to living in and living out God's reign. In sum, the opposites of martyrdom show that a Christian properly refuses to submit to walking a path other than Christ's and refuses to kill another.

Not all Christians are executed for their faith and witness. At most times and in most places today, governments do not execute Christians for being disciples. Indeed, modern liberal democracies profess to be religiously neutral. Such polities do not make martyrs. Our commodified culture seduces us with attractive goods that distract us from God's work.[10] Such polities do make it easy for us to be traitors. But one can still live in the reign of God by engaging in the practices of reconciliation. We can engage in virtuous ascetic practices that help us recognize and avoid or resist the seduction of our desire for God into desires for things. There are other patterns of discipleship that image Christ in different ways in contexts where martyrdom is unlikely, and that is the rainbow of Christian life: we refract Christ in many different ways.

Leonardo Boff has argued that contemporary Christian asceticism must develop new virtues. The ancient ascetics sought to develop the stoic virtues into a Christian pattern that would overcome the vices of "piggishness, lechery, greed, depression, hatred, inability to care, bragging and egotism."[11] Those vices are still with us, and we still need to develop graced and graceful virtues so as to live in God's ways. Boff suggested that we also need virtues that counter contemporary vices.

> Solidarity with one's class, participation in community decisions, loyalty to the solutions that are defined, the overcoming of hatred against those who are the agents of the mechanisms of impoverishment, the capacity to see beyond the immediate present and to work for a society that is not yet visible and will perhaps never be enjoyed. This new type of asceticism, if it is to keep the hearts pure and be led by the spirit of the beatitudes has demands and renunciations of its own.[12]

Boff, of course, had an audience in mind that was composed not of wealthy North Americans but of poor Latin Americans and the priests, religious, and laity who would minister to them. Yet his point can be generalized. In our own context, in our own class, in our own community, we are to work for reconciliation.

The previous chapter claimed that what God wants for humans is for each and all to flourish. The reconciling practices of Christians are to contribute to the work of saving humans from alienation and reconciling them to God and each other. That reconciliation is the key constituent in human flourishing. We cannot expect that

---

10. For a discussion of commodification, see Terrence W. Tilley et al., *Religious Diversity and the American Experience: A Theological Approach* (New York: Continuum, 2007), 35-41, and the literature cited therein.

11. This rendering of the vices is found in William Clebsch, *Christianity in European History* (New York: Oxford University Press, 1979), 76.

12. Leonardo Boff, O.F.M., "The Need for Political Saints: From a Spirituality of Liberation to the Practice of Liberation," trans L. Rivera and L. King, *Cross Currents* 30, no. 4 (1981): 375-76.

we will finish the job. Only God can do that. But if we are agents of reconciliation in practice, then the point of reconciling practices is human flourishing.

The minimum standards for human flourishing were outlined by Pope John XXIII (in a noninclusive translation, alas, and in "rights language" that might be out of vogue). He wrote:

> Any well-regulated and productive association of men in society demands the acceptance of one fundamental principle: that each individual man is truly a person. His is a nature, that is, endowed with intelligence and free will. As such he has rights and duties, which together flow as a direct consequence from his nature. These rights and duties are universal and inviolable, and therefore altogether inalienable. . . .
>
> Man has the right to live. He has the right to bodily integrity and to the means necessary for the proper development of life, particularly food, clothing, shelter, medical care, rest, and, finally, the necessary social services. In consequence, he has the right to be looked after in the event of ill health; disability stemming from his work; widowhood; old age; enforced unemployment; or whenever through no fault of his own he is deprived of the means of livelihood.
>
> Moreover, man has a natural right to be respected. He has a right to his good name. He has a right to freedom in investigating the truth, and— within the limits of the moral order and the common good—to freedom of speech and publication, and to freedom to pursue whatever profession he may choose. He has the right, also, to be accurately informed about public events.
>
> He has the natural right to share in the benefits of culture, and hence to receive a good general education, and a technical or professional training consistent with the degree of educational development in his own country. . . .
>
> Also among man's rights is that of being able to worship God in accordance with the right dictates of his own conscience, and to profess his religion both in private and in public.
>
> Human beings have also the right to choose for themselves the kind of life which appeals to them: whether it is to found a family—in the founding of which both the man and the woman enjoy equal rights and duties—or to embrace the priesthood or the religious life. . . . [13]

The list does not end here. Humans have rights to have good work, to receive just wages, to own property "which entails a social obligation as well,"[14] to associate,

---

13. Pope John XXIII, *Pacem in Terris*, promulgated April 11, 1963, §§9, 11-14, available at http://www.vatican.va/holy_father/john_xxiii/encyclicals/documents/hf_j-xxiii_enc_11041963_pacem_en.html (accessed August 2, 2007).

14. Ibid., §22.

to emigrate, to immigrate, to participate in political life, and so on. Correlated with each of these rights is a duty to promote these rights for all: one's "natural right gives rise to a corresponding duty in other men; the duty, that is, of recognizing and respecting that right. . . . Hence, to claim one's rights and ignore one's duties, or only half fulfill them, is like building a house with one hand and tearing it down with the other."[15] The encyclical lays out further obligations based on people's relationships with public authorities, nations' relationships with each other, and nations' relationships in a global community.

The reign of God is the reign of human flourishing. It seems obvious that our world as a whole is far from the reign of God, yet Christian communities can engage in appropriate forms of reconciling practices. All of the areas cited by John XXIII clamor for commitment. To engage in practices that allow each to flourish is to fulfill the law of Christ (Gal. 6:2) in the contemporary world. But human flourishing, as *Pacem in Terris* noted, is not merely individual flourishing; it is the flourishing of all of the communities and structures needed this side of heaven. Just as martyrdom is both a political and a religious act, so the practices of reconciliation—the practices in line with God's will for human flourishing—are both political and religious.

To promote human flourishing is to make available the basic conditions for humans to thrive, continuing the practices of the reign of God: healing, exorcising, sharing table fellowship, forgiving, and teaching. If those basic conditions are not met, human beings are not flourishing. Because our world is far removed from first-century Galilee and Judea, our range of practices must be somewhat different, but they can and should be rooted in the practices of the first members of the Jesus-movement, whom Jesus first taught how to live in and live out God's reign. The practices that lead to the reconciliation of humans with themselves, each other, and God are the practices of reconciliation, the practices that realize God's reign, the practices that empower all to flourish together. Yet the enduring power of oppressive patterns, structures, and practices does not bode well for the immediate future.

The point of a practical christology can be found in Robert Barron's summary of his work in *The Priority of Christ*.

Throughout these writings, I have been insisting on the embodied, the iconic, the incarnational. We know God and ourselves, I have maintained, through a particular first-century Jew who walked the hills of Galilee—and through the saints who function as the living icons of Jesus up and down the centuries. . . .

What solves the problem [of the modern understanding of God as a being who is over and against the world], what indicates a way forward, is not an abstraction or a new philosophical conception, but this Jesus, this incarnate Lord, crucified and risen from the dead. It is this Christ who rubs healing salve into sin-sick eyes; it is this Christ who, reflected iconically in his

---

15. Ibid., §30.

saints, provides the template for right living; it is this Christ who knows the face of God.[16]

Indeed, this Christ not only *knows* the face of God but *is* the face of God for us. The divine agency that Jesus incarnated gracefully empowers the practices of Christians who serve as God's (secondary) agents in the world. To know who Christ is, is to learn how to live in God's reign, practicing reconciliation at every level.

In line with *Pacem in Terris*, however, I would add that a reconciling practice is not only healing individuals but also working for a health-care system that makes it possible for all people to receive healing. Healing the sick is a good thing, but ministering to the individual sick person when the whole system of health care is failing to enable millions to flourish is like rearranging the deck chairs on the Titanic. Healing individuals is a good, but the alienation and separation between those who can afford clean water and those who cannot is a horrible chasm. The divide between those who have basic health care and those who do not is a canyon that must be bridged. Similar comments could be made about other issues raised in *Pacem in Terris*.

Not everyone, alas, is gifted with elevated virtue that flourishes by accepting God's grace (Barron offers Mother Teresa as one of his exemplars of elevated virtue). Some of us are called to the practices of developing the social patterns and structures that make it more likely that all, even those without elevated virtue, can contribute to the project of "the proper development of life," which requires "food, clothing, shelter, medical care, rest, and, finally, the necessary social services . . . to be looked after in the event of ill health; disability . . . widowhood; old age; enforced unemployment," as John XXIII put it. Because we are all not Mother Teresas, and because her kind are few and far between, we need social structures that allow those of us with far less elevated virtue to contribute to a system that provides to all the basic needs for human flourishing.

The call for reconciliation is typically rooted in the eschatological parable of the sheep and the goats (Matt. 25:31-46). This story is a parable about knowing Christ and living in God's reign. It is often interpreted as a warning: be like the sheep, not the goats. But that interpretation falls short. Here is the parable:

> When the Son of Man comes in his glory, and all the angels with him, then he will sit on the throne of his glory. All the nations will be gathered before him, and he will separate people one from another as a shepherd separates the sheep from the goats, and he will put the sheep at his right hand and the goats at the left. Then the king will say to those at his right hand, "Come, you that are blessed by my Father, inherit the kingdom prepared for you from the foundation of the world; for I was hungry and you gave me food,

---

16. Barron, *Priority of Christ*, 342-43. Barron sees Jesus as an icon of God rather than as God's agent, which shapes his use of historical material and his christology in a way somewhat different from the one developed here. Nonetheless, he makes points I can wholeheartedly endorse. I would suggest that the "template" is not merely a model but a gracious empowerment.

I was thirsty and you gave me something to drink, I was a stranger and you welcomed me, I was naked and you gave me clothing, I was sick and you took care of me, I was in prison and you visited me." Then the righteous will answer him, "Lord, when was it that we saw you hungry and gave you food, or thirsty and gave you something to drink? And when was it that we saw you a stranger and welcomed you, or naked and gave you clothing? And when was it that we saw you sick or in prison and visited you?" And the king will answer them, "Truly I tell you, just as you did it to one of the least of these who are members of my family, you did it to me." Then he will say to those at his left hand, "You that are accursed, depart from me into the eternal fire prepared for the devil and his angels; for I was hungry and you gave me no food, I was thirsty and you gave me nothing to drink, I was a stranger and you did not welcome me, naked and you did not give me clothing, sick and in prison and you did not visit me." Then they also will answer, "Lord, when was it that we saw you hungry or thirsty or a stranger or naked or sick or in prison, and did not take care of you?" Then he will answer them, "Truly I tell you, just as you did not do it to one of the least of these, you did not do it to me." And these will go away into eternal punishment, but the righteous into eternal life. (NRSV)

This story, remembered and shaped by Jesus' disciples,[17] is told in the context of the hope of Israel that the covenant God made with one nation would be expanded to all the earth. Israel was to be a light unto the nations. Thus, God's reign could extend over all the earth when they saw the light.

The typical interpretation of the significance of the parable is that the sheep and the goats have made decisions in relation to Jesus: the sheep made good decisions, the goats bad decisions. The significance, then, according to one interpretation, is "that the decisions made by man now in relation to Jesus are determinative of their destiny in the age to come."[18] Yet this interpretation is incomplete. It rightly notes that what we do now shapes who we are and what we will be. But the point of the story is different. The king does not separate the sheep from the goats on the basis of their decisions, but because of their vision and practices. Both sheep and goats have the same question, "When did we see you?" The issue is not decision, but vision and practice. For who would not help the king if one recognized the king in distress? The point is to have the vision and to engage in the practices.

If this parable were a dire warning about decision, the king would be somewhat arbitrary. He blesses those who did not know him but acted rightly anyway. He curses those who didn't know him and failed to act rightly. But even if we say that the judgment of the king was based on the practices of those judged, we have ignored the perplexity of both the sheep and goats. To take the story as a "moral"

---

17. See James D. G. Dunn, *Jesus Remembered*, vol. 1 of *Christianity in the Making* (Grand Rapids: Eerdmans, 2003), 423 n. 219.

18. Howard Clark Kee, "The Gospel According to Matthew," in *The Interpreter's One Volume Commentary on the Bible*, ed. Charles M. Laymon (Nashville: Abingdon, 1971), 639.

that we should be on the side of the sheep assumes that we should not recognize the king or that it doesn't matter if we do!

I would suggest that we understand this parable as an invitation to vision that leads to reconciling practice. The point is to see all the members of the king's family ("brethren" in more traditional versions) as incarnating or showing forth the presence of the king. Whoever can see the king in the suffering people will do what is right. The story warns us to be neither blind (but good) sheep nor blind (and bad) goats. Rather, if we see the king present in each and all, but especially in the marginal,[19] then we will engage in the reconciling practices of God's reign. In reconciling with each of these, we are also reconciling ourselves with God.

"God was in Christ reconciling the world to Godself" (2 Cor. 5:19). Focus on this powerful phrase has led people to remember the life, death, and resurrection of Jesus. But all too often, people ignore the verses around it. Consider the following, which contextualizes the statement "All things are of God who reconciled us to Godself through Christ and gave us the service (*diakonia*) of reconciliation. That is, God was in Christ reconciling the world to Godself, not reckoning others' trespasses to them and having put in us the word (*logon*) of reconciliation" (2 Cor. 5:18-19). To be a disciple of Christ, then, is to engage in the practices that constitute the service of reconciliation. This service is what Christians do proximately as God's agents; ultimately, the final and complete reconciliation is not in our hands, but God's.

This reconciliation is liberation. It is not that Christ does something for us and we have no part in it save to suffer our redemption. Rather, we are in the service of reconciliation. His showing how to be disciples is not merely a model or an example but an empowering practice. Hence, Jon Sobrino, reflecting on the Latin American bishops' meeting at Medellín, wrote:

> Christ's work cannot be understood only as beneficent, but has to be understood formally as *liberations*; this, of course, recovers the original etymological meaning of the term "redemption," in Latin *redemptio*, restoration by means of payment of the slave's freedom, and in Hebrew *gaal*, "recovery by God of what is his and has been stolen, orphans, widows. . . ."[20]

Reconciliation takes different forms depending on what needs to be reconciled. And, if we are to believe the reality of the martyrs, executed by political officials or their agents, and the variety of rights that constitute the basic needs for human flourishing, then to ignore the political aspect of reconciliation is to deny that

---

19. In contrast to many "supersessionist" views that treat Jesus as an exception to Jewish practice in his treatment of the marginal, John R. Donohue noted that in Jesus' teaching, as "in the Old Testament the marginal ones become the touchstone for the doing of justice" in "Biblical Perspectives on Justice," in *The Faith That Does Justice*, ed. John C. Haughey (New York: Paulist, 1977), 105.

20. Jon Sobrino, *Jesus the Liberator: A Historical-Theological Reading of Jesus of Nazareth*, trans. Paul Burns and Francis McDonagh (Maryknoll, NY: Orbis Books, 1993), 18.

the practices of discipleship can and should permeate all the spaces in which we live.

We are not God. We cannot bring about God's reign. Only God can do that. But we are God's and can live in and live out a tradition we call the Jesus-movement, the body of Christ, or the church that incarnates immanently the reconciliation that is our flourishing together and the will of God for all. In Jesus, the human will and the divine will are perfectly in tune. He was sinless. Our wills are partially in accord with the divine. Thus, we both sin and participate in the work of God. Unlike him, we can incarnate atonement, God's work in Christ, only in fractured and partial ways.[21]

---

21. In taking religious practices as primary and theological theory as secondary, the "doctrine" of the atonement is re-placed. It must be addressed in terms of the practices of at-one-ment, the practices of reconciliation that Jesus' reconciling work makes possible. This is an advantage over a systematic approach simply because theories of the atonement are fraught with difficulties that seem insoluble if they are taken as a description of an event or transaction. See, e.g., Anthony W. Bartlett, *Cross Purposes: The Violent Grammar of Christian Atonement* (Harrisburg, PA: Trinity Press International, 2001). As Lisa Sowle Cahill notes, today there is "a chorus of voices" that finds "the atonement paradigm sanctifies violence; . . . worships a divine sadist; . . . turns God into an omnipotent child abuser; . . . speaks no word of salvation to African American women and others resisting oppression; . . . and provides murderous fanatics, fascists, and torturers with validating symbols" (see her "The Atonement Paradigm: Does It Still Have Explanatory Value?" *Theological Studies* 68, no. 2 [2007]: 418-32, and the extensive literature cited therein; quotation at 419-20). I agree with Cahill that the "atonement paradigm of salvation when tied to resurrection and accompanied by soteriologies of incarnation and ethics of the reign of God and option for the poor, can inspire communities of vicarious sacrifice for others that can make a difference in the world around us" (432). However, that inspirational value, that God so loved the world that Jesus—in the harmony of divine and human wills—accepted execution as the price for enabling his disciples to become graced agents who engage in reconciling practices that overcome sin, and that others may have to pay such a price too, is not an explanation, but an image or metaphor. This image, licensed by the many images of atonement in the New Testament, helps us place our practices as we attempt to be disciples of Jesus. Jesus died for sin in the sense that he showed how *but also empowered people* to live in God's reign. Jesus was not merely an exemplar, but the one who shared his own agency with his disciples who could then go out and make disciples of others. Even in death, God reconciles the world to Godself. Even in a situation where God seems to have absconded, God is present as God was present to and in the crucifixion, so we can hope for final and ultimate reconciliation even *in extremis*. W. Anne Joh (*Heart of the Cross: A Postcolonial Christology* [Louisville: Westminster John Knox, 2006]) takes the cross as a "signifier of redemptive agency" while recognizing that traditional interpretations have been problematical (118). She sees the cross as both reflecting and subverting patriarchal power. I would say that realizing that the atonement is always spoken of in image and metaphor in scripture, rather than in theory or explanation, is a good thing, as it provides a basis for avoiding the critiques of the misuse (all too common) of theories of atonement but allows the use of atonement images. It is not the metaphors of the atonement that are the problem, but drawing inferences from them by systematizing theologians (not a legitimate practice—remember "Juliet is the sun," like all metaphors, cannot properly be placed as the middle term in a syllogism and that logical deductions from metaphors always flirt with disaster). Images and metaphors of the atonement are *not* literal descriptions. Ian Ramsey (*Christian Discourse: Some Logical Explorations* [London: Oxford University Press, 1965], especially chap. 2) shows the problems with taking "atonement theology" as a descriptive explanation.

Incarnating Atonement

In chapter 15 above, I wrote of forgiveness and individual reconciliation. The reconciliation of Cardinal Bernardin and his accuser is an example of the grace of reconciliation, the active presence of God's powerful love in this world, enabling those who were alienated to be reconciled. But as much as individual reconciliation is important, there is also social reconciliation.

Robert Schreiter, in *The Ministry of Reconciliation*,[22] notes five elements in the practice of reconciliation, elements he derives from St. Paul.

- First, reconciliation is God's work in and through Christ. "The experience of reconciliation is the experience of grace—the restoration of one's damaged humanity in a life-giving relationship with God" (15). In line with the sort of work detailed in chapter 18 on God's agency and human agency, Schreiter notes that "God's action is not some thunderbolt over and apart from human action. The communion between the human and the divine involves divine initiative coming through human action" (15). As God was in Christ reconciling the world to Godself, so God's agency empowers us also to be reconciling agents—although we too often can and do resist God's will.

- Second, reconciliation, though requiring strategies, is more a spirituality, a practice of being "ambassadors for Christ" (2 Cor 5:20). To actually live in God's grace is to be impelled to act; to resist God's grace is to impel oneself to act ill or not to act at all.

- Third, the new relationship between the wrongdoer and the victim that is central to the reconciling process makes of both "a new creation" (17). The past is not lost or repressed but reincorporated in a new self. In some forms of psychotherapy, for example, the point is to *recover* the lost memories of the past so that one can *integrate* them into one's ongoing life. That ongoing life, whether personal, interpersonal, or social, is a new creation, not *ex nihilo*, but reconstructing the disparate parts of the past for a good future.

- Fourth, the "master narrative" for this process is found in the life, death, and resurrection of Jesus (18) as remembered in and through the practices of the Jesus-movement.

- Finally, the process is never finished by us, but can only be completed by God eternally. As Schreiter puts it:

> As we become aware of the complexity that must be untangled in a reconciliation process, and the enormity of the task of doing this, we are humbled before the charge to bring about reconciliation. It becomes ever more evident that reconciliation is God's work, with our cooperation. The final state of reconciliation, that new creation, is not the inexorable unfolding of a preconceived scheme programmed to happen from the very

---

22 Parenthetical references in this section are to *The Ministry of Reconciliation*. I have reversed Schreiter's order of presentation of topics.

beginning. It involves human agency and the coming together of a myriad of contingent events. Reconciliation can only be grasped as involving "all things, whether on earth or in heaven, by making peace through the blood of his cross" (Col. 1:20). (19)

Reconciliation, whether personal or social, proximate or ultimate, always begins with empowerment by God.

Schreiter details the practices of social reconciliation in its various forms. These practices realize, in particular times and places, God's reign. Reconciliation is the healing that is sought for the evils of alienation and violence, practices or actions that have ruptured the community and destroyed the peace. Reconciliation is the blessed peacemaking that belongs to the reign of God. At-one-ment is reconciliation.

Schreiter begins by noting that there are multiple actors in any reconciliation process. First are the victims and the survivors (108). Second are the wrongdoers, who, to "the extent that they maintain power . . . will try to block there being a reconciliation effort at all" (109). Third are the bystanders who did nothing to stop the victimization. Fourth are those who are both victims and wrongdoers, often oppressed people co-opted by the oppressors. The dead are fifth. The process of reconciliation with the dead[23] is different from that with the living; in this world, we can perhaps only bury and remember them, as those who took Jesus' body down from the cross did and expected to do. The sixth is the future generations— how the children of the future will relate to the deeds of the past; one aspect of this is our care for the environment in which our children will live in the future. A seventh group is the neighbors who might be minimally involved in the alienation or oppression but who need to be part of the process at least to the extent of their involvement. The eighth is God: "How do the groups—and how does the process itself—stand before God?" (110). The social reconciliation needed when societies end a war, whether cold or hot, requires finding the truth "amid the tangled lies of evidence" (112) in order to begin reconstructing the moral order of society. While societies differ in many ways—and the global society is even more complex—such reconciliation requires a strengthening of law, a democratic and verifiable process, so as to make possible the participation of all, and avenues of reparation not for the sake of vengeance but so that victims can recover "at least some measure of what they have lost" (113-14). How each of these groups and persons is to be reconciled will vary widely. No simple blueprint can be given. The imaginative exercise of practical wisdom, *phronēsis*, is required in each case.

---

23. As with the martyrs, any reconciliation of the dead is in God's hands. Nonreligious accounts typically have no place for reconciling with the dead. Hence, I would claim that religious commitment to a Power that can reconcile all despite appearances is superior to such secular accounts. Helmut Peukert (*Science, Action and Fundamental Theology: Toward a Theory of Communicative Action* [Cambridge, MA: MIT Press, 1984]) has persuasively argued that commitment to a power so powerful as to reconcile even with the dead is a needed constituent of comprehensive reconciling practice. In his brilliantly argued, if densely written, text, he analyzed the holes in the secular communication theory of Jürgen Habermas.

That the church can contribute sacramentally is clear. The sacrament of reconciliation both initiates and celebrates the forgiveness of sin that leads to reconciliation. What the church can and should do beyond recognizing and proclaiming human rights in the national and international spheres varies with the situation. But those who profess to be Jesus' disciples are to engage in reconciling practices in a myriad of ways, realizing the at-one-ment that is found in and through Jesus, the first among equals and the divine agent who empowers his disciples by showing them how to engage in the reconciling practices that form our relationships when we live in and live out God's reign.[24]

Although no simple pattern can be discerned in the lives of the saints, they incarnate at-one-ment. What saints in the broad sense of the term—that is, disciples of Jesus, members of the Jesus-movement—do is to give their lives to and for reconciliation. Saints are the human agents through whom the divine agent, perfectly present in Jesus, continues to work in and for the world. Saints make the power of Christ present in the world. As atonement is properly at-one-ment, the practice of healing divisions, so this reconciliation is the practice of the saints. The notion of a community of people who are so united with each other that they are responsible for each other, led by those who are responsible to the whole, is a story of a community of reconciliation. This is a form of life in which all bear each other's burdens, "and thus fulfill the law of Christ" (Gal. 6:2).

However, the price to be paid may be life itself. This is not an easy consequence to accept. Certainly Peter at Caesarea Philippi had trouble with it. The variety of practices is as wide as the variety of the saints. It may be difficult to discern an underlying unity, but there is a measure for all of them: the stories of recognition and interrogation detailed in part 2. Insofar as Christian lives can find part of their story in those stories, they carry on the ways of God. Christians can have the mind of Christ within them.

An incident from the life of Clarence Jordan, a U.S. Baptist theologian, translator of the "Cotton Patch Version" of the New Testament and founder of an interracial communal farm in Georgia in the 1940s, Koinonia Farm (from which Habitat for Humanity developed), can show this:

> As so often, a bit of remembered Jordan dialogue may come nearest to clarifying his notion of discipleship. In the early fifties, it is told, Clarence approached his brother Robert Jordan, later a state senator and justice of the Georgia Supreme Court, asking him to represent Koinonia Farm legally.
>
> "Clarence, I can't do that. You know my political aspirations. Why, if I represented you, I might lose my job, my house, everything I've got."
>
> "*We* might lose everyting too, Bob."
>
> "It's different for you."
>
> "Why is it different? I remember, it seems to me, that you and I joined

---

24. Some of the contributions of the church to reconciliation can be found in the collection of studies of the church's involvement in reconciliation practices, *The Reconciliation of Peoples: Challenge to the Churches*, ed. Gregory Baum and Harold Wells (Maryknoll, NY: Orbis Books, 1997).

the church the same Sunday, as boys. I expect when we came forward the preacher asked me about the same question he did you. He asked me, 'Do you accept Jesus as your Lord and Savior.' And I said, 'Yes.' What did you say?"

"I follow Jesus, Clarence, up to a point."

"Could that point by any chance be—the cross?"

"That's right. I follow him to the cross, but not *on* the cross. I'm not getting myself crucified."

"Then I don't believe you're a disciple. You're an admirer of Jesus, but not a disciple of his. I think you ought to go back to the church you belong to, and tell them that you're an admirer, not a disciple."

"Well now, if everyone who felt like I do did that, we wouldn't *have* a church, would we?"

"The question," Clarence said, "is 'Do you have a church?'"[25]

To be a disciple, a member of the Jesus-movement, is to engage in the reconciling practices that characterize that movement. To the degree that one's practices reincarnate Jesus' practices and his presence in the world, one is a healthy member of the body of Christ. Insofar as one passes the test of the cross, one is a saint.

But why become a disciple of Christ? In a world where numerous spiritualities are on offer in the spiritual marketplace, why follow Jesus? Why seek to know him and what discipleship means? Sobrino put the answer clearly and simply: "[K]nowing Jesus means, first and foremost, being attracted by him to follow him."[26] But what attracts people to follow him is the lives of his disciples. Living in and living out the reign of God by engaging in reconciling practices is the heart of mission. Why follow Jesus? Because his ways are God's ways, not human ways. Because when all the optimism that one has for progress is shattered, the life of the disciples is a life of hope in God.

Resurrection, Reconciliation, and Mission

One of the constant challenges to Christians is that since the coming of the prince of peace, wars have continued to rage. The reign of God has not come. Moreover, Christians go to war and kill both other Christians and people who live in different, or no, religious traditions. There is little room for optimism. Despite Jesus, despite the saints, people are alienated from one another and wars go on.

While there may be little room for optimism, there is room for hope. Optimism presumes progress. While humanity has made progress in science and technology, it is not clear that we have made any progress in overcoming patterns of alienation and oppression. Claims of progress are often true; the expected life span of humans in the developed world increased markedly in the twentieth century. But claims to

---

25. McClendon, *Biography as Theology*, 127-28.
26. Sobrino, *Jesus the Liberator*, 49.

progress also whitewash the suffering of many and the lack of progress in moral and spiritual realms. The twentieth century featured some of the most violent wars in human history. Optimism is a structure blown apart by the winds of war and atrocity.

Hope, on the other hand, is a virtue rooted in imagination and memory—key practices for Christians, if the argument here is correct. Contrasting hope with optimism, Dermot A. Lane notes:

> In contrast, hope struggles with the ambiguity of existence and responds to it by taking up a particular posture of imagining new possibilities, inspired by the impulses of human experience. It is principally in the midst of darkness and out of darkness that one can truly struggle in hope towards the light. It is very often only in the midst of alienation and estrangement that we can move forward in hope towards wholeness and reconciliation.[27]

Hope is an affair of memory and imagination. We remember that things are not the way they have to be. We imagine other possibilities. We can imagine how things ought to be and can be empowered to work to make them so.

Those possibilities are crystallized in the resurrection of Jesus from the dead. The death on the cross was not the end of Jesus or of the movement. It would be hard to see reason for optimism in the narratives of the New Testament. The disciples were scattered and the Jesus-movement seemed to have been disbanded, if not destroyed. Yet something almost unimaginable and terribly important happened. As Dunn put it, "As a historical statement we can say quite firmly: no Christianity without the resurrection of Jesus. As Jesus is the single great 'presupposition' of Christianity, so also is the resurrection of Jesus."[28] The resurrection of Jesus triggers hope, reunites the disbanded, and recreates what has been destroyed.

Yet the appearances of Jesus in his resurrected state can be understood as healing, reconciling events. Schreiter noted that each of the stories in the New Testament is not merely a story of Jesus' appearance, but each is also a story in which Jesus' appearance embodies the reconciling power of God.[29] The stories vary wildly. Yet there is a pattern in them. The disciples are in dire straits. They have lost hope. They quake with fear. Then someone appears—their identifications are mistaken or their vision is occluded. But then something happens. They recognize Jesus. In recognizing him they are energized. Hope has returned. The mission of the disciples to engage in the reconciling practices of the reign of God can go on.

Jesus' appearances gave the disciples reason for their hope. The memory of the resurrection carried in the Jesus-movement offers the hope that despite the powers arrayed against it and the lures of other ways of life, there is hope that God will ultimately reconcile all to Godself. This hope doesn't let us off the hook, but it

---

27. Dermot A. Lane, *Keeping Hope Alive: Stirrings in Christian Theology* (New York/Mahwah, NJ: Paulist, 1996), 60.

28. Dunn, *Jesus Remembered*, 826.

29. Schreiter, *Ministry of Reconciliation*, 23-102. These interpretations of Jesus' appearances are the bulk of the book.

does mean that hope is alive in the reconciling practices of discipleship because Jesus, even after death, brought and brings reconciliation in practice.

Hope has two fundamental dimensions, as Dermot Lane points out, personal and social. Each of us who does not fall into despair hopes, perhaps minimally, for the future. But that minimal, sometimes narrow, hope can be deepened and broadened in communion with others.

> I am enabled to hope only because of my radical relationality to others and the support of that relationality within the story of the universe. The expression of this basic primordial hope is to be found in the human, historical hopes of the world such as the promotion of goodness, the struggle for justice, the establishment of human rights, the pursuit of happiness, the care of the earth, and a commitment to social and political reform—without, however, being reduced to any one of these particular expressions.[30]

However, these hopes are realized only in the practices of reconciliation empowered by the memory of the resurrection. Hope is the virtue of imagining new possibilities and of acting on them. As Karl Barth put it, "hope takes place in the act of taking the next step; hope is action."[31]

In Matthew's Gospel, after the resurrection, Jesus tells the disciples, "Go make disciples of all the nations, baptizing them in the name of the Father, the Son and the Holy Spirit, teaching them to keep all I have commanded you" (Matt. 28:19-20).[32] The Great Commission may be less a memory than a communal creation, but it is nonetheless instructive. It begins with an injunction: to make disciples. The injunction is not to make them *my* disciples or to make them *worshipers* of Jesus. In light of the argument of this book, the point is to empower all peoples to engage in the reconciling practices of discipleship. The point of the Great Commission is to emphasize the spread of the practices of the Jesus-movement beyond the bounds of Palestinian Judaism to encompass the "whole world" or, more realistically, the cities of the Greco-Roman world. The Great Commission is not to bring everyone to worship Jesus.

The injunction to baptize—more commonly in the name of Jesus or the Spirit at other points in the New Testament—is sometimes thought of as an initiation rite in contrast to circumcision. Yet the contrast should be with John's baptism, a baptism for repentance of sins. For Jesus, this "repentance" is turning around to become a person who engages freely in the practices of reconciliation, practices that realize the *basileia tou theou*. Such a commission is to empower many with the Spirit, not necessarily to induct them into a club. The injunction to teach

---

30. Lane, *Keeping Hope Alive*, 66.

31. Ibid., 66, citing Karl Barth, *Church Dogmatics* IV/3 (second half), ed. G. W. Bromiley and T. F. Torrance, trans. T. F. Torrance, new ed. (Edinburgh: T&T Clark, 2003; 1st German ed., 1932), 938.

32. Material in this paragraph relies on Reginald H. Fuller, *The Formation of the Resurrection Narratives* (Philadelphia: Fortress, 1980), 83-89; Pheme Perkins, *Resurrection* (Garden City, NY: Doubleday, 1984), 133-35; Hurtado, *Lord Jesus Christ*, 331; and Dunn, *Jesus Remembered*, 853.

should then be understood as an injunction not to teach *what to believe* but to teach *how to engage in the practices Jesus empowered the disciples to perform.* To make disciples of all is not necessarily to make all people into Christians but to empower them to engage in the practices of reconciliation that constitute the practices of the Jesus-movement.

Should we want all people to worship the God incarnate in Jesus of Nazareth? Discussing the emergence of a gentile church from a Jewish movement, Amy-Jill Levine comments about Christians' proselytizing in general and Paul's injunctions against eating idol-meat or even worshiping the gods of the city:

> From the gentile perspective, the claim that followers of Jesus must cease being followers of the gods was horrifically unpatriotic, for the gods of the city were its protectors. Forsake the gods, and the gods will forsake you. No wonder Jews in local synagogues were upset, for the message about a Jewish messiah, proclaimed by Jews, would impact them. Having the Gentiles forsake their gods and their pagan practices in the messianic age is desirable; having them do it before the end has come is suicidal.[33]

The odd monotheism of the Jews was evidently mostly tolerated in the Roman Empire because the Jews did not proselytize. But these proselytizing Jews-for-Jesus were preaching sedition, not to mention courting bad luck from gods who would become angry. Moreover, by forcing the gentiles to abandon their gods, proselytizers also courted opposition. That opposition, of course, flamed into persecution at various times and places, although it is hard to see those persecutions as due merely to denying the gods, even if Christians were a-theists regarding any other god but God incarnate in Jesus Christ.

However it was with worship in the ancient world, where the gods and the powers were opposed to Jews and Christians, at best tolerating them and at worst persecuting them, is that determinative for worship in the modern world? Ancient religion had little moral entailment other than loyalty to the city or the empire. Contemporary faith traditions are not always so constrained. Can they not be seen as having "positive salvific significance" and thus be appreciated for the good they contain?[34] Do they not, as reconciling practices, glorify God even as constituents of faith traditions that do not recognize God? That they contain good should not stop us from witnessing to Jesus in our reconciling practices or testifying that God has empowered us through him. Perhaps we Christians should hope that all will

---

33. Amy-Jill Levine, *The Misunderstood Jew: The Church and the Scandal of the Jewish Jesus* (San Francisco: HarperSanFrancisco, 2006), 71.

34. These questions are debated in a series of articles. See Terrence W. Tilley, "Christian Orthodoxy and Religious Pluralism," *Modern Theology* 22, no. 1 (January 2006): 51-63; and the following articles in *Modern Theology* 23, no. 3 (2007), Gavin D'Costa, "'Christian Orthodoxy and Religious Pluralism': A Response to Terrence W. Tilley" (435-36); Tilley, "'Christian Orthodoxy and Religious Pluralism': A Rejoinder to Gavin D'Costa" (447-54); D'Costa, "'Christian Orthodoxy and Religious Pluralism': A Further Rejoinder to Terrence Tilley" (455-62); and Gavin D'Costa and Terrence W. Tilley, "Concluding Our *Quaestio Disputata* on Theologies of Religious Diversity" (463-68).

worship God rightly when the messiah comes to them, but perhaps we should not be optimistic about converting people here and now.

Mission is not necessarily seeking out converts. William R. Burrows has proposed that the church in Asia has and ought to have not a mission *to* the people (*missio ad gentes*) as much as a mission *among* the peoples (*missio inter gentes*). Burrows's view can provide a different, practical way of thinking about mission and of responding to the Great Commission.[35] To have a *missio inter gentes* is to witness to the *basileia tou theou* in a minority situation—a situation that characterizes not only Asia but Europe and North America as well. If all in the world are to be disciples, then discipleship cannot be a foreign import that people will resist as colonialist and hegemonic or a Trojan horse that will destroy what is good in indigenous traditions. Rather, such traditions can be seen not as enemies but as "potential allies against real, *mutual* enemies—'the structural power of evil and Mammon as selfish attachment to wealth and pleasure.'"[36]

In terms used in this text, Christians can find allies among other religious folk in opposing the practices and structures of domination. Christians can find allies in those who engage in the practices of reconciliation, for these practices constitute being disciples and these practices glorify God. Proclaiming Jesus not by attempting to get others to abandon their historic ways, if those ways are practices of reconciliation, not domination, but by engaging in the reconciling practices that realize the reign of God among the peoples. Cooperating with others as they live in and live out their own faith traditions shows how the Jesus-movement can provide light "where religious conflict is rampant, where religious traditions are subverted to political ends, and where secularist ideologies trample the rights of human beings."[37] Our primary mission is to make disciples by our practices, not to force those who would join us in reconciling practices to worship God in Christ.

But if people in other faith traditions engage in practices of reconciliation, why should we evangelize them? Why proclaim the gospel at all? Cardinal Walter Kasper put it this way in the context of explicating for a Catholic and Jewish joint committee the 2000 Declaration of the CDF *Dominus Iesus*:

> In strict theological language, *evangelisation* is a very complex and overall term, and reality. It implies presence and witness, prayer and liturgy, proclamation and catechesis, dialogue and social work. Now, presence and witness, prayer and liturgy, dialogue and social work, which are all part of *evangelisation*, do not have the goal of increasing the number of Catholics. Thus *evangelisation*, if understood in its proper and theological meaning, does not imply any attempt of proselytism whatsoever.

---

35. William R. Burrows, "A Response to Michael Amaladoss," *Proceedings of the Catholic Theological Society of America* 56 (2001): 15-20. "*Missio inter gentes*" is a phrase coined by Burrows as a way of capturing Amaladoss's proposal ("Pluralism of Religions and the Proclamation of Jesus Christ in the Context of Asia," *Proceedings of the Catholic Theological Society of America* 56 [2001]: 1-14).

36. Burrows, "Response," 17.

37. Ibid.

On the other hand, the term *mission*, in its proper sense, is referred to conversion from false gods and idols to the true and one God, who revealed himself in the salvation history with his elected people. Thus mission, in this strict sense, cannot be used with regard to Jews, who believe in the true and one God. Therefore—and this is characteristic—it [*sic*] does not exist any Catholic missionary organisation for Jews. There is dialogue with Jews; no mission in this proper sense of the word towards them. But what is *dialogue*? Certainly—as we learned from Jewish philosophers such as Martin Buber—it is more than small talk and mere exchange of opinions. It is also different from academic dispute, however important academic dispute may be within dialogue. Dialogue implies personal commitments and witness of one's own conviction and faith. Dialogue communicates one's faith and, at the same time, requires profound respect for the conviction and faith of the partner. It respects the difference of the other and brings mutual enrichment.[38]

The point of reaching out to others is not to convert them as much as it is to benefit from mutual enrichment. If the others are empowered by the one true God, then no mission is appropriate. If we or they are not, then proclamation and catechesis are proper. What is to be done depends on the circumstances.

What Cardinal Kasper has written about the Jews may apply also to other faith traditions. I have argued elsewhere that the Christian tradition should recognize what is good and holy in all traditions as indicating the reality of God's grace being in them.[39] Hence, the Christian theologian can recognize the acceptance of that grace—whether so denominated in those traditions or not—as, in Christian terms, the seeds of an authentic faith, though not full faith. Rather than seeing Judaism as the (likely) sole exception as the only tradition that leads to the one true God, the only other tradition that carries grace and faith as a tradition, I would suggest that we recognize that it is the first tradition that we have (finally) come to recognize as clearly God-given, though not the only one that, in some sense, conveys grace and thus has a "positive salvific efficacy." Our mission should be to those whose practices show that they cannot be worshiping the God who loves all there is into being, no matter their tradition.

Burrows wrote as if these conditions of being a minority in a plural society afflicted only Asia, but they are the conditions in which disciples of Jesus live throughout the world. His conclusion also applies much more broadly than just to Asia:

The chief *missio inter gentes* of Christians in Asia, Amaladoss proposes, is one of trying to bring about shalom among peoples riven by myriad

---

38. Walter Cardinal Kasper, "Dominus Iesus," Exchange of Information Session, International Catholic-Jewish Liaison Committee Meeting, New York, May 1-4, 2001, online at http://www.usccb.org/seia/kasper.shtml (accessed August 20, 2007). One might also argue that "mission" does not properly apply to Muslims either, if one thinks they worship the one, true God.

39. See D'Costa and Tilley, "Concluding Our *Quaestio Disputata*," 467.

divisions. He roots that mission in the ministry of the historical Jesus. How the experience of acting in the name of Jesus translates into Christology, as Asians read the *via crucis* of historical commitment and relationship to the risen Christ, remains to be seen. The crucial thing for us in the West, I believe, is to become better informed about this *missio inter gentes*, so that we may be in solidarity with our sisters and brothers in the global Body of Christ.[40]

Christology must be reconciling practice, bringing shalom to the peoples and allowing the peoples to enrich us with their understandings of reconciliation. Otherwise it is sound and fury, signfying nothing worth living in or living out.

Jonathan Yun-Ka Tan has noted that this approach fits with the approach of the Federation of Asian Bishops' Conferences to evangelization and dialogue.

At its Fifth Plenary Assembly, in 1990, the FABC defined mission in Asia as "being with the people, responding to their needs, with sensitiveness to the presence of God in cultures and other religious traditions, and witnessing to the values of God's Kingdom through presence, solidarity, sharing and word," and therefore, "[m]ission will mean a dialogue with Asia's poor, with its local cultures, and with other religious traditions." Simply put, the task of mission in Asia is a mission among the Asian peoples with their ancient cultures and deep religiosity on the one hand, and marginalizing life experiences on the other. While the FABC affirms that "the proclamation of Jesus Christ is the center and primary element of evangelization," it explains that this proclamation means to live like Christ, in the midst of our neighbors of other faiths and to do Christ-like deeds by the power of grace.[41]

The *missio inter gentes* embodies in practice an insight of Walter Ong, noted above in chapter 16. The church may be universal in the end, when God reconciles all things to Godself. But now the church is catholic, *katholikos*, "the leaven in the lump." The church is the Jesus-movement engaging in the reconciling practices *inter gentes*. And if Christianity is a strain of yeast whose saints ferment goodness (to play off William James's images of saints' practices), Christians should welcome and even help develop by shared practices those other strains that ferment the goodness of reconciliation and human flourishing. Rather than demanding that others accept our whole ideological structure, Christians are called to be prophetic. To paraphrase James, we are to treat those whom we meet, in spite of the past, in spite of all appearances, as worthy. In so doing as agents of God's grace, we stimulate them to *be* worthy. Saints have "transformed them

---

40. Burrows, "Response," 20.

41. Jonathan Yun-Ka Tan, "Mission *Among* the Peoples: A Lesson from the Church in Asia," *National Jesuit News,* online at http://puffin.creighton.edu/jesuit/dialogue/documents/articles/njn_tan. html (accessed August 3, 2007).

by their radiant example and by the challenge of their expectations."[42] Such is the goal of the practical proclamation of the reign of God.

Yet this is not merely a contemporary approach. It is the approach of the *Apophthegmata Patrum* of the patristic period, as shown in the previous chapter. Practices can unite an ideologically diverse community. What Burrows and Tan are recognizing is that we do not need to proselytize by proclaiming theological orthodoxy, but we can form communities by orthopraxis. We can form community with those of other traditions by sharing the practices of freeing religious practices and institutions *from* engaging in religious conflict, *from* supporting dominating polities, and *for* supporting the rights of human beings, the fundamental requirement for at-one-ment in particular contexts in this world. While I would not advocate keeping silent about doctrines, as the editors of the *Apophthegmata* likely did, I would advocate not making them a litmus test for sharing practices and forming communities of resistance and solidarity.[43] Doctrines divide where practices can unite. Let the future settle the ideological disputes whenever possible; let the present find ways to share projects and practices, to engage in mutual enrichment, to live like Christ among our neighbors, and to seek reconciliation—thus fulfilling the law of Christ that all should thrive and creating an even larger community that undertakes reconciling practices.

The necessity of the church is a sacramental necessity. God acts in and through the church as God acts in and through the bread and wine of the Eucharist. This necessity can be understood in a number of ways. Just as the sacrament of baptism classically was construed as having three modes depending on the circumstances (baptism of water as the ordinary way, of blood for those catechumens who were martyred before being baptized, and of desire for those who were not Christians but were oriented to the Good that is God in their lives), so perhaps we can think of the sacramental presence of the church as multimodal. The way the church was in the fifth or sixth century may not necessarily be the way the church should be to serve the peoples in Asia or in any of the nations that form today's global economy. The way the church was in the history of "Christian Europe" is not necessarily the way the church should be in a "postsecular" age.[44] Burrows's and Tan's concept of the *missio inter gentes* is a profound way to understand the situation in which we are to be the Body of Christ, the Jesus-movement that welcomes the work of other traditions that also work for reconciliation.[45]

---

42. James, *Varieties of Religious Experience,* 283.

43. This phrase alludes to an important book by American theologian Sharon D. Welch, *Communities of Resistance and Solidarity: A Feminist Theology of Liberation* (Maryknoll, NY: Orbis Books, 1985). Welch suggests that we ought to construe our resistance to injustice not in terms of universal truths, but in terms of "universal accountability" (81), a point made in a different way by Schreiter when he numbers the actors in the process of reconciliation.

44. That Europe has become not only post-religious, but post-secular as well, is argued by Lieven Boeve, *God Interrupts History: Theology in a Time of Upheaval,* trans. Brian Doyle (New York: Continuum, 2007), 14-28.

45. In *Religious Diversity and the American Experience,* 50-63, I argued that there were four key principles informing the Catholic Church's position on religious diversity. Formulated (with tongue in cheek) these principles are:

For one to be a member of the movement, one may not have to be a baptized Christian. Rather, there are many ideologies or religions that can participate in the divine emancipatory wisdom movement. One may or may not be a disciple of Jesus. But one can become part of this movement in practice by participating in the reconciling practices of one's own tradition. Just as Chalcedonian and non-Chalcedonian monks were united in practice, if differing in ideology, so Christians, Jews, Muslims, Buddhists, Vaishnavites, and others can be united at least in some practices while differing in ideology. As George M. Soares-Prabhu put it, "Christian mission must not forget the primacy of God's Reign, and so the ultimate primacy of God. Like all Christian life, Christian mission is theocentric, not Christocentric—much less ecclesiocentric. It is always God and God's Reign that is the goal. . . ."[46] From a practical perspective, promoting the reign of God is first; Christ and the church follow.

Why do people follow Christ? Because they are attracted to him. How are they attracted to him? They are attracted when the disciples proclaim him through their witness by engaging in reconciling practices. Thus, people can come to understand how they can live the graced life that is incarnated in the Jesus-movement to this day. To follow Jesus is to live in and live out the practices of the reign of God; perhaps those who live such a life yet do not confess Jesus as lord can come to do so eventually. "Practice first, theology second."

To do christology is to keep hope alive in and through the reconciling practices that respond creatively to the empowering grace of God, making Christians agents of reconciliation. To do christology is to practice the active memory of the life, death, and resurrection of the first among us, Jesus of Nazareth, who is God's agent, truly human and truly divine, the person whose human will was in perfect accord with God's will for him. To do christology is to actively imagine and realize what peace can be. In short, to do christology is to be disciples of Jesus who live out their commitment to him by engaging in reconciling practices that in this life constitute living in and living out God's reign, and hope for eternal life with and in the God who has loved us all into being.

I. Thou shalt not deny God's universal salvific will.

II. Thou shalt not deny the sufficiency of God's salvation in and through Jesus Christ.

III. Thou shalt not deny the necessity of the church for salvation.

IV. Thou shalt affirm the dignity of each and all human persons.

I would argue that this approach of the practical *missio inter gentes* is compatible with Catholic principles regarding religious diversity and with the heart of Chalcedonian christology even if transliterations of Chalcedonian terms are not used or take a less significant place. A practical christology is carried out as the leaven in the dough of humanity, as *missio inter gentes*.

46. George M. Soares-Prabhu, *The Dharma of Jesus*, ed. Francis Xavier D'Sa (Maryknoll, NY: Orbis Books, 2003), 256.

EPILOGUE

*A*fter this book was completed and in the hands of the publisher, two major texts on Jesus of Nazareth were published: Gerard Sloyan's *Jesus: Word Made Flesh* (Collegeville, MN: Liturgical Press, 2008) and Gerald O'Collins, S.J.'s, *Jesus: A Portrait* (Maryknoll, NY: Orbis Books, 2008). Both priest-theologians have woven critical historical research on scripture and tradition into presentations of Jesus that are faithful to historic Chalcedonian orthodoxy. These texts bring together lifetimes of these senior scholars' reflections in christology. While using materials developed by biblical critics working in the "historical Jesus" more than the "historic Jesus" paradigm, both scholars seek to present Jesus as the historic figure whose life and work ignited the church. Both scholars affirm the true humanity and true divinity of Jesus. I have deep respect and admiration for both authors and both texts.

Yet the present book differs from those texts and from other more traditional texts in christology. The key difference in approach is that other books begin with the *texts* of scripture and the *formulations* of traditional doctrines. The present book begins with the *actions* of Jesus remembered by disciples and written in texts and executed in the practice of following him. Additionally, the present text relies much more heavily on work done by feminist and Jewish authors than either Sloyan or O'Collins does. Of course, there are also similarities. Neither Sloyan nor O'Collins nor the present author treats these topics naïvely. All seek to assimilate the warranted results of criticism while avoiding the rejections of Catholic views that many critics have advocated. Yet the differences between their texts and the present one lead to books quite differently shaped.

In contrast to the more traditional "textual" orientations of Sloyan and O'Collins, the present essay may seem problematic in a number of ways. Two seem especially critical.

First, the present text deals very lightly with the issue of revelation in biblical interpretation. The first section below shows how the present text is rooted in the Dogmatic Constitution on Divine Revelation (*Dei Verbum*) of the Second Vatican Council. This brief description of the present approach to revelation in action and practice needs further development to resolve all the issues that might be raised. Nonetheless, the discussion here indicates, first, that changing the default assumption in understanding revelation from text to act is in line with *Dei Verbum*'s shift from a primacy of word to a primacy of deed; and, second, that a rich concept of primary and secondary agency can generate the basis for a viable "practical" theology of revelation. The key is that revelation can be understood both as God's originating, primary act and an ongoing, secondary act of God's people empowered by God, in, by, and through the Spirit in whom we dwell and who dwells in us.

Second, the present text does not focus on the resurrection as do both Sloyan's and O'Collins's works.[1] Raising Jesus from the dead is an act of God, not merely an historical event.[2] Talking of an act of God as if historical events or observations provided evidence for the actuality of such an act is confused. I take it as historically plausible that (1) Jesus' body was not in his tomb; (2) a number of his disciples saw or "saw" him after his death; (3) that the Easter witnesses were women and that because women's testimony was devalued at that time, it was unlikely that their stories were made up out of whole cloth; had the stories been pure fabrications, more reliable witnesses—that is, men—would be more likely to be named as witnesses. As witnessing or testifying to an act of God is clearly a constituent of (but not necessarily a reason for or foundation of) a person's or community's faith, and as no talk of God can properly be literal, talk of the resurrection as an act of God must be indirect. Indeed, the reticence of the Gospels to describe or even narrate what God did in raising Jesus from the dead or what the act looked like can be taken as beginning a pattern of indirect—analogical or metaphorical—discourse to convey an act of God.

The second section below, then, is a slightly edited version of a previously published meditation for Easter.[3] In chapter 19, I wrote about the significance of the resurrection but did not deal with the resurrection as God's act. Here I write in a confessional, if breezy, style about what Jesus' disciples can affirm about the resurrection of Jesus. While perhaps unconventional in its style, I think that a meditation on the resurrection is a fitting way to bring *The Disciples' Jesus* to its conclusion.

Revelation in a Practice-Based Theology: Reflections on *Dei Verbum*[4]

Catholic theologians have long contested the best ways to understand divine revelation.[5] One of the hidden assumptions in this discussion has been the textualist

---

1. Compare Sloyan, *Jesus*, 135-45, and O'Collins, *Jesus*, 183-200.

2. The significance of this distinction is explored in my *History, Theology, and Faith: Dissolving the Modern Problematic* (Maryknoll, NY: Orbis Books, 2004), 40-54, but is also invoked in the following section on the resurrection.

3. Terrence W. Tilley, "'More Than a Kodak Moment': What to Look for in the Resurrection," *Commonweal* 130, no. 7 (April 11, 2003): 13-16. I retain the title that editor Paul Baumann gave the meditation and have not corrected the time elements as doing so would ruin the flow of the piece; so "recently" in section two, below, refers to a time over five years before this book was published.

4. An earlier version of this section was presented as a paper at the Annual Meeting of the College Theology Society, Contemporary Theologies Section, Spring Hill College, Mobile, AL, June 2005. My graduate assistants Matthew Minix and Louis Albarran helped with the research. I also am indebted to a paper exploring the links between revelation, incarnation, and religious diversity that Minix wrote for a seminar in which we participated.

5. The magisterial work of Avery Dulles, S.J., *Models of Revelation*, 2nd ed. (Maryknoll, NY: Orbis Books, 1992; 1st ed., 1983) critically surveys the different understandings of revelation; the new preface to the second edition places his typology in dialogue with some more recent publica-

assumption. Whether in the form of the approach in modern hermeneutics that assumes that texts are the primary subject of interpretation, or in the form of postmodern strategies where the Derridean motto "There is nothing but the text" has been taken to enable interpreters to treat every event, action, person, or monument as if it were a text to be interpreted or even deconstructed, textualism has shaped the discussions of revelation. One indicator of this is the common use of "symbol" as the crucial category for understanding revelation.[6]

What if we assume that *acts* are more fundamental than texts; that texts are the *products* of acts; and that the first thing that needs to be understood in understanding divine revelation is not its symbolism but the act that God performs in revealing through human acts and ordinary events. I claim that this approach fits *Dei Verbum* exceptionally well (see n. 9, below). God's revelation is not a text but an act. Hence, we begin not by interpreting a text but by reacting to or responding to an action.

Some problems in theologies of revelation arise because scholars interpret an *action* of God using hermeneutical theories developed to deal with *texts*, rather than using theories of action. In revelation, God acts in and through agents and/ or events, not a book, which is the *result* of collecting and editing *texts* that result from human acts responding to God. Taking seriously the relationship of primary and secondary agency discussed in the main text may avoid some of those problems.

Changing the default setting from texts to acts changes the perspective and approach to theology.[7] First, I presume *Dei Verbum* to be primarily an *action* of the council. However, *Dei Verbum* cannot be understood apart from the actions the council took in reaction to the problems with theologies of revelation they had inherited, so I attend to those briefly. Second, I then explore the significance of a practical, action-centered, rather than a textual, approach to revelation in the wake of *Dei Verbum*.

---

tions. I will not comment at length on Dulles's work here, but, like all who write after Dulles on revelation, I take my bearings from his work. I also have discussed Dulles's own symbolic model at length in *Inventing Catholic Tradition* (Maryknoll, NY: Orbis Books, 2000), 170-77. The contributors to *Divine Revelation,* ed. Paul Avis (Grand Rapids: Eerdmans, 1997) are Protestants and Catholics who have sought to extend the discussion of revelation theology. I am indebted to these authors. One of the key issues in revelation theology is the relationship of divine revelation to living faith traditions other than Judaism and Christianity. Given the extensive range and intensity of debates on these issues, that issue will not be considered here.

6. Dulles (*Models of Revelation*, especially 266-83) provides a contemporary example of the "symbolic" approach.

7. "The default setting means that when you want to create something different, you need constantly to resist the default setting, you need consciously to change or alter it. But when you turn your attention elsewhere, the default setting, the pre-set preference, reasserts itself" (James D. G. Dunn, "Altering the Default Setting: Re-envisaging the Early Transmission of the Jesus Tradition," *New Testament Studies* 49 [2003]: 139-75, at 140). Here I am seeking to understand revelation as a divine performance, not as a divinely given text or a text that in some sense contains divine revelation. On the present view, revelatory texts are a product of our responses to divine action.

Dei Verbum

The first word about Revelation in *Dei Verbum* is that it pleased God to reveal Godself (*Placuit Deo in sua bonitate et sapientia Seipsum revelare* [*DV* 2; see *DV* 6]).[8] Revelation is characterized by an inner unity of deeds and words—just as who a person is is shown by what she or he does and says. Hence, doctrines of revelation and incarnation are intrinsically linked because Jesus the Christ is both the incarnation and the revelation of God. Doctrines of incarnation and revelation both refer to God's issuing the Divine Word. They both talk of God's *action*, for to *issue* the Word, to reveal, is to *act*.[9]

The act of responding to God's revealing (*oboeditio fidei*) is a full commitment freely given, a full submission (*obsequium*) of intellect and will, freely consenting to the Revelation given by God (*et voluntarie revelationi ab Eo datae assentiendo* [*DV* 5]).[10] God truly gives the gift of God's very self to which the response in awe, a response of *oboeditio fidei et obsequium*, is appropriate.

The consent we are to give is not to propositions, but to God, who acts to reveal Godself. This form of consent is best characterized by Mary's consent: "Let it be to me according to your word" (Luke 1:38 RSV). It is a consent to an act of God, an *obsequium et oboeditio* like Mary's. We may formulate propositions to represent what God gives, but propositions are not given by God; God acts to give

---

8. Latin quotations from the text of *Dei Verbum* are found at http://stjosef.at/concilium/dei_verbum.htm (accessed June 25, 2008) as in *AAS* 58 (1966): 817-36. Translations are mine, but done in light of the published translations of Abbott and Austin Flannery (*Documents of Vatican II* [Grand Rapids: Eerdmans, 1984]). At many points the translations inevitably turn out to be identical. Where Abbott and Flannery diverge, I follow one or neither, depending on the context.

In his introduction to *Dei Verbum*, R. A. F. McKenzie, S.J., found that the document showed that revelation was a "manifestation by God—primarily of Himself; secondarily of His will and intentions. . . ." That manifestation is a communication that is "part of a larger pattern . . . destined ultimately for the good of all. . . ." This communication is public, not private, and "has to be made known to others by the testimony of its recipient. Passed on orally, it becomes tradition; recorded in writing, it becomes Scripture" (R. A. F. McKenzie, S.J., "Revelation," in *Documents of Vatican II*, ed. Walter M. Abbott, S.J., and Joseph Gallagher [New York: Guild Press, America Press, Association Press, 1966], 106). Hence, scripture and tradition *contain* revelation, but not all of scripture or tradition *is* revelation; however, the relationship between revelation, on the one hand, and scripture and tradition, on the other, is not to be conceived as between a part and a whole, but as scripture and tradition in some way sacramentally bearing revelation. This discussion is indebted to McKenzie's insights and to Herbert Vorgrimler, ed., *Commentary on the Documents of Vatican II*, 5 vols. (New York: Herder & Herder, 1967–).

9. Thomas Norris ("On Revisiting *Dei Verbum*," *Irish Theological Quarterly* 66 [2001]: 317) suggests that the "deeds, then, seem to have a certain priority"; also see D. C. Schindler, "Surprised by Truth: The Drama of Reason in Fundamental Theology," *Communio* 31 (Winter 2004): 606 n. 34: "at the center of revelation lies not *merely* an aesthetic/intelligible form, but in fact a *deed*. . . ." I would agree, as the next section shows.

10. Abbott and Gallagher render *datae* as "truths" (Flannery has "Revelation"). But *datae* are not *sententiae* nor *veritates*. The word is derived from "*dare*," to give. The givens revealed by God are certainly "truths" in some sense; but not necessarily propositions. The Flannery rendering fits better with the fundamental insight that God reveals Godself, not propositions. I render *assentiendo* as "consent" rather than "assent," because in English one consents to acts, but assents to claims.

Godself, especially in the incarnation, and it is that gift to which we consent, not to propositions *about* the giving.

God's revelation is carried in some sense by scripture and tradition. These are not sources of revelation, but the vehicle, "mirror," or "window" (*DV* 7: *speculum*) in which the community sees God, accepts everything from God, until it sees God face to face (*DV* 7: *in quo Ecclesia in terris peregrinans contemplatur Deum, a quo omnia accipit, usquedum ad Eum videndum facie ad faciem sicuti est perducatur*). The writers are inspired by the Holy Spirit to place in the text of scripture what God has revealed (cf. *DV* 11). Indeed, taking the composition of the Gospels as a paradigm, the writers' work can be understood as their engaging in a practice in which they are inspired to compose in writing the oral traditions which they had heard (cf. *DV* 7, 19). Tradition also "develops in the church with the assistance of the Holy Spirit" (*DV* 8: *sub assistentia Spiritus Sancti in Ecclesia proficit*). Scripture, tradition and the magisterium are together to provide for the salvation of souls (cf. *DV* 10). *Dei Verbum* claims that God acts to inspire the authors of Scripture and to assist the church as it is on pilgrimage.

Dei Verbum, as promulgated by the council, is profoundly different from the schema first presented for consideration in that it offers different solutions to key problems than did the preparatory schema.

The first problem was the relationship of scripture and tradition. The preparatory schema had followed the common pattern of the post-Tridentine handbooks of theology which found two sources of revelation (not a claim made explicitly by the Council of Trent) opposing the Protestant *sola scriptura*. *Dei Verbum* finds God to be the source of revelation, and scripture and tradition a *speculum* for seeing God. In so doing, the council embraced a fundamentally "personalist" as opposed to "propositionalist" understanding of revelation and one that did not recapitulate anti-Protestant rhetoric.[11]

The second problem was the relation of scripture and revelation: whether scripture is revelation and whether all revelation is contained in scripture. The preparatory schema had claimed plenary inerrancy for Scripture.[12] Rather than simply asserting scriptural inerrancy and sufficiency, the commission authored a text that considered the truth scripture faithfully teaches to be the truth (*veritatem*)

---

11. This is not to claim that some propositions cannot be found to be necessary for expressing what God has revealed. However, propositions can be formulated in many different sentences. This is not to say that "anything goes," that any formulation might articulate a proposition. But there must be many "right" sentences in various languages at various times in various places with various commonalities that are specific to the time and place in which the sentences are uttered that do express the same proposition, even though those sentences are not necessarily equivalent to each other. Differing sentences must be appropriate expressions of complex and/or abstract propositions (or, in my view, of any proposition, properly understood, at all). Sometimes expressions in severe tension with each other must both be good, if timely rather than timeless, expressions of a proposition; for example, personalist and social models of the Trinity may both be good, but not finally exhaustive expressions of the proposition that the One God subsists triunely.

12. See Gabriel Daly, "Revelation in the Theology of the Roman Catholic Church," in Avis, ed., *Divine Revelation*, 37.

for our salvation (*nostrae salutis*) that God placed in scripture (cf. *DV* 11).[13] Avoiding plenary inspiration, absolute scriptural sufficiency, and the theory once wrongly attributed to biblical scholar Alfred Loisy that some parts of the scripture were inspired and others were not, the council focused not on the content of revelation, but on the *action* of God revealing and the *purpose* for which God acted: our salvation. Scripture is not revelation but the result of God's revealing act.

Moreover, the council left open the question of whether all revelation was contained in scripture. It claimed that the church does not draw its certainty about everything that has been revealed from scripture (*DV* 9: *quo fit ut Ecclesia certitudinem suam de omnibus revelatis non per solam Sacram Scripturam hauriat*), a claim that was designed to leave the issue of scriptural sufficiency open. Additionally, a notable omission from the document—and a key hermeneutical principle for interpreting Vatican documents is that the omission of expected claims is always significant—is the omission of the traditional formulation that revelation ended with the death of the last apostle. The council simply doesn't mention it—in omitting that point, we can say it did *not* teach that point.[14]

A third problem was the historicity of the Gospels and, by extension, of historical narration in the Bible more generally. The council recognized the Gospels as constructs by their authors, but truthful constructs:

> The holy authors thus composed the four Gospels, selecting items from many oral or written traditions, redacting them into a synthesis, or explicating them for the situation of the churches, retaining the form of a proclamation, while they always communicated with us the honest truth about Jesus (*DV* 19: *Auctores autem sacri quattuor Evangelia conscripserunt, quaedam e multis aut ore aut iam scripto traditis seligentes, quaedam in synthesim redigentes, vel statui ecclesiarum attendendo explanantes, formam denique praeconii retinentes, ita semper ut vera et sincera de Iesu nobiscum communicarent*).[15]

The council at this point refers to the 1964 instruction of the Pontifical Biblical Commission which recognized the legitimacy of critical methods of biblical

---

13. Since the council, numerous authors have highlighted that the purpose of revelation is essentially for our salvation, including Augustin Cardinal Bea, *The Word of God and Mankind* (Chicago: Franciscan Herald Press, 1967), 26; Joseph Ratzinger, "The Transmission of Divine Revelation," in Vorgrimler, ed., *Commentary on the Documents of Vatican II*, 3:171-72; Catherine Cory and Corrine Patton, "Toward a Scriptural Understanding of Revelation: God Inserts God's Self into History," in Raymond A. Lucker and William C. McDonough, *Revelation and the Church: Vatican II and the Twenty-First Century* (Maryknoll, NY: Orbis Books, 2003), 48; Carmen Aparicio, "Bishop Paul-Joseph Schmitt and Vatican II: Jesus Christ, the Fullness of Revelation," in *The Convergence of Theology: A Festschrift in Honor of Gerald O'Collins, S.J.*, ed. Daniel Kendall, S.J., and Stephen T. Davis (Mahwah, NJ: Paulist, 2001), 102.

14. Daly, "Revelation in the Theology of the Roman Catholic Church," 37.

15. This sentence is open to different translations as the style of the prose is not quite "fitting well" with English style.

scholarship. In effect, the council found the Gospels to be purposefully constructed, selectively composed, and historically accurate. The Gospels were shaped by their authors; they are not literalistic chronicles of the uninterpreted events. They offer us "Jesus Remembered."

Dei Verbum is the council teaching about revelation while responding to the challenges of modern biblical scholarship, of biblical literalism, and of the burden of painful relationships with Protestant denominations shaped in the history of polemics about revelation between Protestant and Catholic theological traditions. The council does so by teaching about the God who acts revealingly.

In effect, the council shifts the whole debate about revelation and scripture into a different register. It changed the "default setting." No longer should debates about revelation center on propositions or doctrines, but on the God who actively reveals who God is through the acts we call revelation and incarnation.

To a Revealing God: Toward a Theology of Revelation as Divine Action

"Revelation is essentially a relational concept; it is the revealing of something by someone to someone else"[16] for a purpose. Divine revelation is God showing Godself to humanity for the sake of our salvation. It is a gracious act of the Triune God[17] showing that abiding in love is salvation. "When we come finally to abide in love, we are utterly transformed, because God is love."[18] Such abiding in God's reign is not merely a future hope, but also a present reality for those who engage in reconciling practices. We live out salvation as we live in love of God and neighbor.

In changing the register for discussing divine revelation, Vatican II shifted the focus from the words God uttered to the act God performed. This act is necessarily an empowering act. It is not an act that God performed *on* humanity. Humanity is not merely hearers of the word God uttered. Rather, revelation comes from God's primary agency, through which God empowers those who respond in the obedience of faith to act: to live and proclaim the Good News. As Jesus is both divine agent and first among equals who leads and empowers a movement, so revelation is an empowering act of God for reconciling all with Godself. The people of God are thus the doers and speakers of the word, secondary agents of revelation. Active faith in practice coinheres with active revelation, for the

---

16. Maurice Wiles, "Revelation and Divine Action," in Avis, ed., *Divine Revelation*, 100.

17. Thomas Norris ("On Revisiting *Dei Verbum*," 315-17) suggests that there are two languages in *Dei Verbum* regarding revelation, one more philosophical centered on creation and one more theological centered on the Trinity, citing Brendán Leahy, "Revelation and Faith," in *Evangelizing for the Third Millennium: The Maynooth Conference on the New Catechism, May 1996*, ed. Maurice Hogan, S.C., and Thomas Norris (Dublin: Veritas, 1997), 65-66. I do not find these "languages" so much in tension with each other as complementary.

18. Cory and Patton, "Toward a Scriptural Understanding of Revelation," 48.

ongoing community continues to show forth, to reveal, what it is to live in God's reign, in relationship with God, in the presence of God.[19]

The key for developing this insight is an assumption contained in *DV* 12: "Sacred Scripture is to be read and interpreted in the same Spirit in whom it has been written" (. . . *Sacra Scriptura eodem Spiritu quo scripta est etiam legenda et interpretanda sit . . .*).[20] The Spirit in whom scripture was written is the Spirit of God who acts to show Godself, not God who dictates propositions. To read the scripture is one thing. But to interpret it is not to *say* what the text means, but to *act out*, to *show*, what it means, to live a life together in the Spirit of reconciliation and peace.[21]

If the default assumption is that we need first to attend to acts rather than texts, then we need focus on the practices that are reactions to God's act of revealing Godself. Reading and interpretation are practices of faith in response to the revealing act of God. One can claim to understand God's action only if one knows how to act out the word. But I also want to suggest an even richer notion of agency here by utilizing a form of a Thomistic distinction between primary and secondary agency developed in chapter 18 above.

It is clear that God in Christ is the primary agent of divine revelation; God is in Christ not only revealing, but saving us (and God reveals salvifically). Jesus the Christ, then, can be seen as the person in whom primary (divine) and secondary

---

19. One way of putting this correlation in a more textual manner, though one that recognizes the act of God and human active responses, is found in Dulles, *Models of Revelation*:

> On the one hand, revelation precedes faith inasmuch as, before anyone can believe there must be symbols wherein God expresses what he is, and wills to be, for the world. These symbols, before their meaning is understood and accepted, are virtual revelation. When believers accept revelation, they allow their minds to be determined by the meaning they find in the symbols. Thus revelation shapes their faith.
>
> On the other hand, faith exists before revelation inasmuch as the symbols do not yield their meaning except to religious inquirers or believers who are actively committed to the search for truth. The quest itself involves a kind of implicit faith—a confidence that the search is not a futile one and that God's revelation, if it exists, can be recognized. When the search has succeeded, faith actively receives revelation and provides it, so to speak, with a dwelling place in the mind. Since revelation cannot exist as such outside a created mind, revelation may be said to presuppose faith. (279-80)

Hence, for Dulles, revelation is not a foundation for Christian faith and practice, but the correlate of faith within a tradition of the practice of faith. For a brief account of the history of the use of revelation as a foundational category in Catholic theology, see Francis Schüssler Fiorenza, *Foundational Theology: Jesus and the Church* (New York: Crossroad, 1994), 256-59, 266-67. His alternative hermeneutical approach is summarized on pp. 285-311.

20. Thomas J. McGovern, "The Interpretation of Scripture 'in the Spirit': The Edelby Intervention at Vatican II" (*Irish Theological Quarterly* 64 [1999]: 245-59) highlights the significance of this concept. McGovern finds it a "restatement of a fundamental principle of patristic exegesis" and "a corrective to the over-emphasis on critical exegesis" (258-59), but it can be read much more richly.

21. "For as the rain and the snow come down from heaven, and do not return there until they have watered the earth, making it bring forth and sprout, giving seed to the sower and bread to the eater, so shall my word be that goes out from my mouth; it shall not return to me empty, but it shall accomplish that which I purpose, and succeed in the thing for which I sent it" (Isa 55:10-11 NRSV).

(human) agency are not identical, but in full or perfect accord. Yet we are also (imperfect) secondary agents of revelation—for ourselves, for each other, and for the world. Divine revelation is not merely something that happened once upon a time a long time ago. God's revealing is not over and done with. God continues to act revealingly in and through the community that forms the Jesus-movement, the body of Christ.

The intimacy of primary and secondary agency avoids the "either/or" of claiming that if we do something, God does not; and that if God does something, we do not do it. This is a "both/and" intimacy. It is not that "we do it" and God does not. Rather, when we practice our faith gracefully, we are God's agents through whom God works. When we engage in those practices we should avoid, we effectively obstruct God's action. We cannot finally obstruct God's purpose, of course, nor can we think we are the only secondary agents God uses—the entire created world and everything in it in and through which God acts is in some way at least potentially God's secondary revelatory agents. In this "practical" perspective, the "Great Commission" of Matthew 28 is, as discussed in chapter 19, a commissioning of Jesus' disciples to be God's agents and thus to reveal God to the world in and through acts of reconciliation, exemplified as preaching and baptizing.

The change in default setting applies not only to what I will call primary revelation—God's act in revealing Godself to us—but in secondary revelation—the acts secondary agents perform in revealing God to themselves and others. Scripture is faithfully and revealingly interpreted not primarily by exegetes working in the academy, but by the church itself insofar as it dwells in the Spirit and shows what it means to live in the Spirit. Scriptural interpretation in this act-centered approach is divine revelation in the mode of secondary agency or secondary causality.

The infinite power of God does not preclude the need for finite powers exercised in this world by finite agents who participate in and further the agency of infinite love. God's infinite agency and infinite power are not on the same level with nor exercised in the same way as finite power. Finite and infinite power and agency cannot be in competition with each other. Salvation, the reconciling all-that-is in divine love, reveals not only who Christ—Emmanuel, God with us—is, but also what God does in the present. Insofar as the church is in an analogous sense the body of Christ, God shows Godself now through the church in the acts God performs in, through, and with this body. Our acts, when gracious, reveal who God is and what God does. Of course, we are not perfect secondary agents, but sinners whose acts conceal the love of God—sometimes more than we reveal it!

God's revealing is an exercise of primary agency. As uncreated grace, it is God's very presence as an agent to us. Faith is revelation considered as secondary agency. Uncreated grace produces created grace, that is, the grace that possesses and is possessed by disciples (and even others!). An Orthodox theologian could well recast this as the presence of the Spirit in the community, actively energizing the community to do God's work and show God's love. So to say that we can know of uncreated grace only through the reality of created grace, we could also say that we can know of the Triune God only through the power of the Spirit that possesses us and that we possess. If we are recipients of grace, if we live in the Spirit, the grace that is created in us is the result of our relationship with God which is God's very presence to and action on and in and with us. Our actions and our secondary agency are created grace resulting from uncreated grace, the empowering presence of the Spirit, the very relationship we have with and in God.

Where the present approach may differ from St. Thomas (or at least some of his followers) is that it construes created grace as creative.[22] For better or for worse, we humans in particular (and the cosmos is general—but that's another story) are interdependent creators of stability and novelty. It is not that God creates things; God creates creative agents—God's Spirit as the spirit of creativity works in and through them. In classical language, what God creates is not entities, things, events, actions, or states of affairs, but *being*.[23] But God's being is pure act, and God's agency and creativity are primary. Analogously, then, our being is also act (not "pure act," but act sometimes thwarted by sin) as secondary creative agents. But the key is that grace is not some "thing" superadded to our being, but it is what we are as graced humans, as creative agents. To put it quickly, to be graced is to be graceful in what we do. And when we act gracefully we reveal how God acts and thus show in the "speculum" of our deeds who God is.

The upshot of this is that discerning what constitutes the practice of discipleship, our actions and our agency, is also discerning divine revelation, for discerning what acts are exercises of a gracious practice is also discerning what we can of that relationship of God being present to us in a relationship of uncreated and created grace. If we have a doctrine of revelation correlated with a doctrine of faith, then, what we understand of and as revelation must arise—as do all doctrine and all theology—out of the practice/praxis of the faith in discipleship. The practice of discipleship then becomes not merely the "formal" source of revelation but the "material" source as well. In sum, divine revelation and divine faith are related as primary and secondary agency, uncreated and created grace, God's response and

---

22. Too often we read Thomas's motto *gratia perficit naturam* in a Neo-Thomist way, as if *perficit* means "builds upon." The image thus created is of a static nature that is somehow capped by grace, as if grace were the second scoop of ice cream on a cone. One obvious example of this interpretation can be found in the influential book of H. Richard Niebuhr, *Christ and Culture* (New York: Harper & Row, 1950), in which Niebuhr characterized Thomas and the Catholic tradition as placing Christ "above" culture. But *perficit* comes from *per* + *facio* – an image of making (*facio*) intensified (*per*) and perhaps even understandable as "making through." Grace perfects nature not additively, but by making nature what it is to be. Henri de Lubac and (*pace* John Milbank) Karl Rahner do this by "supernaturalizing the natural" all the way down—that is to say, there is no un-graced nature in the actual world, even if there are possible worlds where there is an ungraced or partially graced nature.

23. I owe this point to a presentation by James Ross at an Annual Meeting of the American Academy of Religion in the distant past. Austin Farrer put a similar point as follows: "If God creates energies, he creates going activities. What he causes to be is their acting as they do. We cannot even say that he causes them to act, for it is by their action that they are" (Austin Farrer, *Faith and Speculation: An Essay in Philosophical Theology* [London: A. & C. Black, 1967], 82; cf. 62, 65, 154).

the response of God's spirit working in and through us unless we obstruct God's agency by sin. We can recognize God's revelation only in faith.

More generally, we can recognize God's act only in faith, only as disciples. This applies especially to the act of God Christians identify as the resurrection of Jesus.

"More Than a Kodak Moment":
What to Look for in the Resurrection

In 1996, independent film maker Beth Harrington produced a wonderful film, *The Blinking Madonna*. The film focuses on a video clip from the production of her 1991 film, *Moveable Feast*, one of her documentaries about the feast of the Madonna del Soccorso, patroness of fishermen, as celebrated by Italian-Americans in Boston. While the statue of the Madonna was being carried through the streets in procession, the video camera recorded her blinking. I have seen the film a number of times. On two of those occasions, Harrington was present to discuss the film. There is no doubt that her camera "recorded" the event of the Madonna blinking. It is unmistakable. But, of course, the blinking could easily be the result of an anomaly caused by the automatic shutter.

Did the Madonna blink? Or was it just a technical glitch?

"The tape caught it. That's evidence. It must be real. The statue blinked. Right?" So would my true believer friends say.

"It was a glitch. Don't be silly. Statues don't blink." So goes the gospel according to my more skeptical friends.

The problem is that the true believers and the skeptics think they're talking about the same thing—events that occurred. They're not. They're talking about different things entirely.

"If there had been a video camera around on Easter morning, what would it have recorded?"

A colleague asked me this question during a "social" dinner for local theologians recently. We were enjoying drinks, canapés, and a nice buffet supper in the basement dining hall of a nearby seminary on a cold Friday night in January.

The conversation had turned to future plans—and my upcoming sabbatical.

"What will you do?" was the polite inquiry.

"Well," I said, "I've got a couple of books to write—one on the relationship of theology and history, and another on christology as rooted in disciples' imaginations." After some polite talk, the discussion turned again to the litmus-test question: "What would the camera have seen?" (as if to say, "If a camera had been available at the moment of the resurrection, then we'd have proof, right?").

"That's an illegitimate question," was my response. "It can't be answered." I continued more or less in this vein: "It's counterfactual—there were no cameras around. At best, any answer would be completely speculative—no shred of evidence is available to warrant any answer to the question."

It *is* a bad question. But I know now that there is a better response to my friend's "social dinner" question: "My friend, if a camera had been there, the camera would have recorded an act of God—but not all could see it." Like the sheep and the goats who failed to recognize the king when he was present to them, not all can see God's actions or God's presence.

―――――――――――

The following Tuesday, I was at my parish church for choir practice. I didn't realize it until a few days later, but preparing for Easter helped hatch the better answer.

We picked up our new music on the way into the choir loft. We were beginning our preparation for Easter. I was delighted to see that we would do—for the second year in a row—the complex, eight-voice, two choir, *a capella* "This Is the Day" by Jacobus Gallus (Handl), who lived 1550-1591. We had spent so many months rehearsing last year (we are all amateur singers, and music of such precision and complexity is hard for us). Now we could sing this beautiful, moving piece again.

We sing this only twice, once at the Easter Vigil, and once at the main Sunday Mass—not a lot of "performance time" for so much practice time, but enough.

―――――――――――

"God raised Jesus from the dead. The camera would have photographed it. Right?" So would my true believer friends full of their certainty say.

"It was an illusion. Don't be silly. Dead men don't walk. There would be nothing for any camera to show." Thus goeth the gospel according to my more skeptical friends.

The root problem is that people think of the resurrection as either a historical event or not a historical event. They think it one in a series of one damn thing after another—arrest, trial, crucifixion, resurrection. This thinking misleads them. The agents who arrested, tried, and crucified Jesus of Nazareth were human. The agent who raised him up was divine. If they're all "events," they're not of the same kind. The agents are as different as divine nature is different from human nature.

How can one understand this?

―――――――――――

Questions about videotapes from Jesus' tomb are as useless as questions about whether the Madonna blinking was a miracle. Would these tell us who raised Jesus or who made the Madonna blink? Or who didn't act to raise Jesus or who didn't make the Madonna blink? These questions are confused.

Events *happen*. Acts *are performed by agents*. To turn an act of God into an *event* is to erase the *agency*. This is the confusion.

———————

The scriptures record testimony to the risen Lord. Early testimony is passed on by Paul: "For I passed on to you as of first importance what I also received, that Christ died for our sins after the scriptures and that he was buried and that he was raised on the third day after the scriptures and that he appeared to Cephas, then to the twelve, and then he appeared to over five hundred disciples at one time, most of whom live, but some have fallen asleep and then he appeared to James and to all apostles. At the end (*eschaton de pantōn*) he appeared to me, one untimely born" (1 Cor. 15:3-9; adapted from RSV).

Whatever the cause, it is a fact that a whole bunch of people, apparently independently, testified that Jesus appeared to them. Maybe this sort of flat listing by Paul makes people think that these acts of God were events that might have been photographed and put into an album or transferred to a DVD.

———————

Consider the following dialogue from scene 1 of George Bernard Shaw's *Saint Joan:*

JOAN. I hear voices telling me what to do. They come from God.
ROBERT [DE BAUDRICORT]. They come from your imagination.
JOAN. Of course. That is how the messages of God come to us.
[BERTRAND DE] POULENGEY. Checkmate.

———————

These are facts: Joan reported that she heard voices; Jesus' disciples reported that he appeared to them after his death; the camera—glitches or no—recorded the Madonna blinking.

Perhaps God did these things. Perhaps God did use Joan's imagination. Perhaps God had the Madonna blink—whether by manipulating the statue or utilizing a technical glitch in a video camera shutter. Perhaps God raised Jesus and had Jesus appear to the others. Perhaps one or more of these are miracles, acts of God.

Or perhaps these are just natural events, fully explicable by physics or psychology without reference to God. Perhaps those "with eyes to see" and "ears to hear" are simply seeing illusions and hearing delusions.

We *can* figure such events as illusions. We *can* explain away acts of God as natural events. We may explain things away more often than we imagine. But for those who have eyes to see, that we don't *need* God to explain events does not mean that they are not or cannot be God's *acts*. The events of my daughters' births can be explained without reference to God. Yet is it silly or stupid to recognize the messy and painful joy of new life aborning as not in some way the result of an act of God as well as natural events?

———————

However it may have been done, God raising Jesus from the dead was an act of *God*. So Christians believe, then and now. We cannot talk about it "straight" or as just another event in a set. We have to use charged metaphorical language. So did Paul. Even the verb "raise" is figurative. I can raise my hand to my mouth, the salt shaker to the shelf, or my children to adulthood. To "raise" Jesus from the dead—as many theologians have reminded us—is itself to use figurative language. "Raising" here is a trope, a figure of speech.

There is no other language for an act of God than metaphorical, figurative language. Only figured language can tell of God's acts rather than of mere events. The question is whether some figures are better than others, not whether we can avoid figurative talk for acts of God. If we give up metaphors and figures, we give up talking of God and God's acts. All our talk of God is analogical. All analogies limp. Analogies drawn from finite agents to an infinite Agent cannot but limp badly.

———————

Events *happen*. Acts *are performed*. Facts are *stated*. Too often we fail to keep these distinctions straight.

———————

To say one believes in the resurrection is to state a fact (among other more profound things one does in confessing one's belief). The question is, what kind of fact? One like "Caesar crossed the Rubicon"? Or one like "God became incarnate in the man Jesus who lived in Galilee and Judea in the first third of what we call the first century C.E."? Or one like "the Madonna blinked"? There are many ways to figure these facts in order to state them.

The question is, How do we figure the fact of the resurrection?

———————

The late William A. Clebsch, in *Christianity in European History*, noted that no "available *historical* method can distinguish the way men and women personally and socially understood their universe from the way their universe actually was then and there. . . ." Their universe may well not be the contemporary historian's universe. But that does not give a historian *as a historian* permission to say that they were deluded or only thought they experienced what they reported. Historians cannot reduce the experience in the past to what fits in the contemporary worldview. As Clebsch put it, "A license to rule out, as illusion or mere apprehension, everything testified to which lies outside the historians' own experience would collapse their narratives into little more than autobiography."

Are acts of God outside a twenty-first century historian's experience? Perhaps so. Does that make them impossible? Why would one infer *that*? Perhaps our contemporary historian's experience is too limited? Perhaps her universe is different from Paul's?

Clebsch reminds us that "critical history issues no warrant for changing what happened into an apprehension of what happened." What happened is that Paul reported what was handed on to him. Unless he was lying, that was the way it was for Paul and the witnesses.

Perhaps they were deluded. Or perhaps God raised Jesus from the dead and Jesus appeared to a whole bunch of people.

"Critical historians" cannot warrant *on grounds proper to the discipline of history* that those appearances must be somehow illusions. Skeptics can explain away and *redescribe* or *re-represent* what Paul presented. But on what grounds do they do that? Not on those proper to doing historical reconstruction and analysis.

The discipline of history has nothing to say about God's acts, however much it may describe events. Its factual statements are about events; God is an agent whose acts are beyond the historian's range.

Of course, we can *argue* for skepticism about the resurrection based on our views of social psychology or our commitments to allowing only natural explanations of events. We can argue that Paul and the disciples and apostles must have been deluded or self-deluded because social psychology "explains" better what happened than Paul did. Or we could say that we "know" that whatever happens in the space-time continuum is explained only by science. We can say that we "know better" and that what they saw and reported was highly unlikely or impossible.

Such revisions of the story are possible and even commonplace. They help accommodate the strangeness of the past to our naturalistic understanding in the present.

But notice that such revisions can speak only of events and natural acts, not of the divine act which brings whatever exists into being. The question is not the event, but the agent. Were these events sustained by God or illusions in the minds of the witnesses? Could they be both? (Remember St. Joan).

The word we received is that God performed the act; disciples were witnesses.

We can change this if we want, I suppose. We could say, for example, that the New Testament testimony must be only "sensible representations" of something insensible or "symbolic vehicles for expressing faith in and asserting the reality of Jesus' resurrection" or "merely etiological cult legends explaining why we pray to Jesus." But should we? On what grounds? In doing so, might we not erase any chance of recognizing an act of God in and through these events?

Would this not be worse than asserting that the Madonna *could not have* blinked or Joan could not have heard voices? Specific events occurred and were recorded or reported. On what grounds should we argue that these events were not also God's acts?

———————

Take it one step further. Would understanding just what happened as if caught by a video camera enable us to understand the resurrection? The camera can record an event. Can it record the presence or absence of an act of God?

Isn't this reducing the *meaning* to the mechanism, as though our photograph of the risen Jesus would tell us the meaning of the event? Would a snapshot or a DVD help us understand that this event was God's act?

———————

Sometimes, if we know the mechanism we can distinguish bogus from authentic meanings. When Toto pulled aside the screen, the grand and glorious Oz was shown to be a fake. When we see the mechanism of a Penn and Teller trick, we know the meaning of the act: it is a magician's trick. Magic tricks and deceptions are within a historian's experience. Acts of God may well not be.

———————

On Easter Sunday in my church (built in 1905, Romanesque in style, German-American baroque in decoration) there will be a two-story grotto in front of a side altar. It will be built by the men's (and women's) club out of lumber, scaffolding, and lovingly preserved, half-century old, stone-colored canvas. It will have a running stream of holy water used in the baptisms at the Easter Vigil. This "realistic" scene will have statues of angels, a light source in the cave, a discarded crown of thorns, abandoned grave cloths, an empty cross, and other kitsch (including a rock near the pool at the end of the stream with the label, "Thou shalt not plunge the candle too deeply," installed after a previous pastor's vigor at the Easter Vigil caused a big leak).

We will sing again and again, "This is the Day the Lord has made. Let us rejoice and be glad in it. Alleluia."

This grotto is no less and no more figurative or metaphorical a representation of God's act than an empty tomb story or a translated sixteenth-century hymn. All represent that this *is* the day that the Lord has made. All call for us to respond. But how to respond?

There will be cameras in our church this Easter. Videos and pictures will be taken of travelers and parishioners and biennial visitors in front of our seasonal grotto. Those who have eyes to see will see the risen Lord in them. They will recognize an act of God. They will state it as a fact as they speak of it figuratively, since there is no other way to speak of God's acts.

Others will no doubt say it all can be explained away naturally, that the disciples thought "lovely thoughts." Such skeptics are like those who would explain away love by hormones, joy by brain chemicals, the savory taste of chocolate by neurological processes. Are these not all cases of reducing the *meaning* to the *mechanism*, analogous to reducing a miracle to something like a videotape recording?

We cannot say what mechanism God used in raising Jesus. We have no access to God's view of what God did. All we have are records of witnesses who saw the results: an empty tomb, a man in a garden, an unrecognized traveler cooking fish, and many more. So the real question is whether *we* dare testify that what we see in these events *is* an act of God. The question is whether *we dare* proclaim, "He is risen. Alleluia."

The real question is what would a camera record if one took pictures in our church? Some *events* that would prove God acted? Or didn't? I think not. It might record some events, but not God's acts or God's presence. God acts through events. The camera only records those events. Can we see in those pictures an act of God? Can we recognize that *this* is the day the Lord has made? Can we rejoice and be glad in it? If so, we can recognize the resurrection as an act of God (even if we have some difficulties with blinking Madonnas). Had the camera been present at the resurrection, it would have recorded some events, but for those disciples who have eyes to see, whatever it recorded would be an act of God; for those with sheeps' or goats' eyes, it would not be God's act.

As for me, I hope that when I sing "This Is the Day," I will see the risen Lord, *eschaton de pantōn.* And for me—or any disciple—to *see* him this or any Easter will take an act of God.

BIBLIOGRAPHY

Abbott, Walter M., S.J., ed. *The Documents of Vatican II*. New York: America Press, 1966.

Amaladoss, Michael, S.J. *The Asian Jesus*. Maryknoll, NY: Orbis Books, 2006.

————. "Pluralism of Religions and the Proclamation of Jesus Christ in the Context of Asia." *Proceedings of the Catholic Theological Society of America* 56 (2001): 1-14.

Aparicio, Carmen. "Bishop Paul-Joseph Schmitt and Vatican II: Jesus Christ, the Fullness of Revelation." In *The Convergence of Theology: A Festschrift in Honor of Gerald O'Collins, S.J.*, ed. Daniel Kendall, S.J., and Stephen T. Davis, 87-108. Mahwah, NJ: Paulist, 2001.

Aristotle. *Nicomachean Ethics*. Translated by H. Rackham. Loeb Classical Library. Cambridge, MA: Harvard University Press, 1975.

Augustine of Hippo. *De Doctrina Christiana*. Available at http://www.newadvent.org/fathers/12023.htm (accessed August 21, 2007).

Avis, Paul, ed. *Divine Revelation*. Grand Rapids: Eerdmans, 1997.

Bach, Kent. "Conversational Implicature."Available at http://userwww.sfsu.edu/~kbach/impliciture.htm (accessed February 22, 2005).

Bailey, Kenneth E. "Informal Controlled Oral Tradition and the Synoptic Gospels." *Asia Journal of Theology* 5 (1991): 42-45.

Barrett, Michèle. *The Politics of Truth: From Marx to Foucault*. Stanford, CA: Stanford University Press, 1991.

Barron, Robert. "The Metaphysics of Co-Inherence: A Meditation on the Essence of the Christian Message." In *Handing on the Faith: The Church's Mission and Challenge*, ed. Robert Imbelli, 77-90. New York: Crossroad, 2006.

————.*The Priority of Christ: Toward a Postliberal Catholicism*. Grand Rapids: Brazos, 2007.

Bartchy, S. S. "Table Fellowship." In *Dictionary of Jesus and the Gospels*, ed. Joel B. Green and Scott McKnight, 796-97. Downer's Grove, IL: InterVarsity, 1992.

Barth, Karl. *Church Dogmatics* IV 3/2. Edited by G. W. Bromiley and T. F. Torrance. Translated by T. F. Torrance. New ed. Edinburgh: T&T Clark, 2004 (first German edition, 1932).

Bartlett, Anthony W. *Cross Purposes: The Violent Grammar of Christian Atonement*. Harrisburg, PA: Trinity Press International, 2001.

Baum, Gregory, and Harold Wells, eds. *The Reconciliation of Peoples: Challenge to the Churches*. Maryknoll, NY: Orbis Books, 1997.

Bea, Augustin Cardinal. *The Word of God and Mankind*. Chicago: Franciscan Herald Press, 1967.

Boethius, Anicius Manlius Severinus. *The Consolation of Philosophy*. Translated with introduction and notes by Richard Green. Indianapolis: Library of Liberal Arts, 1962.

————.*Tractates/De Consolatione Philosophiae.* Translated by H. F. Stewart, E. K. Rand, and S. J. Tester. New Edition. Loeb Classical Library: Latin authors, no. 74. Cambridge, MA: Harvard University Press, 1973.

Boeve, Lieven. *God Interrupts History: Theology in a Time of Upheaval.* Translated by Brian Doyle. New York: Continuum, 2007.

Boff, Leonardo, O.F.M. "The Need for Political Saints: From a Spirituality of Liberation to the Practice of Liberation." Translated by L. Rivera and L. King. *Cross Currents* 30, no. 4 (1981): 369-76.

Boraine, Alex, Janey Levy, and Ronell Scheffer, eds. *Dealing with the Past: Truth and Reconciliation in South Africa.* Capetown: IDASA, 1994.

Borg, Marcus J. *Conflict, Holiness, and Politics in the Teaching of Jesus.* New York: Edwin Mellen, 1984.

Borg, Marcus J., and N. T. Wright. *The Meaning of Jesus: Two Visions.* San Francisco: HarperSanFrancisco, 1999.

Boyarin, Daniel. *Border Lines: The Partition of Judaeo-Christianity.* Philadelphia: University of Pennsylvania Press, 2004.

Bronkhorst, Daan. *Truth and Reconciliation: Obstacles and Opportunities for Human Rights.* Amsterdam: Amnesty International, 1995.

Brown, Raymond E. *The Death of the Messiah: From Gethsemane to the Grave: A Commentary on the Passion Narratives in the Four Gospels.* Anchor Bible Reference Library. New York: Doubleday, 1994.

————. *The Gospel According to John: Introduction, Translation, and Notes.* 2 vols. Anchor Bible 29, 29A. Garden City, NY: Doubleday, 1966, 1970.

————. *An Introduction to New Testament Christology.* Mahwah, NJ: Paulist, 1994.

————. *New Testament Essays.* Milwaukee: Bruce, 1965.

Buckley, James J. "*Lectio Divina* and Arguing over Jesus: An Ascetic for Christological Rebukes." In *Who Do You Say That I Am? Confessing the Mystery of Christ,* ed. John C. Cavadini and Laura Holt, 87-108. Notre Dame: University of Notre Dame Press, 2004.

Bultmann, Rudolf. *The History of the Synoptic Tradition.* Translated by John Marsh. Rev. ed. New York: Harper & Row, 1968.

Burke, Alexander J., Jr. *The Raising of Lazarus and the Passion of Jesus in John 11 and 12.* Lewiston, NY: Edwin Mellen, 2003.

Burrell, David. *Faith and Freedom: An Interfaith Perspective.* Oxford: Blackwell, 2004.

Burrows, William R. "A Response to Michael Amaladoss." *Proceedings of the Catholic Theological Society of America* 56 (2001): 15-20.

Cahill, Lisa Sowle. "The Atonement Paradigm: Does It Still Have Explanatory Value?" *Theological Studies* 68, no. 2 (2007): 418-32.

————. "Christology, Ethics and Spirituality." In *Thinking of Christ: Proclamation, Explanation, Meaning,* ed. Tatha Wiley. New York: Continuum, 2003.

Carlson, Jeffrey, and Robert A. Ludwig, eds. *Jesus and Faith: A Conversation on the Work of John Dominic Crossan, Author of the Historical Jesus.* Maryknoll, NY: Orbis Books, 1994.

Cavadini, John C., and Laura Holt, eds. *Who Do You Say That I Am? Confessing the Mystery of Christ.* Notre Dame: University of Notre Dame Press, 2004.

Chia, Edmund. "Interreligious Dialogue in Pursuit of Fullness of Life in Asia." *Seventh Plenary Assembly Workshop Discussion Guide.* FABC Paper No. 92k. Available at http://www.ucanews.com/html/fabc-papers/fabc-92k.htm (accessed July 15, 2007).

Chilton, Bruce, and J. I. H. McDonald. *Jesus and the Ethics of the Kingdom*. Biblical Foundations in Theology. London: SPCK, 1987.

Clebsch, William. *Christianity in European History.* New York: Oxford University Press, 1979.

Comstock, Gary. "Two Types of Narrative Theology." *Journal of the American Academy of Religion* 55, no. 4 (1987): 687-717.

Congregation for the Doctrine of the Faith. "Notification on the works of Fr. Jon Sobrino SJ." Rome: Office of the Congregation of the Doctrine of the Faith: 26 November 2006. Available at http://www.vatican.va/roman_curia/congregations/cfaith/documents/rc_con_cfaith_doc_20061126_notification-sobrino_en.html (accessed March 16, 2007).

Cory, Catherine, and Corrine Patton. "Toward a Scriptural Understanding of Revelation: God Inserts God's Self into History." In *Revelation and the Church: Vatican II and the Twenty-First Century,* ed. Raymond A. Lucker and William C. McDonough, 32-48. Maryknoll, NY: Orbis Books, 2003.

Crossan, John Dominic. *Jesus: A Revolutionary Biography*. San Francisco: Harper-Collins, 1994.

Crowley, Paul G., S.J., ed. *Rahner beyond Rahner: A Great Theologian Encounters the Pacific Rim.* Lanham, MD: Rowman & Littlefield, 2005.

Cuneo, Michael W. *American Exorcism: Expelling Demons in the Land of Plenty*. New York: Doubleday, 2001.

Daly, Gabriel. "Revelation in the Theology of the Roman Catholic Church." In *Divine Revelation,* ed. Paul Avis, 23-44. Grand Rapids: Eerdmans, 1997.

Davies, Brian, O.P. *The Reality of God and the Problem of Evil*. New York: Continuum, 2006.

D'Costa, Gavin. "'Christian Orthodoxy and Religious Pluralism': A Response to Terrence W. Tilley." *Modern Theology* 23, no. 3 (2007) 435-46.

———. "'Christian Orthodoxy and Religious Pluralism': A Further Rejoinder to Terrence Tilley." *Modern Theology* 23, no. 3 (2007) 455-62.

D'Costa, Gavin, and Terrence W. Tilley. "Concluding Our *Quaestio Disputata* on Theologies of Religious Diversity." *Modern Theology* 23, no. 3 (2007) 463-68.

Denzinger, Henricus, and Adolfus Schönmetzer, S.J. *Enchiridion Symbolorum: Definitionum et Declarationum de Rebus Fidei et Morum.* 36th ed., amended. Freiburg: Herder, 1965.

Donahue, John R., S.J. "Biblical Perspectives on Justice." In *The Faith That Does Justice,* ed. John C. Haughey, S.J., 68-112. New York: Paulist, 1977.

Dulles Avery, S.J. *Models of Revelation.* 2nd ed. Maryknoll, NY: Orbis Books, 1992.

———. "Tradition as a Theological Source." In idem, *The Craft of Theology: From Symbol to System,* 87-104. New York: Crossroad, 1996.

Dunderberg, Ismo, Kari Syreeni, and Christopher Tuckett, eds. *Fair Play: Diversity and Conflicts in Early Christianity: Essays in Honour of Heikki Räisänen.* Leiden: Brill, 2002.

Dunn, James D. G. "Altering the Default Setting: Re-envisaging the Early Transmission of the Jesus Tradition." *New Testament Studies* 49 (2003): 139-75.

———. *Christology in the Making: A New Testament Inquiry into the Origins of the Doctrine of the Incarnation.* Philadelphia: Westminster, 1980.

———. *Jesus' Call to Discipleship.* New York: Cambridge University Press, 1992.

———. *Jesus Remembered.* Vol. 1 of *Christianity in the Making.* Grand Rapids: Eerdmans, 2003.

Dupuis, Jacques. *Who Do You Say I Am? Introduction to Christology.* Maryknoll, NY: Orbis Books, 1994.

Farrer, Austin. *Faith and Speculation: An Essay in Philosophical Theology.* London: A. and C. Black, 1967.

Ferguson, Everett, ed. *Encyclopedia of Early Christianity.* New York and London: Garland, 1990.

Finlan, Stephen. *Problems with Atonement: The Origins of, and Controversy about, the Atonement Doctrine.* Collegeville, MN: Liturgical Press, 2005.

Fiorenza, Francis Schüssler. *Foundational Theology: Jesus and the Church.* New York: Crossroad, 1994.

Fitzmyer, Joseph A. *The Gospel According to Luke: Introduction, Translation, and Notes.* 2 vols. Anchor Bible 28, 28A. Garden City, NY: Doubleday, 1981, 1985.

Flannery, Austin. *Documents of Vatican II.* Grand Rapids: Eerdmans, 1984.

Fowl, Stephen E. *The Story of Christ in the Ethics of Paul.* Journal for the Study of the New Testament Supplement 36. Sheffield: JSOT Press, 1990.

Fredriksen, Paula. *From Jesus to Christ: The Origins of the New Testament Images of Jesus.* 2nd ed. New Haven: Yale University Press, 2000.

———. *Jesus of Nazareth, King of the Jews: A Jewish Life and the Emergence of Christianity.* New York: Knopf, 1999.

———. "What Does Jesus Have to Do with Christ? What Does Knowledge Have to Do with Faith? What Does History Have to Do with Theology." In *Christology: Memory, Inquiry, Practice,* ed. Anne M. Clifford and Anthony J Godzieba, 3-17. College Theology Society Annual Volume 48. Maryknoll, NY: Orbis Books, 2003.

Fulkerson, Mary McClintock. *Changing the Subject: Women's Discourses and Feminist Theology.* Minneapolis: Fortress, 1994.

Fuller, Reginald H. *The Formation of the Resurrection Narratives.* Philadelphia: Fortress, 1980.

———. *The Foundations of New Testament Christology.* London: Collins, 1976.

———. *The Mission and Achievement of Jesus.* Chicago: Alec R. Allenson, 1954.

Funk, Robert W. "The Good Samaritan as Metaphor." *Semeia* 2 (1974): 74-86.

Gelpi, Donald. *Peirce and Theology: Essays in the Authentication of Doctrine.* Lanham, MD: University Press of America, 2001.

Georgi, Dieter. "The Interest in Life of Jesus Theology as a Paradigm for the Social History of Biblical Criticism." *Harvard Theological Review* 85, no. 1(1992): 51-83.

Goizueta, Roberto S. *Caminemos con Jesús: Toward a Hispanic/Latino Theology of Accompaniment.* Maryknoll, NY: Orbis Books, 1995.

Greeley, Andrew. "Theology and Sociology: On Validating David Tracy." *Journal of the American Academy of Religion* 59, no. 4 (1991): 643-52.

Grice, H. Paul. *Studies in the Ways of Words.* Cambridge, MA: Harvard University Press, 1989.

Gutiérrez, Gustavo. *A Theology of Liberation.* Translated by Sr. Caridad Inda and John Eagleson. 2nd ed. Maryknoll, NY: Orbis Books, 1988.

Haack, Susan. "Confessions of an Old-Fashioned Prig." In eadem, *Manifesto of a Passionate Moderate: Unfashionable Essays,* 7-30. Chicago: University of Chicago Press, 1998.

Haight, Roger. *Jesus Symbol of God.* 2nd ed. Maryknoll, NY: Orbis Books, 2000.

Harmless, William, S.J. "Desert Silence: Why Christology Is Missing from the *Apophthegmata Patrum.*" Paper, Fifteenth International Patristics Conference, Oxford University, August 10, 2007, unpublished.

Harnack, Adolf. *What Is Christianity?: Sixteen Lectures Delivered in the University of Berlin during the Winter Term, 1899-1900.* London: Williams & Norgate, 1901 (first German ed., 1900).

Harvey, A. E. *Jesus and the Constraints of History.* Philadelphia: Westminster, 1982.

Harvey, Van. *The Historian and the Believer.* New York: Macmillan, 1966.

Hauerwas, Stanley. *Character and the Christian Life: A Study in Theological Ethics.* San Antonio: Trinity University Press, 1975.

———. "Jesus: The Story of the Kingdom," in idem, *A Community of Character: Toward a Constructive Christian Social Ethic,* 36-52. Notre Dame: University of Notre Dame Press, 1983.

———. *Performing the Faith: Bonhoeffer and the Practice of Nonviolence.* Grand Rapids: Brazos, 2004.

———. *Truthfulness and Tragedy: Further Investigations into Christian Ethics.* Notre Dame: University of Notre Dame Press, 1977.

———. *Vision and Virtue: Essays in Christian Ethical Reflection.* Notre Dame: Fides, 1974.

Hauerwas, Stanley, and James Fodor. "Performing Faith: The Peaceable Rhetoric of God's Church." In Stanley Hauerwas, *Performing the Faith: Bonhoeffer and the Practice of Nonviolence,* 75-110. Grand Rapids: Brazos, 2004.

Hengel, Martin. *Between Jesus and Paul.* London: SCM, 1983.

———. *The Charismatic Leader and His Followers.* Edited by John Riches. Translated by James C. G. Greig. Studies of the New Testament and Its World. Edinburgh: T&T Clark, 1996 (first German ed., 1968).

———. "Christology and New Testament Chronology." In idem, *Between Jesus and Paul,* 30–47. London: SCM, 1983.

Hengel, Martin, and Anna Maria Schwemer. *Paul between Damascus and Antioch: The Unknown Years.* Louisville: Westminster John Knox, 1997.

Hollenbach, Paul W. "Jesus, Demoniacs, and Public Authorities: A Socio-Historical Study." *Journal of the American Academy of Religion* 49, no. 4 (1981): 567-88.

Holmer, Paul. *The Grammar of Faith.* New York: Harper & Row, 1978.

Hooker, Morna D. "Adam *Redivivus*: Philippians 2 Once More." In *The Old Testament in the New Testament: Essays in Honour of J. L. North,* ed. Steve Moyise, 220-34. Journal for the Study of the New Testament Supplement 189. Sheffield: Sheffield Academic Press, 2000.

———. "Philippians: Phantom Opponents and the Real Source of Conflict." In *Fair Play: Diversity and Conflicts in Early Christianity: Essays in Honour of Heikki Räisänen,* ed. Ismo Dunderberg, Christopher Tuckett, and Kari Syreeni, 377-95. Leiden: Brill, 2002.

Horsley, Richard A., and Jonathan A. Draper. *Whoever Hears You Hears Me: Prophets, Performance, and Tradition in Q.* Harrisburg, PA: Trinity Press International, 1999.

Hügel, Friedrich von. "Official Authority and Living Religion." In idem, *Essays and Addresses in the Philosophy of Religion.* 2nd series. London: J. M. Dent and Sons, 1926.

Hurtado, Larry W. *How on Earth Did Jesus Become a God? Historical Questions about Earliest Devotion to Jesus.* Grand Rapids: Eerdmans, 2005.

———. *Lord Jesus Christ: Devotion to Jesus in Earliest Christianity.* Grand Rapids: Eerdmans, 2003.

———. *One God, One Lord: Early Christian Devotion and Ancient Jewish Monotheism.* Philadelphia: Fortress, 1988.

Imbelli, Robert, ed. *Handing on the Faith: The Church's Mission and Challenge*. New York: Crossroad, 2006.

Isasi-Díaz, Ada María. "Christ in *Mujerista* Theology." In *Thinking of Christ: Proclamation, Explanation, Meaning*, ed. Tatha Wiley, 157-76. New York: Continuum, 2003.

James, William. *The Varieties of Religious Experience: A Study in Human Nature*. London: Longmans, Green, 1902. Reprint, New York: Collier Books, 1961.

Jeremias, Joachim. *The Prayer of Jesus*. Translated by John Bowden. London: SCM, 1967.

Joh, W. Anne. *Heart of the Cross: A Postcolonial Christology*. Louisville: Westminster John Knox, 2006.

John XXIII (Pope). *Pacem in Terris*, promulgated April 11, 1963, §§9, 11-14. Available at http://www.vatican.va/holy_father/john_xxiii/encyclicals/documents/hf_j-xxiii_enc_11041963_pacem_en.html (accessed August 2, 2007).

John Paul II (Pope), and His Holiness K. Mar Dinkha IV. *Common Christological Declaration*. Delivered at St. Peter's Basilica, Rome, November 11, 1994. Available at http://www.vatican.va/roman_curia/pontifical_councils/chrstuni/documents/rc_pc_chrstuni_doc_11111994_assyrian-church_en.html (accessed July 17, 2007).

Johnson, Elizabeth A. *Consider Jesus: Waves of Renewal in Christology*. New York: Crossroad, 1990.

———. "Does God Play Dice? Divine Providence and Chance." *Theological Studies* 57, no. 3 (1996): 2-18.

———. *Truly Our Sister: A Theology of Mary in the Communion of Saints*. New York: Continuum, 2003.

Johnson, Luke Timothy. *The Real Jesus: The Misguided Quest for the Historical Jesus and the Truth of the Traditional Gospels*. San Francisco: HarperSanFrancisco, 1996.

"Jon Sobrino—Dossier." *Concilium*, no. 3 (2007): 125-34.

Jones, L. Gregory. *Embodying Forgiveness: A Theological Analysis*. Grand Rapids: Eerdmans, 1995.

Josephus. *The Jewish War*. Revised edition, new introduction, notes and appendicies by E. Mary Smallwood. Translated by G. A. Williamson. London: Penguin Books, 1981.

Kähler, Martin. *The So-Called Historical Jesus and the Historic Biblical Christ*. Edited by Carl E. Braaten. Philadelphia: Fortress, 1964 (first German ed., 1892).

Kasper, Walter Cardinal. "Dominus Iesus." Exchange of Information Session, International Catholic-Jewish Liaison Committee Meeting, New York, May 1-4, 2001. Available at http://www.usccb.org/seia/kasper.shtml (accessed August 20, 2007).

Kee, Howard Clark. "The Gospel According to Matthew." In *The Interpreter's One Volume Commentary on the Bible*, ed. Charles M. Laymon, 609-43. Nashville: Abingdon, 1971.

Kerr, Fergus. *Twentieth-Century Catholic Theologians*. Oxford: Blackwell, 2007.

Lampe, G. W. H., ed. *A Patristic Greek Lexicon*. Oxford: Clarendon, 1961. Reprint, 1987.

Landgraf, Artur. *Dogmengeschichte der Frühscholastik*. 4 vols. in 9. Regensburg: Pustet, 1952-56.

Lane, Dermot A. *Christ at the Centre: Selected Issues in Christology*. Dublin: Veritas, 1991.

———. *Keeping Hope Alive: Stirrings in Christian Theology*. New York/Mahwah, NJ: Paulist, 1996.

———. *The Reality of Jesus: An Essay in Christology*. New York: Paulist, 1975.

Lash, Nicholas. "Letter to the Editor." *The Tablet* [London], March 24, 2007.

Laymon, Charles M., ed. *The Interpreter's One Volume Commentary on the Bible.* Nashville: Abingdon, 1971.

Leahy, Brendán. "Revelation and Faith. In *Evangelizing for the Third Millennium: The Maynooth Conference on the New Catechism, May 1996,* ed. Maurice Hogan, S.C., and Thomas Norris, 64-84. Dublin: Veritas, 1997.

Levine, Amy-Jill. *The Misunderstood Jew: The Church and the Scandal of the Jewish Jesus.* San Francisco: HarperSanFrancisco, 2006.

Lindbeck, George A. *The Nature of Doctrine: Religion and Theology in a Postliberal Age.* Philadelphia: Westminster, 1984.

Loewe, William P. *The College Student's Introduction to Christology.* Collegeville, MN: Liturgical Press, 1996.

———. "The Sobrino File: How to Read the Vatican's Latest Notification." *Commonweal* 134, no. 10 (March 18, 2007). Available at http://www.commonwealmagazine.org/print_format.php?id_article=1939 (accessed July 19, 2007).

Loisy, Alfred. *The Gospel and the Church.* Translated by Christopher Home. London: Isbister, 1906 (first French ed., 1902).

Lysaught, M. Therese. "Love Your Enemies: Toward a Christoform Bioethic." In *Gathered for the Journey: Moral Theology in Catholic Perspective,* ed. David Matzko McCarthy and M. Therese Lysaught, 307-28. Grand Rapids: Eerdmans, 2007.

MacIntyre, Alasdair. *After Virtue: A Study in Moral Theory.* Notre Dame: University of Notre Dame Press, 1981.

Macy, Gary. "The Doctrine of Transubstantiation in the Middle Ages." In idem, *Treasures from the Storeroom: Medieval Religion and the Eucharist,* 81-120. Collegeville, MN: Liturgical Press, 1999.

Marion, Jean-Luc. *God Without Being: Hors-Texte.* Translated by Thomas A. Carlson. Chicago: University of Chicago Press, 1995.

Marshall, Mary J. "Jesus: Glutton and Drunkard." *Journal for the Study of the Historical Jesus* 3, no. 1 (2005): 47-60.

Martin, Ralph P. *Carmen Christi: Philippians 2:5-11 in Recent Interpretation and the Setting of Early Christian Worship.* Rev. ed. Grand Rapids: Eerdmans, 1983.

Martin, Ralph P., and Brian J. Dodd, ed. *Where Christology Began: Essays on Philippians 2.* Louisville: Westminster John Knox, 1998.

Martini, Cardinal Carlo Maria. *Praying as Jesus Taught Us: Meditations on the Our Father.* Translated by John Belmonte, S.J. Lanham, MD: Sheed & Ward, 2001.

McCarthy, Michael C., S.J. "Religious Disillusionment in a Land of Illusions." In *Rahner beyond Rahner: A Great Theologian Encounters the Pacific Rim,* ed. Paul G. Crowley, S.J., 101-12. Lanham, MD: Rowman & Littlefield, 2005.

McClendon, James Wm., Jr. *Biography as Theology: How Life Stories Can Remake Today's Theology.* Nashville: Abingdon, 1974.

———. *Systematic Theology,* vol. 1, *Ethics*; vol. 2, *Doctrine.* Nashville: Abingdon, 1985, 1994.

McGovern, Thomas J. "The Interpretation of Scripture 'in the Spirit': The Edelby Intervention at Vatican II." *Irish Theological Quarterly* 64 (1999): 245-59.

Meier, John P. *A Marginal Jew: Rethinking the Historical Jesus,* vol. 2, *Mentor, Message and Miracles.* Anchor Bible Reference Library. New York: Doubleday, 1994.

Meyer, Ben F. *The Aims of Jesus.* London: SCM, 1979.

Michaels, J. Ramsey. *Servant and Son: Jesus in Parable and Gospel.* Atlanta: John Knox, 1981.

Migne, J.-P. *Patrologia Latina*. Available at http://pld.chadwyck.com.avoserv.library. fordham.edu/ (accessed August 20, 2007).

Miranda, José Porfirio. *Communism in the Bible*. Translated by Robert Barr. Maryknoll, NY: Orbis Books, 1981.

Moltmann, Jürgen. *The Way of Jesus Christ: Christology in Messianic Dimensions*. Translated by Margaret Kohl. San Francisco: HarperSanFrancisco, 1990.

Murphy, Catherine M. *John the Baptist: Prophet of Purity for a New Age*. Collegeville, MN: Liturgical Press, 2003.

Neill, Stephen, and Tom Wright. *The Interpretation of the New Testament 1861-1986*. 2nd ed. Oxford: Oxford University Press, 1988.

Neusner, Jacob. "Two Pictures of the Pharisees: Philosophical Circle or Eating Club?" *Anglican Theological Review* 64, no. 4 (1982): 525-38.

Newman, John Henry. *An Essay on the Development of Christian Doctrine*. 2nd ed. London: James Toovey, 1846.

Norris, Richard A., Jr. *The Christological Controversy*. Philadelphia: Fortress, 1980.

Norris, Thomas, "On Revisiting *Dei Verbum*." *Irish Theological Quarterly* 66 (2001): 315-37.

O'Collins, Gerald, S.J. *Christology: A Biblical, Historical and Systematic Study of Jesus*. Oxford: Oxford University Press, 1995.

———. "Jesus as Lord and Teacher." In *Who Do You Say That I Am? Confessing the Mystery of Christ*, ed. John C. Cavadini and Laura Holt, 51-62. Notre Dame: University of Notre Dame Press, 2004.

Ong, Walter J., S.J. "Realizing Catholicism: Faith, Learning and the Future." In *Faith and the Intellectual Life*, ed. James L. Heft, S.M., 31-42. Notre Dame: University of Notre Dame Press, 1996.

Orsi, Robert A. *Thank You, St. Jude: Women's Devotion to the Patron Saint of Hopeless Causes*. New Haven: Yale University Press, 1996.

Passion of the Christ, The. Produced by Bruce Davies, Mel Gibson, and Steven McEveety. Directed by Mel Gibson. 126 Minutes. Icon Productions, 2004.

Pearson, Birger A., ed., in collaboration with A. Thomas Kraabel, George W. E. Nickelsburg and Norman R. Petersen. *The Future of Early Christianity: Essays in Honor of Helmut Koester*. Minneapolis: Fortress: 1991.

Perkins, Pheme. *Peter: Apostle for the Whole Church*. Columbia: University of South Carolina Press, 1994.

———. *Resurrection*. Garden City, NY: Doubleday, 1984.

Perrin, Norman. *Jesus and the Language of the Kingdom*. Philadelphia: Fortress, 1976.

———. *The New Testament: An Introduction*. New York: Harcourt, Brace, Jovanovich; 1974. 2nd ed., 1982.

Peukert, Helmut. *Science, Action and Fundamental Theology: Toward a Theory of Communicative Action*. Cambridge, MA: MIT Press, 1984.

Plantinga, Alvin. *God, Freedom and Evil*. New York: Harper & Row, 1974.

———. *God and Other Minds: A Study of the Rational Justification of Belief in God*. Ithaca, NY: Cornell University Press, 1968. Reprint, 1990.

Poon, William C. K. "Superabundant Table Fellowship in the Kingdom: The Feeding of the Five Thousand and the Meal Motif in Luke." *Expository Times* 114, no. 7 (2001): 224-30.

Powell, Mark Allan, and David R. Bauer, eds. *Who Do You Say That I Am? Essays on Christology*. Louisville: Westminster John Knox, 1999.

Principe, Walter. *William of Auxerre's Theology of the Hypostatic Union.* Toronto: Pontifical Institute of Mediaeval Studies, 1963.

Quesnell, Quentin. "The Women at Luke's Supper." In *Political Issues in Luke-Acts,* ed. Richard J. Cassidy and Philip J. Sharper, 59-79. Maryknoll, NY: Orbis Books, 1983.

Rahner, Karl. "Current Problems in Christology." In idem, *Theological Investigations* I. Translated by Cornelius Ernst, O.P., 149-200. New York: Herder & Herder, 1961 (German original, 1951).

Rahner, Karl, and Herbert Vorgrimler. *Theological Dictionary.* Translated by R. Strachen. New York: Herder & Herder, 1965.

Ramsey, Ian. *Christian Discourse: Some Logical Explorations.* London: Oxford University Press, 1965.

Ratzinger, Joseph [Pope Benedict XVI]. *Jesus of Nazareth: From the Baptism in the Jordan to the Transfiguration.* Translated by Adrian J. Walker. New York: Doubleday, 2007.

———. "The Transmission of Divine Revelation." In *Commentary on the Documents of Vatican II,* ed. Herbert Vorgrimler, 3:181-98. New York: Herder & Herder, 1967–.

Rees, B. R. *Pelagius: A Reluctant Heretic.* Wolfeboro, NH: Boydell, 1988.

Regnault, Lucien. "Les apophtegmes des pères en Palestine aux Vᵉ-VIᵉ siècles." *Irenikon* 54 (1981): 320-30. .

Reinhartz, Adele. "The Gospel of John." In *Searching the Scriptures,* vol. 2, *A Feminist Commentary,* ed. Elisabeth Schüssler Fiorenza, 561-600. New York: Crossroad, 1994.

Russell, Robert John, Nancey Murphy and Arthur Peacocke, eds. *Chaos and Complexity: Scientific Perspectives on Divine Action.* Vatican City: Vatican Observatory; Berkeley: Center for Theology and Natural Science, 1997.

Russell, Robert John, Philip Clayton, Kirk Wegter-McNelly, and John Polkinghorne. *Quantum Mechanics: Scientific Perspectives on Divine Action.* Vatican City: Vatican Observatory; Berkeley: Center for Theology and the Natural Sciences, 2002.

Sanders, E. P. *The Historical Figure of Jesus.* London: Penguin, 1993.

———. *Jesus and Judaism.* London: SCM, 1985.

Schillebeeckx, Edward. *Jesus: An Experiment in Christology.* New York: Seabury, 1979.

Schindler, D. C. "Surprised by Truth: The Drama of Reason in Fundamental Theology." *Communio* 31 (Winter 2004): 587-611.

Schleiermacher, F. D. E. *The Christian Faith.* Edited by H. R. MacKintosh and J. S. Stewart. Translation of 2nd German ed. Edinburgh: T&T Clark, 1928; German ed., 1830.

Schneiders, Sandra. *The Revelatory Text: Interpreting the New Testament as Sacred Scripture.* 2nd ed. Collegeville, MN: Liturgical Press, 1999.

Schottroff, Luise. *The Parables of Jesus.* Translated by Linda Maloney. Minneapolis: Fortress, 2006.

Schreiter, Robert J., C.Pp.S. *The Ministry of Reconciliation: Spirituality and Strategies.* Maryknoll, NY: Orbis Books, 1998.

Schüssler Fiorenza, Elisabeth. *But She Said: Feminist Practices of Biblical Interpretation.* Boston: Beacon, 1992.

———. *In Memory of Her: A Feminist Theological Reconstruction of Christian Origins.* New York: Crossroad, 1983.

———. *Jesus: Miriam's Child, Sophia's Prophet: Critical Issues in Feminist Christology.* New York: Continuum, 1994.

———. *Jesus and the Politics of Interpretation.* New York: Continuum, 2000.

Schüssler Fiorenza, Elisabeth, ed. *Searching the Scriptures.* Vol. 2, *A Feminist Commentary.* New York: Crossroad, 1994.

Schweitzer, Albert. *The Quest of the Historical Jesus.* London: A. and C. Black, 1910 (first German ed., 1906).

Searle, John R. "Consciousness and the Philosophers." *New York Review of Books* 44, no. 4 (March 6, 1997). Available at http://www.nybooks.com/articles/1258 (accessed January 29, 2007).

Smith, Dennis E. "Table Fellowship as a Literary Motif in the Gospel of Luke." *Journal of Biblical Literature* 106, no. 4 (1987): 613-28.

Soares-Prabhu, Georges M. *The Dharma of Jesus.* Edited by Francis Xavier D'Sa. Maryknoll, NY: Orbis Books, 2003.

Sobrino, Jon. *Christ the Liberator: A View from the Victims.* Translated by Paul Burns. Maryknoll, NY: Orbis Books, 2001.

———. *Jesus the Liberator: A Historical-Theological Reading of Jesus of Nazareth.* Translated by Paul Burns and Francis McDonagh. Maryknoll, NY: Orbis Books, 1993.

Sokolowski, Robert. *The God of Faith and Reason: Foundations of Christian Theology.* Notre Dame: University of Notre Dame Press, 1982.

Starr, Paul. *The Social Transformation of American Medicine.* New York: Basic Books, 1982.

Strzelczyk, Grzegorz. *Communicatio Idiomatum: Lo scambio delle proprietà: Soria, status questionis e prospettive.* Rome: Pontificia Università Gregoriana, 2004.

Tan, Jonathan Yun-ka. "*Missio Inter Gentes*: Towards a New Paradigm in the Mission Theology of the Federation of Asian Bishops' Conferences." Discussion guide for the Eighth Plenary Session of FABC at Taejon, Korea, August 2004. Available at www.ucanews.com/html/fabc-papers/fabc-109.htm (accessed July 15, 2007).

———. "Mission *Among* the Peoples: A Lesson from the Church in Asia," *National Jesuit News.* Available at http://puffin.creighton.edu/jesuit/dialogue/documents/articles/njn_tan.html (accessed August 3, 2007).

Taylor, Charles. *The Ethics of Authenticity.* Cambridge, MA: Harvard University Press, 1991.

Taylor, Vincent. *Forgiveness and Reconciliation: A Study in New Testament Theology.* New York: St. Martin's Press, 1960.

Theissen, Gerd, and Annette Merz. *The Historical Jesus: A Comprehensive Guide.* Translated by John Bowden. Minneapolis: Fortress, 1998.

Theissen, Gerd, and Dagmar Winter. *Quest for the Plausible Jesus: The Question of Criteria.* Translated by M. Eugene Boring. Louisville: Westminster John Knox, 2002.

Thiel, John. *Senses of Tradition.* New York: Oxford University Press, 2000.

Tilley, Maureen A. "The Ascetic Body and the (Un)Making of the World of the Martyr." *Journal of the American Academy of Religion* 69, no. 3 (1991): 467-79.

———. "Philippians 2:6-11 and the Question of Pre-Existence." M.A. thesis, St. Michael's College, Colchester, Vermont, 1985.

Tilley, Terrence W. "Christian Orthodoxy and Religious Pluralism." *Modern Theology* 22, no. 1 (2006) 51-63.

———. "'Christian Orthodoxy and Religious Pluralism': A Rejoinder to Gavin D'Costa." *Modern Theology* 23, no. 3 (2007) 447-54.

———. *The Evils of Theodicy.* Washington, DC: Georgetown University Press, 1991. Reprint, Eugene, OR: Wipf & Stock, 2000.

———. *History, Theology, and Faith: Dissolving the Modern Problematic.* Maryknoll, NY: Orbis Books, 2004.

———. "Incommensurability, Intratextuality and Fideism." *Modern Theology* 5, no. 2 (1989): 87-111.

———. "The Institutional Element in Religious Experience." *Modern Theology* 10, no. 2 (1994): 185-212.

———. *Inventing Catholic Tradition.* Maryknoll, NY: Orbis Books, 2000.

———. "O Caesarea Philippi: Starting Christology at the Right Place." In *Theology and Sacred Scripture,* ed. Carol Dempsey, O.P., and William P. Loewe, 135-64. College Theology Society Annual Volume 47. Maryknoll, NY: Orbis Books, 2002.

———. *Story Theology.* Wilmington, DE: Michael Glazier, 1985. Reprint, Collegeville, MN: Liturgical Press, 1990, 1991, 2002.

———. "The Systematic Elusiveness of God: On the 50th Anniversary of Ian Ramsey's *Religious Language.*" *Horizons* 34, no. 1 (2007): 7-25.

———. "Teaching Christology: History and Horizons." In *Christology: Memory, Inquiry, Practice,* ed. Anne M. Clifford and Anthony J. Godzieba, 265-76. College Theology Society Annual Volume 48. Maryknoll, NY: Orbis Books, 2003.

———. "Towards a Creativity Defense of Belief in God in the Face of Evil." In *Physics and Cosmology: Scientific Perspectives on the Problem of Natural Evil,* ed. Nancey Murphy et al., 195-215. Vatican City: Vatican Observatory Press, 2007.

———. *The Wisdom of Religious Commitment.* Washington, DC: Georgetown University Press, 1995.

Tilley, Terrence W., and Gavin D'Costa. "Concluding Our *Quaestio Disputata* on Theologies of Religious Diversity." *Modern Theology* 23, no. 3 (2007) 463-68.

Tilley, Terrence W., et al. *Postmodern Theologies: The Challenge of Religious Diversity.* Maryknoll, NY: Orbis Books, 1995.

Tilley, Terrence W., et al. *Religious Diversity and the American Experience: A Theological Approach.* New York: Continuum, 2007.

Tracy, David. *The Analogical Imagination: Christian Theology and the Culture of Pluralism.* New York: Crossroad, 1981.

Tuckett, Christopher. *Christology and the New Testament: Jesus and His Earliest Followers.* Louisville: Westminster John Knox, 2001.

Tyrrell, George. *Christianity at the Crossroads.* London: Allen and Unwin, 1963.

Volf, Miroslav. *Exclusion and Embrace: A Theological Exploration of Identity, Otherness, and Reconciliation.* Nashville: Abingdon, 1996.

Wainwright, Elaine. *Women Healing/Healing Women: The Genderization of Healing in Early Christianity.* London: Equinox, 2006.

Weber, Max. *On Charisma and Institution Building: Selected Papers.* Edited by S. N. Eisenstadt. Chicago: University of Chicago Pres, 1968.

Welch, Sharon D. *Communities of Resistance and Solidarity: A Feminist Theology of Liberation.* Maryknoll, NY: Orbis Books, 1985.

Wells, Samuel. *Improvisation: The Drama of Christian Ethics.* Grand Rapids: Brazos, 2004.

Wiles, Maurice. "Revelation and Divine Action." In *Divine Revelation,* ed. Paul Avis, 100-11. Grand Rapids: Eerdmans, 1997.

Wiley, Tatha, ed. *Thinking of Christ: Proclamation, Explanation, Meaning.* New York: Continuum, 2003.

Williams, D. H. *Retrieving the Tradition and Renewing Evangelicalism: A Primer for Suspicious Protestants.* Grand Rapids: Eerdmans, 1999.

Williams, Rowan. "'Tempted as We Are': Christology and the Analysis of the Passions." Opening Lecture, Fifteenth International Conference on Patristic Studies, Oxford University, August 6, 2007, unpublished.

Wink, Walter. "Response to Luke Timothy Johnson's *The Real Jesus.*" *Bulletin for Biblical Research* 7 (1997): 1–16.

Wise, Michael O., and James D. Tabor. "The Messiah at Qumran." *Biblical Archaeology Review* 18, no. 6 (1992): 60-61, 65.

Witherington, Ben, III. *The Christology of Jesus.* Minneapolis: Fortress, 1990.

Wolterstorff, Nicholas. *Divine Discourse: Philosophical Reflections on the Claim That God Speaks.* Cambridge: Cambridge University Press, 1995.

Wrede, William. *The Messianic Secret.* Cambridge: J. Clarke, 1971 (first German ed., 1901).

Wright, N.T. "Quest for the Historical Jesus." In *The Anchor Bible Dictionary,* ed. David Noel Freedman. 6 vols. 3:796-802. New York: Doubleday, 1992.

Yoder, John Howard. *The Politics of Jesus: Vincit Agnus Noster.* 2nd ed. Grand Rapids: Eerdmans, 1994 (first ed., 1972).

INDEX

act: versus text, 20-22, 263
acts: versus events, 53n13, 273-77
Acts of the Apostles: healing and
    exorcising in, 146
agency
    distinction between primary and
      secondary, 31
    of Jesus, 59-66
    power and, 31
    and revelation, 267-70
Amaladoss, Michael
    on Jesus as sage, 230
    on Jesus' teaching practice, 151-52
anamnesis: meaning of, 127
anti-Judaism, Christian, 74-75
Arianism, 211-12
asceticism, 237-38
atonement
    as at-one-ment, 251
    doctrine of, 248n21
    incarnating, 249-52
    soteriology and, 27-28
    See also reconciliation
Augustine
    on figurative and literal language, 220
    on nearness of God, 226

Bailey, Kenneth: and orality, 55
Barron, Robert
    on agency and power, 31n38
    on Aquinas on morality, 227
    on Chalcedon, 225-26
    on existence of God and creatures, 225
    on Jesus as icon of God, 245n16
    on monothelitism, 31n41, 230-31
    on nearness of God, 226
    on practical christology, 244-45
Bartchy, S. S.: on Jesus and table
    fellowship, 176

Barth, Karl: on hope, 254
basileia tou theou, 1, 24, 43, 65, 70, 95,
    101, 121, 130, 142-47, 150, 152,
    153, 158-62, 170, 172, 174, 178-82,
    186, 195, 228, 229, 240, 244, 256.
    See also God: reign of
beatitudes, 160-64. *See also* Jesus/Christ:
    teaching of
believing. *See* faith
Benedict XVI (pope)
    on beatitudes, 160-61
    on continuity between Jesus and
      disciples, 134n18
    and indifferentism, 10
    on Jesus' self-understanding, 153n7
    on parables of Jesus, 157n19
    and relativism, 10
Bernardin, Joseph Cardinal, 172-74, 249
Bible
    audience response criticism and, 54
    fundamentalism and, 202n14
    Gospels, 104-7; historicity of, 266-
      67; inscribing practices of Jesus-
      movement, 131-32; meal imagery
      in, 178-81; Petrine confession
      in, 80n8; process of composition
      of, 56-57; as scripts for oral
      performance, 51-52, 73-77, 94-
      95n33, 130; versions of Last Supper
      in, 182-85
    historical-critical interpretation of, 43-
      44
    historical narrative in, 266-67
    inspiration of, 266
    interpretation of: in Spirit, 268
    New Testament: as book, 76;
      interrogations of, 2; New Adam
      christology of, 229-30; orality and,
      152; rhetorical context of, 35;

Of Related Interest

The Resurrection Effect
Transforming Christian Life and Thought
Anthony J. Kelly
ISBN 978-1-57075-770-9

Explores the resurrection as the living center of Christian life, an event that should focus and shape our vision of Christian existence.

Acknowledging that the resurrection, like a work of art, eludes any single point of view, Kelly shows why it remains the key to God's relationship to Jesus and ourselves, the most critical horizon from which to grasp the meaning and pattern of life, and the basis of our ultimate hope.

Jesus
A Portrait
Gerald O'Collins
ISBN 978-1-57075-783-9

An informed, inspirational portrayal of the one who launched the path followed by billions over the course of two millennia.

In a work filled with wisdom and insight, the reader gains new perspectives on such perennial treasures as the Beatitudes and the Lord's Prayer. *Jesus* is a portrait of one who gives us the courage to be in the world.

Please support your local bookstore or call 1-800-258-5838.
For a free catalog, please write us at

Orbis Books, Box 302
Maryknoll, NY 10545-0302

or visit our website at www.orbisbooks.com.

Thank you for reading *The Disciples' Jesus*.
We hope you profited from it.